COOKING
WITH
Confidence

COOKING

WITH

Confidence

FRASER STEWART

HOW TO USE THE RECIPES

Approximate preparation and cooking times are given for each recipe, with the following symbols where appropriate:

Ease ① easy to prepare and cook
⑪ requires care ⑪⑪ complicated

Cost £ inexpensive ££ moderately priced
£££ for special occasions

Freezing ❋ freezes particularly well

Plan ahead 🕐 can be cooked ahead of time; this symbol in the steps indicates that the dish can be prepared ahead to this point.

Weights and measures Both metric and imperial measurements are given, but are not exact equivalents; work from one set only. Use graded measuring spoons levelled across.

Ingredients ● Flour is plain white flour unless otherwise stated ● Sugar is granulated unless otherwise stated ● Eggs are medium (EEC size 4) unless otherwise stated ● Vegetables and fruits are medium-sized and prepared, and onions, garlic and root vegetables are peeled unless otherwise stated ● Butter for sweet dishes should be unsalted ● Block margarine may be substituted for butter, although the results may be different in flavour, appearance and keeping qualities.

Cooking Dishes should be placed in the centre of the oven unless otherwise stated.

Calorie counts When the number of servings for a recipe is variable (eg 4-6), the calorie/kilojoule count is given for the minimum number of people served. Optional ingredients are not included in calorie counts.

This edition published by
Fraser Stewart Book Wholesale Ltd
Abbey Chambers
4 Highbridge Street
Waltham Abbey
Essex EN9 1DQ

Produced by Marshall Cavendish Books
(a division of Marshall Cavendish Partworks Ltd)
119 Wardour Street
London W1V 3TD

Some of this material has previously appeared in the Marshall Cavendish partwork *WHAT'S COOKING?*

c o n t e n t s

f o r e w o r d

*C*ooking with Confidence *is not just a recipe book, it is an invaluable work of reference and a guide to both simple and more complicated cooking skills. The book is divided into four main sections: Basic foods and techniques; Starters; Main courses; and Desserts and cakes. These are sub-divided into chapters, each devoted to one theme, usually a food, a technique or a cooking method.*

The chapters are packed with practical information on equipment, ingredients, planning ahead, freezing and microwaving. All the delicious, easy-to-follow recipes are illustrated and clear step-by-step photographs will help you through even the most complicated process, giving you the chance to improve your skills and learn new techniques. You will find out how to achieve perfect results – and if the finished dish isn't quite right, there is information on what might have gone wrong and why. Whether you are a beginner or a more experienced cook, Cooking with Confidence *will provide you with all the secrets of successful cooking.*

Basic foods and techniques

*T*his section contains the basic building blocks for successful cooking. Each chapter provides the essential information you need to understand how individual recipes work. You will find facts about each food or technique along with fully illustrated step-by-step instructions on how to achieve the best results. Cooking with Confidence *helps you steer clear of any pitfalls, but offers helpful hints and advice if problems do occur.*

However, this section is not purely instructional – there are over 50 fabulous recipes, with cook's tips, suggestions for varying a basic recipe, and serving ideas. Many of the basic foods and techniques covered in this section – pastry, bread and pasta, for example – are based on the same simple ingredients: flour and fat combined with water, milk or eggs. Like many basic foods, they can be bought ready-made in larger supermarkets, yet there is nothing quite like the real thing.

The simplest pastry, shortcrust, takes only moments to mix together, yet it is quite an art to achieve perfect, crisp, melt-in-the-mouth results. The specialist chapter sets out the basic rules, and there is plenty of useful advice on how to get the best results and what equipment to use. There are similar sections on hot water crust and puff pastry, plus tips and sugges-

tions for all sorts of decorative finishes, from a simple forked design to more elaborate cut-out decorations, as well as lattice patterns, tassels and leaves.

Where would we be without our daily bread? Freshly baked bread is a treat to eat and fun to make. Although kneading by hand sounds like hard work, if you follow the step-by-step guide you will find that it is easy – even relaxing. And once you have perfected bread, you can graduate to pizzas. The specialist chapter covers everything from bases to toppings, which range from simple tomato to the hearty sausage and egg.

Pasta is yet another staple of the storecupboard. Cooking with Confidence shows just how quick and easy it is to make at home, whether you leave it plain or flavour and colour it with spinach or tomato. There are lots of pasta facts and cooking tips, including information about different shapes and which sauce,

either simple or more adventurous, to serve with it.

Sauces form the basis of a great many dishes; they are an essential part of any cook's repertoire. The specialist chapter explains how to make them the right consistency, and how to keep them lump-free. It also suggests classic variations on a simple white sauce, such as Béchamel, aurore and cheese, and includes delicious recipes using both basic and enriched sauces. A separate chapter deals with mayonnaise.

Essential for so many sauces, stews and soups is a good stock. Here the basic ingredients and techniques are given, followed by various recipes based on different types of stock.

For speed and versatility, choose eggs. Cooking with Confidence guides you through a wide range of egg dishes, from simple folded omelettes to spectacular hot soufflés.

Melt-in-the-Mouth Pastry

Shortcrust pastry is the foundation of many delicious dishes, ranging from savoury quiches to sweet pies and flans. Mastering the art of making it is not difficult, just a matter of observing some basic principles

*A*S ITS NAME suggests, the texture of this pastry is 'short' — it should be crisp to bite, but then melt in the mouth. It should not be over-rich, but set off the flavours of the filling it contains. Plain shortcrust pastry is made from nothing more than plain flour, fat, milk or water and a little salt. The fat can be butter, margarine, lard or vegetable fat, or a mixture. Use butter alone for best flavour, margarine for economy, vegetable fat or lard for the crispest texture. A 50:50 mixture of butter and lard or vegetable fat is a good combination.

Sweet shortcrust pastry is made by adding sugar to the flour before rubbing in the fat.

Keys to success

Pastry-making does not lend itself to creative improvisation: break the basic rules and you will get disappointing results.

Measure your ingredients: for ordinary shortcrust the proportion is usually half fat to flour with just enough liquid to bind the mixture.

Keep cool: have your equipment, ingredients and hands as cool as possible. A marble slab is the best surface for rolling out as it is smooth and cool. The liquid should be well chilled — even iced in hot weather — and the fat cool, but not too hard, otherwise it will not bind properly with the flour. Use fingertips to rub the fat into the flour.

Work lightly and quickly: when rubbing the fat into the flour, lift the mixture high and let it fall back into the bowl. This helps to lighten the pastry by introducing air.

Relax the dough: make the pastry in advance and chill for at least 30 minutes, wrapping it in greaseproof, stretch wrap, or foil first. Chill the pastry for another 30 minutes after rolling it out and lining the container. Uncooked pastry can be kept for one to two days in the refrigerator.

Correct rolling out: sprinkle the work surface and the rolling pin with a very little flour. Lightly form

Fruit barquettes (page 13)

the dough into roughly the correct shape and then roll in one direction, turning it round frequently. This will produce an even thickness and shape. If making small circles or other shapes, divide the dough into the required number of pieces before rolling each one out.

Preheat the oven: shortcrust pastry is normally cooked at 200C/400F/gas 6. The heat of the oven causes rapid expansion of the air trapped in the dough, giving the pastry its light texture.

Pastry containers

Pastry cases can be made in a variety of tins or dishes. For quiches and flans the ideal is a loose-bottomed tin or a flan ring, which make it easy to unmould the delicate pastry. Metal is the best heat conductor, and therefore makes a crisper pastry. But ceramic or glass containers look more attractive, and a quiche or flan cooked in one can be left unmoulded. Do remember that ceramic or glass dishes will need more cooking time than metal.

For pies with a top crust only, use a deep glass, ceramic or enamel dish with a lip round the edge. Double-crust pies can be baked in pie plates with a broad rim, or shallower pie dishes with a narrower rim. Small tartlets are usually cooked in multi-hole tins; unusual items like barquettes need specially shaped individual tins.

Baking blind

Baking a pastry case without its filling is known as baking blind. Prepare and chill the pastry case, then line it. Meanwhile, preheat the oven and a baking sheet to 200C/400F/gas 6. Put the case on the baking sheet and bake for 10-20 minutes. Then reduce the heat to 180C/350F/gas 4 and remove the beans and paper.

For a fully-cooked case return to the oven for another 10-15 minutes or until the pastry is golden and set. For a partly cooked case bake for only 8-10 minutes – not long enough for the pastry to colour.

Small cases (10cm/4in) cook more quickly. Bake at high temperature for 10 minutes, then for 5 minutes at the lower temperature.

Basic shortcrust pastry

This makes enough pastry to line a 23-25cm/9-10in flan tin.

● *Preparation: 15 minutes, plus 30 minutes chilling*

225g/8oz plain flour
¼tsp salt
100g/4oz butter
4-6tbls cold milk or water

1 Sift the flour and salt into a large bowl. Cut the butter into 5mm/¼in dice.

2 To cut the butter into the flour mixture use two knives or a pastry blender until all the pieces are about half their original size and coated in flour. Then use your fingertips to rub the butter and flour together until the mixture resembles breadcrumbs.

3 Sprinkle a little cold milk over the surface of the mixture and stir it in with a knife. Continue stirring in milk, a little at a time, until the mixture clings together in small lumps. When three-quarters of the pastry is holding together, gently draw it into a ball using one hand.

4 Put the dough on a very lightly floured surface and knead lightly until smooth. Wrap it in stretch wrap and chill for 30 minutes before rolling out.

Variations

To make wholemeal pastry use 175/6oz wholemeal flour mixed with 50g/2oz plain flour, or half and half. Dough made with all wholemeal flour is soft and unmanageable.

Cook's tips

If you forget to remove your butter from the refrigerator, try coarsely grating it into the flour before rubbing in.

Freezer

Unbaked shortcrust pastry dough freezes well so you can make it up in advance ready for use when needed. Wrap the ball of dough in foil or stretch wrap and freeze for up to 3 months. Defrost, wrapped, at room temperature for 2-3 hours. You can also freeze baked unfilled pastry cases. Wrap well, then freeze for up to 6 months. Unwrap, then defrost for 2 hours in the fridge or 1 hour at room temperature.

Rubbing in fat

Use only the tips of your fingers to rub fat into flour, and raise your hands well above the bowl. This way you avoid overhandling and incorporate plenty of air, so the pastry turns out light and flaky.

PROCESSOR PASTRY

To make pastry in a food processor, sift the flour and salt into the bowl and add the diced fat. Process for 10-15 seconds until the mixture looks like fine breadcrumbs. Sprinkle over 3tbls cold milk or water and process for another 20 seconds or until the pastry clings together in a loose ball. Knead lightly to form a smooth dough.

Beef and walnut parcels

- **Preparation: 1 hour, plus 30 minutes chilling**

- **Cooking: 2½ hours, plus cooling**

450g/1lb braising steak, cut into
  2cm/¾in cubes
25g/1oz seasoned flour
2tbls oil
2 small leeks, thickly sliced
50g/2oz walnuts, chopped
225ml/8fl oz red wine
about 300ml/½pt beef stock
grated zest of 1 small orange
salt and pepper
½ × Basic shortcrust pastry
  (see left)
1 small egg, beaten

- **Serves 4**

- **670cals/2815kjs per serving**

1 Dust the meat with seasoned flour. Heat the oil in a flameproof casserole and fry the meat, turning often, until browned on all sides. Add the leeks and walnut pieces and cook for another 2-3 minutes, stirring occasionally. Add the wine and enough stock to just cover the meat. Add the orange zest, bring to the boil, then reduce the heat, cover and simmer gently for 1½-2 hours or until the meat is tender, adding more stock if necessary. Add salt and pepper to taste and leave to cool.

2 Roll out the pastry about 5mm/¼in thick. Assemble four 175ml/6fl oz ramekins. Cut out four slightly larger lids. Brush the rims of the ramekins with water.

3 Heat the oven to 200C/400F/gas 6. Spoon the filling into each dish, piling the meat slightly higher in the centre so that the crust will not sink. Place the lids over each dish, press firmly to seal, then trim the edges. Pierce a hole in the centre of each lid to allow the steam to escape. Brush the pies with beaten egg to glaze, then decorate with pastry trimmings. Bake the pies for 25-30 minutes or until the crust is golden brown. Serve hot.

Serving ideas

These pies are delicious served with mashed potatoes, steamed broccoli and buttered carrots.

You could also serve a green side salad dressed with a walnut-oil flavoured vinaigrette.

How to ...line a flan tin

Roll the pastry out so that it is 3mm/⅛in thick and about 4cm/1½in larger than the flan tin all round. Roll it round the rolling pin and unroll over the tin.

Starting in the centre, press the pastry gently into the shape of the tin. Do not stretch it: it will only shrink back during baking. Use a bent forefinger to make it fit snugly.

Fold the excess pastry over the rim of the tin and run the rolling pin over the top. This will cut it off neatly and leave a clean edge. Press the pastry gently into the flutes.

Prick the base all over with a fork to release any trapped air. Chill. Line with greaseproof paper or foil and fill it with dried beans (or rice), pushing them up against the sides.

Strawberry flan

- *Preparation: 1 hour,*
  plus 1 hour chilling

- *Cooking: 40 minutes, plus cooling*

1 × Basic shortcrust pastry
(page 10), sweetened with
50g/2oz caster sugar (see below)
butter, for greasing
4tbls raspberry jam
For the filling:
450g/1lb full-fat soft cheese
50g/2oz caster sugar
juice and grated zest of 1 orange
225g/8oz strawberries, sliced

- *Serves 6-8*

- *480cals/2015kjs per serving*

1 Make the pastry, adding the sugar before rubbing in the fat. Wrap in stretch wrap and chill for 30 minutes.

2 Use the pastry to line a greased 24cm/9½in loose-bottomed fluted flan tin and chill. Meanwhile, heat the oven to 200C/400F/gas 6. Line the case,

then bake for 20 minutes. Reduce the heat to 180C/350F/gas 4, remove the lining and the beans and return to the oven for a further 10-15 minutes, until the pastry is completely dry on the surface and a golden brown colour. Leave in the tin to cool, then remove to a serving plate.

3 Make the filling: put the cheese, sugar, orange juice and zest in a blender or food processor and blend until completely smooth. Turn into the cooled pastry case and spread evenly. Arrange the strawberry slices in neat circles on top of the filling.

4 Put the jam into a small saucepan with 1tbls cold water and heat gently, stirring occasionally, until melted. Sieve, then brush evenly over the strawberries. Chill for 1-2 hours before serving.

Microwave hints

Use your microwave to make the glaze: put the jam and water into a small bowl and microwave at 100% (high) for 30-60 seconds, stirring twice, until melted.

WHAT WENT WRONG?

Pastry case collapses while baking: make sure the greaseproof paper or foil lining covers the sides of the case and that there are enough beans to cover the whole of the base and to stack up against the sides of the shell to support it.

Pastry case shrinks while baking: the dough was insufficiently relaxed. Remember to leave it in the fridge for another 30 minutes after fitting it into the mould.

The top crust of a fruit pie is soggy underneath: start and end with layers of fruit — sugar sprinkled on fruit directly under the crust causes the sogginess.

Soggy pastry parcels: the steam given off by the filling is unable to escape and so is absorbed into the pastry. Always prick pastry parcels well to make holes for the steam to escape.

Chilled lemon tartlets

- **Preparation: 1¼ hours, plus 3 hours chilling**
- **Cooking: 30 minutes, plus cooling**

½ × Basic shortcrust pastry
  (page 10), sweetened with
  50g/2oz caster sugar (see below)
150ml/¼pt milk
50g/2oz sugar
½tsp cornflour
2 large egg yolks
1½tsp powdered gelatine
50ml/2fl oz lemon juice
grated zest of ½ lemon
150ml/¼pt double cream,
  lightly whipped
1 large egg white, lightly beaten
lime zest, to decorate

- **Makes 4**

- **585cals/2455kjs per tartlet**

1 Make the pastry, adding the sugar before rubbing in the butter. Wrap in stretch wrap and chill for 30 minutes. Roll out and line four buttered tartlet tins, 9cm/3½in across and 2.5cm/1in deep. Chill for 30 minutes. Meanwhile, heat the oven to 200C/400F/gas 6. Line the cases, then bake for 10 minutes. Reduce the heat to 180C/350F/gas 4, remove beans and paper or foil and return the tins to the oven for 5 minutes or until the pastry is golden.

2 Gently heat the milk in a small pan with 25g/1oz sugar, stirring until it has dissolved. Remove from the heat when it is just coming to the boil.

3 Whisk cornflour with the egg yolks and the remaining sugar until the beaters leave a ribbon trail when lifted. Gradually pour in the scalded milk, whisking constantly, and return to the pan. Heat slowly, stirring constantly, until thick enough to coat the spoon; cool.

4 Meanwhile, put 2tbls cold water in a cup and sprinkle on the gelatine. Leave for 5 minutes or until softened, then put the cup in a pan of hot water and heat until dissolved; do not stir. Cool slightly. Pour the gelatine into the cold custard in a continuous stream, whisking constantly. Add the lemon juice and zest. Put the mixture over a bowl of ice and stir until it is on the point of setting.

5 Fold the cream into the custard. Brush the pastry cases with egg white, then pour in the cream mixture. Refrigerate until set; about 2 hours. Top with lime zest to serve.

Fruit barquettes

- **Preparation: 1 hour, plus 1 hour chilling**
- **Cooking: 25 minutes, plus cooling**

½ × Basic shortcrust pastry
  (page 10)
3tbls ground almonds
1 ripe apricot, stoned and
  quartered
½ ripe peach, stoned and sliced
  into 8 slivers
50g/2oz tiny seedless grapes
50g/2oz redcurrants
6tbls apricot jam
1tbls brandy

- **Makes 8**

- **125cals/525kjs per barquette**

1 Roll out the pastry 3mm/⅛in thick and use to line eight barquette moulds. Prick all over and chill for 30 minutes.

2 Meanwhile, heat the oven to 200C/400F/gas 6, with a shelf above the centre. Divide the ground almonds between the barquettes. Bake for 20 minutes, then leave to cool in the moulds for 10 minutes. Remove from the moulds and place on a wire rack to cool completely.

3 Divide the fruit between the barquettes as shown.

4 Make the glaze: put the apricot jam and brandy into a small saucepan over low heat and stir until dissolved. Rub through a nylon sieve, then spoon some of the glaze over each barquette. Chill for 1-2 hours before serving.

Lining barquette moulds

Put a mould upside down on the pastry and cut round it about 1cm/½in away from the edge, following the shape exactly.

Lift the pastry ovals into the moulds and press gently with a ball of scrap pastry until they fit perfectly. Trim edges.

Broccoli and mushroom quiche

- **Preparation: 40 minutes, plus 1 hour chilling**

- **Cooking: 1 hour**

1 × Basic shortcrust pastry
   (page 10)
butter, for greasing
2tbls olive oil
1 onion, chopped
1 garlic clove, crushed
225g/8oz broccoli, cut into small
   florets
100g/4oz button mushrooms,
   sliced
2tbls chopped parsley
salt and pepper
75g/3oz Cheddar cheese, grated
75g/3oz Gruyère cheese, grated
150ml/¼pt double cream
125ml/4fl oz milk
2 eggs, beaten

- **Serves 4-6**

- **690cals/2900kjs per serving**

1 Use the pastry to line a greased 23cm/9in flan dish and chill. Meanwhile, heat the oven to 200C/400F/gas 6. Line the case, then bake for 10-15 minutes. Remove the beans and paper.

2 Meanwhile, heat the oil in a large frying pan over moderate heat and fry the onion and garlic until soft but not browned. Add the broccoli florets and cook, stirring occasionally, until slightly softened. Add the mushrooms and parsley and season with salt and pepper to taste. Continue cooking for 20-25 minutes over low to medium heat until the vegetables are cooked through.

3 Put the vegetable mixture into the pastry case, spreading it evenly. Sprinkle over the grated cheeses.

4 Mix the cream and milk together in a jug, add the beaten eggs and season to taste. Pour the egg mixture evenly over the vegetable filling. Return the quiche to the oven and cook for 20-25 minutes or until the egg mixture is set and golden. Serve hot or cold.

Cook's tips

To prevent the base of a quiche from becoming soggy when the moist filling is poured in, make sure the baking sheet on which the tin is to stand is really hot by putting it in the oven while it is heating up. This will ensure that the bottom of the pastry becomes really crisp.

WATCHPOINTS

Too much fat produces an over-rich and crumbly pastry. Too much flour makes the pastry dry and hard. Too much liquid results in a pastry which is likely to shrink, but too little produces an unmanageably dry dough.

Handle pastry as gently and quickly as possible, otherwise the gluten in the flour will strengthen and toughen the pastry, and the fat will become oily, giving a greasy, heavy result.

Once made, relax the dough by chilling it. This makes the pastry easier to roll out and will help prevent the dough from shrinking in the oven.

Always cook shortcrust pastry at the temperature stated in the recipe. If the oven is too hot the pastry will burn before the filling is cooked; if it's too cool the pastry will be tough.

Classic
White Sauces

Master a basic white sauce and you can transform vegetables into creamy dishes, pasta into cheesy golden bakes and chicken into dinner-party elegance

Cheesy macaroni florentine (p.18)

A BASIC WHITE sauce consists of butter and flour cooked together, then simmered with milk and seasoned. This simple mixture can be varied by adding flavourings such as cheese or onion, and enrichments such as eggs or cream. You can also change the thickness to produce either a thin sauce for pouring over food, a thicker sauce for coating or masking it, or an even thicker sauce for binding foods.

Making a roux
Most sauces are thickened with a roux — equal quantities of butter and flour combined over low heat. Making a roux is a very simple

procedure, but needs attention.

If you find making a roux difficult, cook it in the top pan of a double boiler over simmering water. This will guarantee that it does not cook too quickly, colour or burn.

Melt the specified quantity of butter over a very low heat in a small pan. Add plain flour and stir with a wooden spoon or wire whisk for 2-3 minutes only, until smooth and beginning to bubble.

Adding the liquid
The liquid used gives the finished sauce much of its character. Milk, used for a basic white sauce, does not give much flavour so, when

time allows, make Béchamel sauce, in which the milk is flavoured with onion and herbs before mixing it with the roux.

To minimize the risk of lumps, have the milk warm or hot when adding it to the roux, and take the pan off the heat. Add the milk very gradually, stirring or whisking constantly. Return the pan to the low heat and bring to the boil, still stirring, then simmer gently for 5 minutes to make sure the flour is cooked through.

Some recipes recommend cooking a white sauce for much longer —

30 or 40 minutes. This is the French method and requires adding more liquid (half as much again), which is then reduced by long simmering to the required consistency. It is best done in a double boiler to avoid any risk of the sauce burning. This method produces a very smooth sauce with a concentrated flavour.

The end result should be perfectly smooth, and thin enough to flow if it is a pouring sauce, or thick enough to coat the back of a wooden spoon if it is a coating sauce. For a super-smooth finish, strain the sauce into a clean pan and reheat gently before using.

Additions and enrichments

To make a white sauce richer and more flavoursome, egg yolks or cream may be whisked in at the end, or lemon juice added.

Egg yolks especially need careful handling or they will curdle. Before adding them, remove the pan from the heat and allow the sauce to cool slightly. Beat in the yolks, then cook in the top pan of a double boiler over very low heat, whisking constantly. Do not allow the sauce to boil.

Cream is less tricky, but again, do not allow the sauce to boil once it has been added. Stir in lemon juice after cooking is complete.

White sauce variations

Most of these are best made with a Béchamel base, but plain white would be preferable for strongly flavoured sauces such as onion and cheese. Stir the flavourings into 300ml/½pt of hot sauce.

Anchovy: add 1tsp anchovy essence. Serve with fish.

Cheese (known as Mornay if made with Béchamel base): add 50g/2oz grated hard cheese (Cheddar, Parmesan or Gruyère) and ½tsp mustard powder. Serve with vegetables, pasta, eggs or fish.

Curry: add 1tbls curry powder and ½ cooking apple, finely chopped; simmer until cooked. Serve with fish, poultry, eggs or vegetables.

Onion: add 2 onions, chopped and cooked in salted water until soft. Use the cooking liquid to replace some of the milk. Serve with eggs, tripe, lamb or veal.

Asparagus and mushroom gratin

● **Preparation: 45 minutes**

● **Cooking: 1 hour 15 minutes**

*900g/2lb fresh asparagus, trimmed
  from the bottom to equal lengths
50g/2oz mushrooms, thinly sliced
25g/1oz butter
2tbls single cream
300ml/½pt Béchamel sauce of
  coating consistency (see Using
  white sauces, page 18)
salt and pepper
2tbls grated Parmesan cheese*

● *Serves 4*

● *165cals/695kjs per serving*

1 Tie the asparagus in a bundle and, if you don't have an asparagus steamer, stand it upright in 7.5cm/3in boiling water in a narrow-based saucepan. Wearing oven gloves, tightly fix a domed lid of foil over the asparagus tips so that they cook in the steam. Cook in boiling water until a stalk is tender and can be pierced with a knife point. The time can vary from 15-45

minutes. When the stalks are tender, drain the asparagus and reserve.

2 Meanwhile, fry the mushrooms in butter until just tender. Drain.

3 Stir the mushrooms and cream into the hot Béchamel sauce. Adjust the seasoning if necessary.

4 Heat the grill to moderate. Arrange the asparagus in a flameproof serving dish with the tips facing both ways. Cover with the sauce, sprinkle over the Parmesan cheese and grill for 5-6 minutes until the top is golden brown.

WHAT WENT WRONG?

Lumpy sauce: the roux was not cooked enough, or the liquid was added too quickly, without enough stirring. Remedy: sieve the sauce.

Over-thin sauce: the proportion of liquid was wrong, or the roux was undercooked. Remedy: boil rapidly, stirring to prevent burning, to reduce the liquid.

Over-thick sauce: either the wrong proportions were used, or the sauce was cooked too fast so that too much liquid evaporated. Remedy: gradually beat in more liquid.

Greasy sauce: too much fat was used, or the roux was overcooked. Remedy: use absorbent paper to remove excess fat.

Chicken with cucumber sauce

In this dish, a cucumber purée is added to a basic white sauce enriched with cream.

- **Preparation: 10 minutes**
- **Cooking: 35 minutes**

1 cucumber, peeled
  and roughly chopped
425ml/³/4pt chicken stock
150ml/¹/4pt dry white wine
¹/2 small onion, finely chopped
6 black peppercorns
1 bay leaf
salt
4 chicken breasts, skinned and
  boned
cucumber slices, to garnish
For the sauce:
25g/1oz butter
40g/1¹/2oz flour
150ml/¹/4pt milk
150ml/¹/4pt single cream
freshly grated nutmeg

- **Serves 4**
- **485cals/2035kjs per serving**

1 Steam the cucumber pieces in a sieve set over a saucepan of boiling water and covered. Steam for about 5 minutes and, when just soft, purée in a food processor or blender.

2 In a large saucepan, bring the chicken stock and wine to the boil. Add the onion, peppercorns, bay leaf and salt to taste. Add the chicken breasts, cover the pan and simmer gently for about 15 minutes or until the chicken is tender.

3 To make the sauce, melt the butter in a saucepan and stir in the flour. Cook for 1-2 minutes, then remove from the heat and gradually add the milk and the cream, stirring constantly. Return the pan to the heat and stir in 1-2tbls liquor from the simmering chicken breasts. Beat well to make a smooth sauce and season to taste with salt and nutmeg.

4 Add the cucumber purée and simmer gently for a few minutes.

5 With a slotted spoon, transfer the chicken breasts to a warmed serving dish. Pour the sauce over the chicken and garnish with cucumber slices.

Serving ideas

Accompany the dish with saffron rice, made by adding a few strands of saffron to the water when boiling the rice. Alternatively add a teaspoon of turmeric, which is much cheaper, and gives a good golden colour though not the same flavour.

How to ... make a white sauce

Melt the butter in a heavy saucepan. Add an equal quantity of flour and blend into the fat. Cook for 2-3 minutes, stirring constantly.

Add the liquid slowly, whisking all the time to prevent the formation of lumps. Bring to the boil and season. Simmer for 5 minutes until cooked.

To thicken and enrich the sauce, remove the pan from the heat and whisk in finely diced butter. Do not reheat or the sauce will separate and become fatty.

Cheesy macaroni florentine

● **Preparation: 10 minutes**

● **Cooking: 50 minutes**

450g/1lb frozen chopped spinach
75g/3oz butter, plus extra for
*   greasing*
salt and pepper
225g/8oz macaroni
100g/4oz onion, finely chopped
40g/1¹/₂oz flour
425ml/³/₄pt milk
225g/8oz grated Gouda cheese
3 tomatoes

● **Serves 4-5**

● **655cals/2750kjs per serving**

1 Heat the oven to 180C/350F/gas 4. Grease a 1.7L/3pt casserole. Cook the spinach and drain well. Cut 25g/1oz of the butter into small pieces and mix into the spinach. Season to taste with salt and pepper.

2 Cook the macaroni in boiling, salted water for 8-10 minutes, or until *al dente* (tender but still firm to the bite). Drain and reserve.

3 Melt the remaining 50g/2oz butter in a large saucepan. Add the onion and cook gently until soft. Stir in the flour and continue stirring for ½-1 minute to make a pale roux. Remove the pan from the heat.

4 Warm the milk separately, then gradually add to the roux, stirring constantly. Return the pan to the heat and bring to the boil. Cook for 2 minutes, stirring, then stir in 175g/6oz of the cheese. Add the macaroni to the sauce, toss until well coated and season with salt and pepper to taste.

5 Spread the spinach mixture over the bottom of the prepared casserole and pour in the macaroni cheese. Slice the tomatoes and arrange in an even layer on top. Sprinkle with the reserved grated cheese.

6 Place in the oven and bake for 20 minutes or until the top is golden. Serve at once.

Eggs with aurore sauce

This dish can be served as a starter or, accompanied by a salad, as a light lunch

● **Preparation: 50 minutes**

● **Cooking: 5 minutes**

2tbls tomato purée
300ml/¹/₂pt Béchamel sauce
salt and white pepper
1tbls single cream (optional)
fresh herbs, finely chopped
*   (optional)*
4 eggs, hard-boiled and cut in half
*   lengthways*
parsley sprigs, to garnish

● **Serves 4**

● **175cals/735kjs per serving**

1 Over medium heat, stir the tomato purée into the hot Béchamel sauce and season with salt and pepper to taste. Mix in the cream and herbs, if wished.

2 Arrange the eggs on individual plates, pour over the hot sauce and garnish.

Béchamel sauce

● **Preparation: 5 minutes,**
**   plus 25 minutes infusing**

● **Cooking: 10 minutes**

300ml/¹/₂pt milk
¹/₂ onion, chopped
1 bay leaf
1 clove
4-6 peppercorns
15g/¹/₂oz butter

15g/¹/₂oz flour
salt and white pepper

● **Makes 300ml/¹/₂pt**

1 Put the milk in a small pan with the onion, bay leaf, clove and peppercorns. Bring slowly to the boil, remove from the heat, cover and leave to infuse for 25 minutes. Strain and discard the flavourings.

2 Melt the butter in a small pan over low heat, stir in the flour and cook, stirring, for 1-2 minutes without allowing the mixture to colour.

3 Remove the pan from the heat and gradually add the flavoured milk, stirring or whisking constantly. Return to the low heat and bring to the boil, then simmer very gently for 5 minutes. Season.

USING WHITE SAUCES

Vary the liquid content of your sauces according to what they are to be used for. Béchamel sauce (left) makes a sauce of pouring consistency. For a coating consistency, use 25g/ 1oz each of butter and flour.

If you have to keep a sauce warm, cover the top with dampened greaseproof paper or run a spoonful of stock or milk over the top to stop a skin from forming.

Amazing Mayonnaise

Home-made mayonnaise is rich and delicious, and despite the mystique that clings to its making, the technique is really quite simple

THE MYSTIQUE SURROUNDING mayonnaise probably grew up because it is such a magical creation – simply by beating together egg yolks and oil, you produce a thick creamy sauce.

There is no magic, however; all you have done, by beating, is to make an emulsion. But the way in which the beating is done, and the temperature of the ingredients, are critical to its success.

Ingredients

Fresh egg yolks and good-quality oil (preferably olive, for best flavour) are the foundation ingredients. Basic mayonnaise is simply flavoured with lemon juice or vinegar, which also help the emulsifying process, plus mustard, salt and pepper (white so as not to introduce dark specks into the pale sauce). Although rich and delicious, it is quite bland, and so lends itself to any number of variations – see page 21 – which can affect both its flavour and colour.

Making mayonnaise

The first rule for success is that all the ingredients must be at roughly the same temperature, and neither too hot nor too cold. So, if you keep your eggs in the fridge, get them out an hour or so ahead of time.

The second rule for success is to add the oil extremely slowly at first; as you go along you can work a little faster. If too much oil is added at once, the egg cannot absorb it, the emulsion breaks down and the mayonnaise curdles.

Storing

Mayonnaise can be made in advance: add 1tbls of boiling water to keep it from turning or separating. Cover the bowl with stretch wrap to prevent a skin from forming and store in the bottom of the refrigerator. Hand-made mayonnaise will keep for up to a week, whereas blender mayonnaise will last for a few days longer.

Aubergine salad (page 22)

Artichokes with prawns

- **Preparation: 25 minutes**
- **Cooking: 45 minutes, plus 1 hour cooling**

4 large artichokes
salt and pepper
juice of 1 lemon
1tbls olive oil
100g/4oz cooked, peeled prawns
200ml/7fl oz mayonnaise
watercress sprigs and 100g/4oz
  unpeeled prawns (optional), to
  garnish

- **Serves 4**
- **500cals/2100kjs per serving**

1 Prepare the artichokes: cut off the stalks with a sharp knife, trim the bases so they stand level and pull off the tough outer leaves.

2 Bring a large pan of water to the boil. Add salt, 2tbls lemon juice and the olive oil, then the artichokes. Cover and cook for 35-45 minutes or until just tender. Drain thoroughly and leave, upside down, for about 1 hour to cool.

3 Gently open the outer leaves. Carefully remove the inner leaves, leaving the choke exposed. Scrape this away with a teaspoon, making sure that no prickly bits remain. Immediately brush the freshly exposed base with lemon juice to prevent discoloration.

4 Divide the prawns among the artichokes and dress with mayonnaise.

Garnish with a sprig of watercress, and extra prawns if using; serve at once.

Variations

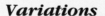

For a more peppery-tasting filling, add 2tsp lemon juice or a pinch of cayenne pepper or mustard powder to the mayonnaise. Or for added flavour and colour, chop up a bunch of watercress and stir into the mayonnaise.

WHAT WENT WRONG?

Mayonnaise can curdle for any of the following reasons:
Ingredients at different temperatures.
Ingredients too cold.
Oil added too quickly.
Insufficient whisking when adding the oil.
Stale egg yolks.

The remedy is simple: break another egg yolk into a clean bowl and gradually beat the curdled mixture into it. Slowly add any remaining oil.

How to ... *make mayonnaise*

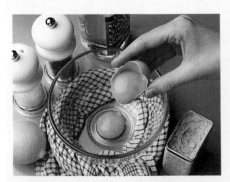

Twist a cold wet cloth around the bottom of a small bowl to keep it cool and steady. Add the egg yolks, mustard and salt and pepper and beat to a smooth paste.

Beat in a little lemon juice. Now add 50ml/2fl oz olive oil, literally drop by drop, beating constantly. When the oil has all been absorbed, add a little more lemon juice.

Add more oil, in a thin stream, whisking all the time. Continue doing this until all the oil has been incorporated and the mayonnaise is thick and smooth.

Basic mayonnaise

- **Preparation: 15 minutes**

2 egg yolks
½tsp French or dry mustard
salt and white pepper
2-3tsp lemon juice
300ml/½pt olive oil

- **Makes about 300ml/½pt**

- **2535cals/10645kjs total**

1 Put the egg yolks in a small bowl with the mustard and salt and pepper to taste. Wring out a tea-towel in very cold water and twist it around the bottom of the bowl to keep it steady and cool.

2 Using a wooden spoon, wire whisk, balloon whisk or fork, beat the mixture to a smooth paste. Add a few drops of lemon juice.

3 Add about 50ml/2fl of the oil, drop by drop, beating constantly. Add a little more lemon juice, then some more oil, beating all the time.

4 Continue adding the oil in a thin stream, beating constantly, until the mayonnaise is thick and smooth. Taste and adjust the seasoning, adding more lemon juice if necessary to sharpen the flavour.

Variations

Cucumber mayonnaise: add a 7.5cm/3in length of cucumber, finely chopped, and 1tbls finely chopped parsley.
Garlic mayonnaise: add 1 crushed garlic clove.
Mustard mayonnaise: use additional mustard, to taste.
Horseradish mayonnaise: use plenty of lemon juice and, just before serving, stir in 2tbls freshly grated horseradish.
Russian mayonnaise: add 2tbls tomato ketchup, a dash of hot pepper sauce or Worcestershire sauce and 1tsp each of snipped chives and canned pimiento.
Saffron mayonnaise: add a few lightly toasted and crushed saffron strands to give a pronounced golden colour and exquisite flavour.

LEFT-OVER EGG WHITES

Store egg whites in a cup covered with stretch wrap in the fridge for up to 4 days. Alternatively, beat them very lightly with a little salt and freeze for up to 6 months.

MAKE IT SAUCY

The following sauces are based on the basic mayonnaise recipe (see left).
Sauce chantilly: stir in about 50ml/2fl oz stiffly whipped cream just before serving. Serve with cold asparagus.
Sauce rémoulade: flavour the mayonnaise with 1tbls each of finely chopped fresh tarragon, basil and parsley, 1 crushed garlic clove, 1 pounded anchovy fillet and extra mustard. Garnish with 1tsp capers and 2 small gherkins, finely chopped. Serve with cold meat or shellfish.
Sauce tartare: make the mayonnaise using 4 hard-boiled egg yolks, finely sieved, and 1 raw egg yolk. Mix 2tsp each of chopped capers, gherkins, parsley and tarragon into the finished sauce. Serve with fish.
Sauce verte: plunge 25g/1oz each of fresh watercress, parsley and chervil sprigs into boiling water, simmer for 5 minutes, drain and press dry in absorbent paper. Purée in a blender or food processor and mix into the mayonnaise. Serve with cold salmon or duck.

Anchovy egg mayonnaise

- **Preparation: 30 minutes**

4 large eggs, hard boiled
40g/1½oz canned anchovy fillets, drained
3tbls mayonnaise
2tsp chopped fresh thyme or other herb
1 small lettuce
75g/3oz jar of capers, drained

- **Serves 4**

- **210cals/880kjs per serving**

1 Cut the eggs carefully in half horizontally and remove the yolks to a small bowl. Finely chop half of the anchovy fillets, add to the egg yolks along with 1tbls of the mayonnaise and mash together, then stuff the egg halves.

2 Mix the herbs into the remaining mayonnaise. Line four serving plates with lettuce leaves and put the eggs on top. Mask them with the mayonnaise. Garnish with the remaining anchovy fillets, cut into thin strips, and arranged in a lattice, with capers in between.

minutes, or until the onion has softened, stirring occasionally. Add the tomato purée, wine, stock and seasoning; cook for a further 3-4 minutes. Remove from the heat and leave until cold.

2 Prepare the rice salad: put the oil and vinegar into a small screw-topped jar, season to taste with salt and pepper and shake to mix. Stir into the rice along with the raisins and apricots. Spoon onto a serving dish.

3 Mix the mayonnaise and chutney into the dressing and fold in the chicken. Spoon on top of the rice salad and garnish.

Aubergine salad

- **Preparation: 20 minutes, plus 1 hour draining and chilling**

- **Cooking: 10 minutes**

1 large aubergine
salt and pepper
3tbls olive oil
200ml/7fl oz mayonnaise
200ml/7fl oz yoghurt
1 small onion, finely chopped
1½tsp dried marjoram
1tsp clear honey
1tsp horseradish sauce
1tsp lemon juice
cayenne pepper and flat-leaved parsley, to garnish
pitta bread, to serve

- **Serves 4**

- **645cals/2710kjs per serving**

1 Wipe the aubergine with a clean damp cloth but do not peel it. Cut in half and chop each piece into very fine strips. Put on a plate, sprinkle liberally with salt and leave for 30 minutes to draw out excess water. Then put the strips in a colander, rinse well under cold running water and shake well to drain.

2 Put the olive oil in a large frying pan over medium heat. When it is nearly smoking add the aubergine and cook for 10 minutes, stirring occasionally. Remove from the pan and drain on absorbent paper. Leave until cold.

3 Meanwhile put the mayonnaise and yoghurt in a large bowl. Add the onion, marjoram, honey, horseradish sauce and lemon juice and mix thoroughly.

4 Add the cold aubergine, season to taste with salt and pepper, mix well and chill for 30 minutes.

5 Pile the mixture onto a serving dish, sprinkle with a pinch of cayenne pepper, garnish with parsley and serve.

Coronation chicken

- **Preparation: 45 minutes**

- **Cooking: 20 minutes**

450g/1lb boneless cooked chicken, cut into chunks
lemon slices and coriander, to garnish
For the dressing:
1tbls oil
1 small onion, finely chopped
2tsp Madras curry powder
2tsp tomato purée
2tbls red wine

2tbls chicken stock
salt and pepper
125ml/4fl oz mayonnaise
2tbls mango chutney
For the rice salad:
2tbls oil
1tbls wine vinegar
100g/4oz long-grain rice, cooked
2tbls raisins
4tbls chopped dried no-soak apricots

- **Serves 4**

- **675cals/2835kjs per serving**

1 First make the dressing: put the oil, onion and curry powder in a small pan over medium heat and cook for 5-6

How to ··· make blender mayonnaise

Put a whole egg in the goblet with 1tbls lemon juice, ½tsp each of mustard powder and salt and a pinch of pepper. Add 2tbls cold water, cover and process at maximum speed for 5 seconds.

Remove the centre of the lid and, still working at maximum speed, add 300ml/½pt olive oil in a thin, steady trickle until it is all absorbed and the sauce is thick and smooth. Taste and adjust the seasoning.

Classic Crêpes

Making crêpes, or pancakes, is an art, but one that's soon learnt. And it's not even necessary to toss them and risk disaster!

PANCAKES ARE SO versatile and delicious, forming the basis of countless sweet and savoury dishes, that it's not surprising countries all over the world have their own versions: German *pfannkuchen*, Russian *blinis*, Jewish *blintzes*, Mexican *tortillas*, Indian *parathas*, to name but a few. Crêpes are the French version. They are richer than the English pancake, containing more egg, and a little oil or butter which helps stop the crêpes sticking. Savoury crêpes made from buckwheat are called *galettes* in Brittany and Normandy.

Properly made, a crêpe should be thin and delicate, yet substantial enough to wrap round a filling without coming apart.

The crêpe pan

A good pan is the key to success. It should be heavy, so that the batter heats up evenly; rounded sides are an advantage as it is easier to slip a palette knife under the crêpes to loosen them. The ideal is a well-seasoned pan not used for other things, and not washed after use – just wipe it clean with absorbent paper. If any batter has stuck, rub it off with salt. If you keep a special omelette pan you can use this for crêpes too. Alternatively use a heavyweight non-stick pan.

It's vital to heat the pan before greasing it, to just the right temperature; if it's either too cool or too hot the batter will stick. Test by sprinkling on a little cold water; this should form drops and sizzle away almost at once. Wipe the pan with a wad of absorbent paper dipped in oil. Do not overgrease: the aim is to lubricate the pan, not provide fat for the crêpes to fry in. To make absolutely certain the crêpes don't

Italian pancake pie (page 27)

stick wipe the pan out again after cooking each one, then grease lightly.

The crêpe batter
Although the batter is very simple it must be just right; absolutely smooth, with the consistency of thin cream. Use your judgement when adding the liquid; different flours take up different amounts, and eggs vary in size. Do not beat it any more than necessary to combine the ingredients. Overbeating makes for tough crêpes.

Cook the batter as shown in the photographs. Don't be disappointed if the first one doesn't turn out too well; this often happens, especially if the pan is used for cooking other things. Throw it out if it's really hopeless, regrease the pan and start again. Tossing pancakes is just for show-offs; flipping them over with a palette knife is quicker and safer.

As with many fried foods the first side cooked is the best looking; the second usually develops unattractive dark spots. So always roll or fold crêpes with the first side out.

Keep each crêpe warm as you cook the rest. For rolling or folding the crêpes should be slightly soft: stack these on an upturned soup plate over a pan of hot water and cover with a folded tea-towel. For stacking, crisper crêpes are preferable; keep warm in a low oven.

Reheating and storing crêpes
Warm crêpes up gently or they may become rubbery. Put them over hot water, as when keeping warm, and gently heat the water. Stuffed crêpes can be reheated in a moderate oven, gently fried in butter or put under a moderate grill.

Crêpes keep well in the refrigerator, provided that they are absolutely cold before going in; if still warm they may go rubbery. Stack them up and wrap them in an airtight plastic bag and they will keep for several days.

To freeze crêpes stack them with a sheet of lightly oiled greaseproof between each one to stop them sticking together. Wrap in foil or a plastic freezer bag, make sure all the air is expelled and seal tightly. Freeze for up to 8 weeks.

Ham and mushroom crêpes

- **Preparation: making crêpes and sauce, then 30 minutes**
- **Cooking: 40 minutes**

12 × 12cm/5in crêpes
tomato sauce (see Linguini steps 1, 2, and 3, page 33)
For the filling:
225g/8oz mozzarella cheese
4 thin slices cooked ham
50g/2oz butter, plus extra for greasing
100g/4oz button mushrooms, sliced
4tbls flour
300ml/1/2pt milk, heated
1/2tsp grated nutmeg
pinch of cayenne pepper
salt
2 egg yolks
300ml/1/2pt double cream

- **Serves 4**
- **945cals/3970kjs per serving**

1 Heat the oven to 180C/350F/gas 4. Cut the mozzarella into 12 slices. Dice the remainder; also dice the ham.

2 Melt half the butter in a frying pan and fry the mushrooms until they are lightly browned. Keep on one side.

3 Melt the remaining butter in a saucepan. Add the flour and cook, stirring, until smooth. Gradually add the hot milk and continue cooking, stirring constantly, until the mixture thickens. Add the nutmeg, cayenne pepper and salt to taste.

4 Beat the egg yolks and mix in the cream. Pour in a little of the hot sauce and whisk until smooth. Stir the egg and cream mixture back into the sauce and add the diced cheese, ham and mushrooms. Cook over low heat until the mixture is thick and smooth. Do not allow to boil or the eggs will curdle.

5 Spread a thin layer of tomato sauce over each crêpe, then cover generously with the ham and mushroom filling and roll up. Generously grease a baking dish. Lay the crêpes in the dish, spoon a little tomato sauce over each crêpe and top with a strip of mozzarella cheese. Bake for about 20 minutes until the crêpes are heated through. Serve at once.

Variations

Instead of baking the crêpes, fill the crêpes as above, using hot crêpes and tomato sauce, then roll up and arrange on a pool of hot tomato sauce. In this case, you will need only 100g/4oz mozzarella.

For ham and sweetcorn crêpes, replace the mushrooms with 100g/4oz drained canned sweetcorn.

How to ... make perfect crêpes

Heat a heavy frying pan and then grease it: rub it all over with a thick wad of absorbent paper dipped in oil. Keep your fingertips clear of the hot frying pan.

Pour a tablespoon of batter in the centre of the pan, and another one or two around the edge. Tilt the pan to make the pools of batter spread evenly over its surface.

Cook the crêpe over medium heat until it becomes opaque and dry on top, and little bubbles of air start to form underneath. The first side cooked is always the best-looking.

Slip a palette knife around the edges of the crêpe to free it from the pan. Then use the knife to flip the crêpe over. Do not overcook the second side; 1 minute is usually ample.

Basic French crêpes

- *Preparation: 10 minutes, plus standing*
- *Cooking: 20 minutes*

75g/3oz flour
½tsp salt
2 eggs, lightly beaten
2tbls oil, plus extra for greasing
about 150ml/¼pt milk

- *Makes 8-12 crêpes*

1 Sift the flour and salt into a bowl. Add the eggs and oil and stir gently until smooth. Gradually stir in enough milk to obtain a batter with the consistency of single cream. Strain through a fine sieve if not absolutely smooth. Leave to stand for 30 minutes.

2 Put a heavy frying pan over medium heat, then grease it. (Use a 12.5cm/5in diameter pan for small crêpes, an 18cm/7in pan for larger ones.) Spoon in 2 or 3tbls of batter, according to the size of the pan. Tilt the pan so that the batter thinly coats the surface. Cook for 1 minute, until bubbles start to form underneath.

3 Slip a palette knife under the edges of the crêpe and flip it over. Cook for 1 minute on the second side. Do not overcook: the heat of a heavy pan may be enough on its own.

4 Repeat until all the batter is used up, greasing the pan between crêpes. Stack the crêpes as you make them and keep warm over hot water or in a very low oven, if wished.

Mocha crêpes with pears (page 26)

Mocha crêpes with pears

- **Preparation: 30 minutes, plus standing**
- **Cooking: 40 minutes**

ingredients for Basic French crêpes (page 25) without the oil
1tbls cocoa
1tbls instant coffee powder
25g/1oz melted butter
For the filling:
300ml/½pt double cream
1-2tbls rum
icing sugar
For the garnish:
5 ripe pears
150g/5oz sugar
1tbls lemon juice
few drops of vanilla essence

- **Serves 4-6**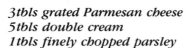
- **750cals/3150kjs per serving**

1 First prepare the garnish. Peel, core and thinly slice the pears. Put the sugar in a saucepan with 300ml/½pt water and the lemon juice. Stir over low heat until the sugar has dissolved. Bring to the boil and boil, without stirring, for 1 minute. Add the vanilla essence, then slip the pears into the syrup and poach gently for 5-10 minutes or until tender but not mushy. Remove with a slotted spoon and set aside.

2 Make the crêpe batter, adding the cocoa and coffee powder to the flour and beating in the butter after adding the milk. Leave to stand for 30 minutes.

3 Use the batter to make 12 x 12.5cm/ 5in crêpes. Keep them warm.

4 Whip the cream and sugar until thick and fold in the rum. Spread the crêpes with the mixture and half the pears, roll up and top with the remaining pears. Serve at once.

Spinach crêpes

- **Preparation: making crêpes, then 20 minutes**
- **Cooking: 30 minutes**

4 × 18cm/7in crêpes
450g/1lb spinach
pinch of grated nutmeg
salt and pepper
25g/1oz butter, plus extra for greasing
1tbls flour

3tbls grated Parmesan cheese
5tbls double cream
1tbls finely chopped parsley

- **Serves 2-4**
- **560cals/2350kjs per serving**

1 Heat the oven to 180C/350F/gas 4. Wash and pick over the spinach. Drain well, then cook over medium heat with no added water, stirring frequently, until limp and just tender.

2 Put the spinach in a colander and press firmly to remove any remaining moisture. Chop very finely and season with nutmeg and salt and pepper to taste.

3 Melt half the butter in a saucepan, then add the flour and cook over low heat, stirring, to make a pale roux. Add 2tbls Parmesan cheese and the cream; cook, stirring constantly, until the cheese has melted. Add the spinach and heat through. Taste and adjust the seasoning.

4 Spread a quarter of the hot spinach mixture over each crêpe and roll up. Butter a shallow ovenproof serving dish and lay the crêpes in it. Dot with the remaining butter and sprinkle with the remaining Parmesan mixed with the parsley. Heat through in the oven for 5-10 minutes and serve at once.

Serving ideas

Serve one crêpe per person for a starter, or two for a light lunch, accompanied by a tomato salad.

Crêpes Suzette

- *Preparation: making crêpes, then 15 minutes plus standing*
- *Cooking: 50 minutes*

12 × 12.5cm/5in crêpes
quartered orange slices, to decorate
For the orange butter:
100g/4oz butter
25g/1oz caster sugar
finely grated zest of 1 large orange
2tbls Cointreau
5tbls orange juice
To flame:
1tbls caster sugar
2tbls Cointreau
2tbls brandy

- *Serves 6*
- *330cals/1385kjs per serving*

1 To make the orange butter, melt the butter in a large frying pan and add the sugar, orange zest, Cointreau and orange juice. Simmer over low heat for 3-4 minutes or until slightly reduced.

2 Keeping the heat low, immerse a crêpe in the bubbling butter and, using a fork and spoon, fold it in half and then in half again. Push it to the side of the pan and repeat with the remaining crêpes.

3 To flame, first sprinkle the surface of the crêpes with the sugar. Then pour the Cointreau and brandy into another small pan and heat through gently. Light a taper and, standing well clear, set the alcohol alight. Quickly pour it over the crêpes and serve at once, decorated with quartered orange slices.

Cook's tips

When flaming, make sure you take the usual safety precautions: use long kitchen matches or tapers, never a lighter; make sure there is nothing above or near the pan to catch fire; keep hair and long sleeves out of the way.

SWEET CRÊPES

Once you have mastered the art of making crêpes, use different accompaniments and fillings to make a variety of simple desserts. Vary the way they look, too, by either rolling them up, or folding in quarters.

Traditional lemon: Sprinkle the crêpes with caster sugar and serve with lemon wedges.

Orange: Use wedges of orange instead of lemon and squeeze some orange juice over the crêpes before rolling or folding.

Normandy: Spread with sweetened apple purée.

Jam: Spread with a thin layer of raspberry, strawberry or apricot jam.

Parisian: Fill with a mixture of whipped cream and crushed macaroons or ratafia biscuits.

Italian pancake pie

- *Preparation: making crêpes and tomato sauce, then 30 minutes*
- *Cooking: 1½ hours*

10-12 × 18cm/7in crêpes
2tbls oil, plus extra for greasing
1 onion, finely chopped
1 garlic clove, finely chopped
700g/1½lb minced beef
tomato sauce (see Linguini steps 1, 2 and 3, page 33)
225g/8oz ricotta cheese
150g/5oz mozzarella cheese, finely chopped
25g/1oz grated Parmesan cheese

- *Serves 6*
- *620cals/2605kjs per serving*

1 Heat the oil in a large frying pan, add the onion and garlic and fry over low heat, stirring occasionally, until the onion is soft and transparent. Add the minced beef and cook, breaking it up with a wooden spoon, until it changes colour. Drain off excess fat.

2 Add about half the tomato sauce to the beef and simmer gently, uncovered, for about 30 minutes or until the meat is tender.

3 Heat the oven to 190C/375F/gas 5. Brush a deep 23cm/9in ovenproof ▶

serving dish or cake tin with oil. Assemble the pie: put a crêpe in the dish and spread it with about 3tbls of the meat mixture. Dot with 1tbls ricotta cheese and sprinkle with mozzarella cheese. Continue layering crêpes, meat and cheeses until they are all used up, finishing with a crêpe.

4 Spoon the other half of the tomato sauce on top of the pancake pie. Scatter the grated Parmesan cheese on top of the sauce. Cover loosely with foil and bake for 20 minutes, then remove the foil and cook for a further 15-20 minutes until the top is bubbling and golden brown.

5 Transfer to a warmed serving dish using two fish slices, if necessary, and serve at once.

Freezer

The pancakes, meat mixture and tomato sauce may all be frozen. Pack the cooled meat mixture and tomato sauce in rigid containers, cover and freeze for up to 3 months. Defrost overnight in the fridge.

Plan ahead

The pancake batter can be made up to 24 hours ahead of time. Cover it lightly and store in the fridge.

CRÊPE CREDENTIALS

Traditionally served on Candlemas and Shrove Tuesday, pancakes celebrate good fortune and future happiness. A French saying goes, if you toss a crêpe holding a coin in your hand on New Year's Day, the coin will multiply each day of the year. In French rural society, crêpes symbolized allegiance — farmers offered them to their landowners.

Deep-fried cheese crêpes

● **Preparation: making crêpes, then 25 minutes, plus setting**

● **Cooking: 20 minutes**

8 × 18cm/7in crêpes
1 egg, beaten
100g/4oz fine dry white breadcrumbs
lime slices, to garnish

For the filling:
25g/1oz butter
2tbls flour
300ml/½pt milk
125g/4½oz Gruyère cheese, grated
pinch of paprika
salt and pepper
2 egg yolks, beaten
oil, for greasing and deep-frying

● Serves 4-8

● 660cals/2770kjs per serving

1 To make the filling, melt the butter. Stir in the flour and cook, stirring constantly, for 2-3 minutes to make a pale roux. Gradually add the milk, stirring the sauce with a whisk. Cook over medium heat for about 5-10 minutes, whisking occasionally.

2 Add the cheese and continue cooking until it melts. Season with paprika and salt and pepper to taste, then remove from the heat and beat in the egg yolks. Pour the mixture into an oiled shallow baking dish or tin about 18cm x 18cm/7in x 7in and leave about an hour to cool and set. When set, cut the filling into eight rectangles.

WHAT WENT WRONG?

Doughy crêpes: batter too thick, or too much used.
Crêpes tear: batter too thin, or not enough egg in it.
Crêpes stick: pan unseasoned or not heavy enough; or too hot or too cool when greased.
Rubbery texture: reheated crêpes not allowed to cool before refrigeration; or warmed up too quickly.

3 Pour oil into a deep-fat fryer or deep saucepan to fill it no more than halfway up and heat to 180C/350F; at this temperature a cube of day-old bread turns golden in 1 minute.

4 Put a cheese rectangle into the middle of each crêpe. Fold over the two sides, brush with beaten egg to seal, then fold over the top and bottom, sealing with egg. Repeat with the remaining crêpes. Brush the cheese crêpes with beaten egg, then coat carefully and thoroughly with breadcrumbs.

5 Deep-fry four of the cheese crêpes for 1½ minutes or until golden brown. Repeat with the second batch. Drain on absorbent paper, garnish and serve.

Pasta Mania

Beat the Italians at their own game by making fresh pasta at home; team it up with a sauce or dressing and you've made a meal that 'mama' would be proud of

FRESH PASTA HAS a flavour that dried pasta cannot match — apart from the fun of making it yourself. The main ingredients of a pasta dough are flour and eggs in the proportion of four large eggs to 450g/1lb flour. It is best to use strong flour, the high gluten flour used to make bread, which is nearer to the durum flour used in Italy than plain flour.

Basic pasta dough is made by combining the flour and eggs together until the dough forms a stiff ball, then it is kneaded, just like bread, for 15 minutes or so. The dough must then be left to relax. If you have a pasta machine, the dough can then be rolled and cut by the machine; otherwise, roll out the pasta very thinly and cut it into noodles of the required width, using a very sharp knife. The noodles should then be left to dry out before cooking.

The basic egg pasta will be a familiar pale golden colour, but you can add spinach or tomato purée to the dough to make beautiful green or pink noodles (see page 34).

Handling the pasta dough

The first thing that will probably strike you when you start mixing the ingredients is that there is far too little liquid to hold the dough together. Keep at it a bit longer and add more water. Of course, flours vary and some absorb more liquid than others, but with a little more effort you will be able to force in all the flour.

Now start kneading in real earnest. If you can develop a smooth, relaxed, regular kneading rhythm, you will find it much less tiring.

After about 15 minutes steady kneading, the dough will have become smooth and elastic, though still very firm. Little air blisters just under the surface are a sure sign that it has had enough.

Linguini with tomato (page 33)

Rolling the dough at this stage would be very difficult indeed. The answer is to wrap the ball loosely in a polythene bag (to prevent the surface drying out) and leave it to rest for a minimum of 1 hour at room temperature.

Rolling out the dough

When dealing with a large amount of dough you will find it easier to roll it out a piece at a time. Cut off a quarter and return the remainder to its polythene bag to keep moist.

Flour your working surface lightly and flatten the piece of dough out with the palm of a lightly floured hand. Don't knead the dough at this stage: it will revive its elasticity and make it more difficult to roll.

Dust your rolling pin with flour and start rolling the dough, using short light strokes, in one direction only, and always working outwards from the centre to make a circle. Check occasionally that the sheet of dough has not stuck to the working surface, flouring a corner of the surface from time to time and swishing the sheet of dough over it to ensure that the underside keeps dry. The sheet of dough will resist all the way, but with perseverance you will finally get it paper-thin. Press it firmly: it should leave only the faintest indentation.

When making stuffed ravioli-type pasta, the dough should be used as soon as it is rolled, but for noodles it is safer to leave it for 10-15 minutes to dry slightly.

Cutting the pasta

When it is ready for cutting, flour your hands lightly and sweep them over the surface of the dough. Fold the dough loosely, over and over, until it resembles a wide sausage, or roll it up into a Swiss roll shape. Using a very sharp knife which will slice through the dough with minimum pressure, trim off the uneven ends, then cut to the required width (see Pasta shapes, page 34).

Ham and pasta salad

- **Preparation: making pasta, then 20 minutes**

- **Cooking: 5 minutes**

250g/9oz tagliatelle
175g/6oz cooked ham, in one piece
350g/12oz tomatoes, skinned, seeded and quartered
For the dressing:
½tsp Dijon mustard
2tbls wine vinegar

salt and pepper
6tbls olive oil
1tbls finely chopped parsley
1tbls finely chopped mixed herbs
   (such as thyme, fennel, tarragon)

- **Serves 4**   ① ££

- **515cals/2165kjs per serving**

1 Bring a large saucepan of salted water to the boil. Add the pasta and cook until *al dente*.

2 Slice the ham into batons, 4cm/1½in long and 5mm/¼in thick.

3 Drain the cooked pasta, refresh it under cold water; drain again.

4 For the dressing, put the mustard into a salad bowl. Add the vinegar, salt and pepper to taste and the oil. Beat vigorously with a fork until the mixture emulsifies. Add the finely chopped parsley and mixed herbs and stir until well blended. Add the cooked drained pasta, the ham batons and the prepared tomatoes. Toss lightly and serve immediately.

Cook's tips

Although this salad is served cold, it is unwise to prepare it much in advance or the pasta will become soggy.

How to ... *knead pasta dough*

Make a stiff dough. Knead well – push the ball of dough down and away from you with the heel of your hand.

Lift the end of the piece of dough up as you draw back your fingers and slap the dough back into a ball.

Give the dough a quarter turn, then push it out again as before. Try to develop a rocking rhythm; it is much less tiring.

PASTA MACHINES

A machine which rolls and cuts the dough is useful if you make a lot of pasta or want to make spaghetti.

Some food processors have pasta-making attachments which can be adjusted easily to give different widths and shapes of pasta.

Home-made egg pasta

This recipe makes about 450g/1lb of fresh pasta

● **Preparation: 45 minutes, plus relaxing and drying**

450g/1lb strong flour, plus extra for dusting
1tsp salt
4 large eggs
1tbls olive oil

● **Serves 4-6**　　　(m) (£) (⏰) (❄)

● **505cals/2120kjs per serving**

1 Sift the flour and salt into a large bowl. Make a well in the centre. Break the eggs into the well. Add the oil and 3tbls cold water. With the fingers of one hand, gradually draw flour from the sides into the liquid. Then work the dough until it holds together in a very stiff ball. Add a little more water if necessary, but remember the dough will soften quite a lot after kneading and resting.

2 Knead the dough, pushing the ball down and away from you with the heel of your hand. Then lift up the end of the oblong with your fingers as you draw your hand back and slap the dough into a ball. Then give the dough a quarter turn, so that the next time it is stretched in a different direction. Push it out again in the same way: like this every part of it is kneaded. Knead for about 15 minutes, or until the dough feels smooth and elastic; little air blisters under the surface of the dough mean that it is ready.

3 Roll the dough into a ball. Wrap it loosely in a polythene bag and leave it to relax at room temperature for at least 1 hour. If you want to leave it overnight put it in the refrigerator, but do not seal the bag.

4 When you are ready to roll the dough, divide the ball into four equal pieces and return three of them to the polythene bag. Dust your work surface and rolling pin with flour and roll the dough out as thinly as possible. Use more flour as necessary to prevent the dough sticking.

5 If cutting noodles by hand, it is best to leave the sheet to dry for 10-15 minutes at this point, so that the ribbons do not stick together, then roll the dough out and use a sharp knife to cut the pasta so that it does not drag or squash the dough. Repeat with the three other balls of dough. The noodles should then be left to dry before cooking. (⏰)

Freezer

Both the unrolled dough and cut strips can be frozen for 6 months or more. Eventually, however, they dry out and lose the characteristics that distinguish them from dried pasta.

COOL IT

Because fresh pasta can easily overcook, some people add cold water to the cooking water before draining, or rinse the drained pasta in cold water, to stop it cooking any more.

Pasta ribbons with spinach

- **Preparation: making pasta, then 25 minutes**
- **Cooking: 15 minutes**

450g/1lb spinach
75g/3oz butter
2tbls olive oil
1 onion, finely chopped
100g/4oz full-fat soft cheese
25g/1oz freshly grated Parmesan cheese
40g/1½oz canned anchovy fillets, drained and chopped
3tbls single cream
¼tsp grated nutmeg
pepper
450g/1lb pink tagliatelle
lemon slices, to garnish

Drying the noodles

Lay the pasta strips out on a clean cloth dusted with flour. If leaving overnight, cover with another clean cloth.

- ● **Serves 4-6** ① ££
- ● **875cals/3675kjs per serving**

1 Wash the spinach leaves well and shake off excess water. Place in a saucepan and cover tightly. Cook over low heat for 5 minutes or until tender, stirring once or twice. Place the cooked spinach in a sieve and press out excess moisture with the back of a wooden spoon. Chop the spinach finely.

2 Heat the butter and oil in a saucepan, add the onion and cook gently for 5 minutes or until tender. Stir in the spinach, the cheeses and the anchovies. Cook over low heat until smooth and heated through, stirring often. Stir in the cream and season to taste with nutmeg and pepper. Keep the sauce warm.

3 Meanwhile, cook the tagliatelle until *al dente*. Drain thoroughly. Transfer the pasta to individual serving dishes and spoon the spinach and anchovy sauce on top. Serve immediately, garnished with lemon slices.

Serving ideas

Serve this pasta dish accompanied by a side salad of watercress and sliced raw mushrooms, tossed in a light vinaigrette dressing.

DRYING OUT

Fresh home-made noodles must be left to dry out for at least an hour before cooking (or preferably overnight) until they feel hard, if not exactly brittle like bought pasta. If they are not dry enough they will absorb too much of the cooking water and turn slimy. You can use one of two methods:

On a tray: dust a clean cloth with flour and, as you slice the noodles, shake them out onto the cloth. If you intend to leave them overnight, lay another cloth over the top to cover them completely. Do not overlap the ribbons.

Hanging up: Place two kitchen chairs back to back with a scrubbed broomstick between them, and hang the noodles over this to dry in the warm air of the kitchen.

Linguini with tomato sauce

- *Preparation: making pasta, then 10 minutes*

- *Cooking: 40 minutes*

4tbls olive oil
1 onion, finely chopped
2 garlic cloves, crushed
400g/14oz canned chopped
tomatoes
salt and pepper
½-1tsp sugar
1-2tsp dried oregano, basil or
marjoram
450g/1lb linguini
basil sprigs, to garnish
freshly grated Parmesan, to serve

- *Serves 4-6*

- *675cals/2835kjs per serving*

1 Heat the oil in a saucepan, add the onion and garlic and cook over low heat for 5 minutes or until the onion is soft but not brown, stirring occasionally.

2 Add the tomatoes and their juice, salt and pepper to taste, the sugar and the herb. Stir well, cover and simmer gently for 15-20 minutes, stirring occasionally.

3 Remove the cover and continue simmering for a further 10-15 minutes to allow the sauce to reduce slightly.

4 Meanwhile, cook the linguini until *al dente*. Drain thoroughly and transfer to a heated serving dish.

5 Pour the tomato sauce over the pasta, garnish with basil and serve immediately, with Parmesan cheese.

Variations

For a delicious seafood sauce, combine 225g/8oz cooked peeled prawns and 100g/4oz sliced mushrooms with 150ml/¼pt dry white wine in a saucepan and simmer for 5 minutes. Add to the tomato sauce.

FASTA PASTA

Cooking home-made pasta is very quick and easy. Bring a large pan of salted water to the boil, add the pasta, bring back to the boil then test a strand or two after just 30 seconds. Keep testing every 30 seconds as it will only take a maximum of 2 minutes to cook.

SAUCES, OF COURSES!

Not content with inventing well over a hundred different pasta shapes, the Italians then married each one to the right dressing – rich, thick sauces that would cling to ropes and ribbons, rather thinner sauces to flow through and around tubed noodles.

Sometimes a plate of perfectly cooked steaming noodles will be served with just a dollop of butter and a bowl of freshly grated Parmesan cheese. Another favourite is to add one or two raw egg yolks and a little cream to this basic recipe – the heat of the noodles fuses these ingredients into a creamy sauce. Or try a light dressing of warmed, fruity olive oil, barely coloured with garlic and parsley.

Lemony courgette pasta

- *Preparation: making pasta, then 15 minutes*

- *Cooking: 15 minutes*

2tbls olive oil
75g/3oz butter
1 small onion, finely chopped
1 garlic clove, crushed
4 courgettes, cut into 5mm/¼in
slices
grated zest and juice of ½ lemon
2tbls chopped parsley
salt and pepper
450g/1lb spaghetti

- *Serves 4-6*

- *735cals/3085kjs per serving*

1 Place the oil and butter in a large saucepan over low heat until melted. Add the onion and garlic and cook gently for about 5 minutes or until the onion is soft but not brown.

2 Add the courgettes, lemon zest and juice to the onion mixture and stir well. Cook for 5-8 minutes or until the courgettes are tender when pierced with a knife. Stir in the parsley and season with salt and pepper to taste. Keep warm.

3 Meanwhile, cook the spaghetti until *al dente*. Drain thoroughly. Stir into the courgette sauce and transfer to a heated serving dish. Serve immediately.

COLOURED PASTA

The recipe for green pasta, *pasta verde*, breaks the proportion rule of four large eggs to 450g/1lb flour. Half the eggs are replaced by spinach. There is no need to add extra water to the dough as the spinach will add sufficient moisture. Start by adding 5tbls cooked, puréed spinach — if you find the dough is too dry add more spinach, 1tbls at a time.

There are different ideas about how to tint pasta pink for *pasta rosa*. Some people incorporate beetroot but the colour can come out during cooking. The best thing to use is tomato purée, which produces an orange-tomato colour — tantalizing when mixed with plain pasta. Blend the eggs and 3tbls tomato purée in a blender, then add to the flour.

cook until tender, about 3-4 minutes. Remove the ham and mushrooms from the pan with a slotted spoon.

3 Add 15g/½oz of the remaining butter to the pan and sauté the onion until it is transparent. Remove from the pan with a slotted spoon and add to the reserved ham mixture.

4 In a clean pan melt the remaining butter, add the flour and cook, stirring constantly, for 2-3 minutes. Add the cream and stir until the sauce starts to thicken. Do not let the sauce boil, and once it has thickened remove the pan from the heat. Add the ham mixture to the sauce and season with salt, pepper and cayenne pepper to taste.

5 Drain the noodles and, while they are still very hot, toss them in a clean saucepan with the olive oil. Add the sauce to the noodles and heat through gently. Serve immediately, with a generous amount of freshly grated Parmesan cheese.

Cook's tips

It is important not to let the ham and mushroom sauce boil or it will separate. If, however, the heat has become too high and the sauce has separated, remove the saucepan from the heat and stir in 1-2tbls cold milk. This will make the sauce emulsify again.

Noodles with ham and mushrooms

● *Preparation: making pasta, then 25 minutes*

● *Cooking: 15 minutes*

salt and pepper
225g/8oz green noodles
225g/8oz egg noodles
2tbls olive oil
freshly grated Parmesan cheese, to serve
For the sauce:
175g/6oz cooked ham, cut into 5mm/¼in cubes
50g/2oz butter
225g/8oz mushrooms, cut into 5mm/¼in cubes
¼ onion, finely chopped
1½tbls flour
150ml/¼pt double cream
pinch of cayenne pepper

PASTA SHAPES

Linguini: narrow ribbons 2.5mm/⅛in wide.
Fettuccelle or tagliolini: narrow strips 2.5mm-5mm/⅛in-¼in wide.
Tagliatelle (known in Rome as fettucine): slightly wider version of fettuccelle, 5mm/¼in wide.
Lasagne: cut long strips 5cm/2in wide. Unravel and divide into 10cm-15cm/4in-6in lengths.
Cannelloni: 10cm/4in squares to roll around a filling.

● *Serves 4-6*

● *920cals/3865kjs per serving*

1 Bring a large pan of salted water to the boil. Add the green noodles and egg noodles and cook until *al dente*.

2 While the water is coming to the boil, start cooking the sauce. Sauté the ham in 25g/1oz of the butter. As the ham begins to colour, add the mushrooms and

Taking Stock

Good stocks are the foundation of many dishes, especially soups and sauces, so every good cook should know how to make them when required

A HOME-MADE STOCK will give any dish or sauce a superior flavour, and is free from the additives and excessive salt used in most commercial stock cubes. So although most of us use stock-cubes for everyday purposes, it's worth learning the technique for a really special soup or sauce.

You will need a large, heavy saucepan (about 4.5L/8pt capacity), to accommodate the bulky ingredients. For meat stocks you also need a butcher who will sell you beef and veal bones chopped into large chunks ready for use.

Basic ingredients

Bones are the essential ingredient, as in addition to flavouring the stock they contain gelatine, which gives the stock body: a good stock should set lightly when chilled. Beef, veal and poultry bones are all used (and fish bones for fish stock). A few pork bones can be included; lamb and ham bones have too strong a flavour, but can be used alone to make lamb or ham stock. Veal knuckle bones are particularly high in gelatine; so are chicken feet, which is why they are used, if available. The more scraps of meat adhering to the bones the better; marrow bones are ideal. For a really rich brown stock pieces of lean meat are included.

Vegetables used for stock are mainly carrots, onions, leeks and celery. Starchy vegetables – potatoes, peas and beans – make a stock cloudy, as does any cooked vegetable. Turnips and members of the cabbage family are too strong-tasting for meat or fish stock, but suitable for vegetable stock. Scraps and peelings are fine, provided they are clean and fresh, but remember that onion skins will turn the stock yellow. Mushroom stalks and ripe tomatoes add flavour and colour.

Herbs and spices are also important: bay leaf, thyme and parsley (a bouquet garni) are the usual ones. Parsley stalks are just as good as a whole sprig. Season bone stock with peppercorns, but not salt, as the considerable reduction in the

Blue cheese onion soup (page 38)

How to ... *skim stock*

Wait until a thick layer of scum forms on the surface, then remove it with a skimmer or shallow spoon.

Sprinkle with salt and continue to skim until the surface is clear, then add vegetables, herbs and seasoning.

volume of liquid may result in over-saltiness. A sprinkling of salt is used to help draw scum out of meat bones; but adjust the seasoning when you use the stock.

Stock-making techniques

Making a classic meat stock involves five or six separate stages.
Brown, simmer and skim: for a brown stock the bones and vegetables must be browned in the oven. Then they are put into plenty of cold water and brought slowly to the boil. The heat must then be turned right down, so that the stock barely simmers; if it boils scum will be drawn into the liquid and make it cloudy. As the scum is drawn out of the bones it is skimmed off using a skimmer.
Reduce, strain and degrease: the stock is then reduced by long slow simmering, partially covered to allow steam to escape. This takes 3-4 hours for a classic brown stock, but only 30 minutes for fish stock. The stock is then strained and sieved; never leave stock with bones and vegetables still in it for any length of time as it will turn sour. Finally the stock is degreased. This is easiest to do by cooling and chilling the stock, then scraping or lifting the fat off when it is solid. But for immediate use cool for 5 minutes, then spoon off the bulk of the fat and mop up the rest with absorbent paper. Alternatively, use a bulb baster.

Chicken stock

- **Preparation: 20 minutes**

- **Cooking: 4 hours**

1.8kg/4lb boiling fowl with its feet, cut up roughly if wished
salt
6 peppercorns
2 leeks, thickly sliced
2 large carrots, roughly chopped
1 large onion, halved and stuck with 2 cloves
2 celery stalks, roughly chopped
1 bouquet garni
1 garlic clove

- **Makes 1.7L/3pt**   ① ££ ◔ ❄

1 Put the boiling fowl in a large saucepan or flameproof casserole and pour in 3.5L/6pt cold water. Sprinkle lightly with salt and bring slowly to the boil.

2 Reduce the heat so that the water barely bubbles, then skim off the scum. Add the peppercorns. Partially cover and simmer gently for 1 hour, skimming again if necessary.

3 Add the vegetables, bouquet garni and garlic and continue to simmer for 30 minutes or until the chicken is meltingly tender.

4 Remove the chicken and vegetables. Reserve the chicken to use as required. Continue to simmer the stock for 1-2 hours or until it has reduced to 1.7L/3pt. Strain the stock through a fine sieve into a large bowl. Cool quickly and degrease. ◔

STORING STOCK

Cool stock as rapidly as possible and keep it in the refrigerator for no more than four days for meat stock, and only two days for fish stock. Vegetable stock will keep for three days but needs boiling up daily. Make sure to bring any stock to the boil when using it.

For longer storage freeze the stock. To save space first boil the stock to reduce it by half. Freeze and dilute before use. Or freeze in ice-cube trays and turn into plastic bags. Frozen meat stock will keep for two months, fish and vegetable stock for one month.

VEGETABLE STOCK

Finely chop about 450g/1lb mixed vegetables: mostly carrots, celery, leek and onion. Fry lightly in a little butter and oil until lightly coloured, then cover the pan tightly and 'sweat' the vegetables over a low heat for 10-15 minutes. Pour in 1L/1¾pt cold water, add a bouquet garni and a squashy tomato if available; season with salt and pepper. Simmer gently for no more than 1 hour, then strain.

Brown beef stock

- **Preparation: 30 minutes**
- **Cooking: 4 hours**

*1kg/2¼lb veal knuckle bones,
  roughly chopped*
*450g/1lb beef knuckle bone,
  roughly chopped*
3 Spanish onions
4 large carrots
2 celery stalks
2 leeks, thickly sliced
*25-50g/1-2oz beef dripping or
  butter*
*1.4kg/3lb shin of beef, cut into
  12 pieces*
a few mushrooms stalks
3 over-ripe tomatoes
salt
3 parsley sprigs
*1 sprig of fresh thyme or a pinch of
  dried thyme*
1 bay leaf
1 clove
9 black peppercorns

- **Makes 1.7L/3pt**

1 Heat the oven to 240C/475F/gas 9. Put the pieces of veal and beef bone in a large roasting tin. Roughly chop two of the onions, the carrots and celery and put them around the bones along with the leeks. Dot with the dripping or butter. Roast for 40-45 minutes, turning occasionally, until richly browned.

2 Cut the remaining onion in half, then sear the cut sides by placing the onion halves, cut sides down, straight on a hot, ungreased frying pan, until golden brown.

3 Transfer the contents of the roasting tin to a very large saucepan or flameproof casserole and pour over 3L/5½pt cold water. Add the shin of beef, the mushroom stalks, the tomatoes cut in quarters and the browned onion.

FISH STOCK

This is much quicker and easier to make than meat stocks. Get about 1.1kg/2½lb of fish trimmings from your fishmonger (heads are good, but discard any black skin from fish pieces). Chop roughly and put in a pan with 850ml/1½pt cold water. Bring slowly to the boil, allow the scum to rise, then skim once. Add a roughly chopped onion, carrot and celery stalk, a bay leaf and 2-3 parsley sprigs or stalks. Season with six white peppercorns (no salt) and the pared zest of ½ lemon. Simmer gently, uncovered, for no more than 30 minutes, then strain.

4 Add 300ml/½pt cold water to the roasting tin, put it over medium heat and bring to the boil, scraping the base and sides of the tin with a wooden spoon to detach the sediment. Add this to the stock pot.

5 Bring the stock slowly to the boil over low heat, then reduce the heat so that it barely bubbles. Skim off the scum several times. When the surface is quite clear add the herbs and spices. Partially cover and simmer very gently for 2½-3 hours or until the stock has reduced to about 1.7L/3pt.

6 Strain the stock through a colander, then through a fine sieve into a large bowl. Cool quickly and degrease.

Cook's tips

Adapt this recipe to make a cheaper stock by using 1kg/2¼lb of chopped beef bones and a chicken carcass if you have one available. Omit the veal knuckle bones and the shin of beef, and reduce the number of carrots and onions to two. Follow the same method.

White veal stock

- **Preparation: 20 minutes**
- **Cooking: 3½ hours**

*1.4kg/3lb veal knuckle bones,
  roughly chopped*
salt
3 large carrots, roughly chopped
3 celery stalks, roughly chopped
3 large onions, roughly chopped
1 leek, thickly sliced
3 over-ripe tomatoes, quartered
3 parsley sprigs
*1 sprig of fresh thyme or a pinch of
  dried thyme*
1 bay leaf
2 cloves
8 white peppercorns

- **Makes 1.7L/3pt**

1 Put the pieces of veal bone in a large saucepan or flameproof casserole and pour in 3.5L/6pt cold water. Bring slowly to the boil over low heat.

2 Reduce the heat so that the water barely bubbles. Skim off the scum several times, sprinkling with salt. When the surface is quite clear, add the vegetables, herbs and spices. Partially cover and simmer very gently for 2½-3 hours or until the stock has reduced to about 1.7L/3pt. Skim again if necessary. ▶

3 Strain the stock through a colander to remove the bones and vegetables, then through a fine sieve into a large bowl. Cool quickly and degrease.

Cook's tips

Use this stock in soups, stews and delicate sauces. It has a neutral flavour, so can be used with almost any meat or poultry.

Blue cheese onion soup

● *Preparation: making stock, then 35 minutes*

● *Cooking: 1½ hours*

75g/3oz butter, plus extra for
  spreading
3tbls olive oil
½tsp caster sugar
600g/1¼lb onions, thinly sliced
  into rings
1.5L/2½pt Brown beef stock
  (page 37)
75g/3oz blue cheese
4tbls brandy (optional)
salt and pepper
4 slices French bread,
  each 3cm/1¼in thick
4tbls grated Gruyère cheese

HAM STOCK

This can be made by straining and reserving the water used to boil a bacon joint. When chilled it will turn into a rich jelly. It is very salty, so be sure to use it diluted with water.

● *Serves 4* ⑪ ££ ◷

● *445cals/1870kjs per serving*

1 Put 40g/1½oz of the butter in a large saucepan with the oil and sugar. Add the onion rings and cook over moderate heat for 15-20 minutes, stirring frequently, until the onions are golden brown.

2 Gradually stir in the stock and bring to the boil. Lower the heat, cover and simmer gently for about 1 hour, by which time the soup should have reduced to about 1.1L/2pt.

3 Heat the grill to high. Put the blue cheese, remaining butter and 2tbls hot stock from the pan into a bowl. Mash with a fork to a smooth paste.

4 Stir the cheese mixture into the soup, along with the brandy and walnuts, if using, until well blended. Season with salt and pepper to taste.

5 Toast the slices of French bread and spread them on one side with butter. Put a round into each of four flameproof soup bowls. Ladle the soup into the bowls and wait a few seconds until the toast rises to the top. Sprinkle each round with Gruyère cheese. Put the bowls under the grill for 3-4 minutes or until the cheese is melted. Serve hot.

Chicken blanquette

● *Preparation: making stock, then 30 minutes*

● *Cooking: 1½ hours*

1.4-1.6kg/3-3½lb oven-ready
  chicken (or cooked boiling fowl
  from making stock)
600ml/1pt boiling Chicken stock
  (page 36)
50g/2oz butter
100g/4oz button mushrooms,
  halved
juice of ½ lemon
15g/½oz flour
salt and pepper
150ml/¼pt double cream
2 egg yolks
chervil sprigs and lemon wedges, to
  garnish

● *Serves 4* ⑪ ££

● *580cals/2435kjs per serving*

1 If not using a cooked boiling fowl, heat the oven to 180C/350F/gas 4. Put the chicken in a large casserole with enough stock to half cover it. Cover and put in the oven for 1½ hours or until tender and cooked through.

2 Melt 25g/1oz of the butter in a small saucepan, add the mushroom caps and lemon juice and simmer for 5 minutes. Remove the mushrooms with a slotted spoon and keep warm. Remove the chicken from the oven or the boiling fowl from the pot and keep warm. Strain the cooking liquid or stock and reserve for making the sauce (you'll need about 600ml/1pt).

3 To make the sauce, melt the remaining butter in a saucepan and stir in the flour. Stir for 2-3 minutes, until the mixture is smooth but has not changed colour. Stir in the reserved liquid a little at a time. Bring to the boil, season to taste and simmer very gently for 15-20 minutes.

4 Mix the cream and egg yolks together in a bowl and pour in a little of the sauce, stirring constantly. Return to the rest of the sauce, stirring well. Heat gently, stirring constantly, until the sauce thickens; do not boil. Add the mushroom caps and correct the seasoning.

5 To serve, divide the chicken into eight pieces (remove the skin if it is a boiling fowl). Arrange on a heated serving dish and spoon the sauce over the top. Garnish and serve hot.

Bread Winners

Home-made bread, served warm and fragrant from the oven with lashings of butter, is a rare treat. Making it is a skill that's surprisingly easy to master

*M*AKING BREAD IS an ancient craft, and even today many people find it a very rewarding branch of cookery, for special occasions if not on a regular basis. The techniques are really very simple, but the basic rules must be followed exactly if you are to achieve a loaf which is crisp and crusty on the outside, soft and melting inside; not a heavy, soggy and indigestible lump.

Basic ingredients
Yeast is a living plant which raises or leavens the bread by multiplying rapidly inside the dough. It dies if it gets too cold or too hot, so all liquid used must be lukewarm. The exact temperature is 43C/110F, but this is not critical – so long as it feels neither cold nor hot, it's OK.

Flour: strong plain flour is best for most breads because the high gluten content makes it light and airy. Plain flour can be used, but it gives a different-textured bread. Self-raising flour is unsuitable. Bread made with wholemeal flour has a more solid texture; for a lighter loaf substitute one-third strong white flour. For a high-fibre loaf use 600g/1¼lb wholemeal flour with 100g/4oz bran.

Working with yeast
These recipes are made with easy-blend yeast as it keeps almost indefinitely and is the most convenient to use. But remember it *must* be added to the dry ingredients before any liquid if it's to work.

If you have some ordinary dried yeast check the packet date – if more than six months old it may

Quick wholemeal bread (page 43)

How to··· *knead bread dough*

Turn the dough onto a lightly floured surface. Push it down and away from you with the heel of one hand, holding the end with the other, until it is about 30cm/ 12in long.

Fold the pushed-away part of the dough towards you to make a ball. Give the dough a quarter turn before stretching it again so that it is being pushed in a different direction each time.

Push and fold the dough with a steady, even rhythm. The texture will change, becoming smoother and more elastic. After about 10 minutes it will develop a sheen and is ready for rising.

not be active. To use, dissolve a little sugar in some of the warm liquid used in the recipe, then sprinkle on the granules and beat in with a fork. Leave until the liquid is very frothy and all the granules dissolved, then mix with the remaining liquid and add to the flour. If it fails to froth it's inactive.

Fresh yeast is hard to get, only keeps for a few days (a month in the fridge), and there's no particular reason to use it. But if you want to try some, just crumble it into a little of the lukewarm recipe liquid and stir until dissolved. Add the remaining liquid.

Making bread dough
First sift the dry ingredients into a bowl, then rub in any hard fat, if used. Next add easy-blend dried yeast, and finally the recipe liquid plus any melted fat or oil. Stir together and knead to make a dough which will leave the sides of the bowl clean.

Kneading: turn the dough onto a floured surface and knead for 10 minutes as shown above. It is ready when shiny and elastic.

Rising: oil a clean bowl lightly, put in the ball of dough and turn it over so it is coated in oil. This is to stop a dry crust forming while it rises. Cover the top of the bowl loosely with oiled stretch wrap. This both keeps the dough moist and con-

serves heat generated by the multi-plying yeast. The bowl should be large enough so that the dough has room to rise without touching the covering. Put in a warm place if you want it to rise quickly, but not too hot or the yeast will be killed. About 21-22C/70-75F is a good safe temperature. A lower temperature will do but delays rising. Wait until the dough has doubled in size, then remove from the bowl and knock it back: punch it to remove any large air pockets.

For some breads, such as the French sticks, the kneading and rising process is repeated to produce a finer texture. Quick whole-meal bread is kneaded briefly and put straight into the tin to rise.

Shaping and proving: for standard bread the risen dough is kneaded again briefly, then shaped as required. Then it is covered and put in a warm place to rise again: this is called proving.

Glazing and baking
The loaves are glazed or topped as required (see Finishing the loaf, page 41), then baked. Follow recipe temperatures and times, but test whether a loaf is done by tapping the bottom with your knuckles. If it does not sound hollow bake for a further 10 minutes, out of its tin and upside-down. Cool bread on wire racks.

FINISHING THE LOAF

For a shiny crust, glaze the bread with egg wash (egg yolk mixed with several tablespoons of water), or with milk.

For an extra-crisp crust, brush the bread with cold water while baking. For an even crisper crust, put a pan of water in the oven while the bread is baking.

For a soft crust (as for baps), sprinkle the dough lightly with flour, then wrap in a clean dry cloth after baking.

For extra flavour and texture, sprinkle the dough with seeds (poppy, caraway or sesame), oatmeal, bulgur, celery or garlic salt, grated cheese or finely chopped nuts.

French sticks

- **Preparation: 30 minutes, plus 3 risings and chilling**

- **Cooking: 1 hour, plus cooling**

15g/½oz butter
1 tbls sugar
700g/1½lb strong white flour, plus extra for kneading and rolling
2 tsp salt
1 sachet easy-blend dried yeast
oil, for greasing
boiling water

- **Makes 3 loaves**

- **895cals/3760kjs per loaf**

1 Stir the butter and sugar into 425ml/¾pt hot water and leave to cool until lukewarm.

2 Sift the flour and salt into a large mixing bowl. Thoroughly mix in the yeast. Gradually add the liquid, beating it vigorously into the flour to make a smooth, soft dough.

3 Use your hands to slap and knead the dough vigorously for 10 minutes, sifting a little more flour over the surface until it begins to lose its tendency to stick to the fingers. This can be done in the bowl if it is large enough, or on a floured work surface.

4 Gather the dough into a ball. Put it in a lightly oiled bowl and turn over so that it is coated in oil. Cover the bowl loosely with oiled stretch wrap and leave to rise in a warm place for about 1½ hours or until doubled in bulk.

5 When risen, turn onto a lightly floured surface and knock the dough back to deflate it. Knead lightly, return to the oiled bowl, then cover and let it rise again until doubled in bulk; about 30-40 minutes. Heat the oven to 200C/400F/gas 6.

6 Punch the dough down and turn it onto a well-floured work surface. With floured hands, knead lightly until smooth, then divide it into three equal portions. Roll each portion into a 20cm x 35cm/8in x 14in rectangle.

7 Roll each piece up tightly like a Swiss roll, starting from a long edge. Pull each roll into shape if necessary. Put the loaves, seam sides down, on an oiled baking sheet. Using a very sharp knife, cut three or four diagonal slashes across the top of each loaf. Brush with oil and cover lightly with stretch wrap. Leave to rise until doubled in bulk, about 1 hour, in a warm place.

8 If necessary, pinch the loaves into shape before brushing with cold water. Pour 2.5cm/1in boiling water into a roasting tin and put it in the bottom of the oven. Put the baking sheet full of loaves in the oven for 1-1¼ hours or until hollow when tapped, brushing the tops with cold water every 15 minutes. If they brown too quickly, cover with crumpled foil. Cool on wire racks.

Cook's tips

The close-textured crumb and crisp crust of this bread is achieved by glazing the bread with cold water and placing a tin of water in the oven to create steam.

Stand back when opening the oven as the steam will come rushing out!

Serving ideas

Serve this crisp bread with a selection of French cheeses and/or pâtés.

How to ...
shape rolls

Bridge rolls: divide the dough into 24 pieces. Form each into a ball, then an oval. Lay on the baking tray 1cm/½in apart so they join up when baked, then glaze with egg wash or milk.

Baps: roll dough out 1cm/½in thick. Cut into 24 rounds with a 7.5cm/3in biscuit cutter. Dust with flour and cover with a cloth after baking for a soft crust.

Coils: divide the dough into 12 pieces. Form into strands about 12cm/5in long. Curl each one up firmly from one end to make a flat coil. Glaze with egg.

White bread

- **Preparation: 40 minutes, plus 2 risings**

- **Cooking: 40 minutes, plus cooling**

400g/14oz strong white flour, plus extra for kneading
2tsp salt
25g/1oz soft margarine
1 sachet easy-blend dried yeast
1 egg, beaten
100ml/3½fl oz lukewarm milk mixed with an equal quantity of tepid water
oil, for greasing
glaze and/or topping (optional)

- **Makes 1 large loaf**

- **1755cals/7370kjs per loaf**

1 Put the flour and salt into a large mixing bowl and rub in the margarine. Mix in the yeast. Make a well in the centre and pour in the beaten egg. Gradually add the milk and water, stirring it into the flour to make a firm dough which will leave the sides of the bowl.

2 Turn the dough out onto a lightly floured work surface and knead for 10 minutes or until the texture becomes smooth and pliable. Put it in an oiled bowl, cover the bowl with a piece of oiled stretch wrap and leave to rise for 1 hour at warm room temperature or until the dough has doubled in size.

3 Take the dough out and knock it back: press it firmly all over with your knuckles to remove any large pockets of air. Knead for 2 minutes.

4 Shape the dough as required and put into a large loaf tin or onto a greased baking tray. Cover loosely with oiled stretch wrap and leave in a warm place to rise again: allow 30-50 minutes rising time for a large loaf, 20-30 minutes for bread rolls. Meanwhile, heat the oven to 220C/425F/gas 7.

5 If wished, brush the top of the dough with glaze and sprinkle with a topping (page 161). Bake for 10 minutes, then reduce the heat to 190C/375F/gas 5 and bake for a further 10-20 minutes or until the bread sounds hollow when tapped on the bottom. Cool on a wire rack.

42

Quick wholemeal bread

Wholemeal flour contains 100% of the wheat grain and produces a dough of closer texture and with less rise than a white dough

- ● **Preparation: 30 minutes, plus 1 rising**
- ● **Cooking: 45 minutes, plus cooling**

1tbls oil
2tbls bulgur (optional)
700g/1½lb stone-ground wholemeal flour, plus extra for kneading
1 sachet easy-blend dried yeast
2tsp salt
1½tsp soft brown sugar
milk, to glaze

- ● **Makes 1 medium loaf** (♈) (££) (🕐) (❄)
- ● **2400cals/10,080kjs per loaf**

1 Grease a 1.4kg/3lb metal loaf tin with a little of the oil. Sprinkle half the bulgur, if using, over the base. Leave the tin in a warm place while you prepare the dough.

2 Put the flour in a large warmed mixing bowl and stir in the yeast, salt and sugar. Stir the remaining oil into about 425ml/¾pt hand-hot water. Stir into the dry ingredients and mix thoroughly by hand to make a moist but manageable dough. If the dough is too stiff add a little more warm water; if it is too wet work in a little extra flour. ▶

FREEZING DOUGH

Unbaked bread dough can be frozen after kneading. Wrap the dough in an oiled freezer bag, seal the bag and freeze for up to 5 weeks.

Clockwise from top left: baps, coils, cottage loaf, plait, crown and bridge rolls – all made from White bread dough

How to··· *shape baking tray loaves*

Plait: form three strands about 30cm/12in long; taper each end. Press together at one end and plait. Pinch the ends together and tuck them under.

Crown: divide the dough into 12; form into rounds. Put one in the centre of each of two sandwich tins, then surround with the remaining rounds.

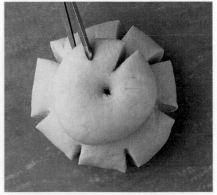

Cottage loaf: form one-third of dough into a round, the rest into another. Put the small one on top and press a floured spoon handle through the middle. Snip edges.

3 Turn the dough out onto a lightly floured surface and knead for 5 minutes. Put it in the prepared tin and press down evenly. Brush with milk and sprinkle over the remaining bulgur, if using, and press it lightly into the dough.

4 Cover the tin loosely with oiled stretch wrap and leave in a warm place for about 30 minutes until the dough has risen just above the top of the tin. Meanwhile, heat the oven to 220C/425F/gas 7.

5 Remove the stretch wrap and bake for 10-15 minutes. Reduce the temperature to 190C/375F/gas 5 and bake for a further 25-30 minutes or until the bread has shrunk slightly from the sides of the tin and is cooked. Cool on a wire rack.

CONVERTING RECIPES

A sachet of easy-blend dried yeast contains 7g/¼oz and is the equivalent of 25g/1oz fresh yeast or 15g/½oz dried yeast. Use the appropriate number of sachets, or part of a sachet, when converting old recipes based on fresh or conventional dried yeast. But be careful to alter the method as well — easy-blend dried yeast *must* be added to dry ingredients. If mixed into liquid like the other types it won't work.

Pumpernickel

- **Preparation: 40 minutes, plus 3 risings**

- **Cooking: 50 minutes**

350g/12oz strong white flour, plus extra for kneading
350g/12oz rye flour
2tsp salt
1 sachet easy-blend dried yeast
350ml/12fl oz lager
150ml/¼pt light molasses
25g/1oz butter, diced
oil, for greasing

- **Makes 2 loaves**

- **3065cals/12,875kjs per loaf**

1 Sift the white and the rye flour into a large bowl, adding any bran left in the sieve, and stir in the salt and yeast. Make a well in the centre.

2 Heat the lager, molasses and butter until the butter has melted. Allow to cool until lukewarm. Gradually pour the liquid into the dry ingredients. Mix in the flour by hand, gradually forming a sticky dough. Turn out onto a floured work surface and knead well, adding more flour if necessary. Knead for 10 minutes or until the dough is smooth and elastic.

3 Shape the dough into a ball. Put it in a lightly oiled bowl and turn so that it is covered with oil. Cover the bowl loosely with oiled stretch wrap and leave the dough to rise for 1-1½ hours or until doubled in bulk.

4 Punch the dough down and knead it again lightly. Return it to the oiled bowl and turn again. Leave to rise for 1 hour or until once more doubled in bulk, loosely covered with oiled stretch wrap.

5 Divide the dough in half. Form into two balls and put on an oiled baking sheet. Brush the tops very lightly with oil, cover with a damp tea-towel and leave to rise in a warm place until they have doubled in size, about 1 hour. Meanwhile, heat the oven to 180C/350F/gas 4.

HIGH RISE

Use your microwave to help dough rise: place it in a very lightly oiled bowl, turning it over once. Place the bowl in a shallow dish of hot water and cover loosely with lightly oiled stretch wrap. Microwave at 10% (warm) for 4 minutes, then stand for 15 minutes. Repeat the two procedures until the dough has doubled in volume, then shape.

6 Bake the loaves for 40-50 minutes or until they sound hollow when tapped. Cool on wire racks.

Cook's tips

Unlike other breads, pumpernickel improves with keeping, which matures the flavour. Wrap it in foil to keep it moist.

Molasses is a syrup derived from sugarcane sap. Look for it in some speciality shops and delicatessens; if you can't find it, use treacle for a sweet loaf.

Pizza Please

A sizzling slice of pizza hot from the oven is hard to beat. Yet a pizza is simple peasant food, easily made: just a round of bread dough baked with a variety of toppings

PIZZAS HAVE BEEN enjoyed for centuries in Italy, where originally they were made in farmhouse kitchens using dough left over after baking a batch of bread or rolls. The toppings feature readily available local ingredients: tomatoes, olives, Mozzarella and Parmesan cheese, slices of salami – and olive oil plays its part too, being used to moisten and flavour both the dough and its topping.

Although these ingredients, with the exception of the invaluable canned Italian tomatoes are not cheap outside Italy, the pizza base makes a little go a long way, so they are still quite an economical dish. They are also incredibly versatile, as the number of different toppings that can be used is virtually limitless, and they can be served as starters, snacks, or make a substantial meal if accompanied by a green salad and some crusty bread.

Pizza dough

The bread dough used for making pizzas is the simple one used to make Italian bread, enriched with a little olive oil. Making it is a simple process, especially if you use easy-blend dried yeast, as in the basic recipe. The most important rule to observe is to have all the ingredients at room temperature, and the recipe liquid lukewarm, so as not to kill the yeast. (Remember, easy-blend dried yeast *must* be mixed with the dry ingredients first; it doesn't work if mixed into liquid like fresh or dried yeast.

Also make sure to knead the dough for at least 10 minutes to make it smooth and elastic. A dough hook on a mixer takes the labour out of this, and a food

Here the tomato filling (page 46) is topped with grated cheese, crushed garlic, onion rings, pepper strips, green olives, smoked ham rolls and chopped fresh herbs

processor is even quicker. Put the dough to rise in a temperature of about 21-26C/70-80F – many people find their airing cupboard is a good place, but check it's not too hot as this would kill the yeast. A cooler temperature is fine but the dough will take longer to rise.

If you want to check on the basic techniques of bread making, or prefer to use conventional fresh or dried yeast, refer to Bread winners, page 39.

Pizza toppings

While the dough is rising you can prepare the topping. The most basic is just a purée of tomatoes and onion (Pizza napoletana); but this is usually enriched with other ingredients, the most familiar being cheese and a lattice of anchovy strips studded with black olives (Pizza romana). Other popular additions include ham, cheese, fish, mushrooms, salami, courgettes and asparagus – singly or in diverse combinations.

The tomato base must be full of flavour, and this is one occasion when canned tomatoes are better than fresh ones. Use English or Spanish onions, according to how strong an onion flavour you like (Spanish ones are much milder), and always include a little garlic for that Mediterranean tang. Similarly always use olive oil, preferably a virgin grade, for its rich taste. Herbs too play an important part: oregano and basil are the characteristic Italian flavours, and if you can get fresh basil so much the better.

The cheese used for pizza is traditionally Mozzarella. Real Mozzarella is made from buffalo milk; that most widely exported is made from cow's milk and less flavoursome. Emmental and Gruyère are good alternatives, or a mixture of either with Parmesan.

Baking pizzas

Cook pizzas in a hot oven, usually 220C/425F/gas 7, just like bread. Check at the end of the cooking time to see if the underside is cooked (lift with a slice to ensure the bottom is golden). If not return the pizza to the oven for 5-10 minutes, covering the top with foil if it is already golden brown. Pizzas are at their mouthwatering best eaten straight from the oven; serve at once.

QUICK SCONE PIZZA

Make a scone base: use 225g/ 8oz self-raising flour, ½tsp salt and 2tbls oil; mix to a soft but not sticky dough with about 150ml/¼pt milk. Press out into a 25cm/10in round, top as required and bake at 220C/425F/ gas 7 for 20 minutes.

Pizza dough

- **Preparation: 30 minutes, plus rising**

225g/8oz strong flour, plus extra for kneading
½tsp salt
½ sachet easy-blend dried yeast
50ml/2fl oz milk
1tbls olive oil, plus extra for greasing

- **Makes 1 thick or 2 thin pizza bases**

- **450cals/1850kjs per serving**

1 Sift the flour, salt and easy-blend dried yeast into a bowl. Make a well in the centre.

2 Mix the milk with 50ml/2fl oz hot (but not boiling) water to give a lukewarm mixture. Stir gradually into the flour mixture, adding just enough to make a firm but soft dough.

3 Turn the dough out onto a floured work surface and knead for 10 minutes or until the dough loses its stickiness and becomes pliable and elastic. You should need very little extra flour.

4 Flatten the dough out and make deep indentations over it with your fingertips. Sprinkle with 1tbls olive oil. Fold the dough up to enclose the oil and knead again until all the oil has been completely absorbed. Roll the dough into a ball.

5 Put the dough into a clean, lightly oiled bowl and turn the ball so that it is coated with oil all over. Cover the bowl with stretch wrap and leave in a warm place to rise about 1 hour.

6 When the dough has risen punch it down again and knead lightly before rolling out to the required shape.

Freezer

If you make two thin bases one can be frozen. Put it on a freezer-proof tray and brush lightly with oil all over. Open freeze, then pack and label. Freeze for up to 2 months. Defrost before cooking.

How to... make a pizza base

Fold in the edge of the dough all round to make a rim about 1cm/ ½in wide. (Alternatively just crimp it up using your fingers dipped in flour.)

Make a neat edging which gives the pizza a professional look and holds in the filling. Brush the dough with olive oil and add the chosen toppings and filling.

Sausage and egg pizza

● **Preparation: making dough, then 25 minutes**

● **Cooking: 30 minutes**

1 × Pizza dough (see left)
flour for rolling
1tbls olive oil, plus extra for
  greasing
1 large onion, finely chopped
1 garlic clove, finely chopped
400g/14oz canned tomatoes,
  drained and chopped
1tbls tomato purée
½tsp dried oregano
salt and pepper
15g/½oz butter
6 chipolata sausages, sliced
6 eggs
50g/2oz grated Parmesan cheese
2tbls grated Gruyère cheese
2tsp chopped parsley
parsley sprig, to garnish

● Serves 3-6   (♙)(££)

● *820cals/3445kjs per serving*

1 Prepare the pizza dough and roll out on a lightly floured surface into a large round – at least 30cm/10in across. Fold in the edge to make a rim about 1cm/½in wide and flatten it gently with the rolling pin. Lift onto a greased baking tray.

2 Heat the oven to 200C/400F/gas 6. Heat the olive oil in a saucepan. Add the onion and garlic; fry for 5 minutes, stirring occasionally.

3 Add the tomatoes, tomato purée, oregano and salt and pepper to taste. remove from the heat and reserve.

4 Heat the butter in a frying pan and fry the sliced sausages for 1-2 minutes until golden brown.

5 Spread the tomato mixture over the pizza, leaving the rim clear, and arrange the partly cooked sausages on top. Bake for 15 minutes.

6 Remove the pizza from the oven and crack the eggs neatly over the top. Sprinkle with the grated cheeses and return to the oven for 5 minutes, until the eggs are set but still soft.

7 Sprinkle with chopped parsley and garnish with a parsley sprig. Serve hot, cut into wedges making sure there is an egg on each wedge.

Cook's tips

Adapt this recipe to serve different numbers of people by varying the number and size of eggs used, and the number of sausages. To serve four use four large eggs and four sausages. Make sure the eggs are fresh or they will spread too much to fit onto the pizza.

Tuna and olive pizza

● **Preparation: making dough, then 40 minutes**

● **Cooking: 20 minutes**

1 × Pizza dough (see left)
flour for rolling
4½tbls olive oil
450g/1lb onions, thinly sliced
165g/6oz canned tuna, drained
  and flaked
2 large hard-boiled eggs, thinly
  sliced
3 tomatoes, thinly sliced
salt and pepper
1tsp fresh oregano or ½tsp
  dried
1tbls fresh basil, or 1tsp dried
1tbls finely chopped parsley
3tbls grated Parmesan cheese
3tbls grated Gruyère cheese
12 small black olives

▶

● *Serves 4* ⑪ ££ ❋

● *545cals/2290kjs per serving*

1 Prepare the pizza dough and roll out on a lightly floured surface into a round about 1cm/½in thick. Fold in the edge to make a rim 1cm/½in wide and flatten it gently with the rolling pin. Lift onto a greased baking tray.

2 Heat the oven to 220C/425F/gas 7. Heat 4tbls olive oil in a frying pan, add the onions and fry over low heat for about 20 minutes until soft and lightly coloured, stirring occasionally.

3 Remove the onions with a slotted spoon, allowing surplus oil to drain off, and spread them over the pizza dough, leaving the rim clear. Cover the onions with the tuna and top with slices of egg and tomato.

4 Season with salt and pepper to taste; sprinkle over the oregano, basil and parsley. Cover with the grated cheeses and arrange the olives round the edge. Drizzle a little olive oil over the pizza and bake for 16-18 minutes. Serve hot, cut into even-sized wedges.

Pizza alla casalinga

● *Preparation: making dough, then 1 hour*

● *Cooking: 15-20 minutes*

1 × Pizza dough (page 46)
olive oil, for brushing
For the topping:
225g/8oz canned tomatoes
2tbls tomato purée
salt and pepper
75g/3oz cooked ham
75g/3oz Mozzarella or Emmental cheese, thinly sliced
1 canned pimento, cut into thin strips
50g/2oz canned anchovy fillets, drained and halved lengthways
6-8 black olives, stoned
1tsp dried oregano
1tsp olive oil

● *Serves 4* ⑪ ££ ❋

● *385cals/1615kjs per serving*

1 Prepare the pizza dough. When it has risen shape it with the palm of your hand into a 25cm/10in round on a baking tray, building up the edge slightly to contain the topping. Brush the surface lightly with olive oil.

2 Make the topping: drain the tomatoes and chop roughly, or rub them through a sieve if you don't want any pips. Add the tomato purée, season with salt and pepper to taste and mix well. Spread over the prepared base to within 1cm/½in of the edge.

3 Cut the ham and cheese into strips about 5cm/2in wide. Lay the ham strips on the topping, then cover with the cheese strips. Criss-cross the surface with strips of pimento and anchovy.

4 Dot the top with the olives and sprinkle with the oregano and olive oil. Leave to rise for 20 minutes, meanwhile heating the oven to 220C/425F/gas 7.

5 Bake the pizza for 15-20 minutes for the thick base, only 10-15 if you have made a thin one. Check that the underside is cooked and if necessary return to the oven for 5-10 minutes. If the top is already brown cover it with foil. Serve hot, cut into wedges.

ALTERNATIVE PIZZAS

Start with the basic tomato, onion and garlic topping and enrich as follows:
Capricciosa: Add ham, mushrooms, artichokes and olives.
Funghi: Add plenty of sliced mushrooms cooked in olive oil.
Margherita: Add chopped basil and percorino cheese.
Prosciutto: Add Parma ham.
Quattro Stagioni (Four seasons): Make a topping in four quarters: one tomato and onion, one sliced fried mushroom, one tuna and one sliced ham.
Würstel: Add slices of German sausage.

Rough and Puff

Featherlight layers of crisp, buttery puff pastry are produced by a complicated, almost magical technique. Mastering it requires meticulous attention to detail, but it is rewarding

*P*UFF PASTRY IS made by repeatedly rolling, folding and turning to produce multiple alternating layers of butter and dough. When baked in a hot oven the pastry rises enormously because of the steam produced by all the air trapped in between the layers. It is a fascinating technique, and one every good cook should know.

Rough puff
Rough puff pastry is the easiest, and the one to start with. To make it all the butter is diced, then mixed with flour and liquid to make a rough paste. The lumps of butter

are gradually eliminated by a series of rolling and folding. The proportion of fat to flour can be as low as 1:2, rising to 3:4.

Puff pastry is more laborious to make, but the technique enables the ratio of fat to flour to be almost 1:1, producing a super-rich and delicious result. The process starts with a basic flour and liquid dough containing very little fat. This is then rolled into a rectangle and wrapped round a block of butter. This parcel is rolled out and folded four times to distribute the butter evenly on the paste and create the different layers.

Raspberry mille feuilles
Layers of rough puff pastry (page 51) sandwiched together with crème patissière or whipped cream topped with fresh fruit and jam.

Simple ingredients

Although the techniques are complex the ingredients are simple. First, strong plain flour – never self-raising flour. Its high gluten content helps give puff pastries a better, stronger structure. Second, butter: unsalted butter is preferable, especially for puff pastry, as there is so much of it that salted butter might produce an over-salty pastry. Third, liquid: ice-cold water is vital, to help keep everything cool; plus lemon juice or white wine vinegar – the acid content helps develop the gluten in the flour. Egg yolk can add both moisture and richness to the light puff pastry.

Keys to success

Keeping it cool: this is even more vital than with shortcrust pastry. Ingredients must also all be at the *same* temperature, so the first step is to put them all, including the water, plus the mixing bowl, in the refrigerator, preferably overnight.

Work on a marble slab if possible, in a cool kitchen, with cool hands. Work quickly and chill the pastry after rolling.

Rolling and handling: Use a long rolling pin in one direction with long smooth strokes. Start in the centre and roll one stroke away from you, then one stroke towards you. This ensures that the pastry is not over-stretched. Do not roll over the edges of the dough, as this makes them thinner than the rest. Do not push hard or stretch the pastry with the rolling pin – this will tear the layers which have been built up.

Lift the pastry up gently now and then to make sure it is not sticking, being careful not to break through the layers with your fingers. As the pastry rectangle begins to take shape knock the sides straight and keep the corners right angled with a ruler. This is important – a rounded edge, falling short, means a loss in that particular area of so many layers.

When folding the pastry, brush off any loose flour from the underside before folding the other side over, to avoid incorporating any unnecessary extra flour. Seal the folded rectangle by pressing the seams gently with the rolling pin or the side of your hand.

Turning: each time you re-roll the slab of pastry it is given a quarter turn (through 90°) to the right, so that every rolling is in a different direction. To remember the position the pastry should be in, imagine it as a closed book: the folded edge is the spine, which should be on the left. Make a note of the number of turns each time you chill the pastry (it is easy to forget!)

Relaxing: when the pastry has been rolled and folded four times enclose it in stretch wrap and chill for at least an hour. This makes the butter firm and the pastry easier to roll out, and also helps the layers to remain well defined after baking.

How to ... *make puff pastry*

Sift the flour and salt into a mixing bowl. Add the finely diced butter and work with your fingers until it is coated in flour.

Add the lemon juice and iced water and work with one hand to a moist but not sticky dough. Add more water if necessary.

Put the remaining butter on a lightly floured board and knock it with your fist into a rectangle measuring 15 x 12.5cm/6 x 5in.

Roll out the pastry to measure 38 x 30cm/15 x 12in. Lay the butter in the centre and fold over the four edges to make a parcel.

Roll the pastry out into a rectangle the same size as before. Fold the bottom third up and the top third down, seal.

Turn the pastry 90°. Fold the short edges to meet in the centre. Then fold one half on top of the other. Seal, chill for 15 minutes.

Puff pastry

● *Preparation: overnight chilling, then 3 hours, plus chilling*

450g/1lb strong flour, plus extra for rolling
2 x 225g/8oz packs unsalted butter
½tsp salt
2tbls lemon juice

● *Made weight of pastry 1.2kg/2¾lb*

1 Put 450-700g/1-1½lb strong flour, the butter, salt and lemon juice in the refrigerator along with the mixing bowl and 250ml/9fl oz water. Leave for several hours or better still overnight.

2 Finely dice 40g/1½oz of the butter. Set the remaining butter aside. Sift 450g/1lb of the flour with the salt into the chilled mixing bowl. Add the diced butter and work with your fingers until the pieces are thoroughly coated with flour. Make a well in the centre.

3 Pour the iced water and lemon juice into the well and work the ingredients with your hand to a moist but not sticky dough. Add 1-2tbls more water if necessary.

4 Turn the dough out onto a floured work surface and knead into a ball, adding flour to the board and dough, until the dough is no longer moist.

5 Flatten the dough ball to 2.5cm/1in thick, enclose in stretch wrap and chill for 15 minutes.

6 Meanwhile put the remaining butter on a lightly floured board and knock and shape it by hand into a rectangle about 15 x 12.5cm/6 x 5in. Chill.

7 With plenty of flour on the work surface, pat the ball of dough down a little with your hands, then roll into a rectangle. Push the sides and corners as straight as possible with the side of a clean ruler.

8 Brush the excess flour off the top of the pastry, put the 'brick' of butter in the centre of the rectangle and fold over the edges to make a parcel. Seal the joins by pressing gently with your fingertips.

9 **First turn:** roll the pastry into a rectangle 38 x 30cm/15 x 12in. Mark it into three equal horizontal sections with your finger; fold the bottom section up to meet the first mark, and fold the top section down on top of it. Seal the edges by pressing gently. Turn the pastry through 90°; note down that it has had one turn.

10 **Second turn:** Roll the pastry out to 38 x 30cm/15 x 12in and mark the centre with your finger. Fold top and

Chicken and prawn vol-au-vent (page 52)

bottom edges in to meet at the mark. Then fold one half on top of the other. Seal the edges and turn through 90° so that the folded edge is on the left. Enclose the pastry in stretch wrap and chill for at least 15 minutes.

11 Repeat both the turns as described above, being sure to start to roll the dough with the long edge towards you. Rest the pastry again, ideally for 1 hour.

12 Roll out to the desired shape and leave to relax in the refrigerator for ½-1 hour before baking.

Cook's tips

If you don't have any lemon juice, 2tbls of white wine vinegar will do just as well.

Rough puff pastry

● *Preparation: 40 minutes, plus chilling*

225g/8oz strong flour, plus extra for rolling
pinch of salt
175g/6oz unsalted butter
1tsp lemon juice

● *Made weight of pastry 450g/1lb*

1 Put all the ingredients in the refrigerator to chill, along with 150ml/¼pt water and the mixing bowl.

2 Sift the flour and salt into the chilled bowl. Dice the butter into 1cm/½in

USING PUFF PASTRY

Roll and shape the pastry as required (cut it with a sharp knife that will not drag at the edges). Score the top lightly in a diamond pattern to help it rise evenly. Rolling pastry stretches it, so put it back in the refrigerator to relax for another 30 minutes before baking, otherwise the finished shape will be distorted. Take it out while preheating the oven.

Glaze the pastry as usual with egg yolk or egg yolk and water, but be very careful not to let it run over the edges or they will not flake as they should. Bake in a hot oven – 220C/425F/gas 7. If the top browns before the filling is cooked cover loosely with crumpled foil and turn the temperature down slightly.

Use puff pastry to make pies, vol-au-vents and cream horns, plus sausage rolls, mince pies, cheese straws, palmiers and a range of sweet pastries from Eccles cakes to mille-feuilles.

cubes and drop them into the flour. Add the lemon juice and 125ml/4fl oz water and mix quickly to a light dough. Add 1-2tbls more water if necessary.

3 Turn the dough onto a lightly floured work surface and roll out to a rectangle 30 x 15cm/12 x 6in. Push the sides straight and corners as square as possible with the side of a clean ruler.

4 Fold one-third of the pastry up towards the centre, then fold the top third down over this. Seal the edges with your hand or a rolling pin. Turn the pastry through 90°. Roll out into a rectangle, fold and turn twice more.

5 Enclose the pastry in stretch wrap and chill for 1 hour before using as required.

Chicken and prawn vol-au-vent

- **Preparation: making pastry, overnight relaxing, then 30 minutes**

- **Cooking: 1 hour**

450g/1lb made-weight Puff pastry (page 51)
four, for rolling
1 large egg yolk, beaten with 1tbls water
For the filling:
425ml/³⁄₄pt milk
¹⁄₂ chicken stock cube, crumbled
40g/1¹⁄₂oz butter
3tbls flour
salt and pepper
50g/2oz Cheddar cheese, grated
225g/8oz cooked chicken, diced
100g/4oz cooked, peeled prawns
paprika

- **Serves 6**

- **595cals/2500kjs per serving**

1 On a lightly floured work surface, roll the pastry into a 22cm/8½in square. Using a saucepan lid or plate as a guide, cut a 20cm/8in diameter circle. Transfer the circle, turning it upside down, to a baking tray. Carefully brush off the surface flour. Using a sharp knife mark the pastry in a circle 4cm/1½in inside the circumference, without cutting through. Score top in a diamond pattern with a sharp knife.

2 Cover with stretch wrap and leave in the refrigerator to relax for at least 1 hour, preferably overnight.

3 Put the milk in a saucepan, bring to the boil and add the stock cube. Melt the butter in another saucepan, add the flour and stir over low heat for 2-3 minutes to make a pale roux. Add the boiled milk gradually, stirring with a wire whisk to prevent lumps forming; bring to the boil. Season with salt and pepper to taste and simmer over low heat for 10 minutes until thickened, stirring frequently. Remove from the heat and set aside. Meanwhile heat the oven to 220C/425F/gas 7.

4 Brush the vol-au-vent case with the egg mixture to glaze it, being careful not to go over the incision or the edge of the pastry. Sprinkle the baking sheet with cold water. Bake for 30 minutes.

5 Return the sauce to a low heat, add the Cheddar cheese and stir until it melts. Add the chicken and keep warm.

6 Carefully cut out and remove the lid from the baked vol-au-vent. Take out any uncooked dough from the centre and transfer to a heated serving plate.

7 Add the prawns to the chicken mixture and season with a pinch of paprika. Cook for 1-2 minutes or until the prawns are warmed through. Taste and adjust the seasoning and ladle the filling into the vol-au-vent case. Put on the lid and serve at once.

Gâteau Pithiviers (page 54)

WHAT WENT WRONG?

Insufficient lift: pastry rolled too thin; too few turns given; baking temperature too low.
Uneven rise: fat not evenly distributed; poor rolling technique or incorrect folding; insufficient relaxing time; large temperature variations during the baking process.
Hard pastry: too much flour or not enough fat in recipe; flour not brushed off when rolling and turning; over-handling.
Soggy pastry: No hole made for steam to escape during the baking process.

Cream horns

- **Preparation: making pastry, then 1 hour, plus chilling**

- **Cooking: 20 minutes, plus cooling**

flour, for rolling
450g/1lb made-weight Puff pastry
 (page 51)
1 large egg yolk, beaten with 1tbls
 water

icing sugar
5-6tbls strawberry or raspberry jam
150ml/¼pt double cream
1-2tbls caster sugar

- **Makes 10-12**

- **315cals/1325kjs per serving**

FREEZER FAVOURITE

Puff pastry freezes extremely well, so it's worth making a large quantity, as in the basic recipe, while you are at it. Rolling, turning and folding will take very little longer. To portion the dough, first flatten it lightly with a rolling pin. Then cut it with a large sharp knife and dip the cut edge in flour to seal the butter. Pack the dough in 450g/1lb or 225g/8oz packs and label. Freeze for up to six months. Defrost before using.

1 On a lightly floured work surface, roll the dough out to 3mm/⅛in thick. Cut it into strips 2.5cm/1in wide and 23cm/9in long. Carefully brush off the surface flour and brush the strips with egg to glaze.

2 Wind a strip of pastry around 10cm/4in cream horn moulds, glazed side out. Start by pressing the pastry firmly onto the pointed end, then start winding it round, overlapping each round slightly. Trim the top level and put each horn, as you finish it, on a baking tray. Chill for 30 minutes. Meanwhile heat the oven to 220C/425F/gas 7.

3 Sprinkle the baking trays with cold water, shake off excess and bake the pastry horns for 10-12 minutes or until golden and crisp brown.

4 Sprinkle with sifted icing sugar and bake for a further 3 minutes or until glazed. Transfer the horns to a wire rack, carefully remove the moulds and cool.

5 About 3-4 hours before serving put the horns in a container just large enough to take them, so that they stand upright. Put 2tsp of jam in the bottom of each horn.

6 Whip the cream until stiff peaks form and fold in sugar to taste. Put the cream in a piping bag fitted with a star nozzle and pipe it into the horns.

Gooseberry pie

- **Preparation: making pastry, then 30 minutes, plus relaxing**

- **Cooking: 30 minutes**

900g/2lb hard green gooseberries
6tbls soft dark brown sugar
4tsp cornflour
flour, for rolling
225g/8oz made-weight Puff pastry
 (page 51)
1 large egg, lightly beaten
1tbls caster sugar
300ml/½pt single cream, to serve
 (optional)

- **Serves 4-6**

- **400cals/1680kjs per serving**

1 Top and tail the gooseberries and put them in a 1.1L/2pt pie dish. Add the sugar and toss the gooseberries.

2 Put the cornflour into a small bowl and mix with 1tbls cold water. Sprinkle the mixture over the gooseberries and toss again.

3 On a floured surface, roll out to 3mm/⅛in thick. Cut a top for the pie larger than the top of the dish. Cut 1cm/½in strips from the remaining pastry. ▶

KNOCK UP AND FLUTE

To knock up pastry means to make horizontal cuts all round the edge of the pastry with the back of a knife. This makes the pastry edges flake more evenly, and also helps to seal them together.

To flute the edges means to pinch them into fluted pattern with your fingers. For a scalloped edge, as on the Gâteau Pithiviers, cut into the pastry at intervals with a knife, judging the spacing by eye.

See Designs on pies, page 71.

◀ 4 Moisten the rim of the dish with water and press the pastry strips on all the way round. Brush the pastry rim with beaten egg and carefully lay the pastry lid on top, pressing the edges lightly together. Carefully brush off all the surface flour with a dry brush.

5 Using the back of a knife, knock up the edge of the pastry, then flute it all round. Cut a slit in the centre to allow steam to escape. Score the pastry lightly in a diamond pattern with a sharp knife. Leave to relax for 30 minutes in the refrigerator. 🕐 Meanwhile, heat the oven to 220C/425F/gas 7.

6 Brush the pastry with beaten egg to glaze. Bake for 25-30 minutes or until the pastry is crisply puffed and golden.

7 Sprinkle the top with caster sugar and serve hot or lukewarm, with whipped or pouring cream if wished.

Gâteau Pithiviers

● **Preparation: making pastry, then 1 hour, plus chilling**

● **Cooking: 25 minutes**

450g/1lb made-weight Puff pastry (page 51)
flour, for rolling
1 large egg yolk, beaten with 1tbls water
For the filling:
100g/4oz butter, softened
100g/4oz sugar
1 large egg
1 large egg yolk
100g/4oz ground almonds
1tbls flour
2tbls rum

● **Serves 6-8**   🍴 £££

● **700cals/2940kjs per serving**

1 To make the filling, beat the butter and sugar together in a bowl until light and fluffy. Beat in the egg, egg yolk and stir in almonds, flour and rum.

2 On a lightly floured work surface, roll out the pastry and cut out a 23cm/9in circle and a 25cm/10in circle. Put the smaller circle on a baking tray, upside down. Carefully brush off all the surface flour from the circle.

3 Pile the almond filling in the centre, leaving a 2.5cm/1in border all round. Brush the border with the beaten egg mixture and put the larger circle on top, upside down, sealing the edges well together. Brush off the excess flour. Knock up the edges and cut into broad scallops. Make a hole in the centre to allow steam to escape and score the pastry like a Catherine wheel with a knife. Chill for 30 minutes. Meanwhile heat the oven to 220C/425F/gas 7.

4 Brush the pastry with egg, making sure that the glaze does not drip over the edges. Sprinkle the baking sheet with cold water, shake off excess. Bake for 20-25 minutes or until the pastry is crisp and golden brown. Remove from the oven and transfer to a wire rack. Allow to cool.

54

Flat or Folded

Whichever way you like them, omelettes are good news: easy to make once you grasp the technique; easy on the pocket and infinitely versatile

*F*ench or folded omelettes are the more familiar of the two and in their basic form, a very light dish. The flat omelette, sometimes known as a Spanish omelette although the French also make them, is more substantial as it contains added ingredients – vegetables, meat and sometimes potato. In addition to these two, there are sweet omelettes, both folded and flat, and the so-called soufflé omelette, savoury or sweet.

Secrets of success

The first essential for making all types of omelette is a good pan. It should have a heavy base with rounded sides and be made of iron, stainless steel, or aluminium with a non-stick finish. Enamelled pans are unsuitable – the eggs will stick. Ideally, keep the pan just for omelettes and wipe it clean whilst still warm with absorbent paper dipped in oil and salt. Otherwise, use any heavy-based frying pan, but make sure it is spotlessly clean.

The pan also needs to be the right size: too small and the omelette will be too thick; too large and it will turn out thin and leathery. For a two- to three-egg one-person omelette, use a 15cm/6in diameter pan. For a five- to six-egg omelette to serve two, use an 18-20cm/7-8in pan. A 23-25cm/9-10in pan will take an eight-egg flat omelette to serve three or four; with folded omelettes it is easier to make two smaller ones to flip over.

The second essential is timing. Cooking an omelette is a precise, fast operation. The butter or oil must be heated just long enough, no longer; the egg cooked just long enough, no longer, then served at once, no waiting.

Use at least two large eggs to make a one-person omelette; or a larger number of smaller ones.

French flat omelette (page 56)

Start on the flat

Flat omelettes are easiest, so master them first. Break the eggs into a bowl and season with salt and pepper to taste. Thin the mixture with a tablespoon of water for every two eggs and beat with a fork or wire whisk just enough to mix yolks and white. Heat the pan over medium heat, then add 1tbls oil for every two eggs and shake the pan so that it coats the base evenly. When hot, pour in the egg mixture, all at once; it should make an audible but not too pronounced sizzling noise. Stir for a second or two, as if making scrambled eggs. As the egg begins to set, lift the edge in several places so that the liquid egg runs underneath. Scatter the cooked filling over the top as soon as the egg begins to set. Continue lifting the edge until there is no liquid egg left, but the set egg is still moist. Shake the pan constantly to stop the omelette sticking to the pan.

Chefs then invert the omelette onto a plate and slide it back into the pan to cook the second side. A much easier way is to pop the pan under a preheated moderate grill for a few seconds.

Flat omelettes can be presented in the pan or turned out; cut into wedges to serve.

Folded and faultless

The French or folded omelette is cooked on one side only, folded and turned out straight onto the serving dish. It can be plain, filled with chopped fresh herbs, or a variety of pre-cooked mixtures such as mushrooms, ham, prawns or bacon. Or it can be filled with jam or fruit and sprinkled with sugar or liqueur, even flambéed.

Cooking: prepare the seasoned beaten egg mixture and heat the pan as for a flat omelette. For a two-egg omelette put 15g/½oz butter in the hot pan and swirl it round to coat the base. When it stops foaming, but before it starts to colour, pour in the egg mixture, all at once. Shake the pan constantly to keep the egg moving and stir the egg mixture gently with the back of a fork until the eggs are just starting to set. Then take a palette knife and lift the edge so that the uncooked egg runs underneath and sets. Continue until all the liquid egg has gone but the top is soft.

Folding: remove the pan from the heat and press the handle downwards so that the omelette slides towards it. When one-third has slid up the edge of the pan fold it quickly towards the centre with the palette knife. Now raise the handle so that the omelette slides one-third up the opposite edge. Hold the pan over the heated serving plate; as the edge of the omelette touches the plate, continue raising the handle so that the pan is upside down and the egg is on the plate.

If you prefer, just fold the omelette in two to form a half-moon shape. Garnish and serve.

French flat omelette

- **Preparation: 15 minutes**
- **Cooking: 8-10 minutes**

75g/3oz butter
175g/6oz smoked bacon (in one piece if possible) cut into small cubes
2 Spanish onions, very thinly sliced
salt and pepper
8 eggs
3tbls olive oil
chopped parsley, to garnish
green salad, to serve

- **Serves 3-4**
- **815cals/3425kjs per serving**

1 Heat 50g/2oz butter in a large saucepan and fry the bacon and onions until soft and golden. Season with pepper to taste. Remove from the heat and cover to keep hot.

2 Break the eggs into a bowl and beat lightly with a fork to mix. Add the remaining 25g/1oz butter in small pieces. Season lightly with salt and pepper. Heat the grill to medium.

3 Heat a 23cm/9in heavy-based frying pan over medium heat. Add 2tbls of the oil, then pour in the egg mixture. Cook the omelette, lifting the edges so that liquid egg runs underneath and shaking the pan to prevent sticking. When the egg begins to set, spread the cooked onion and bacon over the surface.

4 Put the omelette under the grill just long enough to set the top of the omelette. Serve straight from the pan, cut

How to ··· *make a folded omelette*

Lift the edge of the omelette with a spatula so the uncooked egg runs onto the pan.

Tilt the pan so the omelette slides up the near edge; fold one-third into centre.

Slide the omelette the other way; raise the handle to turn the omelette out onto a plate.

base and sides. When the foaming subsides, pour in the egg mixture. Stir lightly with the back of a fork until just beginning to set. Lift the edges with a palette knife so that the soft uncooked egg is released to run onto the pan.

6 When the omelette is set and golden underneath but still moist on top, spread the cheese mixture down the centre. Continue to cook for a few seconds longer to allow it to heat through.

7 Fold the omelette into two or three, as liked. Turn it out onto a heated serving plate and pour the hot tomato sauce on top. Serve at once.

into wedges; or slide it carefully onto a heated serving plate. Cut into wedges, garnish with parsley and serve at once accompanied by a green salad.

Variations

Extra ingredients can be added to the basic onion and bacon mixture to make an even richer, more filling omelette.
Seafood omelette: *add 100g/4oz chopped cooked prawns or whole shrimps.*
Mushroom omelette: *thinly slice 100g/ 4oz mushrooms and fry in butter with a squeeze of lemon juice. Drain well.*
Spanish omelette: *cook 100g/4oz finely diced cooked potato with bacon mixture.*
Tuna omelette: *add 1 small can tuna.*

Italian omelette

- **Preparation: 15 minutes**

- **Cooking: 30 minutes including tomato sauce**

For the tomato sauce:
1tsp olive oil
1tbls finely chopped onion
400g/14oz canned tomatoes
2tbls tomato purée
generous pinch dried basil
pinch of sugar
salt and pepper
For the omelette:
100g/4oz ricotta or sieved cottage cheese
2tbls grated Parmesan cheese
1tbls finely chopped parsley
4 large eggs
15g/¹/₂oz butter

- **Serves 2**   (ⵙ) (££)

- **425cals/1785kjs per serving**

1 Prepare the tomato sauce in advance. Heat the oil in a small saucepan and fry the onion for 3-4 minutes over low heat until softened, stirring occasionally.

2 Add the tomatoes and their juice, tomato purée, basil and sugar; season lightly with salt and pepper (the flavour will intensify as the sauce is reduced). Simmer for 20 minutes until thickened, stirring occasionally. Rub the sauce through a sieve, taste and adjust the seasoning and keep hot.

3 To make the filling, beat the ricotta or cottage cheese in a bowl with 1tbls of the grated Parmesan, the finely chopped parsley and salt and pepper to taste.

4 In another bowl, beat the eggs lightly with a fork to mix, adding the remaining Parmesan and salt and pepper.

5 Heat the butter in an 18cm/7in omelette pan, swirling it round to coat the

Catalan omelette

- **Preparation: 20 minutes**

- **Cooking: 5 minutes and 5 minutes for omelette**

6 tomatoes, skinned
2 green peppers
1 red pepper
3tbls olive oil
3 shallots, finely chopped
3 garlic cloves, finely chopped
salt and pepper
8 large eggs
2 large egg whites
6 black olives, stoned
1tbls finely chopped parsley

- **Serves 4**   (ⵙ) (££)

- **320cals/1345kjs per serving**

1 Chop the tomatoes coarsely, discarding seeds and juice. Cut the green

How to... make a flat omelette

Beat the egg yolk and white lightly with a fork to mix. Pour into the pan and stir once or twice to disperse heat.

Lift the edge in several places as the egg begins to set to allow the liquid egg to run underneath. Shake the pan.

Continue lifting the edge until there is no liquid egg left. Scatter the filling on top; finish under the grill.

peppers in half, deseed them then cut into strips.

2 Heat 2tbls oil in a frying pan and add the peppers, shallots and garlic. Fry over low heat until the shallots are soft and transparent and the peppers still crisp. Add the tomatoes, season with salt and pepper to taste and cook for a few more minutes stirring from time to time.

3 Break the eggs into a mixing bowl and season with salt and pepper. Beat lightly with a fork.

4 Put the egg whites in a large, clean, dry bowl with a pinch of salt and whisk to soft peaks. Gently fold them into the beaten eggs.

5 Heat the remaining 1tbls oil in a 23cm/9in omelette pan and pour in the eggs. Stir the mixture gently with the back of a fork, letting the liquid egg run to the sides so that the omelette cooks evenly. Then leave undisturbed to cook for a few seconds until the omelette is just set but still moist. Remove from the heat.

6 Pour the vegetable mixture onto a warmed serving dish. Fold the omelette in half and slide it on top. Garnish the filled omelette with olives and chopped parsley, serve hot.

Sweet soufflé omelette

- *Preparation: 15 minutes*
- *Cooking: 8 minutes, including grilling*

3 eggs
1tbls caster sugar
1tbls orange juice
finely grated zest of ½ orange
25g/1oz unsalted butter
icing sugar, for dusting

- *Serves 1-2* 🍴 ££

- *530cals/2225kjs per serving*

1 Separate the eggs, reserving all the yolks and two whites (use the third white in another recipe). Put the yolks in a bowl along with the sugar, orange juice and zest. Whisk the whites in a clean dry bowl until stiff but not dry.

2 Whisk the egg yolk mixture until pale and creamy, then carefully fold in the beaten whites.

3 Heat the grill to hot. Stand an 18-20cm/7-8in heavy-based frying pan over medium heat. Heat the butter in the pan, then add the omelette mixture and gently level the surface with a spatula.

4 Cook the omelette until pale gold underneath – do not allow it to brown. Slide the pan under the grill and cook for about 30 seconds, until the omelette is lightly golden and puffed up.

5 Carefully free the edge of the omelette from the pan with a spatula, then slide it gently onto a heated serving plate. Sift icing sugar over the top and serve at once.

Variations

Chocolate: *melt 50g/2oz plain chocolate with 1tbls water and add to the egg mixture before folding in the whites. Serve.*

SEMI-SOUFFLES

A soufflé omelette is all puffed up, resembling a soufflé. To achieve this, separate the yolks and whites and beat the whites to stiff peaks. Then fold the yolks gently back into the whites. Pour the mixture into the pan and cook, without stirring, until just set. Finish off under a hot grill, which causes the omelette to puff up amazingly.

Soufflé omelettes are often sprinkled with sugar.

Show Stoppers

A golden-topped, lightly puffed piping hot soufflé makes a
spectacular start or finish to a dinner party. And they're not
nearly as difficult to make as popularly supposed

*M*AKING SOUFFLÉS IS probably the most mystique-ridden of all culinary operations. They are thought to be not only very difficult to make but extremely temperamental. But given a bit of practice any cook should be able to produce a perfect soufflé: rising high above the dish, with a crisp golden crust contrasting with a light soft inside. The basic requirements are willingness to follow a recipe *exactly*, a reliable oven which delivers the correct temperature, and a timer to make sure the soufflé comes out of the oven and onto the table at the critical moment.

Lemon soufflé (page 62)

Ingredients and dishes

The spectacular appearance of a soufflé is literally all hot air: air beaten into egg whites, then baked in a hot oven. The basis of a savoury soufflé is a thick white sauce, flavoured with cheese or mixed with a fish, meat or vegetable purée, and enriched with egg yolks. A sweet soufflé is usually made with a base of pâtisserie cream, flavoured with one of the following — fruit juice, fruit purée, chocolate, coffee, vanilla or liqueur.

Soufflés are baked in special

round porcelain, china or oven-glass dishes with straight, fairly low sides. To make sure they rise without impediment the inside must be well buttered, especially around the rim. In addition the dish is often coated with breadcrumbs and/or grated Parmesan cheese, providing a rough surface for the mixture to cling to. Granulated sugar serves the same purpose with a sweet soufflé.

Soufflé dishes vary in size from about 150ml/¼pt, for individual servings, to 2L/3½pt ones to serve eight. It's important to use the right size for the amount of uncooked mixture – see chart. This should fill the dish two-thirds to three-quarters full, so the finished soufflé rises well above the rim, but not far enough to topple over.

Making and cooking

Preparation of a soufflé breaks down into four stages.

Making sauce: the white sauce should be thick and well seasoned because adding the egg whites will loosen the consistency and reduce the strength and taste of the sauce. Once enriched with egg yolks and before adding the egg whites, it can be cooled and chilled but warm gently before proceeding.

Pâtisserie cream: making this depends on having a very low heat, otherwise the mixture will curdle. If your stove is rather fierce use a double boiler, or a bowl set over barely-simmering water. This method is much slower – be pre-pared to cook the custard for about 15 minutes after adding the hot milk before it starts to thicken, stirring constantly. The cream can be made ahead and chilled until needed; warm slightly before folding in the egg whites to help get a smoother mix.

Whisking egg whites: stiffly whisked egg whites give the soufflé its texture and height. The volume of whisked egg white should roughly equal the volume of the base mixture. When cooked the soufflé should rise to double the uncooked volume. Whichever type of whisk used, electric or hand, make absolutely sure it is clean and dry; that goes for the bowl as well. The slightest hint of grease or water will prevent the whites from reaching the desired volume. Also avoid any trace of yolk in the egg whites, and have them at room temperature. A pinch of salt helps to stabilize them and hold the fluffy texture. Once you start whisking the whites you must bake the soufflé without delay.

Folding in: Always tip the lighter mixture (the egg whites) onto the heavier one (the base). If this is very thick and heavy lighten it by stirring in a spoonful or two of the whisked egg white. The secret of success is to combine the two mixtures with the least amount of air-deflating strokes: it shouldn't take more than a minute or two. Use a large metal spoon or spatula and work lightly, cutting through at right angles and drawing the sauce or cream over the egg white with a gentle over and under motion. Meanwhile turn the bowl round with your other hand. Spoon the mixture into the prepared dish; level the top lightly with the spatula.

Baking: Preheat the oven to the temperature specified in the recipe, with one shelf just below centre position. Prepare boiling water for a bain marie if specified; this is to ensure even cooking of an egg-rich mixture. Set a timer and cook for the time given without opening the oven. If you like a soufflé to be creamy inside use the shorter time; if you want it to retain its handsome appearance as long as possible use the longer one. A baked soufflé should tremble slightly when shaken, but not wobble. Test it with a skewer – if foamy traces have stuck to it, cook for a few minutes longer.

WHAT WENT WRONG

Mixture curdles: eggs added too quickly without removing pan from heat; or mixture overheated.

Soufflé poorly risen: mixture too liquid; egg whites either over or under whisked; dish wrong size or oven temperature wrong.

Soufflé unevenly cooked: bain marie not used or surrounding water not hot enough.

Soufflé collapsed or rubbery: oven door opened during baking; soufflé left standing before being served.

Quantities for different-sized cheese soufflés

	Serves 2	Serves 4	Serves 6
Dish capacity	600 ml/1 pt	1.5 L/2½ pt	1.7 L/3 pt
Cooking time	20 minutes	25-30 minutes	30-35 minutes
Ingredients	150 ml/¼ pt milk	300 ml/10 fl oz milk	450 ml/16 fl oz milk
	20 g/¾ oz butter	40 g/1½ oz butter	65 g/2½ oz butter
	1½ tbls flour	45 ml/3 tbls flour	5 tbls flour
	1 large egg, separated	4 large eggs, separated	5 large eggs, separated
	40 g/1½ oz strong cheese	75 g/3 oz strong cheese	100 g/4 oz strong cheese
	salt and pepper	salt and pepper	salt and pepper
	1 tsp Dijon mustard	2 tsp Dijon mustard	1 tbls Dijon mustard
	1 large egg white	1 large egg white	1 large egg white

Individual game soufflés

- **Preparation: cooking game, then 20 minutes**
- **Cooking: 30 minutes**

melted butter, for the dish
125g/4oz cooked pheasant, rabbit
   or other game
1 chicken liver, cooked
25g/1oz butter
1tbls beef stock
½tsp Worcestershire sauce
salt and pepper
3 large eggs, separated
1 large egg white

- **Serves 4**
- **225cals/945kjs per serving**

1 Heat the oven to 180C/350F/gas 4. Brush the insides of four ramekins or 150ml/¼pt soufflé dishes with melted butter, greasing the dish well.

2 Put the game and chicken liver through a food processor or mincer. Then pound with the butter and stock until smooth. Season with the Worcestershire sauce plus salt and pepper to taste.

3 Heat this purée in the top pan of a double boiler, without letting it come to the boil, stirring constantly. Remove the purée from the heat and stand on a heatproof surface. Beat in the egg yolks slowly one by one.

How to ... prepare a soufflé dish

Grate some hard cheese very finely: you will need about 1 tbls. Make some fresh breadcrumbs in a food processor. Butter the soufflé dish.

Mix the cheese and crumbs and sprinkle all over the soufflé dish. Take the dish in both hands and rotate to spread the crumbs evenly.

4 Whisk the egg whites in a clean dry bowl until stiff, then fold gently into the game purée.

5 Fill the ramekins with the purée and bake for 12-15 minutes until well puffed up and golden brown.

Easy salmon soufflé

- **Preparation: 15 minutes**
- **Cooking: 50 minutes**

butter and breadcrumbs for the
   dish
50g/2oz butter
4tbls flour
300ml/½pt milk
50g/2oz grated Parmesan cheese
200g/7oz canned red salmon,
   drained
50ml/2fl oz double cream
¼tsp cayenne pepper
salt and pepper
4 large egg whites
5 large egg yolks

- **Serves 4**
- **510cals/2140kjs per serving**

1 Heat the oven to 180C/350F/gas 4. Lightly butter a 1L/2pt soufflé dish. Sprinkle with breadcrumbs, shaking well to distribute to coat the dish evenly and get rid of any excess.

2 Melt the butter in the top of a double boiler or a bowl set over simmering water. Add the flour and stir for 2-3 minutes to make a pale roux. Add the milk and whisk for about 15 minutes or until the sauce has thickened and lightly coats the back of a wooden spoon. Stir in the cheese.

3 Remove any bones and skin from the salmon, break up the flesh with a fork and purée with the cream in a blender or food processor. (Or mash in a bowl and beat in the cream.)

4 Add the salmon purée to the soufflé mixture. Season with the cayenne plus salt and pepper to taste.

5 Beat the egg yolks in a large bowl. Pour the hot soufflé mixture over them and stir until well mixed.

6 Whisk the egg whites in a clean dry bowl until stiff peaks form. Stir 1tbls egg white into the soufflé mixture to soften it. Using a large metal spoon, lightly fold the remaining egg whites into the soufflé mixture, cutting through the mixture with the edge of the spoon

7 Pour the mixture into the prepared dish and bake for 25-30 minutes.

Harlequin soufflé

- **Preparation: 1 hour**

- **Cooking: 1¼ hours**

butter and stale breadcrumbs, for
  the dish
65g/2½oz butter
65g/2½oz flour
375ml/13fl oz milk
7 large eggs, separated
For the pea purée:
125g/4oz frozen peas
15g/½oz butter
4-6 sorrel leaves, shredded
  (optional)
1tbls milk
salt and pepper
lemon juice
For the tomato purée
6-8 tomatoes, blanched and
  skinned
15g/½oz butter
2tbls finely chopped fresh basil
2 shallots, finely chopped
2tsp tomato purée
salt and pepper
For the cheese mixture:
75g/3oz Parmesan cheese, grated
1tbls chopped hazelnuts
3tbls whipping cream
salt and pepper
cayenne pepper

- **Serves 4**

- **605cals/2540kjs per serving**

1 Heat the oven to 200C/400F/gas 6.
Butter a 1.7L/3pt soufflé dish generously and sprinkle with breadcrumbs.

2 To make the basic soufflé mixture melt
the butter in a large saucepan and add
the flour. Stir over low heat for 2-3
minutes to make a roux.

3 Bring the milk to the boil, then
gradually add it to the roux, stirring
vigorously with a wire whisk to stop lumps
forming. Simmer until the sauce has
thickened, stirring constantly. Remove the
pan from the heat and whisk in the egg
yolks one at a time.

4 To make the pea purée melt the butter
in a saucepan, add the frozen peas
and the sorrel leaves if using. Cook until
tender, then process or sieve and pour into
a large bowl. Add the milk; season with
salt, pepper and lemon juice to taste. Add
one-third of the soufflé mixture and mix.

5 To make tomato purée deseed the
tomatoes and chop. Melt the butter in
a frying pan, add the tomatoes, basil and

Salmon soufflé (page 61)

shallots; simmer for 20 minutes. Sieve,
pour into a large bowl, season and add
half the remaining soufflé mixture.

6 To make the cheese mixture add the
cheese, hazelnuts and cream to the
remaining basic soufflé mixture; season.

7 Whisk the egg whites with a pinch of
salt in a clean dry bowl until stiff but
not dry. Divide into three and fold one-
third into each flavoured mixture.

8 Take a rectangular piece of stiff card
twice the length of the diameter of the
soufflé dish, fold in half along the long
side then fold these two halves back on
themselves. Holding the card along its
original fold insert it in the soufflé dish to
form a Y shape that divides it into three
equal compartments. Fill each one with
one of the three mixtures, then gently
remove the card. Bake for 50-55 minutes.

Lemon soufflé

- **Preparation: 20 minutes**

- **Cooking: 30 minutes**

butter and sugar, for the dish
3-4 lemons
3 large eggs, separated
4tbls icing sugar
2tbls flour
225ml/8fl oz milk
1 large egg white
pinch of salt

- **Serves 4**

- **185cals/775kjs per serving**

1 Butter a 1L/2¼pt soufflé dish generously, dust out with sugar and shake
out any excess. Heat the oven to 220C/
425F/gas 7.

2 Grate the zest from one lemon and
squeeze the remaining lemons to get
50ml/2fl oz lemon juice.

3 Put the egg yolks in a heavy-based
saucepan and stir lightly. Sift in the
icing sugar and beat until smooth, then sift
in the flour. Continue to stir until the
mixture is smooth and lump free.

4 Put the milk in another pan and heat
slowly to boiling point. Pour onto the
egg yolk mixture in a thin stream, beating
constantly and vigorously.

5 Put the pan over moderate heat and
cook, stirring constantly, until the
mixture becomes a thick smooth custard.

6 Add the lemon juice and grated zest
and cook for 1-2 minutes to thicken
the sauce again. Pour into a bowl.

7 Select another large bowl, put all four
egg whites in it and add a pinch of
salt. Whisk until stiff but not dry. Fold into
the hot custard with a large metal spoon,
working as quickly and lightly as possible.

8 Spoon the mixture into the prepared
dish and smooth the top. Bake for
12-15 minutes until puffed up and golden.

High, Wide and Handsome

Raised pies, large and freestanding, with high pastry sides as well as pastry tops and bottoms, are a great English tradition well worth continuing

*M*AKING A RAISED PIE takes a little time and trouble, but the end result is so impressive it's worth it for a special occasion. A large one makes an impressive centrepiece for a buffet party; yet they are also ideal for family lunches, or to take on a picnic as the hot water crust pastry makes them robust and easy to transport without damage. The rich meaty filling inside makes them extremely substantial, needing no more accompaniment than a salad.

Pliable pastry

Hot water crust is unlike any other pastry as the fat and water are heated together before being combined with the dry ingredients and egg. The warm pastry is pliable enough to shape into an oblong mould or loaf tin, yet strong enough to hold its shape when raised round a cylindrical mould which is then

Raised chicken pie (page 65)

carefully removed.

To make hot water crust pastry forget all the usual rules: everything must be *warm*, not cool. Warm the mixing bowl in a very low oven, have any milk or egg yolk used at room temperature and keep the pastry warm while working on it or it will harden and be impossible to shape. Start by heating the fat and water (or milk and water) just to boiling point. Lard is always used, never butter, because it has a much higher burning temperature and will withstand the prolonged heat necessary to cook the raw meat filling. It is also much more elastic than butter, enabling the pastry to be moulded and shaped. The boiling liquid is poured into a well in the centre of the flour, stirred in, then kneaded briefly to form a soft dough.

Roll the pastry out as soon as it has cooled enough to handle and while it is still warm and pliable; it should look very greasy and lumpy. It may help to put the pastry between two sheets of stretch wrap; the bottom piece can then be used to lift the pastry into the tin. Work as quickly as possible, whilst keeping warm the piece cut off to make the lid. Put this in a bowl, cover with stretch wrap and place inside a larger bowl half-filled with warm water to keep the pastry pliable.

Lift up the pastry which is on the bottom piece of stretch wrap (if used), and put in a pie mould or loaf tin. Alternatively hand raise it over an inverted mould as shown in the instructions on this page.

Flavoursome fillings

Various combinations of raw meat are used to fill these pies – veal, ham, pork, chicken, game, sausagemeat and bacon. A fairly high proportion of fat is desirable as it helps keep the pie moist. Diced ham or bacon gives the filling an attractive pinkness when sliced. Seasoning should be generously applied to each layer of filling.

Pack the filling into the pastry case as tightly as possible, as when cooked it will shrink away from the sides. Although the gaps will be filled with jellied stock, this should only form a thin layer. The jellied stock is added after baking the pie.

After cooling add stock through the steam holes made specially large for the purpose.

The pie is then chilled to set the jelly. Cut into thick slices to serve, using a large sharp knife.

JELLIED STOCK

The delicious jelly inside a raised pie adds greatly to its attraction. It is easily made: for an average-sized pie use 150ml/¼pt chicken stock and 1½tsp powdered gelatine. A splash of brandy, port or wine will improve the flavour. Sprinkle the gelatine over half the stock. Leave to stand for 5 minutes, then add the remaining stock and stir until the gelatine has dissolved. Season lightly with pepper (don't use salt if the stock was made with a cube) and leave until almost cold.

Use a funnel to pour the syrupy jelly into the steam holes in the pie. Chill for at least 4 hours, or overnight, to set the jelly quite firmly.

Hot water crust

● *Preparation: 10 minutes, plus resting*

275g/10oz flour
½tsp salt
1 egg yolk
75g/3oz lard

● *Makes 275g/10oz quantity of pastry*

1 Sift the flour and salt into a bowl. Make a well in the centre, drop in the egg yolk and sprinkle on some of the flour.

2 Put the lard in a saucepan with 150ml/¼pt water and heat gently until the fat melts, then bring to boiling point. Remove from the heat and pour all at once into the flour and egg yolk mixture. Mix with a wooden spoon until a dough forms which leaves the sides of the bowl clean, it will be hot to handle.

3 Turn the dough out onto a floured work surface and knead for 1 minute until the dough is smooth and pliable and all traces of egg yolk have disappeared.

4 Return the ball of dough to the warm bowl, cover closely with a plate and leave for a few minutes until cool enough to handle before using.

Variations

This is a rich hot water crust pastry suitable for small and medium-sized pies. For larger ones use a more robust pastry without any egg yolk. For the Stuffed chicken raised pie on page 245 use 450g/1lb flour, 1tsp salt, 200g/7oz lard and 215ml/7½fl oz mixed milk and water. Make the pastry as above.

How to ··· *make a pastry mould*

Mould the pastry over an upside-down floured jar. Press out the folds with your fingers, working the pastry to an even depth down the sides and 5mm/¼in thick.

Tie a double thickness of greaseproof paper or foil round the outside of the pastry case. Turn the jar upright and carefully twist it out of the pastry case.

How to ... make hot water crust

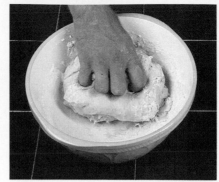

Warm the mixing bowl and sift in flour and salt; make a well in the centre. Heat the lard with water or milk and water; pour in when just boiling and stir.

Cool slightly, then work with the hands to form a dough. Take two-thirds of the pastry and roll out between two sheets of stretch wrap. The remainder forms the lid.

Lift the dough on the bottom sheet of stretch wrap and reverse into the tin. Mould the dough into the tin with the fingertips, leaving a border at the top.

Stuffed chicken raised pie

- **Preparation: 2½ hours, plus chilling**

- **Cooking: 1 hour 20 minutes**

1.4kg/3lb chicken
¼tsp each nutmeg and allspice
salt and pepper
450g/1lb sausagemeat
225g/8oz pie veal, diced
225g/8oz cooked ham, diced
1 large egg, beaten, for glazing
300ml/½pt jellied stock
   (see left)
450g/1lb hot water crust
   (see Variations, left)

- **Serves 10**

- **590cals/2480kjs per serving**

1 First bone the chicken. Make an incision down the backbone from neck to parson's nose. Ease the skin away; cut the meat off the carcass, keeping the knife as close as possible to the bone. Avoid piercing the skin. Cut through the joint where thigh bone meets carcass and continue to cut round until the chicken is boned, with the thighs and drumsticks still attached. Cut round the top of the thigh bone to loose the meat and, with the back of the knife, scrape the meat down to the joint where thigh bone and drumstick meet. Cut through this joint, then cut round the top of the drumstick and scrape the meat down to where foot and drumstick

meet; cut through. Leave the meat attached to the skin.

2 Lay the chicken skin side down and season generously with nutmeg, allspice, salt and pepper. Spread one-third of the sausagemeat over the boned bird; cover with most of the veal and season generously. Cover with most of the diced ham, then another one-third of the sausagemeat, season well.

3 Form the bird into a roll to fit a 9 × 25cm/3½ × 10in tin, bringing the edges of the skin together at the back. Heat the oven to 190C/375F/gas 5.

4 Make the pastry and roll it out to a rectangle 40 × 25cm/16 × 10in. Put in the tin and mould into the sides with the fingers until it is smooth, fairly thin and covers the whole of the inside, leaving a 1cm/½in border around the edge.

5 Put the stuffed bird in the lined tin, join underneath, and fill any cavities with the remaining veal and ham. Top with the remaining sausagemeat. Brush the border with some of the beaten egg.

6 Roll the remaining pastry out into a rectangle to form a lid and put it over the sausagemeat. Pinch the edges of the pastry together, trim off any excess and flute it neatly. Cut a 1cm/½in hole at each end of the pie and put a rolled card in each. Use the pastry trimmings to make decorations (see page 66).

7 Brush the pie with beaten egg. Put the decorations in place and brush them too. Bake the pie for 40 minutes, then reduce the temperature to 170C/325F/gas 3 and bake for a further 40 minutes. Cover

with foil if the top is browning too quickly.

8 Remove the pie from the oven and release the pastry from the tin with the flat blade of a palette knife. If there are any holes in the pastry, fill with butter when the pastry is cold to prevent the jelly seeping through before it has set. Leave the pie until cold; meanwhile prepare the jellied stock for pouring into the pie.

9 When the pie is cold, slowly pour in the almost-set jellied stock through a funnel. Remove the card funnels and chill the pie overnight to set the jelly.

10 Transfer the pie to a long serving platter and serve thickly sliced. To accompany the pie prepare a selection of salads such as potato, beetroot, tomato, mixed green and sliced cucumber. Add dressings just before serving the meal.

MORE PIES

Game pies are perhaps the most delicious of all raised pies. They can be made with any kind of raw game – venison, hare, rabbit or pheasant. As game is dry lean meat, always add 50g/2oz diced pork fat to every 225g/8oz game flesh. Take the flesh off the bones and dice it finely; use the bones to make the stock for finishing the pie.

For a pork pie, use diced lean raw pork with the same proportion of pork fat as for making a game pie.

Finishing a raised pie

Cut one or two steam holes in the pie and disguise with a decoration. Put a rolled card in the hole to keep it open. Glaze, bake and cool. Remove the rolled card and pour in the prepared jellied stock.

Rose decoration

Pile up four layers of pastry trimmings and trim to a 5cm/2in square. Pinch the corners, then cut a cross through the centre. Put over the hole and open out petals.

Veal, ham and egg pie

- *Preparation: making pastry, then 1 hour plus standing and chilling*

- *Cooking: 2 hours 40 minutes*

2 × Hot water crust (page 64)
1 egg yolk, beaten
150ml/¼pt jellied stock
   (page 64)
For the filling:
700g/1½lb pie veal, chopped
175g/6oz lean ham, chopped
50g/2oz lean bacon, chopped
1tbls grated onion
¼tsp dried sage
½tsp salt
¼tsp black pepper
3 eggs, hard boiled

- **Serves 8**

- **620cals/2605kjs per serving**

1 Heat the oven to 200C/400F/gas 6. Cut off two-thirds of the pastry, leaving the remainder covered in a warm place to prevent it drying out. Roll out the pastry to a rectangle about 30 × 20cm/12 × 8in. Put in a greased 1.7L/3pt loaf tin and mould with your fingers up the sides, taking care to avoid a double thickness in the corners. Aim for an even thickness of 5mm/¼in and allow the pastry to overlap the top edges all round. Leave in a cool place for about 1 hour until firm.

2 Meanwhile make the filling: mix together the veal, ham, bacon, onion, sage, salt and pepper.

3 Put about a third of the meat mixture in the pastry case. Shell the eggs and arrange them in a line in the tin. Pack more meat mixture into the spaces round the eggs, top with the remainder and level off.

4 Roll out the remaining pastry to a thickness of about 5mm/¼in to make the lid. Dampen the pastry edges, put on ▶

FINISHING TOUCHES

Raised pies are traditionally quite elaborately decorated. The decoration also has a practical purpose, concealing the large steam holes necessary to allow the jellied stock to be poured in, and using up the pastry left over after trimming the pie.

For how to make all kinds of pastry decorations see pages 70-3.

◀ the lid and pinch the join firmly together. Trim the pastry above the join and crimp the edges (page 71).

5 Brush the pie with beaten egg. Cut two 5cm/2in crosses in the lid and fold back the points to leave two square holes.

6 Use the pastry trimmings to decorate round the holes. Insert a rolled card in each one to keep it open during baking. Brush the pie all over with beaten egg.

7 Bake the pie for 25 minutes, then reduce the heat to 180C/350Fgas 4. Lay a sheet of foil lightly on top of the pie and bake for a further 2¼ hours.

8 Leave the pie to cool in the tin for 1 hour, then turn out. Turn upright and cool. Meanwhile make the jelly.

9 Remove the rolled cards from the holes and pour in the jellied stock. Chill for at least 4 hours before serving.

Chicken and pork pie

● **Preparation: making pastry, then 1¼ hours, plus standing and chilling**

● **Cooking: 2 hours**

Hot water crust (page 64)
1 egg, beaten
oil, for greasing
150ml/¼pt jellied stock
  (page 64)
For the filling:
450g/1lb boneless raw chicken,
  diced
175g/6oz lean pork, diced
100g/4oz pork sausagemeat
finely grated zest of ½ lemon
1tbls finely chopped parsley
½tsp salt
¼tsp black pepper
2tbls chicken stock

● **Serves 6**　　　　　　　　　

● **485cals/2035kjs per serving**

1 Heat the oven to 200C/400F/gas 6. Cut off three-quarters of the pastry, leaving the remainder covered in a warm place to prevent it drying out. Roll out the pastry to a round about 20cm/8in across. Turn a straight-sided jar or tin with a diameter of about 12.5cm/5in upside down and flour the outside well. Put the dough over the top. Mould the pastry down the sides with your fingers for about 10cm/4in, pressing out the pleats to get an even thickness of about 5mm/¼in.

2 Set aside in a cool place for about 2 hours until firm. Meanwhile make the filling by mixing all the ingredients together in a bowl.

3 Measure the depth of the pie sides and cut a double thickness of grease-proof paper or foil to wrap round the outside of the pastry case. Tie with string in two places. Invert the container, then carefully twist and ease the paper or foil out of the pastry case.

4 Put the pastry case on a greased baking tray and pack with the filling, mounding it slightly in the centre. Roll out the remaining pastry to make a lid. Brush the edges with beaten egg and position. Seal the edge firmly all round then cut off ▶

excess pastry with scissors, trimming away the greaseproof paper or foil at the same time. Crimp the edges decoratively.

5 Brush the top of the pie with beaten egg and make a 1cm/½in hole in the centre. Make a pastry tassel from the trimmings (see Designs on pies, page 73) and insert it into the hole. Spread out the strands of the tassel and brush with beaten egg.

6 Bake for 25 minutes, then reduce the heat to 180C/350F/gas 4. Lay a sheet of foil lightly on top and bake for a further hour. Remove the paper or foil tied round the pie. Mix the remaining beaten egg with 1tsp water and use to brush the sides of the pie. Return to the oven for 30 minutes, then leave the pie to cool on the tray. Meanwhile make the jellied stock.

7 Gently lift off the tassel decoration with a sharp knife and pour the almost cold jellied stock into the hole through a funnel. Replace the tassel and chill for at least 4 hours before slicing.

FEELING FESTIVE

Raised pies are ideal for buffet parties as they are relatively easy to cut and eat standing up. After Christmas, these pies can be made with cooked turkey, ham and pork. Cut the cooking time if using cooked meat.

Designs on Pies

*A beautifully decorated crust makes you want to eat a pie
even before you know what is inside. Simple, traditional
patterns are very effective and easy to do*

*T*HE VARIOUS FINISHES and decorations applied to pies and tarts not only make them more appetizing, but serve a practical purpose as well. Treating the edges seals the layers of pastry together and stops the filling from seeping out during baking. And decorations are a marvellous way of using up pastry trimmings.

Pie edges
A pie with a 'lid' will always have a double thickness of pastry around the edge, as the top crust is either folded under or secured to the edge of the dish by a dampened strip of pastry. The edge is then knocked up and fluted or crimped to seal it. Another method of sealing is to press the edges with the prongs of a fork or the tip of a round-bladed knife.

Pastry decorations
A great variety of decorations can be cut from rolled-out trimmings. To seal them to the crust, brush with water underneath, or dip in beaten egg if very small, and then press lightly onto the crust. Traditionally savoury pies were decorated, often quite elaborately, but sweet ones were left plain so that they could be distinguished after baking. Now the choice is yours.

Glazing pastry
Savoury pies are usually finished with an egg yolk glaze to give them a shiny golden surface when baked. Use an egg yolk beaten with a drop of water, or a whole egg beaten with a pinch of salt for a more golden effect. Paint evenly over the pie using a pastry brush, then stick on the decorations and brush the glaze over them too.

Sweet pies are traditionally glazed with milk or egg white, and can be finished with a dusting of caster sugar as well.

*Rhubarb and banana pie
(page 73)*

Open-plate tarts

Open-plate tarts are quick and easy to decorate and a lattice over the top makes them look irresistibly appetizing. Unlike a pie with a solid pastry topping, an open-plate pie does not need glazing.

Lining a pie plate

Chill the pastry for 30 minutes, then roll out on a floured surface to 3mm/⅛in thick and 2.5cm/1in larger than the plate. Roll the pastry over the rolling pin, then unroll it onto the pie plate. Press the pastry gently but firmly into the shape of the plate working from the centre outwards. Prick with a fork and trim the excess pastry to 5mm/¼in beyond the plate. Fold the pastry under to lie flush with the pie plate. The extra thickness will stop the edge cooking more quickly than the rest.

Decorating the edge

Try the following ideas for edges:

Forked: lightly flour the prongs of a fork and gently press all round the edge, with the prongs pointing inwards.

Daisy: flour the handle of a teaspoon and press all round the edge, leaving a very slight gap between each indentation. Keep the 'petals' straight and of equal length.

Sunflower: with the point of a floured sharp knife, cut the pastry at 2.5cm/1in intervals. Then lift the corner of each strip and fold diagonally in half to form a triangle.

Overlapping: with the point of a floured sharp knife, cut the pastry edge at 2cm/¾in intervals. Gently lift the strips and bend them over so that they overlap slightly. Make sure they overlap to the same degree all the way round.

Goffered: slip the floured blade of a knife under the pastry edge, put your thumb and index finger on either side of the knife and pinch together to raise the pastry slightly in a ridge.

Cut-out decorations: surplus pastry can be shaped in many ways and used to decorate the edge. Roll it to a neat shape, with an even thickness of 3mm/⅛in. Cut out the decorations, using small floured biscuit or pastry cutters if you are in a hurry. Dampen them to stick to the pastry edge.

Rich shortcrust pastry

This has a richer flavour than Basic shortcrust and is useful if the pie or tart is to be eaten cold

● **Preparation: 15 minutes, plus 15 minutes chilling**

225g/8oz flour
pinch of salt
150g/5oz butter, cut into small dice
1tbls caster sugar (for sweet recipes only)
1 egg yolk

1 Sift the flour and salt into a mixing bowl and add the butter. Press out the lumps of fat using your thumb and fingertips, keeping your hands high over the bowl so that the crumbs shower back. Continue until the mixture resembles breadcrumbs. Stir in the sugar, if using.

2 Mix the egg yolk with 1tbls cold water and stir in to make a soft, pliable dough, adding up to 1tbls more cold water, if necessary.

3 Turn the dough out onto a lightly floured board and knead lightly. Pat into shape. Wrap and chill for 15 minutes before rolling out.

QUANTITIES OF SHORTCRUST PASTRY

Size of plate	Amount of flour	Made weight
15-18cm/6-7in	100g/4oz	175g/6oz
20-23cm/8-9in	150g/5oz	225g/8oz
25-28cm/10-11in	200g/7oz	300g/11oz
30cm/12in	250g/9oz	425g/15oz

PASTRY DECORATIONS

Make an attractive border or central decoration for a pie with any of the following:

Tiny balls arranged touching each other in the centre or spaced out round the edge.

Small discs, cut with an apple corer or thimble, or heart shapes cut with small aspic cutters, in any repeating pattern.

A plait made from three narrow, even strips. The end of each strip is dampened and all three pressed on top of each other. The strips are then plaited.

Roses made from small balls pressed out to form discs which are then cut in half. One half is rolled up with the straight edge as the base, to make the rose centre. The other halves are wrapped round until the rose is completed.

How to ··· *cover a pie dish*

Roll out the pastry to 3-5mm/⅛-¼in thick and 5cm/2in wider than the dish, using the inverted dish as a guide. Cut a 2.5cm/1in wide strip from the outer edge; place it on the moistened rim of the dish. Brush the strip with water.

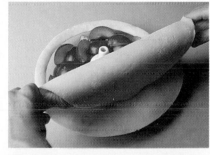

Fill the pie dish, using a funnel in the centre if necessary. Lift the remaining pastry with a rolling pin and lay it over the dish. Press the strip and lid together and trim off any excess pastry with a knife blade held at a slight angle.

Knock up: place the blunt edge of a floured knife against the pastry edge and lay the bent forefinger of the other hand along the pastry rim. Tap the knife round the edge, making several horizontal cuts in each place.

Crimp the edge by pressing a thumb on the rim of the pastry. Push the thumb and forefinger of the opposite hand against the pastry edge on either side of the other thumb to push up the pastry in a pinching action.

Smoked haddock pie

- **Preparation: 20 minutes, plus making and chilling pastry**

- **Cooking: 35 minutes**

350g/12oz smoked haddock fillet, skinned
350g/12oz cod fillet, skinned
150ml/¼pt milk
1 bay leaf
1 × Basic shortcrust pastry (page 10)
1 egg yolk, beaten with a drop of water, for glazing
For the sauce:
25g/1oz butter
25g/1oz flour
2tbls chopped parsley
2 hard-boiled eggs, chopped
squeeze of lemon juice
pepper

- **Serves 4**

- **775cals/3255kjs per serving**

1 Cut the fish into bite-sized pieces and place in a saucepan with the milk, 150ml/¼pt water and the bay leaf. Bring to the boil, cover and simmer very gently for 10 minutes or until just tender. Drain the fish, reserving 300ml/½pt of the cooking liquor for the sauce. Discard the bones, flake the fish and reserve.

2 Melt the butter in a medium-sized saucepan and stir in the flour. Cook gently, stirring, for 2 minutes, then very ▶

gradually add the fish liquor. Bring to the boil, stirring constantly, then simmer for 2-3 minutes. Remove from the heat and carefully stir in the fish, parsley and eggs. Season with lemon juice and pepper.

3 Heat the oven to 190C/375F/gas 5. Spoon the mixture into a 1.1L/2pt pie dish. Roll out the pastry on a lightly floured surface and cut out a narrow strip to fit around the lip of the dish. Brush with water, then cover the pie. Knock up and crimp the edges and cut a steam vent in the centre. Brush with egg yolk to glaze and use the trimmings to decorate the pastry. Bake for about 20 minutes or until golden brown. Serve hot.

Chicken and celeriac pie

- *Preparation: 50 minutes, plus making and chilling pastry*

- *Cooking: 1 hour 45 minutes*

1.1kg/2½lb chicken, jointed
½tsp dried mixed herbs
1 bay leaf
salt and pepper
1 celeriac root, cut into 1cm/½in cubes and sprinkled with lemon juice
2 large carrots, sliced into 5mm/ ¼in rounds
2 onions, sliced
90g/3½oz butter
225g/8oz mushrooms, sliced
pinch of cayenne pepper
40g/1½oz flour
1 × Rich shortcrust pastry (page 70)
4 egg yolks, beaten with a drop of water, for glazing

- *Serves 4-6*

- *980cals/4115kjs per serving*

1 Place the chicken joints in a large pan with the herbs, salt and pepper to taste and just enough water to cover. Slowly bring to the boil, cover and simmer for 35 minutes or until tender. Strain and reserve 425ml/¾pt stock, saving the remaining stock for another recipe, if wished. Cool the chicken quickly, discard the bones and skin and cut the meat into bite-sized pieces.

2 Put the reserved stock in a pan with the celeriac, carrots and onions. Cover and simmer over low heat for 10 minutes or until tender. Drain and keep warm, reserving the stock.

3 Meanwhile, heat 50g/2oz butter in a frying pan and fry the mushrooms for 4-5 minutes or until soft. Drain, season with cayenne pepper and reserve.

4 Melt the remaining butter in a saucepan over low heat, add the flour and cook, stirring, for 2 minutes. Whisk in reserved stock and cook until thickened, whisking constantly.

5 In a large bowl, mix together the chicken, the vegetables and sauce, seasoning to taste. Spoon the mixture into a greased 1.5L/2½pt pie dish and allow to cool.

6 Heat the oven to 180C/350F/gas 4. Place a 1cm/½in strip of pastry on the moistened edge of the pie dish and brush the strip with water. Cover the pie with the rest of the pastry, knocking up and crimping the edges. Cut a small vent in the centre to allow steam to escape during cooking and glaze the pastry with egg yolk. Use the trimmings to decorate the pie with diamonds and small balls arranged to resemble leaves and berries, and glaze these with egg yolk. Bake for 35-45 minutes or until the pastry is golden brown. Serve the pie hot.

Making pastry leaves

Cut the rolled-out trimmings into strips 2.5cm/1in wide. Cut across at an angle to form diamond shapes. Mark veins with the back of a knife and pinch in one end before fixing it to the crust.

Provençale pie

- **Preparation: 45 minutes,
  plus making and chilling pastry**
- **Cooking: 55 minutes**

2tbls olive oil
3 onions, thinly sliced
1 garlic clove, crushed
4 courgettes, cut into 2cm/³/₄in
  slices
2 green peppers, seeded and cut
  into 2.5cm/1in squares
700g/1¹/₂lb tomatoes, skinned,
  thickly sliced and patted dry
3tbls flour
175g/6oz grated Cheddar cheese
salt and pepper
50g/2oz grated Parmesan cheese
1 × Basic shortcrust pastry
  (page 10)
1 egg yolk, beaten with a drop of
  water, for glazing

- **Serves 6**

- **585cals/2455kjs per serving**

1 Heat the oil in a large frying pan. Add
the onions, garlic, courgettes and
green peppers and fry for 10-12 minutes or
until just tender, stirring occasionally.
Carefully stir in the tomatoes. Sprinkle
over the flour and carefully stir in.

Making a tassel

Cut the rolled-out trimmings to a strip
2.5cm/1in wide by 10cm/4in. Cut slits
20mm/³/₄in long at 3cm/1¹/₄in intervals
along the length to resemble a fringe.
Roll up and stand on end. Spread out
the cut strips to form a tassel and
carefully fix to the centre of the pie lid.

2 Place half the mixture in a 1.5L/2½pt
pie dish. Sprinkle with Cheddar; season well. Place the remaining vegetables
on top and sprinkle with Parmesan.

3 Heat the oven to 200C/400F/gas 6.
Roll out the pastry on a lightly floured
surface and cut out a narrow strip to fit
around the lip of the pie dish. Brush with
water, then cover with the rest of the
pastry to form a lid.

4 Press the edges to seal, then knock up
and crimp. Cut a small hole in the
centre and decorate with a pastry tassel
and leaves. Glaze with egg yolk and bake
for 45-50 minutes until golden brown.
Serve hot or warm.

Rhubarb and banana pie

- **Preparation: 15 minutes,
  plus making and chilling pastry**

- **Cooking: 50 minutes**

450g/1lb rhubarb, cut into 2cm/
  ³/₄in lengths
3 bananas, sliced into 2cm/³/₄in
  pieces
175g/6oz caster sugar
juice of ¹/₂ orange
1 piece of stem ginger, finely
  chopped
1tsp ginger syrup
1 x Rich shortcrust pastry (page ⁻0)
1 egg white, beaten, for glazing
cream or ice cream, to serve

- **Serves 4**

- **820cals/3445kjs per serving**

1 Mix the fruit, sugar, orange juice,
ginger and ginger syrup together and
pack into a deep 1.1L/2pt pie dish.

2 Heat the oven to 220C/425F/gas 7. Fit
a pastry strip around the edge of the
dish. Cover the fruit with pastry. Knock up
and flute the edges and cut a slit in the
centre. Brush with egg white. Decorate
with small crescents and small balls made
from the pastry trimmings. ▶

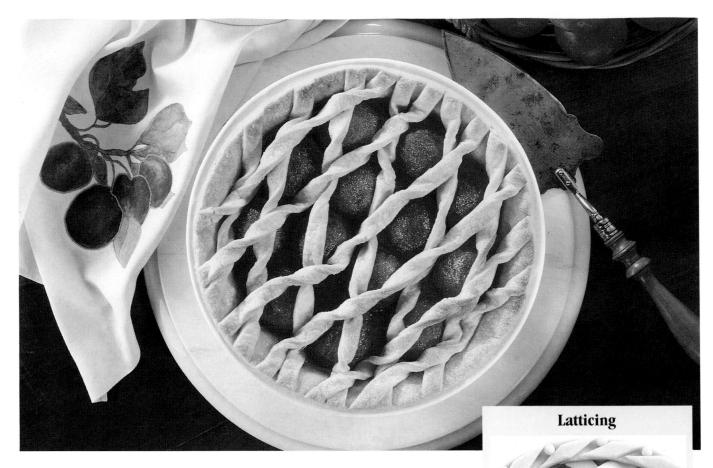

3 Bake for 15 minutes, then lower the heat to 180C/350F/gas 4 and bake for 30-35 minutes or until golden. Serve hot or warm, with cream or ice cream.

Lattice plum pie

- **Preparation: 20 minutes,**
  plus making and chilling pastry

- **Cooking: 1 hour 5 minutes**

700g/1½lb small plums, halved
  and stoned
100g/4oz sugar
1 × Rich shortcrust pastry (page 70)
1 egg white, beaten
3tbls caster sugar
2tsp arrowroot

- **Serves 4-6**

- **710cals/2980kjs per serving**

1 Place the plums in a large saucepan, in a single layer if possible, and cover with 425ml/¾pt water. Add the sugar, cover and poach gently for 10-15 minutes or until just tender but not mushy. Heat the oven to 190C/375F/gas 5.

2 Roll out the pastry to a thickness of 3mm/⅛in and line a 2.5cm/1in deep pie plate, 23cm/9in in diameter. Re-roll the

trimmings and form into long thin strips for the lattice; chill.

3 Brush the pastry in the pie plate with most of the egg white and sprinkle with 2tbls caster sugar.

4 Carefully remove the plum halves from the pan and drain, reserving the juice. Pat the plums dry on absorbent paper.

5 Arrange the plums in the pastry case, cut sides down, pushing them close together. Brush the top rim of the pastry case with water, then arrange the pastry strips on top to form a diamond-shaped lattice. Seal and trim. Brush the lattice with the remaining egg white and sprinkle with the remaining caster sugar. Bake for 30-40 minutes until the pastry is cooked and pale golden.

6 Meanwhile, boil the plum cooking liquid to reduce to 125ml/4fl oz. Blend the arrowroot into the reduced liquid, then simmer for 4-5 minutes to thicken slightly. Pour in as much of the reduced liquid as will go into the pie. Serve hot or warm.

Variations

For a different effect, the strips can be twisted into spirals before being laid in position. Seal and trim as before.

Latticing

Lattices help prevent the filling from drying out. You will need 50g/2oz pastry for a simple lattice and twice that amount for an interwoven one.

To make a simple lattice, roll out the trimmings to 3mm/⅛in thick and 1cm/½in longer than the diameter of the plate. Cut into strips 1cm/½in wide and dampen the edge of the tart. Lay half the strips over the filling in parallel lines. Lay the remaining strips across the first layer, at right angles. Trim the ends so that they are flush with the plate and seal.

To make an interwoven lattice, place half the strips on the tart, then interweave each remaining strip at right angles.

More Classic Sauces

Hollandaise and Béarnaise are classic French sauces of great distinction, similar to mayonnaise but served warm. If you can make mayonnaise, you can soon master these

*T*HESE SAUCES ARE usually served with expensive food. Hollandaise is the classic partner to salmon steaks or asparagus; Béarnaise is the traditional enrichment for a juicy sirloin or fillet steak. But the sauces themselves are not expensive, and can also be used to lift everyday meat, fish and vegetables into the realms of *haute cuisine*. Almost anything becomes a luxury dish with one of these rich golden sauces on top.

Several other sauces are derived from these two 'mother sauces', notably the extremely rich but light Mousseline sauce, made by lacing Hollandaise with whipped cream

Magic emulsions

Hollandaise and Béarnaise are emulsion sauces, made in the same apparently magical way as mayonnaise. The egg particles are separated during beating and held in suspension – in oil in the case of mayonnaise, in liquid unsalted butter for Hollandaise and Béarnaise.

The essential emulsifying agent is an acid: lemon juice or vinegar. Hollandaise sauce is perfectly plain, while Béarnaise is flavoured with chopped herbs, shallots and wine. This makes Béarnaise a sharper sauce, with red meat rather than fish and vegetables.

Sirloin steak (page 164) with Béarnaise sauce (page 77)

Hollandaise sauce is a French invention, nothing to do with Holland, but named after the country which gave its creator his inspiration. Béarnaise sauce was created by a chef from the old French province of Béarn, in honour of his fellow countryman King Henri IV.

Unless you make blender Hollandaise sauce (see page 79) the equipment needed is very simple: a double boiler, or just a bowl set over a saucepan; and a wire whisk. Using a blender is a virtually foolproof method, but you still have to be careful to add the butter slowly in a thin stream.

Keys to success

The technique of making mayonnaise is to beat the oil into the egg yolk drop by drop. Similarly with Hollandaise and Béarnaise, the secret of success is to beat butter into the egg yolk and acid mixture bit by bit until it emulsifies into a thick rich sauce. But this must be done over gentle heat in order to keep the butter soft, which adds an additional complication; if the mixture overheats it will curdle.

Most traditional recipes, and the blender recipe, use melted butter. But in the main recipes here diced cold butter is used instead. As each piece melts slowly in the warmth of the egg yolk and acid mixture there is less danger of there being too much melted butter for the egg yolks to cope with at one time, which also causes the sauce to curdle.

As with mayonnaise, if disaster strikes and the sauce does curdle, fast action can save it. Just throw in an ice cube and whisk furiously, over the hot water, until the sauce emulsifies again. Remove the ice cube as fast as possible.

Always make sure that the water in the saucepan below is hot, not simmering. If the egg gets too hot in the early stages it will cook; later the sauce will curdle. Remove the pan from the heat from time to time while continuing to beat as an extra precaution.

Straining the sauce through a fine nylon sieve before serving is not essential but ensures perfect smoothness and gives an extra gloss to the finished sauce.

Hollandaise sauce

- **Preparation: 5 minutes**
- **Cooking: 15 minutes**

1-2tsp lemon juice
salt and white pepper
4 large egg yolks
100-225g/4-8oz unsalted butter,
diced into 1cm/½in cubes

- **Makes about 175-300ml/6-10fl oz**
- **1000cals/4200kjs total**

1 Put 1tsp lemon juice in the top pan of a double boiler, or a bowl set over a saucepan of hot but not simmering water. Add 1tbls cold water and a pinch each of salt and pepper.

2 Add the egg yolks and one piece of the butter to the lemon juice mixture and stir rapidly with a wire whisk until the butter has melted and the mixture begins to thicken.

3 Add a second piece of butter and continue whisking. As the butter melts add a third piece, stirring from the bottom of the pan until the butter has melted. Continue whisking in the remaining butter piece by piece.

4 Remove the pan or bowl from the hot water and beat for a further 2-3 minutes. Return it to the hot water and beat for 2 minutes more. By this time the sauce should have emulsified and be thick and creamy.

5 Finish with a few extra drops of lemon juice to taste, and salt and pepper if needed. Strain and keep hot over warm (not hot) water.

How to...
make Hollandaise sauce

Put a double boiler containing hot, not simmering, water over very gentle heat. Stir together lemon juice, seasoning, egg yolks and one cube butter.

Add the second cube of cold butter and continue whisking. As the butter melts into the egg yolks the sauce will begin to thicken.

Add the remaining butter bit by bit, stirring constantly from the bottom of the pan. Do not add another cube until the previous one has melted.

Adjust the seasoning with a few extra drops of lemon juice and a little more salt and white pepper. Strain to ensure a smooth glossy sauce. (See column 1, left).

HOLLANDAISE VARIATIONS

Make the sauce with the larger quantity of butter (225g/8oz) in each case.

Horseradish: whisk in 1tbls horseradish sauce after straining. Serve with grilled steak.

Maltaise: Add the juice of ½ blood orange to the lemon juice at the start; add the remaining juice at the end. The zest can be used to garnish the sauce. Serve with asparagus, broccoli or poached fish.

Mousseline: Fold in 5tbls whipped double cream just before serving. Use with fish or boiled vegetables.

Mustard: beat in 2tsp Dijon mustard after straining the sauce. Serve with fried or poached fish.

Béarnaise sauce

- **Preparation: 10 minutes**

- **Cooking: 15 minutes**

4-6 sprigs fresh tarragon, coarsely chopped
4-6 sprigs fresh chervil, coarsely chopped
1tbls chopped shallot
2 black peppercorns, crushed
2tbls tarragon vinegar
150ml/¹/₄pt dry white wine
3 large egg yolks
225g/8oz unsalted butter, diced into 1cm/¹/₂in cubes
salt and cayenne pepper
lemon juice

- **Makes about 300ml/¹/₂pt**

- **1960cals/8230kjs total** ▶

Calabrese with mousseline sauce (page 78)

1 Put half the tarragon and chervil in a saucepan with the shallot, peppercorn vinegar and wine. Bring to the boil and cook over high heat until the liquid has reduced to 2tbls. Remove from the heat and set aside.

2 Beat the egg yolks with 1tbls cold water, then put them in the top pan of a double boiler, or in a bowl set over a saucepan of hot but not simmering water. Strain in the reduced liquid and stir briskly and constantly with a wire whisk until the mixture is light and fluffy.

3 Whisk in the first piece of butter. When it has melted and been incorporated into the egg mixture whisk in a second piece. Continue in this way, waiting until each piece of butter has been incorporated before adding the next.

4 When the mixture begins to thicken start adding a few pieces of butter at a time. Whisk thoroughly all the time, stirring from the bottom of the pan until each piece of butter melts.

5 Remove from the hot water and season with salt, cayenne pepper and lemon juice to taste. Strain through a fine sieve and stir in the remaining chopped herbs. Keep over warm (not hot) water until ready to use.

Variations

For Sauce Choron mix 1-2tbls tomato purée with the reduced wine and herb liquid before adding it to the egg yolks. Serve with roast saddle of lamb, grilled pan-fried meat or poached or fried fish.

Calabrese with mousseline sauce

● *Preparation: making the sauce, then 10 minutes*

● *Cooking: 10 minutes*

900g/2lb calabrese spears
salt
2tsp lemon juice
300ml/¹/₂pt mousseline sauce
(page 77)

● *Serves 4-6*   (❦) (££)

● *370cals/1555kjs per serving*

1 Tie the calabrese spears into a bundle. Boil 5cm/2in water in a large saucepan and add a good pinch of salt and the lemon juice.

2 Stand the bundle of calabrese spears in the boiling water, flower ends up. Cover the pan, return quickly to the boil, then simmer for 7-10 minutes, until just tender. Drain and keep warm.

3 Start making the mousseline sauce while the calabrese is cooking. To serve, arrange the calabrese spears on a heated serving dish and spoon over a little of the sauce. Serve the rest in a heated sauce boat.

Veal with lemon balm hollandaise (see right)

Cook's tips

Use the smaller quantity of butter if you want a rich sauce to serve with the strong flavours of asparagus, broccoli or cauliflower. Use the larger quantity for a milder sauce with the delicate flavours of veal, salmon or a fish mousse.

BLENDER HOLLANDAISE

Use a blender or food processor to make a quick, virtually foolproof Hollandaise sauce. Assemble the same ingredients, but melt the butter over a low heat. Warm the goblet: pour in hot water and let it stand for a few minutes. Empty out the water and dry the goblet.

Put in the egg yolks (or 1 whole egg), 1tsp lemon juice and seasoning. Switch on to mix them together. At medium speed, very slowly pour in the melted butter in a thin stream. The sauce should thicken as you watch. If it seems too stiff beat in 1-2tbls very hot water. Finish with a few extra drops of lemon juice and additional seasoning.

Veal with lemon balm hollandaise

- **Preparation: making sauce, then 10 minutes**
- **Cooking: 10 minutes**

6 x 175g/6oz veal escalopes
black pepper

50g/2oz butter
175ml/6fl oz Hollandaise sauce
(page 76), kept warm
22 lemon balm leaves
lemon slices, to garnish

- **Serves 6**
- **420cals/1765kjs per serving**

1 Season the escalopes with pepper. Melt half the butter in a large frying pan over low heat. Add three escalopes and fry for 3-4 minutes on each side or until cooked through. Remove and keep hot while cooking the rest.

2 Using a pestle and mortar (or a small food processor) pound 10 lemon balm leaves until thoroughly pulverized. Add to the Hollandaise sauce, scraping the sides of the mortar or bowl clean. Mix well and pour over the veal.

3 Serve the veal hot, garnished with the remaining lemon balm leaves and slices of lemon.

Cook's tips

Lemon balm (Melissa officinalis) *is a pretty lemon-scented herb easy to grow from seed in the garden or in pots. Use it to flavour fish, chicken and milk puddings, and in salad dressings.*

Brochettes of mussels

- **Preparation: 25 minutes**
- **Cooking: 40 minutes**

2kg/4¹/₂lb or 2.3L/4pt fresh mussels
2tbls finely chopped shallots
2 sprigs thyme
2 sprigs parsley
1 bay leaf
salt
150ml/5fl oz dry white wine
225g/8oz unsmoked bacon
freshly ground black pepper
melted butter
chopped tarragon
300ml/¹/₂pt Béarnaise sauce
(page 77)

- **Serves 4**
- **885cals/3715kjs per serving**

1 Sharply tap any mussels that are open and discard those which do not close. Pull away the beards, then scrub the mussels clean under cold running water. Scrape off any encrustations with a sharp knife from the shell.

2 Place the mussels in a large saucepan together with the chopped shallots, thyme, parsley, bay leaf, salt and wine. Cover the pan and shake over a high heat for 3-5 minutes, until the shells are well open. Remove from the heat and allow to stand for a few seconds.

3 Strain the mussels into a colander and discard any that are still closed.

When cool enough to handle, remove the mussels from their shells. Cut the bacon into pieces the same size as the mussels. Thread mussels in pairs on small skewers with pieces of bacon between them. Season to taste with pepper.

4 Prepare the Béarnaise sauce. Cover and keep the sauce warm in the top of the boiler (off the heat).

5 Heat the grill to high. Brush the skewered mussels and bacon with a little melted butter then grill for about 4-5 minutes until the bacon is golden, turning the skewers regularly. Just before serving, add a little chopped tarragon to the sauce and transfer to a warmed sauceboat. Serve the brochettes and the Béarnaise sauce separately.

Starters

S*tarters may be served at the beginning of a meal for all sorts of reasons: to whet the appetite before the main course or purely to fill you up. They vary from simple soups and salads to elaborate and relatively time-consuming pâtés and terrines. The choice depends partly on the season, partly on what is to follow.*

Throughout this section, Cooking with Confidence *provides practical information for even the most difficult recipes, including cook's tips and step-by-step guides to the techniques and processes involved. Variations and serving suggestions accompany many of the recipes and, where helpful, you are referred back to the*

Basic foods and techniques section.

The easiest starters do not have to be cooked and are usually simple combinations of ingredients which are quickly prepared, using either fresh or store-cupboard foods, or a mixture of the two. Prawn Cocktail is a classic example of a no-cook starter (see page 84). Chilled soups and dips are also tempting. Salads are a light appetiser, for which it is important to use good-quality ingredients and a complementary dressing.

Soups are another ideal starter. Thick, country-style soups are greatly appreciated in the winter and are extremely versatile as they can be dressed up to serve at a din-

ner party or presented more simply for a family meal. Consommés, either hot or cold, are more delicate and make a delightfully light start to meals throughout the year. These clear soups are time-consuming to prepare, but they can be made well in advance. Cooking with Confidence guides you through the clarifying process, which produces the crystal-clear stock, and suggests various flavours and garnishes.

When you are entertaining in style, pâtés, mousses and terrines are perfect. Pâtés are generally the easiest to make; indeed, several of the recipes need no cooking at all and the smooth purée is either heaped into ramekins or piled onto plates to serve. Savoury mousses are similar to pâtés, but lighter and more delicate. Terrines are often fairly complicated to prepare, but look extremely attractive.

Their name derives from the rectangular dish in which they are usually baked, and they can range from simple, chunky mixtures to impressively layered ones. The Cooking with Confidence step-by-step guide takes the mystique out of the creative process, and there are suggestions for containers, quick cooking tips and serving ideas.

Canapés are often served with drinks at a party, but are perfect if you have lots of guests for a buffet or a casual lunch in the garden. Cooking with Confidence guides you through both choice and preparation, providing countless variations from simple open sandwiches to wrapped and rolled combinations to skewer onto tiny sticks. As ever, there are tips on planning and preparing ahead, and how to present the result in the most attractive way.

No-Cook Starters

Simple, attractive, easy to make – time-saving cold starters are ideal appetizers for a busy cook. And your guests will love them

A LIGHT AND attractive starter makes an ideal beginning to any meal. It does the vital job of tempting you on to the main course, whetting the appetite rather than blunting it.

First impressions

First impressions are always lasting and this is no less true in cooking, so the appetizer you serve will be setting the scene for the whole meal. Colour, presentation and attention to detail are all important. Use finely chopped herbs, not clumsily broken leaves; slice vegetables thinly and evenly in a food processor, or use a sharp knife, and avoid thick uneven chunks. If you are serving hors d'oeuvres, try to present them as inventively as possible on individual dishes and use good olive oil and vinegar to make a perfectly flavoured vinaigrette.

Quick ideas

Canned vegetables and seafood are useful to keep on hand to use for easily prepared appetizers. **Artichoke hearts** cut into thin strips and tossed with mayonnaise or vinaigrette are one idea. Or try canned **red pimento** cut into thin strips and dressed with a delicious garlicky vinaigrette.

You can serve **anchovy fillets** on their own, drained and topped with thin strips of canned pimento and some chopped parsley. Dress with olive oil, a squeeze of lemon juice and freshly ground black pepper to bring out the flavour. Anchovies can also be used to decorate and enhance the taste of other hors d'oeuvres – for example, cut the fillets lengthways and arrange them over a tomato salad.

Toss pieces of well-drained canned **crab** with diced tomato and avocado in a well-flavoured vinaigrette. Or mix the crab with a little chopped onion and green pepper in lemon juice and mayonnaise.

Garnish **sardines** with finely chopped parsley and a squeeze of lemon and serve as part of an hors d'oeuvre. To make fish pâté, mash sardines with lemon juice, curry powder, finely chopped onion and mayonnaise or butter – or use **tuna,** leaving out the curry.

Prawn and avocado cocktail (p.84)

Prawn and avocado cocktail

● **Preparation: 20 minutes**

150ml/¼pt mayonnaise
1tbls lime or lemon juice
4 drops of hot pepper sauce
1tbls grated onion
salt and pepper
2 very ripe avocados
225g/8oz prawns, defrosted
    if frozen
lemon and lime slices and
    unshelled prawns, to garnish

● **Serves 4**

● **565cals/2375kjs per serving**

1 Combine the mayonnaise with the lemon juice, hot pepper sauce and onion. Season with salt and pepper to taste.

2 Cut the avocados in half, removing the stones and gently peeling off the skins. Slice each half into four lengthways and arrange on individual serving plates so that the slices overlap.

3 Divide the prawns between the plates and top with the mayonnaise mixture. Garnish each serving with lemon and lime slices and an unshelled prawn. Serve the cocktail at once.

Cook's tips

To peel an avocado, place one half, cut side down, on a board and, using a small knife, pull or strip away the skin, leaving the flesh unmarked. Thicker-skinned varieties should be stripped one small piece at a time. If you want to make the starter in advance, turn each avocado slice in lemon juice to avoid discolouring.

Chickpea dip

● **Preparation: 15 minutes**

400g/14oz canned chickpeas,
    drained
100ml/3½fl oz yoghurt
juice of 1 lemon
1tbls chopped fresh mint or
    1tsp crushed dried mint (or
    1tbls chopped parsley)
1tbls olive oil
salt and pepper
lemon zest, to garnish

● **Serves 4-6**

● **105cals/440kjs per serving**

PREPARING VEGETABLES WITH A FOOD PROCESSOR

Every brand of food processor has its own particular features, so check the handbook first. These steps are a general guide.
Chopping: cut vegetables into cubes before processing – the smaller the bits, the quicker the chopping. Use the pulse button for more control, allowing the vegetables to drop to the bottom of the bowl.
Slicing: you may have two discs – one for thin slices and one for thick. But the thickness of the slices will vary just by the pressure you exert when pushing the vegetables through.

The gentler the pressure, the thinner the slices will be. Keep the vegetables upright and cut long food shorter than the feed tube. Halve round vegetables first, and for vegetables with tough peel (such as green pepper), push the pieces in with the peel facing towards the centre of the bowl.
Grating carrots: use the grating disc or shredding plate. Peel the carrots and cut into pieces. Stack them in the feed tube and press down with the feeder, controlling the coarseness by the pressure you exert.

1 Place the chickpeas, yoghurt, lemon juice, chopped mint or parsley and olive oil in a food processor or blender and purée. If the mixture is too thick, you may want to add a little water to dilute it. Season to taste with salt and pepper, adding more lemon juice if necessary. Cover and chill.

2 When required, transfer the mixture to a serving dish and garnish with lemon zest, either coarsely grated or cut into thin strips.

Variations

For a crunchy texture, you could add diced green pepper or celery after the dip has been blended.

Serving ideas

This dip is delicious served with hot pitta bread. As an accompaniment to a main course, it can be served with charcoal-grilled kebabs.

How to ··· chop herbs

In a food processor: remove any coarse stalks, place in the processor bowl and then process the herb for 5 seconds.

On a board: push the herbs into a bunch against the flat of your knife and then slice with the knife held against your fingers.

With a mezzaluna (a half-moon shaped blade with two handles): rock it to and fro over the herbs, a small amount at a time.

Using scissors: easiest of all – just hold a bunch of herbs over a board or cup and snip them up with a sharp pair of scissors.

Iced tomato soup

- **Preparation: 25 minutes,
  plus chilling**

600ml/1pt yoghurt, chilled
600ml/1pt tomato juice, chilled
1tsp tomato purée
*½ small cucumber, peeled and
  finely diced*
*1 green pepper, seeded and finely
  chopped*
2 spring onions, thinly sliced
juice and zest of 1 large lemon
pinch of cayenne pepper
1tsp paprika
salt and pepper
1tbls snipped chives
lemon slices, to garnish
lemon wedges, to serve

- **Serves 6**

- **75cals/315kjs per serving**

1 Tip the yoghurt into a large bowl and gradually beat in the tomato juice and ▶

tomato purée until the mixture is smooth and well blended.

2 Stir in the cucumber, green pepper, spring onions, lemon juice and zest, cayenne pepper and paprika. Season with salt and pepper to taste. Cover and chill until needed.

3 Just before serving, stir in the chives. Pour the soup into chilled bowls, garnish with lemon slices and serve very cold, with a lemon wedge for each person.

French hors d'oeuvres

This traditional appetizer is made up of an assortment of raw vegetables dressed with a well-flavoured vinaigrette and arranged in colourful piles on individual serving plates

● *Preparation: 40 minutes*

2 large, ripe tomatoes
3tbls chopped fresh basil or
*   1tbls dried*
1 shallot, finely chopped
2 × Basic vinaigrette (see right)
225g/8oz carrots
1tbls olive oil
juice of ½ lemon
2tbls chopped parsley
salt and pepper
225g/8oz cooked beetroot
2tbls snipped chives
½ cucumber

● *Serves 4*   ⚞⚟ ⚐⚐

●*465cals/1955kjs per serving*

1 Slice the tomatoes and arrange them on the serving plates. Sprinkle with the basil and shallot and dress with half the vinaigrette.

2 Grate the carrots and toss them in the olive oil and lemon juice. Mix in the chopped parsley, season with salt and pepper to taste and arrange on the plates.

3 Dice the beetroot and mix it with half the remaining vinaigrette. Add to the plates and sprinkle with the chives.

4 Very thinly slice the cucumber, arrange on the plates and dress with the remaining vinaigrette. Cover and chill briefly if not serving immediately.

Variations

Try adding chopped spring onions to the sliced tomatoes instead of shallots. Sliced cucumbers are delicious with just a coating of lemon juice and salt and pepper, sprinkled with a little dill.

Crunchy apple starter

● *Preparation: 30 minutes*

4 red dessert apples
2-3tbls lemon juice
2 celery stalks, finely chopped
50g/2oz unsalted peanuts
50g/2oz hazelnuts
50g/2oz sultanas
50ml/2fl oz single cream
50g/2oz full-fat soft cheese
chopped parsley, to garnish

● *Serves 4*   ⚑ ⚐⚐

●*305cals/1285kjs per serving*

1 Core and quarter the apples, then cut each quarter lengthways into two or three slices and toss in 1tbls lemon juice to prevent discoloration.

2 Combine all the remaining ingredients, except the parsley, in a small bowl and mix well, adding lemon juice to taste.

3 Spoon some of the mixture into four individual bowls and then arrange the apple slices on top so that the sides are supported and the fruit forms a rosette shape.

BASIC VINAIGRETTE (see right)

BASIC VINAIGRETTE

In a small jug or cup, stir together ½tsp Dijon mustard and 2tbls wine vinegar. Add 6tbls olive oil and salt and freshly ground black pepper to taste and whisk vigorously with a fork. Use immediately or store in the fridge, covered, then whisk again just before serving.

To vary, add any of the following: 1-2tbls finely chopped fresh herbs (choosing from tarragon, chives, fennel or parsley); a little crumbled Roquefort cheese; a crushed garlic clove; a little finely chopped shallot or a pinch of curry powder.

4 Spoon the remaining mixture into the centre of the apples and sprinkle parsley over each. Serve at once.

Plan ahead

The celery, nut, sultana and cheese mixture can be prepared several hours ahead of time and kept covered in the refrigerator. But do not cut up the apples more than an hour before you plan to serve the starter, otherwise they may discolour.

Hearty Soups

Making your own soup is very rewarding. With very little time and effort, you can make a warming and substantial start to a winter meal

SOUP CAN MEAN anything from a delicate chilled consommé to a rich hot broth that can be either smooth and creamy, or chunky with meat, fish and vegetables. Here, *Cooking with Confidence* is concerned with the latter type: broths, purées, thickened soups and substantial chowders.

Although these hearty soups are sometimes called peasant-style, they are by no means lowly. French *pot-au-feu* is soup on the grand scale, it contains large amounts of beef and is time-consuming to prepare. But a typical peasant soup relies on a good stock and plenty of fresh vegetables to make a small amount of meat or fish go a long way. It will not be difficult to make, though it may call for long cooking. By adding filling items — potatoes, dumplings, rice, pasta or beans — you can turn it into a main meal which is as nutritious as it is delicious to eat.

What's wrong with cans?

Why bother to make soup when every possible kind can be bought in a can or packet? First, because home-made always tastes more interesting than the ready-made kind as you can season it with as much garlic, pepper or spice as you like. Second, because you can make more generous amounts — allow 300ml/½pt per person — containing sizeable chunks of meat, chicken or shellfish. Third, making soup is fun. Bought soups are devised to be the same every time, but you can create subtle differences in the same basic recipe by altering the proportions of ingredients, using an alternative stock or different herbs. Fourth, making soup is a great way of using up all those odds and ends lurking in the fridge and vegetable rack.

Soup does not necessarily involve long cooking. A simple mixed vegetable soup should be cooked for no longer than it takes for the ingredients to become tender.

Spicy tomato soup (page 90)

Types of soup

However much you like to experiment, keep in mind the type of soup you aim to produce.

Broth: this is based on an unclarified stock, and often contains meat, poultry or game, which is cooked in the stock, but may be served separately. The soup is not sieved or puréed and will also contain diced vegetables, and usually some rice or pearl barley. Leek soup with basil is a vegetable broth.

Thickened soup: this is made with a meat, fish or vegetable stock, which is usually thickened with flour. A richer type of thickened soup may be thickened with a mixture of eggs and cream known as a *liaison*. An example is French onion soup.

Purée: here the basic ingredients are puréed to make a smooth thick soup without using any additional thickening agents. Starchy vegetables such as potatoes, peas, beans and lentils are needed to achieve the right consistency, which should be similar to double cream. Spicy tomato soup and Pea souper are two examples.

Chowder: this means a thickened fish and vegetable soup, often including salt pork or bacon, usually served as a main course. Although the word comes from the French *chaudière* (a cooking pot), it is often associated with American soups. Smoky soup is a chowder made with smoked haddock.

STOCK POT OR CUBE?

Some cookery books insist that home-made stock is essential, but most of us don't have the time to make meat stock, which takes many hours. However, vegetable and chicken stocks are quick to make.

Cubes will produce adequate stocks for everyday soups but don't add salt to the soup without tasting it first as most stock cubes are very salty.

Leek soup with basil

- **Preparation: 10 minutes**
- **Cooking: 30 minutes**

25g/1oz butter
1 onion, finely chopped
6 small leeks, sliced
850ml/1½pt chicken stock
225g/8oz canned tomatoes, chopped
1tbls chopped fresh basil or parsley
salt and pepper

- **Serves 4**   ① �£ ⊕
- **100cals/420kjs per serving**

1 Melt the butter in a large saucepan, add the chopped onion and leeks and cook for 5 minutes or until softened but not brown, stirring occasionally.

2 Add the stock, tomatoes and basil, stir well, then cover and cook gently over low heat for 20-25 minutes or until the leeks are tender. Season with salt and pepper to taste. ⊕ Serve hot.

How to ... *degrease soups*

Remove excess fat from the surface of hot soup by blotting with absorbent paper on top.

Alternatively, cool, then chill the soup, then lift off the fat which will have solidified on top.

French onion soup

- *Preparation: 15 minutes*
- *Cooking: 1 hour 10 minutes*

1tbls oil
25g/1oz butter
450g/1lb onions, thinly sliced
1 garlic clove, crushed
1tbls flour
1.1L/2pt hot beef stock
salt and pepper
4 slices of French bread
75g/3oz Gruyère or Cheddar
   cheese, grated
1/2tsp mustard powder
2tbls brandy (optional)

- *Serves 4*
- *385cals/1615kjs per serving*

1 Heat the oil and butter in a large saucepan. Add the onions and garlic, cover and cook very gently for 30 minutes or until very soft and lightly browned, shaking the pan occasionally to prevent the contents sticking.

2 Add the flour and cook for 1 minute, stirring. Gradually add the stock, stir until boiling, then simmer for 20-30 minutes. Season with salt, if needed, and plenty of pepper.

3 Just before the soup is cooked, heat the grill and toast the bread slices on one side only. Mix the cheese with the mustard powder and spread over the untoasted sides. Leave the grill on.

4 Stir the brandy into the soup, if using. Divide it among four heatproof soup bowls and top each with a slice of bread, cheese side up. Put the bowls under the grill, two at a time if necessary, until the cheese bubbles and browns.

Cook's tips

In France onion soup is served in special brown earthenware bowls with straight sides, four of which should fit neatly under the grill. Alternatively, you can put the bowls in a hot oven for 5-10 minutes to melt and brown the cheese.

STORECUPBOARD SOUP

Making soup is a good way of using up vegetables that are slightly past their prime and leftovers too small to do anything else with. Such soups make a good lunch or supper if topped with grated cheese and served with crusty bread.

To serve four, prepare about 450g/1lb of mixed vegetables (an onion, carrot, celery stalk and whatever else you have). Chop and fry gently in 2tbls oil in a covered pan. Add 1.1L/2pt hot stock and simmer gently until the vegetables are just tender. Add any cooked leftovers — diced meat, baked beans, green vegetables — and/or 50g/2oz small pasta shapes or rice 10-15 minutes before serving.

Smoky soup

- *Preparation: 20 minutes*
- *Cooking: 40 minutes*

15g/1/2oz butter
1 small onion, finely chopped
1 celery stalk, thinly sliced
2 streaky bacon rashers, chopped
225g/8oz potatoes, cut into
1cm/1/2in cubes
1 carrot, thinly sliced
225g/8oz smoked haddock fillet
50g/2oz frozen peas
150ml/1/4pt milk
1/2tsp cornflour
pepper
chopped parsley, to garnish

- *Serves 4*
- *200cals/840kjs per serving*

1 Melt the butter in a large saucepan, add the onion, celery and bacon and cook gently for 5 minutes or until softened, stirring occasionally.

2 Add the potato, carrot and 300ml/½pt water, cover and simmer until tender, about 20 minutes.

3 Skin the fish and cut it into 2.5cm/1in pieces, removing any bones. Add to the soup along with the peas and milk and simmer gently for 5 minutes or until the fish is almost cooked.

4 Blend the cornflour with a little cold water and stir it into the soup. Cook for about 5 minutes or until slightly thickened. Season with pepper to taste and serve piping hot, garnished with chopped parsley.

Microwave hints

To defrost 225g/8oz frozen smoked haddock, put it in a large shallow dish and microwave, uncovered, for 5-6 minutes at 20-30% (defrost) until pliable but still icy in the centre, turning and separating once. Cover and leave to stand for 5 minutes.

Spicy tomato soup

● **Preparation: 20 minutes**

● **Cooking: 30 minutes**

1tbls oil
1 onion, chopped
1 garlic clove, crushed
2 bacon rashers, chopped
pinch of chilli powder
225g/8oz potatoes, diced
850ml/1½pt hot vegetable stock
400g/14oz canned tomatoes, chopped
1tbls tomato purée
2tsp chopped parsley
1tsp chopped fresh basil or ½tsp dried
salt and pepper
yoghurt and thin strips of cucumber, to garnish

● *Serves 4*   ① ⓔ ⓒ

● *150cals/630kjs per serving*

1 Heat the oil in a large saucepan. Add the onion, garlic, bacon and chilli powder and cook gently until the onion is soft but not browned, stirring often. Add the potatoes and cook for 5 minutes, stirring occasionally.

2 Add the stock, tomatoes, tomato purée and herbs, and season with salt and pepper to taste. Bring to the boil, then cover and simmer for 15 minutes or until the potatoes are tender.

3 Purée the soup in a blender or food processor or pass it through a vegetable mill or sieve it. ⓒ

4 Return the soup to the rinsed-out pan and reheat gently. Serve in warmed bowls with dollops of yoghurt and a few very thin strips of unpeeled cucumber to garnish.

Variations

If preferred, the soup can be served without puréeing it first.

Grill the bacon until crisp and crumble it over the soup as a garnish instead of the cucumber.

Puréeing soup

Soup can be puréed quite quickly by hand if you use a vegetable mill. Vary the texture by using either a coarse, medium or fine disc.

Pea souper

● **Preparation: 15 minutes**

● **Cooking: 1 hour**

15g/½oz butter
2 back bacon rashers, chopped
1 onion, chopped
1 carrot, chopped
1 leek, chopped
100g/4oz split peas
850ml/1½pt hot ham or vegetable stock
salt and pepper
croûtons, to serve

● *Serves 4*   ① ⓔ ⓒ

● *310cals/1300kjs per serving*

1 Melt the butter in a large saucepan, add the bacon, onion, carrot and leek and cook over low heat until softened, about 15 minutes.

2 Add the split peas, stock and pepper to taste. Stir, cover and bring to the boil, then reduce the heat and simmer for 30-40 minutes or until the peas are tender.

3 Purée the soup in a blender or food processor, or put it through a vegetable mill or sieve. ⓒ

4 Return the soup to the rinsed-out pan, adjust the seasoning and reheat. Ladle into individual serving bowls, sprinkle with croûtons and serve.

Cook's tips

It is not necessary to soak split peas but, if you like, you can do so for 20-30 minutes, and then give the soup less cooking time accordingly.

Terrific Terrines

Crisp and crunchy, smooth and creamy, vegetable pâtés

and terrines are delicious, unusual and full of flavour

PERFECT FOR PARTIES and dinner parties, pâtés and terrines are equally good for light lunches, snacks and picnics. Usually made with meat or fish, they are also delicious made from a wide variety of vegetables.

Pâté or terrine?

At one time, the word pâté was used to describe a meat or fish mixture completely enclosed in pastry and baked in the oven, while a terrine took its name from the oblong ovenproof dish in which it was cooked, again by baking.

Nowadays, the distinction between the two is blurred and as a very rough – though not strictly accurate – guide, the difference between them is one of texture. As a general rule, smooth mixtures are called pâtés while firm, coarse mixtures are called terrines.

The best of the crop

When making vegetable pâtés and terrines, the quality of the produce used is all important. Use fresh, young vegetables that are crisp and flavoursome, not ones that are past their prime.

Shaping up

For terrines, where the vegetables are layered, their colour and shape are vital to the look of the dish. Good vegetables to use for their texture and visual effect are spinach and sorrel leaves (rich green, pliable and excellent used as leafy wrappings), courgettes, green beans, red and green peppers, carrots, celery and turnips. In most cases the vegetables will need to be cut into regular shapes; batons and dice are popular choices.

Creamy vegetable terrine (page 92)

Creamy vegetable terrine

- **Preparation: 50 minutes, plus standing and chilling**
- **Cooking: 10 minutes**

900g/2lb small courgettes
150ml/¼pt chicken stock
450g/1lb carrots, cut lengthways into 8mm/⅓in batons
6tbls aspic powder
425ml/¾pt boiling water
7tbls double cream
7tbls mayonnaise
1tbls white wine vinegar
1tsp lemon juice
2tbls finely chopped fresh parsley
salt and pepper
2 canned pimientos, drained and thinly sliced
sliced tomatoes and parsley sprigs, to garnish

- **Serves 6**
- **280cals/1175kjs per serving**

1 Steam the courgettes, whole, for 10 minutes. Cool quickly under cold running water and slice lengthways into 8mm/⅓in thick batons.

2 Bring the chicken stock to the boil in a saucepan, add the carrots and simmer for 5-6 minutes or until they are just tender. Drain and cool the carrots quickly. (Save the stock for soup.)

3 Put the aspic into a bowl, pour on the boiling water and stir to dissolve. Leave to stand for 10 minutes. Stir in the cream, mayonnaise, vinegar, lemon juice and parsley. Season with salt and pepper to taste. Beat the mixture until all the ingredients are well blended. Chill for about 20-25 minutes or until it has the consistency of unbeaten egg white.

4 While the aspic cream is chilling, layer the vegetables. Rinse a 1.5L/2½pt loaf tin with cold water. Arrange a layer of courgette strips on the base, along the length of the tin. Then place a layer of carrot strips across the tin. Add another four layers of courgettes and three of carrots, in the same way. Then add all the pimientos in one layer. Finish with one more layer each of courgettes and carrots.

5 Pour the aspic cream over the vegetables and rap the sides of the tin so that the cream penetrates all the layers and there are no air bubbles trapped inside. Cover the tin and refrigerate for at least 2 hours or until the cream is firm.

6 Turn out onto a platter. To garnish, halve the sliced tomatoes and arrange them around the terrine, together with the parsley sprigs.

Spinach pâté

- **Preparation: cooking the spinach, then 25 minutes, plus chilling**
- **Cooking: 5 minutes**

50g/2oz butter
6 spring onions, finely chopped
2tbls chopped fresh mint
450g/1lb spinach, cooked, drained and finely chopped
2tbls single cream
225g/8oz full-fat soft cheese
salt and pepper
pinch of cayenne pepper
2tbls lemon juice
4 thin slices of lemon, to garnish
hot granary rolls or toast fingers, to serve

- **Serves 4**
- **450cals/1890kjs per serving**

CLEVER CONTAINERS

Pâtés do not have to be served in a dish. Scooped-out vegetables such as celery sticks, small red or green peppers, tomatoes and courgettes make good containers. If firm enough, pâtés can also be shaped into pieces, then rolled in chopped nuts and herbs.

1 Melt the butter in a pan and sauté the spring onions over moderate heat for 2-3 minutes, stirring occasionally. Add the chopped mint and spinach and mix well. Remove from the heat and leave to cool.

2 When the spinach mixture is cool, stir in the cream, cheese, salt, pepper, cayenne pepper and lemon juice to taste. Reduce to a purée in a blender or food processor.

3 Divide the pâté between four 150ml/¼pt ramekin dishes and smooth the tops. Cover and chill for at least 1 hour,

4 Garnish each ramekin with a slice of lemon, cut and twisted, and serve with hot granary rolls or toast fingers.

Cook's tips

To drain the spinach, immediately after cooking turn the leaves into a colander or sieve and press gently with the back of a wooden spoon to squeeze out the water.

Serving ideas

Pâtés can be used as fillings for sandwiches or pitta bread. To give crispness and texture, add chopped cucumber or spring onions, beansprouts or mustard and cress.

Vegetable and ham terrine

- **Preparation: 1 hour**

- **Cooking: 40 minutes, plus cooling and overnight chilling**

6 carrots
1 young turnip
175g/6oz green beans
1 red pepper, seeded
2 celery stalks
12 large spinach or sorrel leaves
salt and pepper
1 avocado
700g/1½lb cooked ham
2 large egg whites
juice of 1 lemon
2tbls peanut oil
celery leaf and carrot, to garnish

- **Serves 12**   (¶) (££) (◷)

- **185cals/775kjs per serving**

1 Peel the carrots and leave them whole. Peel the turnip and cut it into sticks 1cm/½in square and 5cm/2in long. Top and tail the beans.

2 Cut the red pepper into thin slices. Remove the strings from the celery stalks.

3 Remove the spinach or sorrel stalks, keeping the leaves intact as far as possible, and wash the leaves well. Bring a large saucepan of salted water to the boil, blanch the spinach or sorrel leaves for 10 seconds, then plunge them immediately into cold water to stop the cooking, taking great care not to tear them. Drain the leaves and spread on a cloth or absorbent paper.

4 Cook the carrots, turnips, beans, pepper and celery simultaneously in boiling salted water, in separate saucepans, or one after the other in the same saucepan, until all the vegetables are *al dente*. If using the same saucepan it is not necessary to change the water. Whole carrots will take 8 minutes; the celery stalks 5 minutes; red pepper strips 3 minutes; green beans 2 minutes and the turnip sticks 1 minute. Drain the vegetables, refresh them in cold water and drain again on aborbent paper.

5 Peel and halve the avocado, then halve each piece again, cutting parallel to the first cut.

6 Put the ham and egg whites in a blender or food processor and blend to a fine purée. Add the lemon juice and peanut oil and pepper and blend again.

How to ... *layer a terrine*

Cut the vegetables into regular shapes, then cook in boiling, salted water until *al dente*. Drain, refresh in cold water and drain again on absorbent paper.

Line the bottom and sides of a terrine or loaf tin with spinach or sorrel leaves. Handle them carefully so that they do not tear, and overlap them so there are no gaps.

Spoon in a little mousse to cover the base of the tin, then layer the vegetables, arranging them neatly lengthways and close together. Spoon mousse between each layer.

Finish with a layer of mousse and press down to fill any spaces, then smooth. Fold over any protruding spinach or sorrel leaves. Cover the top with the remaining leaves.

Unmoulding a terrine

Run a knife around the edges of the terrine. Place one hand under the tin and, with the other, invert a serving plate over the top and hold it firmly in place. Turn over the tin and the plate together and shake to release the terrine.

7 Heat the oven to 170C/325F/gas 3. Line the bottom and sides of a 1.7L/3pt terrine or loaf tin with the spinach or sorrel leaves and, using a spoon, add a thin layer of ham mousse. Continue layering the vegetables in the following order, with a layer of ham mousse in between each: whole carrots, turnip sticks, green beans, red pepper, celery and avocado. The whole carrots, turnip sticks and the beans are laid lengthways and close together in the terrine. As you fill the terrine, make sure no gaps are left. Finish with a layer of ham mousse and press down the surface with your fingers to fill any spaces. Smooth the top.

8 Cover the terrine with the remaining spinach or sorrel leaves and seal with foil. Place in a roasting tin, add hot water to come half way up the sides of the dish and then cook the terrine in the oven for 30 minutes.

9 Remove the terrine from the oven and from the roasting tin. Place a 450g/1lb weight on top and cool quickly, then refrigerate overnight.

10 To serve, unmould the terrine, cut into slices and garnish with a celery leaf tied with a piece of carrot.

Carrot and cheese pâté

- *Preparation: 25 minutes, plus chilling*

- *Cooking: 10 minutes*

800g/1¾lb carrots
salt and pepper
350g/12oz full-fat soft cheese
2tsp chopped parsley
2tsp snipped chives
carrot flowers, chives and carrot
    tops, to garnish (optional)

- *Serves 4*

- *300cals/1260kjs per serving*

1 Chop the carrots and cook in boiling salted water for 7 minutes or until tender. Drain the carrots, return them to the rinsed-out saucepan and dry over low heat for 1 minute, shaking the pan occasionally.

2 Mash the carrots with a strong fork or vegetable masher or put them through the coarse grid of a food mill to give a rough-textured purée. Allow to cool.

3 Beat in the cheese, a little at a time, using a fork. Add the parsley and chives, season with salt and pepper to taste and mix until well blended.

4 Line a 12.5cm/5in loaf tin with greaseproof paper. Press the mixture firmly into the tin and level the top with a palette knife. Cover with foil and chill for 3 hours.

5 Run a knife between the pâté and the loaf tin to loosen it. Place a plate on the top and invert, lifting the tin away from the plate.

6 Just before serving, decorate the top of the pâté with the garnishes, if wished. Cut into slices to serve.

PULSE RATE

Pulses make good pâtés as they blend easily with other ingredients such as vegetables, cheeses, nuts and seeds. They add substance, texture and colour, especially red kidney beans, red lentils and peas. For a creamier look, use white or pale yellow beans.

For soft pâtés, the cooked beans are puréed. However, adding breadcrumbs, flakes and oats will give a firmer texture.

Salad Days

*A crisp green salad, made and dressed just before serving,
is simplicity itself, and nothing can beat it for interesting
combinations of texture and flavour*

*T*HERE ARE TWO stages in perfect salad-making — the preparation of the salad itself, and the making of the dressing.

Preparing the salad

Salad greens should be as fresh as possible. There is no kiss of life for a wilted lettuce, although you can keep a fresh lettuce crisp. Wash the leaves carefully under trickling cold water, dry them thoroughly (see page 97). The dressing will not adhere to wet leaves, and any excess moisture will, in turn, dilute the dressing, making its flavour weaker. Lay out the clean, dry leaves on a fresh cloth. Loosely roll up the cloth and chill it in the salad compartment of the refrigerator for at least 1 hour or until you are ready to assemble the salad.

Fresh green herbs — parsley, of course, and mint, chervil, basil, tarragon and chives — can be either snipped over the salad or combined with the dressing.

Preparing the dressing

There is no mystery about a simple French vinaigrette dressing. Olive oil and vinegar are combined, roughly in the proportion of three parts oil to one part vinegar or lemon juice (though some people prefer a four to one mixture). This is seasoned to taste with salt, freshly ground black pepper and perhaps a little French or English mustard, garlic or herbs, then beaten vigorously with a fork until the combination thickens into an emulsion. Alternatively, put all the ingredients into a screw-top jar and shake vigorously. Do not drown your salad with dressing. A small to medium lettuce, round or cos, will take 4-6tbls dressing and a large one 6-8tbls.

Use this chef's trick before assembling your salad: sprinkle a little salt into a salad bowl, add a

Chinese salad (page 98)

garlic clove and mash it into the salt with the back of a wooden spoon. It will now dissolve easily into the oil. Make sure you scoop right to the bottom of the bowl when you toss the salad.

Colour and crunch
There is no end to the additions you can make to your green salad for texture, colour and flavour. Diced celery, crisp green pepper, a touch of finely chopped onion or shallot add texture; while the addition of tomato, cucumber, nuts, raisins, crumbled bacon, diced ham or cheese, sliced hard-boiled egg or stoned black olives will give colour and flavour.

Mange tout and broad bean salad

- **Preparation: 20 minutes**

- **Cooking: 15 minutes**

225g/8oz mange tout
700g/1½lb tender broad beans
   (about 175g/6oz shelled weight)
salt
4 tomatoes, skinned and cut into
   eighths
For the vinaigrette dressing:
½tsp Dijon mustard
2tbls wine vinegar
salt and pepper
6tbls olive oil

- **Serves 6**   ⓘ ££

- **160cals/670kjs per serving**

1 Trim the mange tout and shell the broad beans. (To shell the broad beans, split the pod open with your thumb, pressing down on the curved edge, then run your thumbnail down the edge to open the pod and pull out the beans.)

2 Bring a saucepan of salted water to the boil and blanch the broad beans for 10-15 minutes or until tender. Drain, rinse under cold water and drain again.

3 Meanwhile, bring another saucepan of salted water to the boil. Blanch the mange tout for 2-3 minutes or until tender. Drain, rinse under cold water; drain again.

Bohemian salad (far right)

4 Make the vinaigrette dressing: put the mustard into a small jug or cup and add the wine vinegar. Add the salt and pepper and the olive oil and whisk or shake until the mixture emulsifies.

5 In a bowl, combine the vinaigrette dressing, blanched mange tout, broad beans and tomatoes. Toss lightly to coat the vegetables, then adjust the seasoning and arrange in a serving bowl.

NOTHING BUT THE BEST
Always use the finest olive oil and wine vinegar for a dressing. If your olive oil lacks 'fruitiness', try soaking a few plump black olives (themselves preserved in olive oil) in the bottle of oil. After a week or so the oil will have acquired a totally new, exciting flavour, with plenty of 'body'. The olives can be left in the bottle and the bottle topped up with more oil as necessary.

Freshly ground black pepper is a must, but you should also try substituting coarse salt for table salt. It has an actual flavour of its own, as well as bringing out the flavour of other food.

How to ... *dry salad leaves*

In a salad-spinner: put the washed salad in the inner basket inside the outer container. Replace the lid, then turn the handle or pull the string to spin the inner basket.

In a salad-shaker: put the washed salad into the basket and hang it up to let any water drip away. Alternatively, hold the basket by the handles and whirl it around.

In a tea-towel: shake the washed lettuce in a colander, then put the salad in a clean tea-towel, gather the ends together, hold them firmly in one hand and whirl it around.

Bohemian salad

- **Preparation: 25 minutes, plus chilling and standing**

1 lollo rosso lettuce
1 red oakleaf lettuce
½ head endive
For the dressing:
½tsp mustard powder
½tsp coarse salt
¼tsp caster sugar
3tbls tarragon vinegar
1tsp finely chopped shallot
1tsp finely chopped parsley
½tsp finely chopped fresh
   tarragon
1 garlic clove, lightly crushed, but
   left whole
9tbls olive oil

- **Serves 4-6**   ① ££ 🕐

- **295cals/1240kjs per serving**

1 Separate all the salad leaves, wash and dry them, then wrap in a clean cloth and chill until needed.

2 Meanwhile, blend the mustard, salt and sugar to a smooth paste with the tarragon vinegar. Stir in the shallot, parsley, tarragon and garlic and set aside for 1 hour, to allow the herbs to release their flavours.

3 Remove the garlic clove from the dressing. Stir in the olive oil and reserve until ready to use. 🕐

4 Just before serving, put the leaves into a large serving bowl. Whisk or shake the dressing, pour over the leaves and toss lightly to coat.

Green salad with hot dressing

- **Preparation: 15 minutes**

- **Cooking: 35 minutes**

3 potatoes
salt and pepper
½ large cos lettuce
½ bunch watercress
4tbls finely chopped Spanish onion
2 thin slices of lean bacon, chopped
2tbls wine vinegar

- **Serves 4**   ⑪ ££

- **115cals/485kjs per serving**

1 Scrub the potatoes thoroughly but do not peel them. Drop them into a pan of boiling salted water and cook for 20-25 minutes or until tender, then drain.

2 Meanwhile, separate the lettuce leaves, wash and dry, wrap in a clean cloth and chill until needed. Wash the watercress, discarding the thick stalks and any damaged or yellowed leaves. Divide into small sprigs. Wrap in a slightly damp, clean cloth and chill until needed.

A MATTER OF TIMING

It is a good idea to have salad as a separate course when you are serving wine with the main course. It is generally recognized that the acidity of a salad dressing dulls the palate to the finer points of a wine. By serving the salad after the wine, both will be tasted at their best.

3 Heat a large porcelain salad bowl by dipping it in hot water for a few minutes. Dry thoroughly.

4 As soon as the potatoes are cool enough to handle, peel them. Arrange the lettuce and watercress in the bottom of the salad bowl. Slice the potatoes and put them on top, together with the onion, salt and pepper. Toss thoroughly.

5 Put the bacon pieces in a frying pan and soften over low heat until the bacon is cooked and the fat runs. Stir in 1tbls cold water, mix thoroughly, then bring to the boiling point. Pour this dressing over the salad and toss again. In the same frying pan, heat the wine vinegar and pour it over the salad. Give the salad a final toss and serve immediately, on warmed plates.

Chinese salad

● **Preparation: 20 minutes, plus chilling**

¹/₂ head Chinese leaves
1 head chicory
2 mandarin oranges
2 spring onions
For the honey-soy dressing:
6-8tbls groundnut oil
2tbls white wine vinegar
1-2tsp soy sauce
1tbls clear honey
salt and pepper
large pinch of mustard powder

● **Serves 4-6**   ①£*£

● **250cals/1050kjs per serving**

1 Shred the Chinese leaves, then remove the core from the chicory and separate the leaves. Wash both, dry them, then wrap in a clean cloth and chill until needed.

2 Just before serving, cut the mandarins into segments, removing all the pith and pips. Cut the spring onions on the diagonal. Add the onions to the shredded leaves.

3 Combine all the dressing ingredients and whisk or shake until they form an emulsion.

4 Arrange the chicory leaves, mandarin segments and shredded Chinese leaves and spring onions attractively on each serving dish. Pour the dressing over.

Cook's tips

Although this dressing can be made ahead, it is important not to chill it as this will cause it to thicken too much.

Green salad with flower petals

● **Preparation: 20 minutes**

1 round lettuce
1 small iceberg lettuce
1 bunch of watercress
1 hard-boiled egg, diced
2tbls freshly grated Parmesan cheese
1tbls finely chopped parsley
1tbls finely snipped chives
rose or other edible, clean, unsprayed flower petals (such as nasturtium or primrose)
For the vinaigrette dressing:
2tbls wine vinegar
salt and pepper
¹/₂tsp French mustard
6tbls olive oil

● **Serves 4-6**   ①£*£

● **235cals/985kjs per serving**

1 Separate the lettuce leaves, wash and dry, wrap in a clean cloth and chill until needed. Wash the watercress, discarding the thick stalks and any damaged or yellowed leaves. Divide into small sprigs. Wrap in a slightly damp, clean cloth and chill until needed.

2 Combine all the vinaigrette ingredients and whisk or shake until thickened.

3 Just before serving, assemble the salad. Tear the lettuce leaves across the grain into 2.5cm/1in strips. Place with the watercress in a bowl and toss lightly.

4 Whisk or shake the vinaigrette dressing again, sprinkle over the salad greens and toss until each leaf is glistening. Add half the diced hard-boiled egg, 1tbls grated Parmesan cheese, half the parsley and half the chives. Toss well. Sprinkle with the remaining grated Parmesan cheese, then with the remaining egg, herbs and the petals. Serve.

WELL CONTAINED

Use deep bowls rather than shallow dishes as these give plenty of room for tossing the salad without any leaves falling over the sides.

Wooden bowls are a popular choice but they need special care. Never soak them in hot water or they may warp or crack. Instead, either immerse them quickly in water to wash them or wipe them with a damp cloth. If the wood seems to be drying out, occasionally rub the inside all over with salad oil.

STORING VINAIGRETTE

Make a big batch of dressing while you're at it – simple vinaigrette can be stored in an airtight jar in a cool place for weeks, while dressings with garlic, onion, shallot or fresh herbs should be refrigerated if kept for more than 8 hours.

More-ish Mouthfuls

Making canapés is fun and very creative, as various toppings and bases can be combined and presented in endless different ways

*T*HE GREAT VIRTUE of the cold canapé is that it can be prepared well in advance, leaving you free to entertain. Almost any savoury food can be made into a canapé, provided that it looks attractive and obeys the golden rule that it can be eaten in one, two or at most three bites. And if it is more than one bite, it must not fall apart in the middle once bitten into.

The perfect canapé has eye appeal — use colour contrasts and attractive garnishes — and mouth appeal — contrast creamy or juicy toppings with crisp or crusty bases. Fillings should be tender and strongly flavoured: canapés call for high-quality ingredients such as smoked salmon, asparagus, beef fillet, goose liver pâté, Parma ham and so on. They should be well seasoned as guests will not be able to add any salt or pepper.

Choosing canapés

Select the recipes to give plenty of variety and interest to your canapés. The bases can be anything firm, from a savoury biscuit to a little circle of toast or fried bread (croûte), or a pastry shell or fried bread case (croustade). Choose an assortment of fillings and toppings so that you have some fish, some meat, some cheese and some egg.

For a two-hour drinks party for 30-40 people you can reckon that most of them will eat at least 5-6 canapés, plus nibbles — basically crudités, nuts, olives and crisps.

Presentation

Serve your canapés on fairly small plates. If you use large platters they look terrible when half empty. Pass the plates round and replenish them frequently. Have an assortment of different canapés on each plate so guests can pick something they like.

Garnishes play a very important part in making canapés look appetizing. Use them lavishly and make sure they are edible; the only inedi-

Pumpernickel fingers (page 100)

ble item allowed in a canapé is a cocktail stick.

Plan ahead

Prepare fillings the day before or early in the morning and leave them, covered, in the refrigerator. Pastry cases can be made several days ahead and stored in airtight containers; or weeks ahead if you can freeze them. Other canapé bases can be made on the morning of the party and set aside until they are needed.

If you are making large numbers of canapés to serve at a drinks party you need to make at least the majority well in advance, and put them in the freezer. For mass production you will also need large quantities of stretch wrap and foil, and plenty of freezerproof baking trays. For making barquettes or tartlets it helps greatly if you can buy or borrow plenty of moulds so that the baking can be done in large batches, saving time and energy.

Finding enough space to defrost all the made-ahead canapés can be a problem – you may need to make arrangements to lay them out in a cold spare bedroom.

Pumpernickel fingers

● **Preparation: 30 minutes**

softened butter
6 slices pumpernickel bread
4tbls full-fat soft cheese
1tbls grated horseradish
150g/5oz rare roast beef, thinly
   sliced
salt and pepper
2tbls oil
150g/5oz Roquefort or Stilton
½tsp each finely snipped chives,
   chervil and tarragon
1tbls brandy
paprika
parsley sprigs and finely chopped
   parsley, to garnish

● **Makes 24**

● **90cals/380kjs each**

1 Butter the pumpernickel slices thinly. Cut each slice into four fingers.

2 Put the soft cheese and horseradish into a bowl and mix together. Spread this mixture over half the buttered pumpernickel fingers.

3 Cut the beef into strips to fit neatly over the pumpernickel fingers. Put a strip on top of each cheese-covered finger. Season with salt and pepper to taste and brush lightly with oil.

4 Put the Roquefort or Stilton cheese in a bowl with 75g/3oz butter and blend with a fork until smooth. Beat in the herbs and brandy, then season with salt and pepper to taste.

5 Mound the blue cheese mixture onto the remaining pumpernickel fingers. Sprinkle with paprika and garnish with a line of finely chopped parsley down the centre. Arrange all the fingers on platters, cover and chill. Before serving, garnish the beef-topped pumpernickel fingers with parsley sprigs.

Celery boats

● **Preparation: 20 minutes**

2 celery heads, separated into stalks

175g/6oz full-fat soft cheese
75g/3oz Roquefort or Stilton
   cheese, crumbled
1 large dessert apple
lettuce leaves, to serve
4tbls chopped walnuts, to garnish

● **Makes about 60**

● **20cals/85kjs each**

1 Cut the thick bottom end of each celery stalk into 4cm/1½in 'boats'.

2 Beat the two cheeses together until evenly blended. Peel, core and chop the apple finely and stir it into the cheese mixture. Pile into the celery boats.

3 Line a serving plate with lettuce leaves, arrange the celery boats on top and sprinkle with chopped walnuts.

Cook's tips

Serve Celery boats with drinks or as part of a buffet.

Use only the tender inner stalks to make these canapés. Wrap the stringier outer stalks, and the leafy tops, in a polythene bag and refrigerate to use in soups, stews or stocks.

MORE CANAPE IDEAS

Anchovy: cut buttered toast into small fingers or other shapes and spread with anchovy butter. Decorate with capers and thin slivers of anchovy fillet.
Harlequin: spread diamond-shaped pieces of toast with butter flavoured with French mustard. Lay on alternate strips of smoked salmon, cooked ham or gherkin.
Rollmops: spread fingers of toast with softened butter mixed with pounded anchovy and finely chopped parsley. Top with a slice of pickled cucumber and pickled herring.
Windsor: Spread square cheese biscuits with Potted Stilton (see Shopping Basket page 19) and top each one with a slice of hard-boiled egg.

2 anchovy fillets, drained and
*   pounded*
1tbls finely chopped fresh dill
about 25 anchovy-stuffed olives,
*   halved*

● *Makes about 50*

● *30cals/125kjs each*

1 Heat the oven to 220C/425F/gas 7. On a floured surface, roll out the pastry 3mm/⅛in thick. Using a 4cm/1½in round cutter, stamp out about 50 rounds, rerolling the pastry as necessary.

2 Sprinkle a large baking sheet with cold water and put the pastry rounds on it. Brush their tops with egg yolk, being careful not to let any drip down the sides. Bake for 14 minutes or until puffed and golden brown. Allow to cool for a few minutes, then split the rounds in half horizontally.

3 Using a 5mm/¼in round cutter, cut a hole in the middle of the pastry tops. Discard the cut-outs.

4 Mix together the prawns, Béchamel sauce, anchovies and dill. Spread about ¼tsp of this mixture on each pastry bottom. Cover with the tops and put an olive half into each of the holes on top. Lay the pastries on a tray, cover and chill until 20 minutes before serving. 🕐

Freezer

Freeze the baked pastry rounds for up to 6 months. Defrost and finish on the day.

Anchovy scrolls

● *Preparation: making sauce, then 1 hour, plus soaking*

4 x 45g/1¾oz cans anchovy fillets
milk, for soaking
75g/3oz softened butter
1tbls finely chopped fresh tarragon
25 tiny bridge rolls
150g/5oz canned tuna, drained
1tsp lemon juice
large pinch of cayenne pepper
3tbls Béchamel sauce
*   (page 18)*
salt and pepper
finely chopped parsley, to garnish

● *Makes 50*

● *60cals/250kjs each*

1 Put the anchovy fillets in a small bowl, cover them with milk and soak for 2 hours.

2 Put the butter into another bowl with the tarragon and mix well. Cut the bridge rolls in half and, using half the mixture, spread a little on each piece.

3 Put the tuna into a large bowl. Add the rest of the tarragon butter, the lemon juice, cayenne pepper and Béchamel sauce. Mash together and season with salt, if needed, and pepper to taste.

4 Remove the anchovy fillets from the milk and lay on absorbent paper to dry. Very gently flatten the fillets with the back of a knife. Spread about ¼tsp of the tuna mixture along each fillet; roll up.

BECHAMEL SAUCE

A thick or coating consistency Béchamel sauce is often used to bind a canapé filling together and make it nice and moist. Use the recipe given on page 18 but adapt it to coating consistency by reducing the milk to 150ml/¼pt. Or you could cheat and use a packet sauce, as only a few tablespoons are required.

5 Spread the remaining tuna mixture over the cut side of the bridge rolls and put an anchovy scroll in the middle. Sprinkle with parsley, cover and chill. 🕐

Freezer

Prepare the scrolls except for the parsley garnish, chill, then wrap in freezer foil and freeze for up to 2 months. Defrost overnight in the fridge, then garnish.

Prawn puff pastries

● *Preparation: 45 minutes*

● *Cooking: 15 minutes*

flour, for dusting
225g/8oz Puff pastry (page 51)
2 egg yolks, beaten
200g/7oz cooked peeled prawns,
*   finely chopped*
4tbls thick Béchamel sauce
*   (page 18)*

How to...

make croûtes

Cut out rounds of day-old bread using a 3cm/1¼in round cutter. A dozen slices of bread will yield about 40 rounds.

Pour a good 5cm/2in oil into a large saucepan and heat it gently until the oil just begins to smoke. Do not overheat.

Fry the bread rounds a few at a time over medium heat for 3-4 minutes, until golden brown. Remove them with a slotted spoon and drain thoroughly on absorbent paper.

Tongue and chicken rolls

- *Preparation: making sauce, then 35 minutes*

13 thin slices ox tongue
200g/7oz cooked chicken breast
3tbls thick Béchamel sauce
   (page 18)
1tbls orange juice
3tbls shelled pistachio nuts, halved
grated nutmeg
salt and pepper
ground fenugreek
paprika
¼tsp soy sauce

- *Makes 52*

- *25cals/105kjs each*

1 Cut the tongue slices into quarters and reserve. Finely chop the chicken into a large bowl. Add the Béchamel sauce, orange juice and pistachio nuts and mix well. Season with nutmeg, salt and pepper to taste, plus a large pinch of fenugreek and paprika. Add the soy sauce and mix well.

2 Spread about ¼tsp of the chicken mixture on each quarter slice of tongue. Roll up each slice, then spear it with a cocktail stick. Put the rolls on a large tray, cover with stretch wrap and chill until needed.

Freezer

Once the rolls have been chilled, cover with freezer foil and freeze for up to 3 months. Defrost overnight in the fridge; and serve the Tongue and chicken rolls still slightly chilled.

SANDWICH CANAPES

Even the humble sandwich qualifies as a canapé if it is tiny and cut into an attractive shape or rolled up. Use day-old bread (for firmness), slice it thinly and remove the crusts.
Combinations of brown and white bread add extra interest, while pumpernickel is ideal as it is very firm and cuts easily into shapes. Spread the bread thinly with softened butter and use any highly flavoured sandwich filling that won't drop out: smoked sausage, ham, smoked salmon, rare beef, cheese, pâté and savoury fish spreads.

Gruyère and ham tartlets

- **Preparation: making pastry, then 50 minutes**

- **Cooking: 20 minutes**

flour, for dusting
225g/8oz Basic shortcrust pastry
   (page 10)
100g/4oz Gruyère cheese, cut into
   tiny dice
100g/4oz cooked ham, diced
3-4tbls mayonnaise
2tsp Dijon mustard
pepper
1 large red pepper, seeded and cut
   into tiny strips

- **Makes about 50**

- **40cals/170kjs each**

1 Roll out the pastry 3mm/⅛in thick. Using a 5cm/2in round cutter, cut out about 50 rounds, rerolling as necessary.

2 Heat the oven to 190C/375F/gas 5. Line 50 × 4cm/1½in tartlet moulds with the pastry. Line the pastry with foil and beans and bake blind (see page 10) for 10 minutes.

3 Remove the foil and beans and cook for 10 minutes. Cool in the tins.

4 Combine the Gruyère and ham with the mayonnaise and mustard. Season with pepper to taste. Put 1tsp of the mixture into each tartlet.

5 Garnish the tartlets with a criss-cross of red pepper, arrange them on a platter and cover with stretch wrap. Chill until needed.

Freezer

Open-freeze the baked but unfilled pastry cases and carefully transfer to a rigid container once solid. Freeze for up to 6 months. Defrost and fill on the day.

Herring croûtes

- **Preparation: making croûtes, then 20 minutes**

225g/8oz soft herring roes, cooked
50g/2oz softened butter
¼ Spanish onion, coarsely grated
½ large dessert apple
1tbls finely chopped parsley
1tbls lemon juice
pepper
50 croûtes (page 102)
50g/2oz salted herring fillet,
   finely chopped

- **Makes 50**

- **30cals/125kjs each**

1 Put the herring roes into a large bowl and add the butter and grated onion. Peel and core the apple and grate it into the bowl. Sprinkle with the parsley and lemon juice and season generously with pepper. Stir well.

2 Fit a piping bag with a 1cm/½in star nozzle and spoon in the mixture. Pipe a swirl of the herring mixture onto each croûte, then put them on a large tray. Cover with stretch wrap and chill.

3 Garnish each croûte with a piece of herring fillet. Transfer to a serving platter, cover with stretch wrap and chill until needed.

Freezer

At the end of step 2, cover the croûtes with freezer foil and freeze for up to 3 months. Defrost in the refrigerator the day before and garnish on the day.

Variations

Substitute a little finely snipped fresh dill for the parsley.

   Mix 3-4tbls soured cream or yoghurt with the herring roes instead of the butter; add lemon juice to taste.

Spicy fillet steak balls

Anyone who likes steak tartare will love these little balls of raw fillet steak with a spicy mayonnaise. Make sure the meat is fresh, not frozen

- **Preparation: 40 minutes, plus freezing**

225g/8oz fillet steak in one small,
   round piece
pepper
For the spicy mayonnaise:
4tbls mayonnaise
2tbls capers, very finely
   chopped
1tsp finely chopped fresh
   marjoram
½tsp Dijon mustard
½tsp horseradish sauce
¼tsp cayenne pepper
4tsp grated onion

- **Makes about 50**

- **15cals/65kjs each**

1 If you have an electric slicing machine, put the steak in the freezer for about 1 hour to firm it up slightly, then slice it very thinly on the machine into about 25 slices. Otherwise get your butcher to do it for you.

2 Cover the meat slices with absorbent paper and pat dry. Leave in a cool place while you make the spicy mayonnaise.

3 Mix the mayonnaise with the finely chopped capers, marjoram, mustard, horseradish sauce, cayenne pepper and grated onion.

4 Sprinkle the beef slices generously with pepper and cut each slice in half.

5 Spread ¼tsp of the spicy mayonnaise on each half slice and then roll them up into a little ball. Spear each with a cocktail stick.

6 Arrange the balls on a platter, cover lightly and refrigerate until ready to serve. 🕐 Serve chilled.

Salmon and asparagus barquettes

- **Preparation: making pastry, then 1 hour**

- **Cooking: 20 minutes**

flour, for dusting
225g/8oz Basic shortcrust pastry (page 10)
butter, for greasing
200g/7oz smoked salmon trimmings, finely chopped
25g/1oz softened butter
1-2tsp lemon juice
pepper
450g/1lb canned asparagus tips, drained
4tbls mayonnaise
1tsp tomato ketchup
watercress sprigs, to garnish

- **Makes about 50**
- **50cals/170kjs each**

1 Heat the oven to 190C/375F/gas 5. On a floured surface, roll out the pastry 3mm/⅛in thick and use it to line fifty 5cm/2in long greased barquette moulds (see page 13).

2 Line the moulds with foil and beans and bake blind for 10 minutes. Remove the foil and beans and bake for a further 10 minutes. Let the pastry cases cool in the moulds for 10 minutes before taking them out, then place on a wire rack to cool competely.

3 Put the smoked salmon in a bowl with the butter, lemon juice and pepper to taste. Mash together and divide between the barquettes. Top each barquette with an asparagus tip, trimmed if necessary. Put the canapés on a flat tray, cover with stretch wrap and chill.

4 Before serving, mix together the mayonnaise and tomato ketchup. Fit a small piping bag with a 3mm/⅛in nozzle and spoon in the mayonnaise mixture. Pipe a thin line around the asparagus tip on each barquette.

5 Arrange the barquettes on platters and garnish with watercress. If they are not to be served for some hours, cover with stretch wrap and chill. 🕐

Cook's tips

The more barquette moulds you can muster the better; otherwise you will have to bake the barquettes in batches.

Freezer

Prepare the barquettes to the end of step 3, cover with stretch wrap and freeze for up to 2 months. Defrost in the fridge the day before the party and finish on the day.

GOLDEN RULES

- Choose canapé fillings that will not leave fingers messy. Hand out or provide plenty of napkins.
- Season the food very carefully – remember that guests will not be able to add their own extra.
- Make sure the nibbles are small in size.
- Remember that attractive presentation is most important with food that is passed round. Be lavish and creative with garnishes.

Perfect Pâtés

Home-made pâtés and terrines based on meat, game or fish are easy to make, and can be as elaborate or as simple as you like

*T*HE MAIN INGREDIENTS of a pâté or terrine vary widely: game, pork, veal and liver, plus fish and seafood. Not all are grand affairs that take hours to prepare and days to mature; see Quick salmon pâté, page 106.

Pâtés are often smoother than terrines, but both have a high fat content; this gives the rich taste and smooth texture. Fresh pork fat is usual, but bacon may be substituted if the base meat is highly flavoured. Cream may be added as well, plus lemon juice, wine or brandy, to make the mixture very moist, even sloppy. Don't let this worry you; after being baked for a couple of hours it will attain the desired consistency. Indeed, if the mixture looks stiff and dry, mix in some extra stock or cream.

Seasoning a pâté is difficult, as it's not very pleasant tasting raw minced meat, so people guess and tend to under-season. Allow for the fact that the seasoning will be weaker after cooking and maturing. Pâtés taste much better seasoned with spiced salt (page 106).

Country-style pâtés are coarse-textured, but others are made smooth by processing the ingredients more finely, adding soaked breadcrumbs and even béchamel sauce. A layered pâté may contrast smooth and coarse textures.

Moulded chicken liver pâté (page 107)

Prepare and bake

Pâtés are traditionally cooked in deep glazed earthenware dishes (terrines) which have pierced lids to allow steam to escape. But a loaf tin covered with foil does just as well. To make sure the pâté stays moist during cooking, the dish or tin is often lined with thin slices of pork fat. This may be hard to find nowadays, but streaky bacon rashers do just as well and look attractive when the pâté is turned out. Have the rashers at room temperature and stretch them paper thin with the back of a knife. Very elaborate pâtés may be enclosed in pastry to keep them moist or topped with aspic jelly.

In addition, pâtés are baked at a moderate temperature, standing in a roasting tin one-third full of hot water. This protects the outer layer in closest contact with the heat. To test whether a pâté is done, pierce the centre with a skewer: the juices should run clear, as with meat. The liquid fat surrounding the pâté should be quite transparent and free of pink or red juices. The pâté itself will have shrunk.

Finish and store

As a pâté cools after baking, it will continue to shrink. To ensure a close texture and eliminate air bubles it must be weighted down. Lift the pâté out of the roasting tin and pour away the water. Return the pâté to the tin (to catch any overflowing juices) and put the board or flat dish on top of the pâté (or another loaf tin of the same size). Weight it down with kitchen weights or cans of food until the pâté is submerged in liquid fat and juices. These will flow into any spaces and set to a delicious jelly. Leave until cold and set. The fat should form a seal over the top. Remove the board, dish or tin and chill, leaving the fat undisturbed.

Meat and game pâtés improve in flavour if matured (in the refrigerator) for a few days. They can be kept a little longer – up to a week – provided that the top of the dish is completely sealed with fat. Pour on extra melted lard if necessary, then cool and chill. Eat fish pâtés within a day or two.

Quick salmon pâté

- **Preparation: 20 minutes, plus chilling**

- **Cooking: 20 minutes**

450g/1lb fresh salmon, poached
 and cooled
75g/3oz smoked salmon, chopped
1 small garlic clove, crushed
8tbls double cream
150ml/¼pt olive oil
juice of ½ lemon
salt and pepper
cayenne pepper
quartered lemon slices, to garnish
hot toast and chilled butter,
 to serve

- **Serves 6**

- **430cals/1805kjs per serving**

1 Remove any bones and skin from the cooked, cold salmon and flake the flesh lightly with a fork.

2 In a blender or food processor, combine the flaked salmon, smoked salmon and garlic. Blend lightly.

3 Add half the cream and half the oil to the fish mixture and blend again until smooth. Add the remaining oil and cream alternately until the mixture turns to a creamy and smooth texture.

SEASONING SALT

Spiced salt, similar to the *sel épicé* you can buy in France, will give your pâtés and terrines an extra-delicious flavour. Just mix the finely ground spices and herbs listed with 3tsp salt; keep in an airtight jar ready for use.

¼tsp each grated nutmeg, powdered basil and marjoram
¾tsp each powdered thyme and black pepper
large pinch each powdered bay leaf, ground ginger, ground coriander, cayenne pepper and paprika

This is a basic mixture – try it out, then adapt it to your taste.

4 Turn the pâté into a clean bowl, stir in the lemon juice and season with salt, pepper and cayenne pepper to taste. Chill until needed.

5 Divide the pâté between six individual ramekins and garnish with quartered lemon slices. Serve with hot toast and chilled butter.

Cook's tips

An excellent dish for a starter or as part of a snack lunch. Serve with a crisp green salad and toast or warm granary rolls or French bread. A more economical version can be made with drained canned salmon and smoked salmon pieces.

Moulded chicken liver pâté

● **Preparation: 30 minutes, plus chilling**

● **Cooking: 10 minutes**

425ml/15fl oz canned chicken consommé
2 celery stalks, thinly sliced
1 shallot, finely chopped
2 parsley sprigs
2tsp powdered gelatine
4 radishes, thinly sliced
450g/1lb chicken livers
salt and pepper
50g/2oz butter
225g/8oz full-fat soft cheese
4tbls Madeira
4tbls brandy
1tsp Worcestershire sauce
4tbls finely chopped parsley
radish 'accordions' and watercress sprigs, to garnish
hot toast and chilled butter, to serve

● **Serves 8**

● **350cals/1470kjs per serving**

1 Put the consommé into a saucepan along with the celery, shallot and parsley sprigs. Bring quickly to the boil, then boil for 5 minutes or until reduced to 300ml/½pt. Strain into a measuring jug.

2 Put the gelatine into a small bowl, sprinkle over 2tbls cold water and leave for 5 minutes until softened. Put the bowl in a saucepan of simmering water and leave until dissolved. Pour into the reduced consommé and stir well.

3 Pour 150ml/¼pt consommé into the bottom of a 1.1L/2pt ring mould and put in the refrigerator to set.

4 Arrange overlapping slices of radish at intervals on the set aspic and pour over just enough consommé to cover the decoration. Put in the refrigerator until set, then pour in the remaining consommé and chill until set firmly.

5 Meanwhile drain the chicken livers and pat dry with absorbent paper. Season with salt and pepper. Heat 25g/1oz butter in a large frying pan and fry the livers for 1½-2 minutes each side, turning once during the cooking.

6 Press the cooked chicken livers through a sieve or pass through a food processor into a bowl. Beat in the cheese, then stir in the Madeira, brandy, Worcestershire sauce and parsley. Season with salt and pepper.

7 Melt the remaining 25g/1oz butter in a small saucepan and stir it into the chicken liver pâté. Spread the pâté carefully over the set aspic and put in the refrigerator for 2 hours or until set.

8 When ready to serve dip the mould into a bowl of hot water for a few seconds and turn onto a serving platter. Garnish with radish 'accordions' and watercress sprigs; serve with hot toast and chilled butter.

Terrine du chef

● **Preparation: 20 minutes, marinating, then plus chilling**

● **Cooking: 1¾ hours**

900g/2lb rabbit
900g/2lb boneless pork shoulder
125ml/4fl oz brandy
600ml/1pt dry white wine
4 chicken livers
2tbls Madeira
large pinch each of cloves, nutmeg, ginger and cinnamon
salt and pepper
450g/1lb salt pork, thinly sliced
2 chicken breasts, skinned and boned
3tbls finely chopped parsley
100g/4oz unsmoked streaky bacon
bay leaves and thyme sprigs, to garnish

● **Serves 18**

● **280cals/1175kjs per serving**

1 Remove all the meat from the rabbit bones, cut the pork into 2.5cm/1in cubes and put into a deep bowl along with the rabbit. Pour over the brandy and wine.

2 Trim the chicken livers, quarter and put in a small bowl; sprinkle with Madeira. Cover both bowls and marinate in the refrigerator for 24 hours.

3 Remove the meats from their marinades. Cut the better pieces of rabbit into thin strips about 5cm/2in long.

4 Put the remaining rabbit and half the pork through a mincer or food processor. Add the spices, marinade juices and salt and pepper to taste. Add the chicken livers and mix well with your hands. Heat the oven to 170C/325F/gas 3.

5 Line the base and sides of a 2.3L/4pt terrine or loaf tin with thin slices of salt pork, reserving some for the top. Use thin slices streaky bacon if pork is difficult to find. Spread half the minced mixture in the lined mould and smooth it off.

6 Cut the chicken breasts into 5mm/¼in strips and roll them in the parsley. Arrange with the rabbit strips.

7 Top with the remaining pork cubes and the bacon rashers. Add the remaining minced mixture and cover with the reserved salt pork.

8 Cover with a lid or foil, put in a roasting tin and pour in enough boiling water to come halfway up the sides of the mould. Cook for 1¾ hours.

9 Weight the terrine down and leave about 3 hours. Chill and serve sliced to show off the layers, garnished with bay leaves and thyme.

SERVE TO ADVANTAGE

Turn layered pâtés out and slice fairly thickly. Others can be served straight from the terrine. If you are not going to eat the whole thing, scrape the fat off the surface before serving and keep it to spread over the cut side. Pâté is extremely rich; serve small portions, with toast or French bread.

Smoked mackerel pâté

● **Preparation: 20 minutes**

350g/12oz smoked mackerel
   fillets
150ml/5fl oz soured cream
100g/4oz full-fat soft cheese
salt (optional)
cayenne pepper
1tsp grated orange zest
2tbls orange juice
4 small orange shells or 4 large
   half shells
4 small bay leaves, to garnish

● **Serves 4**

● **370cals/1555kjs per serving**

1 Strip away the mackerel skin and finely flake the fish, discarding any small bones.

2 Put the soured cream, cheese and flaked mackerel into a blender or food processor and process until the mixture forms a soft paste, scraping the sides of the container once or twice if necessary.

3 Season to taste with salt, if needed, and a large pinch of cayenne pepper; add the orange zest and a few drops of the orange juice. Process again; add a little more orange juice and process again. Continue in this way until all the orange juice has been incorporated.

4 Cut a thin slice from the base of each orange shell so that they can stand upright without toppling. Spoon in the pâté and shape it into a mound at the top. Cover loosely and chill until needed.

5 Stick a bay leaf into the top of each mound of pâté before serving.

FREEZER FACTS

With the more elaborate pâtés and terrines which need fairly lengthy preparation, you may want to prepare them in advance and freeze ready for use. Long-term freezing is not advisable, as the pâté will lose both taste and texture. But if you time the operation carefully, the freezing down and defrosting period can be used to mature the pâté. Do not freeze for more than one month. Defrost for 8-24 hours in the refrigerator depending on the amount of mixture and shape of the pâté.

How to ... *prepare fruit shells*

To prepare the decorative orange shells cut them with a zig-zag edge. If using small oranges cut right through the fruit in a zig-zag horizontal line just above the halfway mark; scoop out the flesh.

With large oranges cut the zig-zag line exactly halfway up. Scoop out the fruit from both pieces by loosening the flesh with a grapefruit knife and then scraping the shell with a spoon.

Consummate Consommés

Nothing makes a more elegant beginning to a dinner party than a bowl of crystal-clear sparkling consommé. Making your own is time-consuming but well worth the trouble

THE FIRST STEP to making consommé is to prepare a home-made stock: beef, chicken or fish, as described in Taking stock, page 35. The next step is to clarify the stock – removing all floating bits and pieces, and turning the cloudy liquid into a clear sparkling one. This is done by slowly simmering it with flavouring and colouring additions, also crushed egg shells and/or frothed egg whites. The egg gradually coagulates throughout the soup, gathering up all the bits into a thick head on the top which is discarded. This technique is not difficult, but must be done just as described if the consommé is to emerge absolutely clear.

The consommé is now ready to eat, or it can be chilled, or elaborated into a more complex consommé as in the recipes. It can also be used to make aspic jelly.

Clarifying the stock

Equipment: you will need a large heavy-based saucepan (at least 3.5L/6pt capacity, preferably enamelled or stainless steel); wire whisk or wooden spoon; colander or large sieve; large piece of muslin or a clean tea cloth; large bowl; ladle and slotted spoon.

Both pan and cloth must be scrupulously clean. To prepare them fill the pan three-quarters full of cold water and bring it to the boil. Line the colander or sieve with the cloth and pour the boiling water through to remove any possible trace of detergent. Wring out the cloth and wipe the pan out with absorbent paper.

Clarify the stock as shown in the picture strip on page 110. The

Saffron seafood consommé (page 112)

process is the same for all kinds, except that fish stock is clarified using egg whites only, no shells, and simmered very briefly.

Finishing consommé

The clarified stock will still have some traces of fat in it. If you are going to use it at once remove this by drawing strips of absorbent paper across the surface until no globules remain. Alternatively cool the consommé, then chill and remove the solidified fat from the surface with a fish slice.

Meat or chicken consommé can be stored for up to a week; fish consommé for only a couple of days. All consommé must be reboiled before serving. This applies even if it to be eaten cold, so remember to allow enough time for it to cool again if necessary.

Beef consommé

- **Preparation: making stock**

- **Cooking: 1½ hours**

375g/12oz lean minced beef
2 leeks, trimmed and fairly finely
  chopped
2 celery stalks, fairly finely
  chopped
1 onion, fairly finely chopped
2 soft overripe tomatoes
whites and crushed shells of
  2 eggs
1.7L/3pt cold home-made beef
  stock (page 37)

- **Makes 1.1L/2pt, serves 6** (♈) (££)

- **25cals/105kjs per serving**

1 Put the beef in a large heavy-based saucepan with the chopped vegetables and the tomatoes. Whisk the egg whites until frothy and add to the pan along with the crushed shells. Mix well.

2 Skim all the fat off the stock and bring it to the boil in a separate pan. Pour it a little at a time onto the vegetable mixture, whisking constantly until it comes to the boil, then stop immediately.

3 Turn the heat right down and allow the thick pad of foam to rise to the surface. Simmer, uncovered, for 1 hour.

4 Line a large colander with muslin and stand it over a bowl. Using a slotted spoon gently draw the scum back from ▶

How to ... *clarify stock*

Combine the chopped vegetables and minced meat or fish in a clean saucepan. Whisk 2-3 egg whites to a froth and add, with crushed shells for meat stocks, to the vegetables.

Lift off all fat from the surface of the prepared chilled stock. Pour the stock slowly into a large pan, leaving any sediment behind. Bring to the boil.

Pour the boiling stock onto the vegetable mixture, a little at a time, whisking with a wire whisk or beating with a wooden spoon so that the egg white does not start to cook.

Bring the mixture slowly to the boil, whisking all the time. As soon as it boils stop whisking. Reduce the heat, then allow the thick scum to rise to the surface.

Simmer very gently, uncovered, for 1 hour (5 minutes for fish stock). Do not stir. Remove from the heat and gently draw back the scum to reveal the clear stock underneath the surface.

Line a sieve or colander with scalded muslin and stand it over a bowl. Ladle the clarified stock onto the muslin without disturbing the scum, or use a rubber-topped baster

about one-quarter of the clarified stock. Lower a ladle through the gap and, disturbing the scum as little as possible, ladle the stock onto the muslin. (Alternatively draw off the stock from underneath with a bulb baster.)

5 If the consommé is for later use allow it to cool, then carefully lift off any congealed fat from the surface. Transfer to storage jars, cover and chill until needed. It will keep for up to a week but must be reboiled before use, even if it is to be served cold or jellied.

6 If the consommé is to be used right away remove the fat by drawing strips of absorbent paper across the surface; or draw off the liquid from underneath with a bulb baster.

7 Either serve just as it is, piping hot or lightly chilled; or use to make a more complex consommé.

Variations

Chicken consommé: *use exactly the same method as for beef consommé, but start with 375g/12oz pie veal instead of beef, 2 carrots instead of tomatoes and 1.7l/3pt cold home-made chicken stock (page 36).*

CONSOMME VARIATIONS

Basic consommé can be varied to serve in several simple but delicious ways:

Consommé à l'orange: garnish each bowl of consommé with ½-1tsp finely shredded watercress leaves and half a slice of unpeeled orange, cut into three.

Tarragon consommé: add three sprigs of fresh tarragon to 1.1L/2pt fish or beef consommé. Bring slowly to the boil, cover the pan and leave in a warm place for 20 minutes. Strain through a muslin-lined colander. Garnish portions with 2-3 blanched tarragon leaves or a sprinkling of chopped tarragon.

Madeira or sherry consommé: flavour 1.1L/2pt beef consommé with 1tbls dry (Sercial) Madeira or dry sherry before serving.

Consommé madrilène: Add a cup of raw tomato pulp and serve very cold.

Consommé celestine: garnish chicken consommé with thin slices of rolled pancakes.

Fish consommé

- **Preparation: 35 minutes**
- **Cooking: 30 minutes**

100g/4oz lemon sole, minced
1 onion, finely chopped
1 carrot, finely chopped
1 leek, white part only, finely chopped
3 parsley stalks
3-4 mushroom stalks, finely chopped
10 white peppercorns
1 bay leaf
pinch dried thyme
¼tsp tomato purée
juice of 1 lemon
3 egg whites, whisked to a froth
¼tsp salt
1.1L/2pt cold fish stock (page 37)

- **Makes 850ml/1½pt, serves 4**
- **25cals/105kjs per serving**

1 Put all the ingredients except the stock in a large heavy-based saucepan and mix well.

2 Remove any fat and put the stock in a separate saucepan; bring to the boil. Pour it, a little at a time, onto the vegetable mixture, whisking constantly until it comes to the boil, then stop

---

Consommé orientale

whisking immediately. Turn the heat right down, then allow the thick pad of foam to rise to the surface.

3 Simmer, uncovered, for 5 minutes only, then remove from the heat, cover the pan and leave to infuse for only 10 minutes as fish stock tends to become bitter if left too long.

4 Treat the fish consommé in the same way as beef: push back the scum and ladle it into a muslin-lined colander. Use immediately or cool, degrease and chill.

5 Use fish consommé within two days and bring to the boil beforehand, even if serving cold. Skim off any fat.

Consommé orientale

- **Preparation: making consommé, then 15 minutes**
- **Cooking: 20 minutes**

1.1L/2pt beef consommé (page 110)
For the garnish:
50g/2oz carrot, sliced and cut into small shapes

50g/2oz turnip, sliced and cut into
  small cubes
salt
25g/1oz long-grain rice
pinch saffron powder
50g/2oz cooked beetroot, sliced and
  cut into small shapes

● **Serves 6**

● **45cals/190kjs per serving**

1 Cook the carrot and turnip shapes in boiling salted water until tender but still crisp. Drain and rinse under cold running water.

2 Cook the rice in boiling salted water with a pinch of saffron powder until just tender. Drain well.

3 Put the consommé in a large sauce pan with the carrot and turnip shapes and the saffron rice. Bring to boiling point, then immediately remove from the heat so that it does not boil.

4 Serve the consommé hot or cold, adding the cooked beetroot shapes just before serving. (Do not add the beetroot until the last moment or it will colour the consommé.)

Cook's tips

The classic shape for the vegetables in a Consommé orientale is tiny crescents, but other pretty shapes such as flowers, stars, hearts and diamonds can all be used.

Saffron seafood consommé

● **Preparation: 20 minutes**

● **Cooking: 20 minutes**

4 tightly closed mussels, washed
  and scraped
1/2tsp saffron powder
4tbls dry white wine
1 sole fillet, cut into 4 thin strips
4 oysters (optional)
8 cooked peeled prawns
850ml/1 1/2pt fish consommé
  (page 111)
2 tbls finely snipped fresh chives or
  finely chopped fresh tarragon

● **Serves 4**

● **65cals/275kjs per serving**

1 Put 1cm/½in water in a saucepan, add the mussels, cover and cook over medium heat, shaking regularly, for 2-3 minutes or until the mussels open. Remove the mussels from their shells.

2 Put the saffron in a small saucepan with the wine and bring to a gentle simmer, stirring. Poach the strips of sole in this mixture for 1-2 minutes, until they are opaque. Remove with a slotted spoon, reserving the saffron-wine mixture.

3 Open the oysters, if using, with a strong short-bladed knife, remove from shell, pour off the liquid and poach the oysters in the saffron-wine mixture until they begin to curl at the edges. Remove and trim off the curled edges.

4 Put a mussel, strip of sole, oyster and two prawns in each of four heated soup bowls. Add the consommé to the saffron-wine mixture and bring to the boil. Pour over the fish and sprinkle with chives or tarragon. Serve at once.

OLD FASHIONED BEEF TEA

This is now rather an extravagant invalid dish but it is comforting and nourishing and is much easier than consommé. Remove all fat and gristle from 1lb lean stewing meat. Scrape the meat into shreds or put through a mincer or food processor, collect all the juice. Soak the meat and juice with 600ml/1pt cold water in a heatproof bowl, covered, for 1 hour. Place on top of a saucepan of water so that the water comes halfway up the bowl. Cook for 2 hours, replenishing the water in the saucepan when necessary and stirring the meat mixture from time to time. Strain, check the seasoning and allow to cool. Then remove all surface fat (there should not be very much) and reheat gently before serving. Do not allow it to boil when reheating.

Consommé creole

● **Preparation: making consommé, then 15 minutes**

● **Cooking: 25 minutes**

75g/3oz long-grain rice
1.1L/2pt chicken consommé
  (see Variations, page 111)
For the garnish:
1/4 green pepper, deseeded
4-5 tomatoes, skinned, halved
  and deseeded

● **Serves 6**

● **80cals/335 kjs per serving**

1 Remove excess starch from the rice: rinse in a sieve under cold running water until the water runs clear. Shake out as much water as possible and dab the rice dry with absorbent paper.

2 Put the consommé in a large saucepan and bring to the boil, stir twice then cover and simmer very gently for 15 minutes. Take great care to ensure that the rice is not overcooked.

3 Meanwhile prepare the garnish. Cut two squares from the pepper, each 2cm/¾in across; then cut these down to make nine smaller squares from each one. Cut 18 squares, 1cm/½in across, from the tomato flesh.

4 Add the squares of pepper and tomato to the boiling rice and continue to simmer for 3-5 minutes until the rice is cooked and the vegetables are tender but not overcooked.

5 Either serve the consommé immediately in heated individual bowls, or leave it to cool, then chill the consommé slightly before serving.

Zuppa Pavese

- **Preparation: 5 minutes**

- **Cooking: 10 minutes**

6 rounds French bread
40-50g/1½-2oz butter
3tbls grated Parmesan cheese
6 medium very fresh eggs
1.1L/2pt hot beef consommé (p.110)

- **Serves 6**

- **250cals/1050kjs per serving**

1 Fry the rounds of French bread in butter until golden on both sides.

2 Lay a round of bread at the bottom of each of six large heated soup bowls. Sprinkle each round with 1tbls grated Parmesan cheese.

3 Break an egg into each bowl to one side of the bread, but not over it, taking great care not to break the yolk.

4 Bring the consommé to the boil and, without removing the pan from the heat, carefully ladle boiling consommé into each bowl. Serve at once.

Cook's tips

This famous soup comes from Pavia in north-west Italy. It is very simple to make but you must use very fresh eggs, otherwise the white will run over the bottom of the bowl and turn into a nasty froth when it comes into contact with the boiling consommé.

Consommé italienne

- **Preparation: making consommé, plus 15 minutes**
- **Cooking: 40 minutes**

700g/1½lb ripe tomatoes
2 celery stalks
1.1L/2pt chicken consommé
    (see Variations, page 111)
40g/1½oz tiny pasta shapes
salt and pepper
1-2tbls finely chopped fresh
    parsley
For the garnish:
225g/8oz firm tomatoes
200g/7oz canned pimentos

- **Serves 6**
- **65cals/275kjs per serving**

1 Roughly chop the tomatoes and celery, removing any coarse strings from the celery. Put in a large saucepan with the consommé, bring to the boil and simmer for 30 minutes.

2 Meanwhile make the garnish: blanch, skin and deseed the tomatoes; cut the flesh into 3mm/⅛in dice. Drain the pimentos and cut them into dice of the same size for an extra special touch.

3 Strain the consommé through a muslin-lined colander. Put the consommé in a clean saucepan and bring to the boil. Add the pasta shapes and simmer for 3-5 minutes or until tender. Remove the saucepan from the heat; add the tomato and pimento garnish. Season with salt and pepper to taste. Bring to boiling point and remove from the heat immediately so that it does not boil.

4 To serve hot, ladle the consommé into heated bowls and sprinkle with parsley. To serve cold, chill slightly and sprinkle with parsley just before serving. The pimentos and tomatoes may be cut into fancy shapes with cocktail cutters.

PERFECT ASPIC

Turn your consommé into aspic with powdered gelatine: 2 tbls should be enough for 600ml/1pt consommé. Sprinkle the gelatine onto 3tbls cold consommé, leave to soften, then allow to dissolve in a bowl set over simmering water. Strain this into the rest of the warmed consommé. Use to coat meat or poultry or chop into cubes and use to decorate cold savoury dishes.

Magic Mousses

Savoury mousses, hot or cold, delicate and fluffy or

beautifully moulded, add a superb touch of elegance to a buffet

table or dinner party

THERE ARE THREE main types of savoury mousse. The simplest and easiest is a light fluffy mixture of hot vegetables, served mounded on a plate as an accompaniment to a main dish. A more elaborate type of hot mousse is moulded, then cooked to hold the shape. But the most popular and splendid-looking of the three is the cold moulded mousse, set with aspic jelly. Both of these mousses can be made from meat, fish, poultry or vegetables.

Hot moulded mousses

These are fairly simple to make, and make elegant starters or delicious main courses for a dinner party. The purée of fish, shellfish, meat, poultry or vegetables is mixed with eggs and baked until set in individual dishes. The finished mousses are turned out and often masked with a sauce before garnishing. If you have difficulty in turning out, cook and serve in ramekin dishes.

The trickiest part of making these mousses is getting the right balance of seasoning, as unless you are prepared to taste the raw mixture, or fry a spoonful in butter first, this is a matter of guesswork. Season generously as the ingredients tend to be bland.

Cold moulded mousses

Cold mousses turned out from elaborate moulds were traditional centrepieces for 19th-century buffet parties. Nowadays, they are usually made in plain round or ring moulds, but still look very impressive if attractively garnished and coated with aspic jelly.

The basic ingredient is fish, meat or poultry. This is puréed and added to a base of thick white sauce, with liquid aspic stirred in to stabilize the mixture. Whipped cream and beaten egg white may be folded in

Cold cucumber and prawn mousse (page 116)

for a lighter texture. Once firmly set the mousse is unmoulded as shown on the right. If the outer surface has melted a little, return to the refrigerator to firm.

The key point with this type of mousse is to make sure that the sauce is completely cold before the cream and egg white are added. If it is warm, they will melt, losing air.

Test the setting power of the mousse before committing it to the mould. If it contains too little aspic, it will not turn out satisfactory; too much and it will be dense and rubbery to eat. Spoon a tiny amount of the mixture onto a chilled saucer and freeze for a minute or two until set. If it resembles chewing gum, fold in a little more wine, stock, whipped cream or whisked egg white. If it is too thin, add a little more gelatine, allowing ½tsp powder to each 425ml/¾pt of mousse mixture. Dissolve the gelatine and cool quickly in the fridge or freezer. Fold into the mousse gently.

Taste the mousse and if it lacks flavour add some wine, port, sherry, Madeira, lemon juice, onion juice, Worcestershire sauce or hot pepper sauce to match the flavour.

Added aspic

Aspic jelly is used both as the setting agent for savoury mousses, and for decorating. Making it the traditional way is time-consuming, but the recipe for Quick aspic jelly on page 117 gives good results.

It is advisable to test that the aspic will set properly by making it in advance, then chilling it thoroughly. If it fails the test, there is time to strengthen the mixture with a little extra dissolved gelatine powder. When ready to use, melt it and pour into a small bowl. Stand in a larger bowl full of ice cubes. Stir until on the point of setting. It will be syrupy; use at once.

To coat a cold mousse with aspic, unmould the mousse onto a wire rack and put this over a shallow tray to catch any overflow. Brush the mousse with a thin layer of aspic. Chill until set, then recoat several times. Thinly-cut fancy shapes of colourful vegetables can be used under the layers to decorate a plain mould.

How to ··· *unmould cold mousse*

Run the tip of a knife round the edge of the mould. Hold a hot damp towel round the mould for 1-2 seconds, then put a lightly wetted plate upside down on the mould.

Hold the mould and plate firmly together. Invert them, giving a quick jerk halfway over. When completely inverted, give one or two firm shakes and lift off the mould.

Cold cucumber and prawn mousse

● *Preparation: 1³/₄ hours, plus chilling*

1 large cucumber, peeled, seeded and coarsely grated
1tbls salt
225g/8oz cooked peeled prawns
2tbls lemon juice
pinch cayenne pepper
300ml/¹/₂pt liquid aspic (page 117)
2 egg whites
300ml/¹/₂pt double cream
2tbls each finely chopped chives and parsley
For the garnish:
¹/₂ cucumber, unpeeled and very thinly sliced
shredded lettuce and watercress sprigs
lemon wedges, to serve

● *Serves 6*　　　 (££)

● *250cals/1050kjs per serving*

1 Put the cucumber in a bowl with the salt. Mix well, then turn into a colander to drain for at least 1 hour.

2 Chop the prawns coarsely. Put them in a small bowl with the lemon juice; season with a good pinch of cayenne pepper.

3 Rinse the salt off the cucumber, then press the cucumber in the colander to

remove excess moisture. Dry thoroughly by rolling it in a wad of absorbent paper. Press the prawns in a sieve to remove the excess moisture. Combine with the cucumber.

4 Use the aspic when syrupy and just about to set. Add 8tbls to the cucumber and prawn mixture and mix well.

5 Whisk the egg whites in a clean dry bowl until stiff but not dry. Whip the cream until it holds its shape in soft peaks. Fold the cream into the cucumber and prawn mixture, then fold in the chives and parsley. Gently fold in the egg whites. Taste and season if necessary with lemon juice, salt and cayenne pepper.

6 Wet a 1L/2pt ring mould and put it in a large bowl filled with ice cubes. Spoon ▶

DAMAGE LIMITATION

If you've never made a mousse before, don't do it for a dinner party – practise on the family first. Test the firmness of the mixture as described and allow plenty of time for setting.

Practise holding a mould and plate together and inverting them – turning out a mould is partly a matter of confidence.

If the dinner party mousse still doesn't turn out perfect, don't despair – hide the damage under some mayonnaise and a little finely chopped parsley. If it collapses spoon the mixture into individual dishes and freeze.

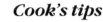

in the mousse mixture, tapping the mould from time to time to prevent air pockets forming. Chill until set; about 3 hours.

7 Unmould the mousse as shown in the step-by-step pictures. Use the remaining liquid aspic to brush over the mousse. Garnish with overlapping circles of cucumber and chill until the aspic has become quite firm.

8 Brush the mousse, including the cucumber, with one or two more coats of syrupy aspic and chill to set.

9 Fill the centre of the mousse with lettuce and watercress sprigs.

Hot sole mousses with watercress cream

- ● **Preparation: 20 minutes**

- ● **Cooking: 35 minutes**

1/2 bunch watercress
350g/12oz sole, halibut or whiting,
   boned and skinned
2 eggs, beaten
150ml/1/4pt double cream
2tbls dry white wine
1/2 chicken or fish stock cube
salt and white pepper
butter, for greasing
For the watercress cream:
1/2 bunch watercress
1tsp cornflour
2tsp white wine vinegar
300ml/1/2pt double cream

- ● **Serves 4**

- ● **540 cals/2270 kjs per serving**

1 Heat the oven to 170C/325F/gas 3. Remove the coarse stalks from the watercress and blanch the leaves in boiling salted water for 3 minutes. Drain, rinse in cold water and drain again, pressing out all excess moisture. Chop very finely, then press through a sieve to make a purée – about 2tbls.

2 Purée the fish in a blender or food processor. Add the eggs, cream and watercress purée. Heat the wine, crumble in the stock cube and stir until dissolved. Add to the fish mixture and process until smooth. Season with salt and white pepper to taste and process again to mix.

3 Butter four 150ml/1/4pt ovenproof soufflé dishes. Divide the mousse mixture between them. Put the dishes in a roasting tin and pour in enough boiling water to come 2cm/3/4in up the sides of the tin. Put over medium heat until the water starts to bubble, then carefully transfer the tin to the oven. Cook for 20-25 minutes, until a skewer inserted in the middle of a mousse comes out clean.

4 Meanwhile prepare the watercress cream. Remove the coarse stalks from the watercress. Mix the cornflour with the vinegar. Gently heat the cream in a pan, then add the cornflour mixture. Do not boil or it will curdle. Add the watercress to the cream mixture, then liquidize or sieve to make it smooth.

5 Carefully turn the mousses onto heated individual serving plates and mask with the carefully reheated watercress cream. Serve at once.

Cook's tips

Serve these delicate little mousses as a light main course with a green salad; or as the perfect starter to precede roast pork.

Quick aspic jelly

- ● **Preparation: 5 minutes**

- ● **Cooking: 10 minutes**

1tbls powdered gelatine
425ml/3/4 pt chicken or beef stock
2tbls each Madeira and dry sherry

- ● **Makes about 600ml/1pt**

- ● **150 cals/630 kjs total**

1 Put the gelatine in a cup or small bowl with 4tbls cold water. Leave for 5 minutes to soften.

2 Strain the stock through a sieve lined with muslin. Transfer it to a saucepan and heat to almost boiling. Add the softened gelatine and stir until the gelatine has dissolved completely.

3 Strain and leave the mixture to cool, then stir in the Madeira and sherry.

Cook's tips

Another way to make quick aspic jelly is to use a commercial brand of savoury aspic powder. Put 600ml/1pt water in a saucepan with one envelope of powder and bring slowly to the boil. Allow to cool before using.

Unused aspic can be chilled for future use. Alternatively set on a flat tray and chop up for garnish when firm.

Cold smoked salmon mousses

● **Preparation: 30 minutes, plus chilling**

225g/8oz smoked salmon
150ml/¼pt single cream
1tbls lemon juice
salt and pepper
grated nutmeg
4tbls liquid aspic (page 117)
2 egg whites
300ml/½pt double cream
For the garnish:
parsley sprigs
small strips of smoked salmon

● **Serves 6-8** 🍮 (£££)

● **295 cals/1240 kjs per serving**

1 Chop the smoked salmon coarsely. Put it in a blender or food processor with the cream, lemon juice and a small pinch each of salt, pepper and nutmeg. Be careful not to over-season. Blend to a smooth purée and transfer to a bowl.

2 Use the aspic when syrupy and just setting. Beat into mixture.

3 Whisk the egg whites in a clean dry bowl until stiff but not dry. Whip the cream until it holds its shape in soft peaks. Fold the cream into the salmon mixture, followed by the egg whites. Taste and adjust the seasoning with a little more lemon juice, salt, pepper or nutmeg.

4 Lightly wet 6-8 small individual dishes. Divide the mousse between them and chill until set; about 1-2 hours.

5 Serve in the dishes, garnished with parsley and salmon strips.

Hot chicken mousses

● **Preparation: 30 minutes**

● **Cooking: 40 minutes**

65g/2½oz butter
50g/2oz flour
300ml/½pt milk
350g/12oz raw chicken meat
50g/2oz cooked ham
4 eggs
175ml/6fl oz double cream
2tsp tomato purée
3tbls vermouth
pinch cayenne pepper
¼tsp crushed juniper berries
¼tsp ground cloves and nutmeg
lemon juice
salt and white pepper
tomato sauce, to serve (see Linguini steps 1, 2 and 3, page 33)
watercress to garnish

● **Serves 8** 🍮 (£££)

● **275 cals/1155 kjs per serving**

1 Heat the oven to 170C/325F/gas 3. Butter eight 150ml/¼pt ovenproof soufflé dishes.

2 Melt 50g/2oz butter in a small saucepan, stir in the flour, then cook over medium heat for 2-3 minutes. Remove the pan from the heat and gradually stir in the milk. Bring slowly to the boil, stirring constantly. Simmer for 1 minute, then remove from the heat.

3 Chop the chicken and ham finely in a food processor, or mince three times. Put in a blender or food processor with the eggs, cream, tomato purée, vermouth, cayenne pepper, juniper berries and spices. Process until smooth. Add the white sauce mixture plus lemon juice, salt and pepper to taste, then process again until smooth.

4 Divide the mixture between the dishes and put in the oven for 20-25 minutes. Meanwhile make the tomato sauce and pass through a blender or food processor.

5 Turn each mousse onto an individual serving plate, mask with warm tomato sauce and garnish with watercress. Alternatively serve in the cooking dishes.

Main courses

*T*his section covers the middle part of a meal – the main course – concentrating on meat-based dishes. It is broken into short chapters based either on cooking technique or type of meat – so that you do not just learn how to follow a recipe, but also discover the secrets of the processes involved.

Grilling is one of the quickest cooking methods. The chapters on lamb and fish contain information about which cuts to use, how to bone and trim and how to marinate. Barbecuing, a form of grilling, has a chapter of its own, with specialized information about the foods to choose and the cooking equipment required.

Casserole-cooking, on the other hand, is one of the slowest methods and is the ideal treatment for dry meats like game and poultry. Cooking with Confidence *explains how this and other moist methods of cooking, such as pot-roasting or braising, are perfect for joints of meat, particularly the less tender cuts of beef and pork, and offal. There are facts about which cuts to choose, and advice on marinating. Bacon and gammon also require moist cooking and* Cooking with Confidence *guides you through the processes of baking, boiling and braising.*

Most joints of meat and whole birds can be roasted, and there are separate chapters on beef, lamb, pork, game and poultry. You will discover which joints respond best to roasting, and how to judge the correct cooking time to achieve the most moist and tender results. There are tips on carving, recipes for gravies and stuffings, and step-by-step guides on how to ensure crisp pork crackling, prepare a crown roast of lamb, and truss a turkey.

Frying (whether stir-frying, shallow-frying or deep-frying) is one of the quickest cooking methods. In the chapter on pan-frying beef, you will find out the importance of a good frying pan, which size and type to buy, and whether or not it needs a lid. The cut of meat, its thickness and shape make a difference to the cooking time, so there is a detailed chart of requisite cooking times in the pork and lamb chapter.

Fish is a slightly different matter: like chicken and turkey, it is best fried in deep oil, covered in a protective wrapping to keep it moist and tender. There is detailed information about types of coating, from the basic dusting of flour to crispy breadcrumbs, and recipes for such classic dishes as Chicken Kiev (see page 192).

Lamb for All Seasons

Lightly grilled lamb is always tender, especially if marinated beforehand, and delicious to eat at any time of the year. What's more it's very quick and easy to cook

GRILLING IS ONE of the easiest ways of cooking meat, and good for the weight-conscious as little or no fat is used. But for best results you need to pick suitable cuts, and get temperature and timing exactly right to achieve a crisply browned surface and succulent, faintly pink interior.

Suitable cuts

When shopping look for lamb which has pink, finely grained flesh, and white or pale cream fat. This shows that it comes from a young animal and will be tender to eat. For best flavour buy fresh home-produced lamb; for economy buy frozen imported lamb and marinate before cooking.

Loin chops: these are so called because they are cut from the loin, or centre back, of the animal. They consist of a lean eye of meat surrounded by fat. A typical loin chop weighs 100g/4oz and is 2.5cm/1in thick.

Chump chops: more compact and meaty looking than loin chops, these are cut from the chump, or lower back area. They have a fairly substantial central bone. Typical weight is 175g/6oz, 2cm/¾in thick.

Leg steaks or gigot chops: being cut from the leg, these are very tender and tasty, and larger than the other cuts: about 250g/9oz in weight and 2cm/¾in thick. They are almost round, with a central bone which some butchers remove.

Cutlets or best end chops: these are cut from the best or lower end of the neck. Although tender and cheap, they are small — allow three per person. After trimming, the cutlet consists of an eye of lean meat backed by a strip of fat, with a strip of bone exposed at one end.

Noisettes: these are rounds prepared from a boned and rolled loin or best end of lamb (see page 123). You can buy ready-prepared noisettes but it is cheaper to buy the meat on the bone and ask your butcher to bone and roll it for you.

Shoulder and leg: these roasting joints can be boned out and the meat cubed to make kebabs or

Lamb with paprika butter (page 124)

brochettes suitable for grilling. A shoulder weighing 900g/2lb will make about 700g/1½lb of kebab meat. Leg is the leanest.

Preparation

If the meat has not been marinated, pat it dry with absorbent paper. Trim off excess fat, but leave a narrow border around the edge of large steaks and chops to keep them moist while cooking. Slash the fat with a sharp knife, or clip with kitchen scissors, to stop it from contracting and curling up when heated. With cutlets and loin chops trim the fat to follow the shape of the meat and make them look neat.

Remove the meat from the refrigerator as much as 2 hours ahead, if possible, to allow it to come to room temperature. Season with pepper and rub in any herbs at this stage so that the flavours have time to penetrate the meat.

Grilling

Preheat the grill on high for 15 minutes, so that it is really hot when the meat goes under. And remember to remove the grid from the pan before preheating; if it is heated, when the meat is put on it will cook in the heat coming from below as well as from the grill above, which would upset the cooking times. Position the grill pan so that the grid is about 7.5cm/3in away from the heat source.

Cook the meat for between 5 and 15 minutes on each side, depending on the cut, its thickness and how you like it. Well-done timings produce meat which is beige all the way through. Medium means that it is brown on the surface but still faintly pink in the centre. Underdone means that it is still raw at the very centre, and lightly cooked outside. Turn the meat once only, using tongs or two wooden spoons. Never pierce it with a fork as this allows juices to escape and toughens the meat.

Testing: to find out whether the meat is done to your liking, slip the point of a small sharp knife between the flesh and the edge of the bone to see what colour it is there. (This is the part that takes longest to cook.)

Noisettes of lamb with mushroom sauce

- **Preparation: 40 minutes, plus overnight marinating**
- **Cooking: 30 minutes**

1.5kg/3¼lb loin of lamb, boned, rolled and cut into 12 × 2.5cm/1in thick noisettes
watercress sprigs, to garnish
For the marinade:
3tbls oil
1tbls lemon juice
1-2 garlic cloves, finely chopped
1tbls chopped fresh rosemary, or 1tsp dried
1tsp Dijon mustard
For the sauce:
1 large onion, chopped
40g/1½oz butter
350g/12oz button mushrooms, thinly sliced
1 garlic clove, crushed
3tbls medium sherry
300ml/½pt beef stock
salt and pepper
125ml/4fl oz dry white wine
150ml/¼pt double cream
1tbls cornflour

- **Serves 6**
- **510cals/2140kjs per serving**

1 Combine the marinade ingredients and coat the noisettes. Place in a dish, cover and refrigerate overnight.

2 Remove from the marinade and bring back to room temperature. Heat the grill without the grid to high. Arrange the noisettes in the grill pan and grill, 7.5cm/3in from the heat, until cooked (10 minutes underdone, 15 minutes medium or 20 minutes well done), turning once.

3 Meanwhile, make the sauce: fry the onion in the butter for 3-4 minutes or until soft. Add the mushrooms and garlic and cook gently until soft, then add the sherry, stock and salt and pepper to taste. Simmer for 5-7 minutes, stir in the wine and cook until simmering again. Remove from the heat and add the cream.

4 Remove 1tbls of the sauce and mix in the cornflour, then stir this paste into the sauce. Return to a very low heat and stir constantly until thickened. Do not boil. Adjust the seasoning.

5 Transfer the noisettes to a warmed serving platter. Pour over the sauce, garnish and serve.

MARVELLOUS MARINADES

The very simplest marinade consists of nothing more than seasoned olive oil. This makes meat more succulent and tasty by stopping it drying out and introducing extra fat into very lean meat as it cooks. To make the marinade tenderize the meat, acid-based liquids are added: lemon juice, wine or wine vinegar.

More sophisticated marinades are made by adding herbs, spices, and vegetables.

Make enough marinade to ensure that the meat remains moist throughout the marinating time. You will need about 150ml/ ¼pt of marinade for every 450g/ 1lb of meat. However, some marinades – like that used for the Moroccan lamb chops on page 123 – are quite dry, containing only enough liquid to moisten and bind together the herbs and spices so that they can be spread over the meat.

How to...
make noisettes

Get your butcher to skin and bone a loin of lamb. Lay it out cut side up and season with pepper and rosemary, if liked. Starting at the thick end, roll the meat up tightly.

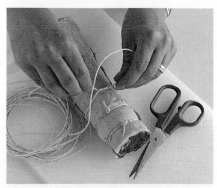

Trim the flap if it is long enough to wrap more than once around the eye of the meat. Tie the roll up tightly with kitchen string at 2.5cm/1in intervals, making sure each piece is firmly knotted.

Take a sharp cook's knife and cut the meat into slices in between the strings. The noisettes should be of uniform thickness so that they cook evenly. Leave the strings in place during cooking.

Moroccan lamb chops

- **Preparation: 20 minutes, plus overnight marinating**

- **Cooking: 25 minutes**

8 loin chops
salt and pepper
flat-leaved parsley and lemon
  wedges, to garnish
For the marinade:
4tbls olive oil, plus extra for
  greasing
2tbls finely chopped parsley
1tbls lemon juice
$\frac{1}{2}$tsp ground cumin
$\frac{1}{4}$-$\frac{1}{2}$tsp cayenne pepper
$\frac{1}{2}$tsp finely crushed black
  peppercorns
$\frac{1}{2}$tsp ground coriander
$\frac{1}{2}$tsp ground ginger

- **Serves 4**

- **360cals/1510kjs per serving**

1 Trim the excess fat from the chops, leaving a narrow border; slash the fat at intervals with a sharp knife. Arrange the chops side by side in a dish just large enough to take them in a single layer.

2 Combine the marinade ingredients in a bowl, stirring until thoroughly mixed. Spread the marinade over both sides of the chops, cover and marinate overnight in the refrigerator, turning occasionally. Remove from the refrigerator well before cooking to allow them to come to room temperature.

3 Heat the grill without the grid to high. Brush the grill grid with olive oil.

4 Remove the steaks from the marinade and place them on the grid. Grill, 7.5cm/3in from the heat, until cooked to your taste (15 minutes for underdone, 20 minutes for medium or 25 minutes for well done). Turn them once while grilling, and brush occasionally with the marinade.

5 Arrange the grilled chops on a serving platter, season with salt and pepper and serve immediately, garnished with flat-leaved parsley and lemon wedges.

123

Lamb steaks with paprika butter

- **Preparation: 15 minutes, plus 1 hour marinating**
- **Cooking: 10 minutes**

5tbls olive oil
3tbls red wine vinegar
4 parsley stalks
1 bay leaf, crumbled
salt and pepper
4 x 175g/6oz lamb steaks, cut
  from the leg
8 bay leaves, to garnish
For the paprika butter:
65g/2¹⁄₂oz butter, softened
1-2 garlic cloves, very finely
  chopped
¹⁄₂tsp paprika

- **Serves 4**
- **550cals/2310kjs per serving**

1 Make the marinade by mixing together the oil, vinegar, parsley stalks, bay leaf and salt and pepper.

2 Put the lamb steaks in a shallow dish and pour the marinade over them. Cover and leave at room temperature for 1 hour, turning occasionally.

3 To make the paprika butter, beat together the butter, garlic and paprika. Rinse a 25cm/10in square of grease-proof paper under the cold tap; squeeze out excess water. Open out the paper and put the butter in the centre. Roll the paper around the butter to form it into a roll about 5cm/2in long; twist the ends like a Christmas cracker. Chill for 1 hour or until ready to serve the steaks.

4 Heat the grill without the grid to high. Grill the lamb steaks for 5-6 minutes on each side or until done to your liking, 7.5cm/3in away from the heat.

5 Transfer the steaks to warmed plates. Top each one with two thin slices of paprika butter, garnish and serve.

Plan ahead

Marinate the steaks for 2-3 hours at room temperature, or overnight in the fridge – they will be even more delicious.

Serving ideas

For a more substantial meal serve the lamb steaks with jacket potatoes or boiled rice. A salad could replace the broccoli.

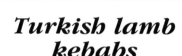

Turkish lamb kebabs

- **Preparation: 30 minutes, plus overnight marinating**
- **Cooking: 30 minutes**

900g/2lb lamb fillet, cut into
  2.5cm/1in cubes
4 small onions, quartered
8 bay leaves
lemon slices and flat-leaved
  parsley, to garnish
For the marinade:
4tbls olive oil
2tbls lemon juice
salt and pepper
3tbls chopped parsley
2 garlic cloves, crushed

- **Serves 4**
- **500cals/2100kjs per serving**

1 Mix the marinade ingredients together. Put the lamb cubes in a shallow dish, pour the marinade over, stir, cover and refrigerate overnight. Bring to room temperature for cooking.

2 Heat the grill without the grid to high. Thread the meat onto four large skewers, adding four onion quarters and two bay leaves to each one.

3 Brush the meat and vegetables with any remaining marinade and grill, 7.5cm/3in from the heat, until done to your liking (15 minutes underdone, 20 minutes medium and 25-30 minutes well done), turning the skewers over every 5-10 minutes. Garnish and serve hot.

SKEWER COOKING

Threading chunks of marinated meat onto skewers and grilling them is a cooking method used in countries all over the world for many centuries, and is still highly popular today. In Turkey and the Middle East they call them *kebabs*; in France and parts of Africa they're *brochettes*; in the Far East and Polynesia they become *satés*.

Eat them as a snack at any time of day, or as a starter or cocktail savoury; they are perfect for barbecues or, accompanied by rice and a salad, they make a simple and substantial main meal.

WHAT WENT WRONG?

Meat tough: the meat was not of sufficiently good quality, not marinated, or overcooked.
Meat burnt outside, raw inside: grill too hot or grid was placed too close to the heat.
Meat lacks colour: either the grill was not hot enough, or the grid was too far away.

Cook's tips

Skewers used for cooking kebabs should be metal, long and flat-sided. If they are round the ingredients may slip and not cook evenly. Ordinary meat skewers are not long enough.

One for the Pot

Game casseroles began as simple peasant food, designed to make tough old birds and beasts edible. But down the centuries great chefs have developed many of the dishes into culinary masterpieces

Rabbit and red wine casserole (page 126)

ROASTING IS THE preferred method of cooking game, but only when it is young and tender. Once a pheasant, for example, is past the first flush of youth, it will be a dry disappointment if roasted. But put it into a casserole with vegetables, herbs and spices, cook slowly in stock, wine or cream, and it becomes a luxury dish fit for a dinner party of special Sunday lunch. It will also cost satisfyingly less to buy than a young bird.

Game can be furred – venison, rabbits and hares – or feathered – pheasants, pigeons and other birds. Strictly speaking, the term refers to wild creatures which are protected during breeding times and hunted outside it. But nowadays most rabbit is bred specially for the table and venison comes from herds of deer farmed like cattle. Game used to be a seasonal delicacy restricted to the autumn and winter months. Today freezing and food farming make much of it available for most of the year, but autumn is still the time when it is most widely on sale.

Furred game

Venison describes the flesh of any deer – roe, fallow or red. It is superb eating, and almost entirely free of fat. This means it is dry by nature and needs marinating and/or generous larding with fat bacon, also careful cooking. The leg, loin and saddle can be roasted or casseroled, but the remainder of the carcass is only suitable for casseroles or pies.

Hare is as richly flavoured as venison and also rather dry, so it needs similar treatment. The traditional way of preparing it, jugged hare, involves using its blood to make a rich dark sauce. A hare carcass is held together by a tough opaque outer membrane and its tenderness will be greatly improved if some of this is stripped away. This allows the marinade or cooking liquid to penetrate better and shortens cooking time.

Rabbit has mild-flavoured, tender meat, very similar to chicken. Although most is bred for the table, often imported, it is still treated and cooked like game. It is at its best cooked by a moist method – use rabbit in chicken casserole recipes and in curries.

Feathered game

Pheasant is an exceptionally beautiful bird, with a flavour to match. The cock bird is the one with the beautiful rainbow plumage, but the brown-feathered hens taste the same. They are often sold paired together in a brace. A cock will serve four; hens are slightly smaller – use two to serve six. Young pheasants make superb roasts, but if you are in any doubt (if it was cheaper, it's probably old) play safe by casseroling it. The moist method will ensure that it is tasty and succulent.

Partridge is more delicately flavoured than most game birds, similar to chicken, but fuller and richer. Only young birds are suitable for roasting; older ones are casserole material. They can be used in most recipes which call for chicken; one plump bird will serve two.

Pigeon meat is dark and well-flavoured; there is not a lot of it on the bones, and you need a whole bird per person. Once again, the meat tends to be dry, so unless you are certain that you have a young bird, casseroling is the best way to cook it. marinating, stuffing or wrapping round with bacon is always advisable. Pigeons are cheaper than most other feathered game used for casseroles.

Wild duck has a much richer flavour than the usually battery-reared tame variety. The birds are much smaller – barely enough for two. To avoid any risk of a slightly fishy taste, put apples, onions or lemons in the cavity before cooking. Wild duck should not be overcooked or it will become dry and tough. Casseroling is the preferred method for older birds.

Rabbit and red wine casserole

- **Preparation: 20 minutes**

- **Cooking: 1¼ hours**

16-20 prunes, stoned
about 250ml/9fl oz red wine
2tbls oil
1 large onion, finely chopped
1.6kg/3½lb rabbit, dressed weight, cut into serving pieces
salt and pepper
mashed potato, to serve

- **Serves 4**

- **600cals/2520kjs per serving**

1 Put the prunes to soak in the red wine. Heat the oil in a frying pan over medium heat, add the onion and fry gently for about 5 minutes until soft and lightly browned, stirring occasionally. Transfer the onions to an ovenproof casserole using a slotted spoon.

2 Heat the oven to 180C/350F/gas 4. Turn the heat under the frying pan up to high, put in the rabbit pieces and fry until lightly browned all over. Add the rabbit portions to the casserole, mixing into the onion. Season generously with salt and pepper.

3 Add a little of the red wine in which the prunes are soaking to the casserole, cover and put in the oven for 45 minutes or until the rabbit is tender. Check occasionally and add a little more wine each time. If the mixture in the casserole becomes dry add a little chicken stock or water with the wine.

4 Add the prunes and remaining wine and cook for another 30 minutes. Taste and adjust the seasoning; serve hot with mashed potato. The potato can be piped in an attractive design around the outside of the serving dish.

How to...
prepare a casserole

Small whole birds like pigeon can be cooked whole or cut in half. Larger birds can be quartered or cut into portions.

Prepare a good selection of root vegetables and sauté in oil and butter. Transfer to a casserole and fry the game birds until brown.

Place the browned game birds in the casserole on top of the vegetables. Pour in wine and stock, season and cook until tender.

Pigeons with lentils

- **Preparation: 25 minutes**

- **Cooking: 2 hours**

4 oven-ready pigeons
4 rashers unsmoked streaky
  bacon
40g/1½oz butter
3tbls olive oil
2 large onions, finely chopped
300ml/½pt chicken stock
1 bouquet garni
salt and pepper
225g/8oz brown lentils
50g/2oz fat salt pork, finely
  diced
1-2 carrots, cut into chunks
¼tsp dried thyme
3 bay leaves

- **Serves 4**

- **615cals/2585kjs per serving**

1 Heat the oven to 170C/325F/gas 3.
Wrap each pigeon in a bacon rasher.
Push a small skewer through one wing,
across the body and out through the
opposite wing to secure the bacon. Tie the
legs together with string.

SMALL GAME BIRDS

In other parts of the world many
small wild birds are shot or
trapped for food, even though
they provide no more than a few
mouthfuls. In Britain, only a few
such birds can legally be taken
and few people would want to
do so in any case. Farmers can
still shoot rooks, which are
classified as vermin, but rook pie
is a dish of the past.

The small wild birds which are
eaten in this country are mainly
quail, woodcock and snipe. Quail
are very similar to partridge;
cook them in the same way but
allow one per person. Nowadays
they are farmed, so available all
year round. Woodcock and snipe
are true game birds, instantly
recognizable by their extremely
long bills. Woodcock is the
larger, but neither makes more
than a single serving. They can
be roasted or casseroled.

2 Heat 25g/1oz butter and 2tbls oil in a
large, heavy, flameproof casserole.
Fry the pigeons for 10 minutes or until well
browned all over. Remove to a plate. Add
half the onions to the fat remaining in the
casserole and fry for 10 minutes until soft
and golden, stirring frequently.

3 Return the pigeons to the casserole.
Add the stock and bouquet garni;
season with salt and pepper to taste.
Cover and cook in the oven for 45 minutes
or until the pigeons are cooked but the
flesh is still firm.

4 Meanwhile melt the remaining 15g/
½oz butter and 1tbls oil in a heavy
saucepan. Fry the remaining onion gently
for 5 minutes. Add the diced salt pork and
carrot and fry over medium heat for 10
minutes or until the onions are a rich
brown, stirring frequently. Stir in the
lentils and cook over low heat for 5
minutes, stirring frequently.

5 Add 600ml/1pt water to the lentil
mixture, along with the thyme, one
bay leaf and pepper to taste. Bring to the
boil, then reduce the heat to low, cover
and cook for 20 minutes or until the lentils
are softened but still very firm. Remove
from the heat and leave, uncovered, until
needed.

6 Remove the pigeons from the casserole. Discard the skewers and strings
and cut the birds in half along the
breastbone. Cut the bacon into thin strips.

7 Add the lentil mixture to the juices in
the casserole and stir together. Bury
the pigeon halves in lentils and add the
bacon strips. The mixture will be rather
liquid at this stage. Cover and return to the
oven for 15 minutes, until the pigeons and
lentils are very tender and much of the
liquid has been absorbed.

8 Remove the bouquet garni, garnish
with bay leaves and serve hot.

Moroccan grouse

- **Preparation: 20 minutes,
  plus marinating**

- **Cooking: 1 hour 10 minutes**

2 grouse, dressed weight 350g/12oz
  each
1 Spanish onion, thinly sliced
225ml/8fl oz olive oil
¾tsp ground ginger
¾tsp ground turmeric
¾tsp ground coriander
¾tsp ground cumin
3tbls finely chopped coriander
  leaves
salt and pepper
4 tomatoes, skinned, de-seeded
  and quartered

- **Serves 4**

- **675cals/2835kjs per serving**

1 Cut each grouse into four serving
pieces, removing the back and breast
bones. Lay the pieces in a shallow dish
and cover with the onion slices.

2 Put the oil in a measuring jug with the
four spices and coriander leaves.
Season with salt and pepper to taste. Pour
over the grouse and turn to ensure they

are well coated. Cover and marinate in the refrigerator overnight.

3 Bring the grouse to room temperature. Put 4tbls of the marinade in a flameproof casserole and brown the grouse and onion. Add the remaining marinade and 300ml/½pt water. Cover and simmer gently for 40 minutes.

4 Cut the potatoes into even-sized wedge-shapes. Put them on top of the grouse after the 40 minutes, along with the tomatoes. Re-cover and cook for a further 20 minutes. Taste and adjust the seasoning; serve hot.

Pheasant in cream sauce

● **Preparation: 30 minutes**

● **Cooking: 1½ hours**

1 pheasant, dressed with liver
  reserved
salt and pepper
50-75g/2-3oz butter
2tbls oil
4tbls finely chopped onion
4tbls finely chopped carrot
¼tsp dried thyme
1 bay leaf, crumbled
2-3tbls brandy
2tbls flour
425ml/¾pt whipping cream (or
  half single, half double cream)
1 large slice of bread, 1cm/½in
  thick, cut lengthways from a
  large loaf
lemon juice

● **Serves 4**

● **695cals/2920kjs per serving**

1 Sprinkle the pheasant inside and out with salt and pepper. Truss in the same way as a chicken (Shopping basket page 80)

2 Heat 25g/1oz butter and the oil in a large, heavy, flameproof casserole. Put in the pheasant and cook over medium heat for 10-15 minutes, turning until browned all over.

3 Reduce the heat to low. Add the onion, carrot, thyme and bay leaf. Cover and cook for 20 minutes. Remove from the heat.

4 Heat 2tbls brandy in a ladle, set alight and pour over the pheasant and vegetables. When the flames die out, remove the pheasant, add the flour and cook for 3 minutes to make a pale roux, stirring constantly.

5 Stir in 300ml/½pt of the cream. Bring to simmering point over low heat, then add the pheasant. Baste with the sauce, cover and simmer very gently until the pheasant is tender and the sauce slightly reduced. Turn the bird occasionally and baste with the sauce to stop it drying out. A young bird will take 30-40 minutes; an older one considerably longer.

6 Shortly before the pheasant is ready, trim the slice of bread to a rectangle large enough to serve as a base for it. Fry in 15-25g/½-1oz butter until golden and crisp on both sides.

7 If necessary, add a further 15g/½oz butter to the pan and fry the pheasant liver over high heat just long enough for it to change colour, turning and crushing it.

8 Transfer the pan contents to a small bowl. Add another 15g/½oz butter and mash to a paste with the fork, flavouring with 1-2 drops of brandy and a squeeze of lemon juice. Season with salt and pepper to taste. Spread the mixture over the fried bread and put it on a warmed serving dish; keep hot.

9 Lift the tender pheasant out of the casserole; discard the skewers and string. Put it on the bread and keep hot.

10 Pass the sauce through a sieve into a clean saucepan, add the remaining 150ml/¼pt cream, season to taste and simmer for 1-2 minutes. Spoon over the pheasant and serve at once.

4 Remove the casserole from the oven and reduce the heat to 170C/375F/ gas 3. Moisten the casserole with the wine, cover tightly and return to the oven for a further 40-45 minutes or until the rabbit is tender. ⏱

5 Untie the strings and discard the bacon. Arrange the rabbit pieces in a shallow heatproof serving dish and return to the switched off oven to keep hot.

6 Strain the contents of the casserole through a fine sieve into a saucepan. Press the vegetables with a wooden spoon to extract their juices without rubbing them through.

7 Mix the cornflour to a smooth paste with 2tbls cold water, then blend in 2-3tbls of the sauce. Stir the mixture into the remaining sauce, bring to the boil and simmer for 2-3 minutes until thickened, stirring constantly.

8 Spoon the sauce over the rabbit joints and surround with the hot noodles.

Jugged hare

● *Preparation: 15 minutes*

● *Cooking: 3¼ hours*

1 hare, jointed, blood reserved
2tbls seasoned flour
50g/2oz dripping, preferably
   bacon
2 onions, chopped
2 carrots, chopped
1 celery stalk, chopped
850ml/1½pt chicken or vegetable
   stock
1 bouquet garni
salt and pepper
150ml/¼pt port
1tbls redcurrant jelly

● *Serves 6-8* 🍴 ££

● *290cals/1220kjs per serving*

KING OF THE MOORS

Grouse comes from the Scottish moors and its flesh is subtly flavoured by the heather it feeds on. Birds are in limited supply – a great deal of aura that surrounds grouse stems from its rarity, as true red or Scottish grouse is found nowhere else. Consequently young birds shot at the beginning of the season – the famous 12th August – are extremely expensive and only enough for one. Older, larger birds suitable for casseroling should be around in late autumn to early winter at much lower prices. These can be split to serve two.

1 If using dried tarragon, put it into a small bowl and pour on 1tbls boiling water. Leave to infuse for a few minutes. Heat the oven to 230C/450F/gas 8.

2 Drain the infused tarragon if using. Mix the fresh or infused tarragon with the mustard. Season each piece of rabbit with salt and pepper, then spread lightly with the tarragon mustard. Wrap in a piece of bacon, securing it with string.

3 Butter a casserole large enough to take the rabbit pieces in one layer. Cover the base with a layer of onion and tomato. Sprinkle this with garlic, thyme, bay leaf and a little salt and pepper. Lay the rabbit pieces on top. Bake, uncovered, for 10 minutes or until the rabbit pieces are lightly coloured.

Rabbit in tarragon sauce

● *Preparation: 20 minutes*

● *Cooking: 1 hour*

2-3tsp chopped fresh tarragon, or
   1tsp dried
900g/2lb rabbit, cut into joints
1tbls Dijon mustard
salt and pepper
about 50g/2oz unsmoked streaky
   bacon rashers
butter, for greasing
2 onions, sliced
4 tomatoes, sliced
2 garlic cloves, chopped
¼tsp dried thyme
1 bay leaf, crumbled
150ml/¼pt dry white wine
2-3tsp cornflour
hot buttered noodles, to serve

● *Serves 4* 🍴 ££

● *525cals/2205kjs per serving*

1 Coat the pieces of hare in seasoned flour, shaking off any excess. Heat the oven to 180C/350F/gas 4.

2 Melt the dripping in a large flame-proof casserole. Add the hare pieces and fry over medium heat until evenly browned all over. Add the onion, carrots and celery and cook for a further 5 minutes, stirring occasionally.

3 Pour in the stock, add the bouquet garni and season with salt and pepper to taste. Put in the oven for 3 hours until the hare is very well cooked and the meat parts easily from the bone.

4 Remove the casserole from the oven. Put the reserved hare blood in a bowl and carefully stir in 3tbls of the hot cooking liquid. Gradually stir the blood mixture into the casserole. Then stir in the port and redcurrant jelly.

5 Put over a very low heat and reheat gently, without boiling, for 5 minutes.

Cook's tips

If you do not have the hare's blood thicken the sauce with cornflour.

Venison hot-pot

- **Preparation: 20 minutes, plus marinating**

- **Cooking: 2 hours 40 minutes**

1kg/2¼lb shoulder or haunch of venison, rolled and tied
600ml/1pt beef stock

450g/1lb baby onions
450g/1lb button mushrooms
225g/8oz canned artichoke hearts, drained
beurre manié, made with 25g/1oz each butter and flour
For the marinade:
600ml/1pt red wine
2tbls wine vinegar
4 garlic cloves, crushed
1tsp allspice
1tsp dried basil
2 bay leaves
2 anchovies, pounded
salt and pepper

● *Serves 6*

● *405cals/1700kjs per serving*

1 Combine the marinade ingredients in a large flameproof casserole or fresh plastic bag and add the joint of venison. Cover and marinate overnight, turning occasionally. The plastic bag makes turning much easier.

2 Heat the oven to 150C/300F/gas 2. Add the stock and onions to the casserole and stir in well. Cover the top of the casserole dish with foil and then put on the lid. Cook in the oven for 2 hours.

3 Add the mushrooms and artichoke hearts to the casserole and return to the oven for another 30 minutes or until the meat is very tender; a fork should pierce it easily. Meanwhile make the *beurre manié* by mixing the butter and flour together.

4 Transfer the casserole to a low heat and add the *beurre manié* in little pieces stirring well between each addition, until the sauce has thickened slightly. Slice the meat and transfer it to a warmed serving dish; pour the sauce over. Serve the vegetables.

BIRDS OF A FEATHER

A game bird bought in the feather — unplucked and undrawn — will need hanging for a short period to develop flavour. This should already have been done when you buy them oven-ready or frozen.

Forget the tales about hanging game birds until reeking and maggot-ridden. For most people's taste, hanging the bird until a tail feather comes out easily when pulled, is quite sufficient. Hang the bird by the neck, in a cool airy place and check it every day. As soon as it passes the feather test, pluck, draw and refrigerate it.

Depending on how warm the weather is, hang the bird in a good current of air — 3 days for a pheasant. Grouse usually needs about 3 days but can hang for 5 depending on the weather. Partridge 3-4 days. Quail, woodcock and snipe can be eaten unhung or hung for up to 3 days.

Joint Effort

A bacon joint can provide anything from an economical
family supper to a substantial Sunday lunch,
while a ham is a luxury item, perfect as the centrepiece for a buffet table

*H*AM IS DRY-SALTED, then lightly or heavily smoked. Most are then cooked, but some, notably the Italian *prosciutto* or Parma ham, are left raw. The most famous types of cooked ham are York and Suffolk from Britain, and American Virginia.

In Britain ham is almost always sold pre-cooked, and often sliced. If you want a whole or half ham for a buffet, order it from a specialist delicatessen or superior grocer.

Bacon is raw pig meat which has been immersed in brine and then hung for a time to mature it. Unsmoked bacon (also called green) is matured for only about a week and has a pale rind and mild flavour. Smoked bacon is matured and then smoked. This gives it a brown rind and a richer, saltier flavour.

The gammon or leg is the prime cut: solid meat with only a thin covering of fat. As a whole one is large, weighing up to 8kg/18lb, it is cut into smaller joints. A middle gammon is about half the weight of the whole one, and is usually sold boned, rolled and cut down into even smaller joints, or gammon steaks. Corner gammon is a triangular piece cut from just above the middle gammon. A hock is cut from the knuckle end of the leg.

Preparing and cooking
Traditionally the first step in cooking any bacon joint was to soak it overnight in cold water to remove excess salt. But refrigerated storage means that bacon is much less heavily salted nowadays. For small joints, 2-3 hours is sufficient.

If time is short, an alternative method with a small joint is to put it into a pan of cold water, bring very slowly to the boil, then drain off the water and cook the joint.

Boiling: this is a misnomer as it takes gentle simmering to make

Braised bacon collar (page 134)

bacon juicy and tender. Starting from when the water boils, allow about 45 minutes per kilogram or 20 minutes per pound for an average-sized joint, plus 20 minutes over. A very large joint or whole gammon will need longer — 30/15 minutes per kg/lb plus 30/15 minutes over.

To preserve maximum flavour, put the joint in a close-fitting pan and barely cover it with cold water. Bring slowly to the boil and, if liked, add flavouring ingredients — peppercorns, a bay leaf and some root vegetables — but no salt. For a sweet taste add a tablespoon of brown sugar or treacle. Cover tightly and simmer gently until a sharp knife penetrates easily.

Remove the meat from the cooking liquid (save this for stock) as soon as it is done and peel off the rind. If it is to be served cold, cool it as quickly as possible (to reduce the risk of bacteria growth); chill.

Baking in foil: this is a convenient method as the joint needs no attention during cooking. Soak and weigh the joint. Allow about 65 minutes per kilogram, 30 minutes per pound at 190C/375F/gas 5. Wrap the joint loosely in foil and put on a rack in a baking tin. Pour a cupful of water into the tin. When cooked, pour off the juices from inside the foil to make a sauce.

Glazing: a bacon joint may be glazed and the cooking finished off in the oven. The initial cooking can be boiling or baking. Remove the joint when it is about three-quarters cooked. Cut off the rind, leaving about 5mm/¼in fat behind: this can be scored into diamond shapes. Brush with a glaze (see Finishing touches, page 134) and bake at 200C/400F/gas 6, basting now and then with the glaze.

Braising: this preserves all the flavour of the meat, so be sure to soak it. Allow 75 minutes cooking time per kilo (35 minutes per pound) plus 35 minutes over, at 180C/350F/gas 4.

To braise, rest the joint on a bed of root vegetables lightly fried in a heavy casserole, then barely covered with stock. Cover tightly during cooking. Serve the meat with the vegetables and a sauce made from the stock.

Spiced glazed gammon

● **Preparation: 15 minutes, plus 3 hours soaking**

● **Cooking: 2 hours 10 minutes**

1.8kg/4lb middle gammon, rolled and tied, soaked for 3 hours, then drained
5 whole black peppercorns
50g/2oz brown sugar
20 cloves
1½tbls flour
300ml/½pt dry cider
pepper
For the garnish:
25g/1oz butter
2 dessert apples, peeled, cored and sliced into rings
parsley sprigs

● **Serves 6-8 plus leftovers**   ⑪ ££

● **355cals/1490kjs per serving**

1 Put the joint in a large saucepan and cover with cold water. Add the peppercorns and bring slowly to the boil. Reduce the heat, cover and simmer for 30 minutes.

2 Heat the oven to 180C/350F/gas 4. Wrap the joint loosely in foil and put on a rack in a roasting tin. Add enough water to cover the bottom of the tin.

3 Roast for 1 hour, then remove from the oven and open the foil. Discard the water in the tin. Raise the oven heat to 200C/400F/gas 6. Remove the string and rind from the joint and, using a sharp knife,

USING THE STOCK

The stock from a good piece of gammon is so rich that it gels when cold. Strain, cool rapidly (to reduce the risk of bacteria growth), then chill. Scrape the soft fat off the top before using.

Gammon stock can be used like any other kind, but it tends to be salty, and may need diluting with vegetable stock or water. It makes a good foundation for soups, or use it to make a sauce for ham or pork, or to give added flavour when boiling root vegetables or rice, but don't add any salt during cooking.

lightly score the thin layer of fat in a criss-cross pattern.

4 Cover the fatty surface with brown sugar, pressing it down onto the fat. Stud the surface with the cloves, following the criss-cross pattern.

5 Leaving the foil open so that it just loosely covers the lean meat surface, return the joint to the oven for a further 30 minutes. Remove, transfer to a serving dish and keep warm.

6 Heat the butter for the garnish in a large frying pan and fry the apple rings until just tender, turning once.

7 Pour the juices left in the foil into the roasting tin. Stir in the flour and cook over medium heat for 2 minutes, stirring. Remove from the heat and stir in the cider, then return to the heat and bring to the boil, stirring constantly. Season to taste.

8 Arrange the apple rings around the joint with a small sprig of parsley in the centre of each one. Serve the sauce separately, in a sauceboat.

How to ··· *carve a knuckle end of ham*

Stand the ham on the flat end and carve a V below the knuckle. Cut slices horizontally towards the bone but do not detach them.

Remove the loosely attached small bone at the knuckle end of the ham. Release the slices by cutting parallel to the bone.

Turn the ham on its side and carve parallel to the bone, cutting neat slices. Turn the ham over and repeat on the other side.

Bacon with hot potato salad

- *Preparation: 25 minutes, plus soaking*

- *Cooking: 1 hour 20 minutes*

1.4kg/3lb forehock joint smoked bacon
900g/2lb waxy potatoes
100g/4oz frozen peas
150ml/¼pt dry white wine or cider
1 Spanish onion, finely chopped
1tbls olive oil
salt and pepper
2tbls chopped parsley
curly endive, to garnish

- *Serves 6* ①£

- *435cals/1825kjs per serving*

1 Soak the joint in cold water for 3 hours, or overnight if you prefer a milder flavour. Drain it and put in a saucepan with enough fresh cold water just to cover. Bring to the boil and skim off any scum. Cover the pan and simmer gently for 1 hour.

2 Cut the potatoes into large chunks, add to the pan with the bacon joint, cover and cook for a further 20 minutes or until tender. Meanwhile, cook the peas, drain and reserve.

3 Using a slotted spoon, lift out the potatoes and put them in a large bowl. Immediately pour over the wine. Stir in the onion and reserved peas and leave to stand for about 5 minutes.

4 Sprinkle the oil over the potatoes and season to taste. Mix the salad gently ▶

◀ to avoid breaking up the potatoes. Transfer to a warm serving dish and sprinkle with parsley.

5 Drain the joint and strip off the rind. Cut the meat into thick slices and arrange on a large warm serving platter. Serve hot accompanied by the potato salad and garnished with sprigs of curly endive.

CARVING

To carve a ham or gammon properly you need a ham knife, which is a very long, slim-bladed, round-ended carving knife. Make sure that it is razor-sharp, so that it slices thinly and evenly. Stand the ham on a large board or plate and use a piece of foil, a clean cloth or a cutlet frill to cover the bone and get a grip on it.

Braised bacon collar

- **Preparation: 15 minutes, plus 3 hours soaking**
- **Cooking: 2 hours 10 minutes**

25g/1oz butter
2 large cooking apples, peeled, cored and chopped
3 celery stalks, chopped
1 onion, finely chopped
300ml/½pt dry cider
1.5kg/3¼lb collar joint of unsmoked bacon, soaked

- **Serves 6-8**
- **365cals/1555kjs per serving**

1 Heat the oven to 180C/350F/gas 4. Melt the butter in a flameproof casserole over low heat, add the apples, celery and onion and cook until softened. Pour in the cider and bring to the boil. Put the drained joint on top of the fruit and vegetables and cover tightly. Cook in the oven for about 1½-2 hours or until the bacon is tender.

2 Remove the joint and peel off the rind. Put the bacon on a warmed serving dish and keep warm. Drain the cooking juices into a jug and remove any surplus fat.

3 Purée the fruit and vegetables in a pan, set over low heat and gradually stir in enough of the reserved juices to make a pouring sauce. To serve, slice the bacon thickly; serve the sauce separately.

Tarragon ham

- **Preparation: 10 minutes**
- **Cooking: 25 minutes**

400ml/14fl oz medium-dry white wine
400ml/14fl oz chicken stock
1 bouquet garni
1-2tsp tomato purée
salt and pepper
4 thick slices cooked ham, each about 100g/4oz
20g/¾oz butter
20g/¾oz flour
1tbls chopped fresh tarragon or 1tsp dried
150ml/¼pt single cream
fresh tarragon, to garnish (optional)

- **Serves 4**
- **370cals/1555kjs per serving**

1 Put the wine and stock in a large pan, add the bouquet garni and tomato purée, stir well and boil steadily until reduced by half. Remove the bouquet garni and season. Add the ham, cover and simmer gently until heated through thoroughly: about 5 minutes. Remove from the heat.

2 Melt the butter in a clean pan and, off the heat, stir in the flour. Cook for 1 minute, stirring, then strain in the ham liquid and the dried tarragon, if using.

FINISHING TOUCHES

Bacon joints can be brushed with a variety of sweet-sour glazes and toppings before baking, designed to complement the salty meat. Joints to be served cold can be glazed or coated with breadcrumbs. Apply all these to the fat surface only.

Honey glaze: mix 2tbls each clear honey and soft brown sugar with 1tsp made mustard.

Apricot glaze: mix 3tbls sieved apricot jam with 1tsp ground cloves, 1tbls soft brown sugar and 2tsp lemon juice.

Crispy topping: mix 1tbls each clear honey and wine vinegar and spoon over the fat. Sprinkle with a 50:50 mixture of brown sugar and dry breadcrumbs.

Bring the sauce to the boil, stirring constantly, until slightly thickened. Reduce the heat, simmer for 3 minutes and stir in the cream and fresh tarragon. Transfer the slices of ham to a warmed serving dish, spoon over the cream sauce and garnish with fresh tarragon, if using.

Variations

If you cannot get the large thick slices of ham needed for this dish, substitute gammon steaks and cook them in wine, water or a mixture of the two before proceeding with the recipe.

Frying Tonight

Deep-frying fish is a simple technique but timing and temperature must be just right to get succulent, moist fish contrasting with a crisp, dry golden coating

*D*EEP-FRYING IS the ideal way of cooking any kind of white fish. Provided that the oil is really hot when the fish goes in the oil, the protective coating of batter, flour or egg-and-breadcrumbs sets, sealing all the juice and flavour inside. In addition, it stops the oil from soaking into the fish. The end result should be a crisp brown coating enclosing succulent, grease-free fish.

Choosing the fish
Fillets of cod or haddock, or portions of other white fish such as halibut or huss, are the most popular choices for deep-frying. These can be cooked in one-portion sizes, cut into strips to make brochettes or goujons, or into small cubes for Japanese bites. Fish such as whitebait or sprats are excellent fried whole, as are small shellfish (scampi and prawns) and rings of squid. Oily fish (trout and herrings) are not suitable.

Whatever type of fish is used, in order for it to cook quickly enough the pieces should be no more than 2.5cm/1in thick. Frozen fish should be completely defrosted.

Coating the fish
Before being plunged into hot oil the fish must be given a protective coating. Batter is delicious but makes a very substantial dish – it can be lightened by adding whisked egg white to the basic mix.

For a lighter dish use a simple coating of flour or egg-and-breadcrumbs. The breadcrumbs can be fresh, which gives the best flavour; or dried, for convenience. But they must be very fine, or they will fall off the fish during cooking.

Very small fish like whitebait, or tiny pieces of fish, can just be coated in seasoned flour.

Cooking the fish
The fish can be cooked in any heavy pan deep enough to hold sufficient oil to cover it completely. A chip pan can be used, but remove the basket for a batter coating as it would stick. A deep-fat fryer is a good buy if you cook this way a lot, as it

Fried squid rings (page 138)

automatically brings the oil to and keeps it at the right temperature.

If using an ordinary pan always test the oil with a frying thermometer or a bread cube (see Temperature test, below), before putting in the fish. Do not fry more than two portions at a time, or as many small pieces as will fit comfortably; if you try to fit too much in at once, you will lower the temperature of the oil. Cook the fish until the coating is crisp and golden brown, turning it once with a slotted spoon or fish slice to brown both sides evenly. This will take 1½-5 minutes, depending on the size and thickness of the pieces. Adjust the heat as necessary. Lift the fish out, drain briefly and lay on absorbent paper.

Temperature test

Heat the oil until it reaches 190C/375F on a deep-frying thermometer. Alternatively, drop in a 1cm/½in square of day-old white bread. It should turn golden brown in 50 seconds.

Fried plaice with spiced mayonnaise

- **Preparation: 20 minutes**
- **Cooking: 20 minutes**

8 small fillets of plaice
flour
1-2 large eggs, beaten
100g/4oz fresh white breadcrumbs
oil, for deep-frying
lemon slices, to garnish
For the spiced mayonnaise:
300ml/½ pt mayonnaise
1 tsp hot pepper sauce
1 tbls each chopped fresh tarragon,
    fennel leaves and basil
1 tbls tomato purée
1 tbls finely chopped spring onion
1 tbls freshly grated root ginger
salt and pepper

- **Serves 4**   (♈♈) (££)
- **980cals/4115kjs per serving**

1 First make the spiced mayonnaise: put the mayonnaise in a bowl, stir in the remaining ingredients, season with salt and pepper to taste, then cover and chill.

2 Dry the fish well on absorbent paper and season with salt and pepper.

3 Put the flour, beaten eggs and breadcrumbs in three separate shallow dishes. Dip each fillet first in flour, shaking off excess, then in beaten egg. Finally coat them in breadcrumbs, patting them on firmly. If possible, chill for 15 minutes to set the coating.

4 Heat the oil to 190C/375F. Fry four of the fillets for 2-3 minutes or until golden brown. Drain and keep hot while frying the remainder.

5 Serve the fish hot, garnished with lemon slices and accompanied by the spiced mayonnaise.

Cook's tips

If serving chips cook them immediately before the fish and keep hot in the oven. Reheat and test the oil again before frying the fish.

How to ··· egg-and-breadcrumb fish

Put flour, beaten egg and breadcrumbs in three separate bowls. First dip the fish in flour; shake off any excess.

Next, dip each piece of floured fish carefully in the beaten egg, making quite sure that it is well coated on all sides.

Last, dip the portions in the bowl of breadcrumbs and pat them firmly into place. Again, make sure that both sides are evenly coated.

Seafood brochettes

- **Preparation: 25 minutes**

- **Cooking: 20 minutes**

2 × 225g/8oz cod fillets
flour
16 large, cooked, peeled prawns
oil, for deep-frying
paprika
lemon slices, to garnish
flat-leaved parsley, to garnish
For the mustard sauce:
25g/1oz butter
1½tbls flour
300ml/½pt hot fish stock
1tbls Dijon mustard
salt and pepper

- **Serves 4**

- **325cals/1365kjs per serving**

WHAT WENT WRONG?

Soggy, greasy fish: the oil was not hot enough, or too much fish was cooked at once.
Coating overdone, fish underdone: the oil was too hot.
Fish unevenly coated with batter: the batter mixture wasn't thick enough.

1 First make the sauce: melt the butter in a saucepan, stir in the flour and cook, stirring constantly, for 1-2 minutes. Gradually pour in the hot stock, stirring with a wire whisk to prevent lumps from forming. Simmer for 5 minutes, stirring occasionally, until the sauce has thickened. Remove from the heat, stir in the mustard and season with salt and pepper.

2 Cut each cod fillet into eight squares. Spread the flour on a flat plate and season well with salt and pepper. Coat the fish and prawns thoroughly with flour, shaking off the excess.

3 Thread eight metal skewers with four pieces of seafood each, rolling the prawns up tightly and alternating them with cod. Heat the oil to 190C/375F in a saucepan fitted with a wire basket.

4 Put four skewers into the wire basket and fry in the hot oil for 1-2 minutes or until lightly golden. Drain on absorbent paper and keep hot. Fry the second batch in the same way.

5 Reheat the mustard sauce gently and divide between four individual plates. Put two skewers on each plate. Season well with salt and pepper and a little paprika, garnish and serve hot.

Cook's tips

The skewers will get very hot, so take care not to pick them up in your fingers. If they have rings at the top you can thread them on a piece of string to lift them in and out.

Japanese bites

- **Preparation: 15 minutes**

- **Cooking: 15 minutes**

4 fish steaks or fillets
seasoned flour, for dusting
oil, for deep-frying
spring onion tassels, to garnish
For the dip:
150ml/¼pt chicken stock
1tbls dark soy sauce
2tbls dry sherry
½tsp sugar
¼tsp ground ginger
1tsp cornflour
For the batter:
1 egg, lightly beaten
1tbls soy sauce
100g/4oz flour

- **Serves 4**

- **405cals/1700kjs per serving**

1 First make the dip: combine the stock, soy sauce, sherry, sugar and ▶

Crisp and dry

Always drain deep-fried fish on several layers of absorbent paper to remove any trace of greasiness and keep the coating crisp. If portions have to be kept warm, line a baking tin with the paper.

◀ ginger in a saucepan. Use 2tbls of the liquid to blend into the cornflour. Stir this into the remaining liquid. Bring to the boil, then simmer for 5 minutes, stirring until slightly thickened. Keep warm.

2 Pat the fish dry with absorbent paper, then cut into 4cm/1½in cubes. Dust with seasoned flour.

3 Make the batter: mix the egg and soy sauce in a bowl. Gradually beat in 7tbls water, then sift in the flour a little at a time, beating well after each addition.

4 Heat the oil in a heavy saucepan to 190C/375F. Dip the fish into the batter and deep-fry in batches for 2 minutes or until golden. Drain, garnish and serve with individual bowls of warm dip.

Microwave hints

Use your microwave to make the dip. Combine all the ingredients in a large jug. Cover and microwave at 100% (high) for 2-2½ minutes or until hot, stirring once.

BETTER BATTER

The batter used for the Fried Squid rings (see right) is a basic fritter batter suitable for deep-frying any fish. Do not beat it more than is necessary to blend the ingredients together – over-beating will make it tough.
For a lighter batter use water or cider instead of milk and add 1-2 stiffly beaten egg whites just before using.

Allowing batter to stand before use improves the texture but is not essential unless it contains alcohol, which needs time to ferment.

Batters can also be chilled for 15 minutes (but no longer). This sets the mixture, making it less likely to fall off.

Fried squid rings

- *Preparation: 30 minutes, plus standing*
- *Cooking: 20 minutes*

8 very small squid
oil, for deep-frying
flour, for coating
1 lemon, quartered
For the batter:
100g/4oz flour
1tsp baking powder
¼tsp salt
1 egg
200ml/7fl oz milk

- *Serves 4*   ⑪ ⑫
- *400cals/1680kjs per serving*

1 First make the batter: sift the flour, baking powder and salt into a bowl. Break the egg into the centre and blend in with a fork. Add the milk and whisk until smooth. Allow to stand for 20-30 minutes if time allows.

2 Prepare the squid: stretch each one out and pull off the head section. Cut off and keep the tentacles and discard the middle part which includes the eyes, ink sac (if present) and intestines. Pull the transparent central bone and discard. Under cold running water, rub the violet outer membrane from the body, then gently turn it inside out and wash well. Dry with absorbent paper. Cut the cone-shaped body into rings. Wash the tentacles and cut into short lengths.

3 Heat the oil in a heavy saucepan to 190C/375F. Dip the prepared squid in flour and then into the batter, allowing any surplus to run off. Fry a few pieces at a time in the hot oil until they are crisp and golden. Drain on absorbent paper and serve on small individual plates with a lemon quarter.

OIL OR FAT?

Deep-frying can be done in oil, lard or a combination of both. But oil is preferable as it reaches the high temperature required quickly and with less tendency to burn.

The oil can be re-used several times, but only for fish as it will retain some flavour. Allow it to cool, then strain through a fine sieve and return to the bottle through a funnel.

Beefing it Up

A succulent joint of beef is always a treat, and even more so when roasted and carved to perfection

ORIGINALLY ROASTING MEANT cooking meat on a rotating spit, but nowadays it usually means cooking it uncovered and without liquid in a closed oven. Technically, it should be called baking.

Only the very best cuts of beef, from the back and hindquarters, are suitable. It must be top quality: a rich red colour, firm and moist to the touch, coarse-grained and flecked with creamy-white fat.

In the past, beef was roasted at high temperatures so that the outside became brown and crusty. Today the average Sunday joint is so small that this would cause too much shrinkage. The modern way is to roast at a much lower tempera-ture (except for a whole fillet which must be cooked quickly to prevent drying out). A boned joint weighing less than 1kg/2¼lb will not roast satisfactorily and should be pot-roasted (that is, simmered in a little liquid).

Suitable cuts

Topside: this is sold boned and rolled, and is the cheapest roasting cut, though not the most flavour-some or tender. It has little or no natural fat so is usually sold already barded (wrapped round with a layer of fat) to prevent it from drying out during cooking. If you like well-done meat, topside is better pot-roasted, as it becomes dry if cooked beyond the rare stage.

Silverside is salted topside, which was traditionally boiled but can also be roasted.

Sirloin: a whole sirloin consists of rib bones and sometimes a section of fillet. A rolled sirloin is minus bones and fillet. Both are very tender, with excellent flavour.

Rib roast: this can consist of wing ribs, top ribs or back and foreribs. It is a magnificent-looking joint, ideal for a very special occasion. On-the-bone rib roast has the best flavour, but it is also sold boned and rolled.

Fillet: although this is the most expensive of roasting joints it is

Rolled roast beef (page 142)

139

very tender, and as it is lean and boneless, a little goes a long way.

How much to buy: If the joint is on the bone, allow 225-375g/8-13oz per person bought weight. If it is boned, 175-225g/6-8oz is sufficient, reducing to 100-150g/4-5oz for fillet.

Preparation and cooking

Take the joint out of the refrigerator 2-3 hours before cooking to allow it to come to room temperature; this improves flavour. Wipe it with a clean damp cloth and trim off excess fat. Season with pepper but not salt as this draws out juices. If it has no natural fat, bard or lard it with fat if the butcher has not already done so. Spread the lean meat with dripping or other fat, and baste the joint while it is cooking.

A rolled joint benefits from being raised above the hot fat on a metal rack, although if it has bones this is not necessary, as they will support it and keep it clear of the fat.

Slow roasting produces moist tender meat, evenly cooked through but without the brown, crusty exterior produced by fast roasting. See Roasting beef, page 80, for times and temperatures.

If the meat is to be served hot, roast it according to your taste: rare, medium or well done. If it is to be served cold have it rare, so that most of the juices are retained and the meat will be tender and moist.

Accompaniments

The traditional accompaniments to a prime roast of beef are gravy made from the meat juices (see page 80), roast potatoes, Yorkshire pudding, a green vegetable and horseradish sauce or mustard.

Yorkshire pudding needs a hot oven, which poses a problem with modern low-temperature roasting. Solve this by making individual puddings in a sectioned tin which will cook in about 20 minutes. At the end of the beef's cooking time turn the oven up to 220C/425F/gas 7 and remove the meat to a warm place. Heat an oiled tin placed on the top shelf then pour the Yorkshire pudding batter into the hot oil and put in the oven. Make the gravy and carve the joint while the puddings cook.

Beef fillet with onion sauce

- **Preparation: 30 minutes**

- **Cooking: 50 minutes – 1 hour 50 minutes, plus resting**

2.3kg/5lb fillet of beef, all fat removed
¼tsp ground coriander
salt and pepper
50g/2oz butter, melted
juice of 2 oranges
parsley sprig and orange slices, to garnish

For the onion sauce:
3 large onions, chopped
40g/1½oz butter
1tbls flour
1-2tsp Dijon mustard
300ml/½pt canned beef consommé
2tbls red wine (optional)

- **Serves 12**　

- **375cals/1575kjs per serving**

1 Heat the oven to 230C/450F/gas 8. Weigh the meat and calculate the cooking time. Allow 10 minutes per 450g/1lb for very rare meat; 14 minutes for medium-rare and 21-22 minutes for well-done. Mix the coriander with ½tsp pepper and rub all over the beef. Fold back the thin end of the fillet and tie it to the thicker part so that the meat is all one thickness. Put in a roasting tin.

2 Brush the meat all over with the melted butter. Put it on a rack in a roasting tin. Cook for the calculated time, testing towards the end. Baste every 20

TESTING TIME

Cooking times for roast meat can never be 100% per cent accurate because no two joints are exactly alike. So test towards the end of the cooking time by inserting a skewer into the centre. If the juice that runs out is red the meat is rare; if it's pink the meat is medium; clear juices indicate well-done meat.

To judge the degree of cooking very precisely invest in a meat thermometer. Insert it into the centre, but not touching any bone. For rare meat it should register 60C/140F, for medium 70C/160F and for well-done meat 80C/180F.

minutes, adding the orange juice to the pan after the first basting.

3 Meanwhile, start making the sauce. Put the onions into a heavy pan with the butter and cook over low heat for 30-40 minutes, stirring frequently, until the onions are very soft and golden – don't let them brown. Then stir in the flour, cook for 4-5 minutes and mix in the mustard. Gradually add the consommé, stirring constantly, and pour in the wine, if using. Cover and simmer for 20 minutes, stirring occasionally.

4 When the meat is cooked, transfer it to a heated platter and leave it to rest for 5-10 minutes at room temperature. Skim the fat from the pan juices, then add them to the sauce. Taste and adjust the seasoning. Carve the beef into thin slices, place on a heated serving dish and garnish with parsley and orange slices. Hand the sauce round separately.

How to ··· *carve a whole sirloin*

Stand the joint upright, backbone down. Cut through the flank, the fatty extension of the main part, and remove it. Carve into thin slices and lay them on a heated serving platter.

Run the knife around the fillet (if present, as here) to free it from the rib bones. Remove the fillet, carve it thinly and arrange on the serving platter with the slices of flank.

Run the carving knife down against the rib bone and then turn and cut across the backbone to loosen the main part of the joint, the uppercut. (This is sometimes called the eye.)

Put the uppercut, fatty side up, on the carving board. Cut the meat into thin slices and add them to the platter. Serve each person with a selection of different slices.

Old English roast beef

- **Preparation: 15 minutes**

- **Cooking: 1 hour 45 minutes–3 hours, plus resting**

2.3kg/5lb sirloin on the bone, or rib roast
2tbls flour
1tbls mustard powder
salt and coarsely ground pepper
50g/2oz dripping or butter
4tbls red wine or water, warmed
sprigs of watercress,
   to garnish
Yorkshire puddings, to serve

- **Serves 6**   ① £££

- **465cals/1955kjs per serving**

1 Heat the oven to 220C/425F/gas 7. Weigh the meat and calculate the cooking time (see Roasting beef, page 80). Put the flour on a baking sheet and cook in the oven until browned. Mix the flour with the mustard and pepper. Spread the beef with the dripping or butter and sprinkle with the mustard mixture. Leave to stand at room temperature until the meat has lost its chill.

CARVING

Beef should be carved thinly, across the grain of the meat. Make sure that you have a freshly sharpened carving knife, and a carving fork to hold the joint down firmly. A boned and rolled joint is easier to carve if set on a spiked platter. Otherwise use a board. Carve standing up – this gives better control.

Let the joint rest for 5-10 minutes to let the fibres relax. Remove any skewers and string which will be in the way as you begin carving, but leave some on to hold the joint in shape.

Serve the slices of meat on very hot plates.

2 Put the beef on a rack over a roasting tin and put in the oven for 15 minutes to brown. Lower the oven temperature to 170C/325F/gas 3 and add the warmed wine or water. Cook for the calculated cooking time, basting occasionally.

3 When the beef is done to your liking, place on a heated serving dish and leave to rest for 5-10 minutes at room temperature while making the gravy. Garnish, then serve with Yorkshire puddings.

MAKING GRAVY

A large joint of beef should produce sufficient meat juices to make a rich brown gravy, but a smaller one will need the addition of some beef stock. A little red wine is always good. Gently pour off as much fat as possible from the roasting tin, leaving the sediment and juices behind. If you like thick gravy, sprinkle on 2-3tsp flour and cook, stirring, for a few minutes until lightly browned. Gradually add stock as necessary, 2tbls red wine (if available) and the meat juices, which will have drained out of the standing joint. Bring to the boil and season.

Rolled roast beef

- **Preparation: 10 minutes**

- **Cooking: 1 hour – 2 hours 30 minutes, plus resting**

1.1-1.8kg/2¹/₂-4lb topside or other boned and rolled beef joint
50g/2oz dripping or other fat
salt and pepper

- **Serves 6-8** ⓘ ££

- **360cals/1510kjs per serving**

1 Heat the oven to 180C/350F/gas 4. Weigh the meat and calculate the cooking time (see Roasting beef, page 80).

2 Put the meat on a rack in a roasting tin and spread the dripping or fat over the ends unprotected by fat. Sprinkle lightly with pepper. Roast for the calculated cooking time, basting several times.

3 When the meat is cooked, put it on a heated serving dish and leave it to rest for 5-10 minutes at room temperature, then sprinkle with salt to taste. Meanwhile, make gravy to accompany the beef (see Making gravy, above), then serve.

Roast beef réchauffé

This recipe is essentially one for 'left overs' but doesn't lack smartness and only takes 15 minutes

- **Preparation: 5 minutes**

- **Cooking: roasting the beef, then 10 minutes**

25g/1oz butter
4 thick slices of rare roast beef
1-2tbls meat juices or gravy left over from roasting
1tbls Dijon mustard
4-6tbls red wine
black pepper
1tbls finely snipped chives
chive bundle, to garnish

- **Serves 4** ⓘ ££

- **335cals/1405kjs per serving**

1 Melt the butter in a frying pan large enough to take the beef slices in one layer. Fry the slices for 1-2 minutes on each side or until warmed through.

2 Remove all the fat from the top of the meat juices or gravy. Add the mustard to the juices and whisk until well blended. Pour the mixture over the meat and simmer for a few seconds.

3 Add the red wine and cook over high heat for 2-3 minutes or until the sauce has reduced to about 5tbls. Season with pepper to taste.

4 Transfer the beef slices to a heated serving dish, overlapping them slightly. Pour the sauce over in two lines on either side of the beef and sprinkle with the snipped chives. Garnish with the chive bundle and serve at once.

Cook's tips

It is important to use really rare, moist beef for this dish to be successful, or it will become overcooked when reheated.

Serving ideas

Serve this with mashed potato and a green vegetable such as broccoli.

ROASTING BEEF

The times apply to all boned and unboned beef joints, except fillet:
Rare: 15 minutes per 450g/1lb plus 15 minutes over
Medium: 20 minutes per 450g/1lb plus 20 minutes over
Well done: 25 minutes per 450g/1lb plus 25 minutes over

SLOW ROASTING: Heat the oven to 180C/350F/gas 4. Weigh the joint and cook for the calculated cooking time.
FAST ROASTING: Heat the oven to 220C/425F/gas 7. Weigh the joint and cook at this temperature for 15 minutes, then reduce the temperature to 170C/325F/gas 3 and cook for the calculated cooking time.

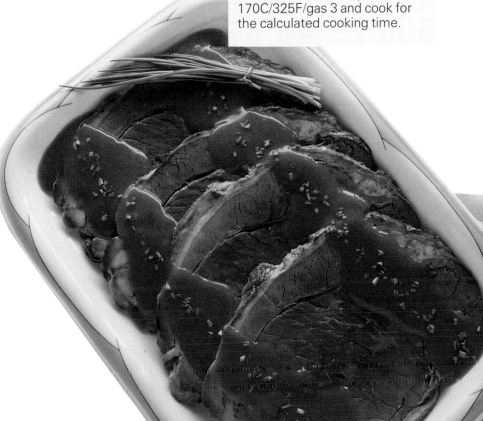

Stir Crazy

Stir-frying is an ancient cooking technique which fits perfectly into the 20th century. Because the food is cooked in minutes, it keeps maximum flavour, texture and vitamin content

*I*F YOUR ONLY experience of stir-fried food so far has been take-away or restaurant meals, don't hesitate to try it. Although the Chinese method of stir-frying is very different from Western shallow-frying, it's easy once you get the hang of it. Also it's very quick, as all the ingredients are cut into small, uniform pieces. The old story that the Chinese housewife starts to cook only when she hears her husband at the garden gate is not so far from the truth.

There's no reason to restrict stir-frying to Chinese-style meals. It's an ideal way of stretching portions of meat or fish, say, to feed unexpected guests, or of using up small quantities of different vegetables.

Equipment

The Chinese use the wok, a wide, curved-bottomed pan, for stir-frying. Its shape allows heat to be concentrated in the base, and food to be pushed up the sides as it gets cooked. They have become quite popular in the West and are now easy to obtain. But to start with a large heavy frying pan will do. If possible, place it on a small ring, so heat is concentrated in the middle. The Chinese use chopsticks to push the food around; a long-handled spoon works just as well.

The only other piece of equipment needed for stir-frying is a large sharp knife (the Chinese use a large cleaver) to cut up the food.

Preparing ingredients

Stir-frying is used for tender cuts of meat — mainly pork in China, but also beef, lamb, chicken and duck.

Shredded pork with cucumber (page 146)

Meat and seafood are often marinated before cooking in a mixture of cornflour, water, soy sauce and sake (rice wine) or dry sherry. This both seals in the juices and adds flavour. Slower-cooking vegetables may be blanched, stir-fried, then moistened with stock and flavoured with soy or oyster sauce and a little sake or sherry.

Prepare all the ingredients before starting to cook, as there won't be time afterwards. Put them ready to hand on separate plates; or prepare in advance, cover with stretch wrap and chill for up to 8 hours.

The way the ingredients are cut is important, as it affects the cooking time as well as the final appearance of the dish. Make sure all pieces of each ingredient are more or less uniform in thickness, so that they will cook in the same time.

Cooking

The Chinese prefer peanut oil, but any light vegetable oil will do. Use very little and make sure that the wok or pan is really hot before adding it. Also, allow the oil to get really hot as this will prevent the food from sticking to the pan. Start by adding the slowest-cooking ingredients first, and fry each ingredient for a few minutes only, just enough to cook wafer-thin slices of meat and for vegetables to become tender but still remain crisp. Stir and toss the ingredients constantly so that every surface makes contact with the hot oil. Add faster-cooking ingredients later, and push items away from the centre as soon as they are cooked. Serve stir-fries at once.

CUTTING TECHNIQUES

Stir-fried food calls for very precise cutting; always sharpen your knife before starting.

Slices: put the point of the knife on the chopping board, push the vegetable or meat under it and bring the cutting edge down sharply. Repeat this rapidly, pushing the item forward after each slice. Cut meat into 5cm/ 2in squares, then slice each square against the grain into strips about 3mm/⅛in thick. This is easier if meat is slightly frozen.

Strips: slice the food lengthways, then make a pile of slices and cut them into matchstick strips. This method is best for carrots and turnips, and also for bamboo shoots.

Cubes and dice: for cubes cut the food into thick slices, reduce the slices to strips, and the strips to cubes. Use the same method for dice, but all the cuts should be made at shorter intervals.

Making carrot flowers

Cut grooves along the length of a carrot using a sharp knife, then cut across into very thin slices.

Sesame vegetables

- **Preparation: 20 minutes**

- **Cooking: 10 minutes**

450g/1lb mixed vegetables
2tbls sesame oil
¼tsp salt
1tbls soy sauce
1tbls dry sherry

- *Serves 4*

- *95cals/400kjs per serving*

1 Prepare all the vegetables and cut into small even-sized pieces. Make sure to cut slow-cooking vegetables such as carrots into very thin slices.

2 Heat the oil in a wok or a large, heavy frying pan. Stir-fry the vegetables for 2-3 minutes, putting the slowest-cooking ones in first.

3 Add the salt and 150ml/¼pt water and stir-fry for a further 2-3 minutes. Add the soy sauce and sherry and stir-fry for 1 more minute. Serve at once.

Cook's tips

For best results, choose fresh seasonal vegetables of contrasting colours and textures. The ones shown in the photograph are carrots, turnips, courgettes, mange tout, red pepper, celery, broccoli, green beans and onion, but you need not use so many.

Variations

If liked, a little finely shredded root ginger or a pinch of ground ginger can be added to the vegetables.

How to ··· *prepare a stir-fry*

Cut the meat and vegetables into even-sized pieces – cubes, dice, slices, strips and florets – before starting to cook the food. Place them in separate dishes and put them near the stove.

Heat the wok or pan and oil. Add the slowest-cooking ingredient and stir constantly with wooden chopsticks or a long spoon, pushing it away from the hot centre as it cooks.

Add the remaining raw ingredients a few at a time, placing them in the centre of the wok or pan. Stir-fry until the meat is cooked through and the vegetables are tender but still crisp in texture.

Four-spiced noodles

- *Preparation: 30 minutes*

- *Cooking: 15 minutes*

375g/13oz Chinese egg noodles
boiling water
6tbls oil
3 garlic cloves, crushed
8 spring onions, finely chopped
2 green chillies, seeded and finely
*   chopped*
2tsp ground turmeric
1tsp ground fenugreek
¹/₂tsp ground ginger
¹/₂tsp ground coriander
1 thick slice of cooked ham (about
*   100g/4oz), diced*
100g/4oz cooked peeled prawns
175g/6oz peas, defrosted
100g/4oz fresh beansprouts
salt and pepper

- *Serves 6-8*   (❛❛)(££)

- *315cals/1325kjs per serving*

1 Put the noodles in a large bowl, pour on boiling water to cover and soak for 5 minutes, separating them with a fork.

2 Heat 3tbls oil in a wok or large frying pan. Add the garlic, spring onions and chillies and stir-fry over medium heat for 3-4 minutes. Add the turmeric, fenugreek, ginger and coriander and stir-fry for 1 minute. Stir in the ham, prawns, peas and beansprouts and stir-fry for 1 minute.

3 Drain the noodles and add to the pan in small batches, stirring well after each addition, and gradually adding the remaining oil at the same time. Lower the heat and continue to cook for 2 minutes, stirring constantly.

4 Season to taste with salt and pepper, transfer to a heated serving dish and serve at once.

Variations

This dish is an excellent way of using up left-over cooked vegetables and various meats or poultry. Alternatively, 175g/6oz frozen mixed vegetables can be used instead of the peas.

Shredded pork with cucumber

- **Preparation: 20 minutes**

- **Cooking: 5 minutes**

250g/9oz pork fillet
1 small cucumber
2–3 spring onions
3tbls oil
1tbls light soy sauce
1tbls dry sherry
1tsp salt

- **Serves 2 on its own, 4 with other dishes**

- **895cals/3760kjs per serving**

1 Cut the pork into matchstick-sized pieces and finely shred the vegetables.

2 Heat a wok or large, heavy frying pan over high heat for 35-40 seconds. Pour in the oil and heat until it smokes. Swirl the pan so that most of the surface is well coated with oil.

3 Add the pork and stir until the colour of the meat changes. This should take less than 45 seconds. Add the soy sauce and sherry and stir a few more times.

4 Add the cucumber and spring onions and season with the salt. Continue stirring until the vegetables are done to your taste and serve hot.

Cook's tips

Instead of cucumber you can use thinly sliced peppers, Chinese leaves, bamboo shoots or whole bean sprouts.

Stir-fried prawns with broccoli

- **Preparation: 15 minutes**

- **Cooking: 5 minutes**

100g/4oz broccoli florets
2tbls dry sherry
3tbls tomato purée
1tsp sugar
1/2tsp Chinese chilli sauce
2tbls soy sauce
3tbls oil
225g/8oz cooked peeled prawns, defrosted if frozen
1tsp finely shredded root ginger
1 garlic clove, crushed
1 spring onion, thinly sliced

- **Serves 2 on its own, 4 with other dishes**

- **370cals/555kjs per serving**

1 Divide the broccoli into small florets. Blanch them in boiling water for 1

Stir-fried prawns with broccoli

minute, then drain them well and set them to one side.

2 Combine the sherry, tomato purée, sugar, chilli sauce, soy sauce and 1tbls oil in a small bowl.

3 Heat the remaining oil in a wok or large, heavy frying pan and stir-fry the prawns for about 30 seconds, until they change colour.

4 Add the ginger, garlic and spring onion to the pan and stir-fry for 1 minute. Add the soy sauce mixture and stir-fry for 1 minute.

5 Add the blanched broccoli florets to the pan and toss over a high heat, then serve immediately.

Variations

As an alternative, use mange tout instead of the broccoli florets. Use the same weight and top and tail the peas before blanching them for 30 seconds.

SERVING STIR-FRIES

To serve stir-fried dishes Chinese style, prepare the same number of dishes of meat or fish and vegetables as there are people, plus a bowl of rice. Put the dishes in the centre of the table, if possible on a table-top warmer to keep them hot. Give each person a small bowl or medium-sized plate and a pair of chopsticks or a fork, so they can all help themselves to the food of their choice. Alternatively, use stir-fried dishes in a Western way, accompanying mainly-meat stir-fries with rice or pasta, or serving stir-fried vegetables with roasts or grills.

Blazing Barbecues

A barbecue party is always great fun, but needs good forward

planning and organization to make it go with a swing

Fresh Air and the delicious smell of charcoal-grilling make people ravenous, so food needs to be plentiful, and either quickly cooked or carefully timed. The basic methods are simple: grilling, skewer cooking, baking in foil and spit-roasting. Marinating is used a lot to make food tender and tasty, and it cuts down on the need to baste during cooking.

Grilling

Meat: steaks, chops, hamburgers, sausages and chicken joints are all suitable for grilling. Always bring them to room temperature before cooking. Trim most of the fat off steaks and chops, or it will drip and make the fire flare up. Snip into the edges of the remaining fat to prevent the meat curling up as it cooks. Cuts of lamb or beef should be about 4cm/1½in thick; pork a bit thinner. Oil the grill rack and put it over the fire about 7.5cm/3in above the coals to heat up before starting to cook.

Fish: whole fish, especially the naturally oily trout or mackerel, and fish cakes are excellent grilled. Fish steaks or thick fillets are best put in a hinged wire grill to keep them whole. Baste frequently to prevent the fish drying out.

Skewer cooking

Kebabs are ideal barbecue food as they are quick to cook and easy to eat with your fingers. Use chunks of meat or fish alternated with suitable vegetables and flavouring items such as lemon wedges and bay leaves. Make sure all the pieces are evenly sized, and use flat skewers so that they don't revolve. Cook on the grill, turning and basting often.

Meat: use boneless top-quality meat, or cheaper cuts such as shoulder of lamb or hand of pork which have been well marinated. Small chicken joints (drumsticks or wings) are also suitable, as are rolled chicken breasts.

Fish: only use firm white fish such as monkfish, cod or halibut. Cut it into large chunks and marinate and/or baste to keep it moist. Prawns and scallops are also good.

Vegetables: the most popular ones for skewer cooking are small tomatoes, button mushrooms and

Marinated salmon steaks with chervil (page 148)

chunks of sweet pepper or aubergine. All will benefit from an oil and lemon marinade.

Baking in foil

This seals in flavour and juices: use a double thickness of foil to make sure it doesn't get pierced. It's good for small cuts of lean meat, gammon steaks, fish steaks or fillets. Add butter or oil and flavourings and put the parcels on the grill. Large whole items – potatoes, onions, corn on the cob and apples – should be wrapped in foil and placed directly in the hot charcoal.

Spit-roasting

If you have a barbecue with a spit this is the ideal way to cook whole poultry or joints of beef or lamb. Make sure the spit passes centrally through the bird or joint so that it turns and cooks evenly. Baste with butter, oil or barbecue sauce and allow plenty of time and fuel.

Marinated salmon steaks with chervil

- **Preparation: 10 minutes, plus marinating and preparing the barbecue**

- **Cooking: 15 minutes**

8 small salmon steaks
For the marinade:
2tbls oil, plus extra for greasing
6tbls dry white wine
juice of ¹/₂ lemon
4tbls chopped fresh chervil
salt and pepper

- **Serves 8**

- **290cals/1220kjs per serving**

1 At least 3¼ hours before barbecueing, trim any fins from the salmon steaks.

2 Mix the marinade ingredients together in a large shallow dish. Turn the salmon steaks in the marinade and leave them for about 3 hours at room temperature.

3 Meanwhile, prepare the barbecue. When ready to cook the steaks, oil the grill and lay them on it. Grill 10cm/4in from the hot coals for 1-2 minutes, turning once and basting with the marinade. Serve hot.

COOKING EQUIPMENT

The simplest set-up is a hibachi-type barbecue standing on a table or bench. You will need a cooking area about 45.5cm/18in across to cook food for eight. Or you can splash out with a brazier-type barbecue incorporating wind shield, warming oven and rotisserie spit. Portable barbecues can be moved to suit the wind direction.

For cooking you need a long-handled fork, spoon and fish slice, plus separate tongs for handling food and coals. Use a long-handled brush for basting, and flat metal skewers for kebabs.

Moroccan beef brochettes

- **Preparation: 30 minutes, plus marinating and preparing the barbecue**

- **Cooking: 15 minutes**

700g/1¹/₂lb rump steak
225g/8oz beef fat
1 Spanish onion, grated or very finely chopped
2tbls finely chopped parsley
1tbls lemon juice
¹/₂tsp ground cumin
¹/₂tsp cayenne pepper
¹/₂tsp crushed black peppercorns
salt
oil, for greasing
finely chopped parsley, to garnish
4 lemon wedges, to serve
hot pitta bread, to serve

- **Serves 4**

- **760cals/3190kjs per serving**

1 Cut the steak into 2cm/³/₄in cubes. Cut the beef fat into squares the same size but only 5mm/¹/₄in thick.

2 Put the onion, parsley and lemon juice into a large bowl along with the cumin, cayenne and crushed peppercorns; mix well. Add the cubed beef and fat. Toss until well coated on all sides, cover and marinate in a cool place for 2-4 hours.

3 Prepare the barbecue. When ready to grill the brochettes, season the meat with salt to taste. Thread four large skewers with alternating pieces of meat and fat.

4 Put the skewer on the oiled grill rack and cook about 7.5cm/3in above the hot coals, turning once. Allow 4-5 minutes each side for rare, 6-7 minutes for medium.

5 To serve, sprinkle the skewers with parsley and accompany with lemon wedges and pitta bread.

Barbecued pork chops with aubergines

- *Preparation: 20 minutes, plus degorging, marinating and preparing the barbecue*

- *Cooking: 15 minutes*

2 aubergines
salt and pepper
4 pork chops, about 2cm/³/₄in thick
paprika
¹/₂tsp dried thyme
¹/₂tsp crushed bay leaves
¹/₂tsp fennel seeds
juice of ¹/₂ lemon
olive oil
2 garlic cloves, halved
oil, for greasing

- *Serves 4*

- *325cals/1365kjs per serving*

1 Cut the aubergines in half lengthways and rub the cut surfaces with salt. Leave to drain, cut side down, in a colander for about 1 hour to allow the salt to draw out any bitterness.

2 Trim excess fat from the chops. Season with salt and pepper to taste and sprinkle lightly with paprika. Lay the chops in a shallow dish and sprinkle with the herbs and fennel seeds, lemon juice and 2-4tbls olive oil. Leave at room temperature for 1 hour to absorb the flavour. Meanwhile, prepare the barbecue.

3 Drain the aubergines, gently squeezing out any remaining bitter juices, and wipe them dry with absorbent paper. Put half a garlic clove into the cut side of each aubergine and moisten generously with

olive oil. Lay the aubergine halves on the oiled barbecue grill. Cook over the hot coals for about 10 minutes, turning occasionally.

4 Drain the chops. Snip the fat on the edge of each one to prevent it curling up during cooking. Lay the chops on the grill with the aubergines and cook for a further 10-12 minutes or until cooked through, turning occasionally. Remove the garlic cloves and serve at once.

Paprika chicken brochettes

- *Preparation: 30 minutes, plus marinating and preparing the barbecue*

- *Cooking: 25 minutes*

4 small courgettes
4 boneless chicken breasts
4 small firm tomatoes, halved
paprika
oil, for greasing
For the marinade:
2 onions, coarsely chopped
150ml/¹/₄pt olive oil
1tbls dried thyme
2 bay leaves
¹/₂tsp paprika
salt and pepper

- *Serves 4*

- *285cals/1195kjs per serving*

1 Combine the marinade ingredients in a large bowl. Cut each courgette into eight and add them to the marinade. Cut each chicken breast into eight even-sized pieces. Add them to the marinade, spoon it over them several times, then leave to marinate in a cool place for 2-4 hours.

2 Prepare the barbecue. Drain the chicken and courgettes, reserving the marinade. Take four 25cm/10in skewers and assemble the ingredients on each as follows: ¹/₂ tomato, eight pieces of chicken alternating with eight pieces of courgette, then ¹/₂ tomato.

3 Brush the brochettes generously with the marinade and sprinkle them with a little paprika. Grill on an oiled rack over the hot coals for 20-25 minutes, or until the chicken is cooked through, brushing occasionally with the marinade and turn- ▶

How to ... light a barbecue

Pour barbecue lighting fluid over the charcoal and leave to soak for a minute before lighting.

Level out the coals when the charcoal is covered with a thin layer of grey ash.

ing the skewers at least twice to ensure even cooking. Serve hot. To serve, grasp one end of each skewer firmly with oven gloves and push the pieces off neatly.

Serving ideas

Accompany the brochettes with saffron rice cooked in the kitchen and kept warm on the barbecue, and a crisp green salad.

SAFETY HINTS

DO have a plastic spray bottle filled with water standing by when dripping fat causes flares.

DO use protective gloves and long-handled tongs and turners.

DO keep children well away from the fire unless supervised.

DON'T have the fire near bushes, trees or wooden buildings, or allow sparks or charcoal to fly onto the grass.

DON'T use petrol, paraffin or lighter fuel, either to light the fire or give it a boost.

DON'T place cans of any of the above near the fire, or any aerosols (including insect repellent).

HEAT CONTROL

To control the heat on a simple barbecue with no mechanism, either move the grid closer to or further from the fire; or move cooked food to the outside edges of the grid. To concentrate the heat, heap the charcoal up using fire tongs. To damp it down, spread the coals further apart. If more fuel is needed add it round the edge to warm up, then push it inwards.

Chilli chicken

- *Preparation: 10 minutes, plus marinating and preparing the barbecue*

- *Cooking: 40 minutes*

1.4kg/3lb chicken, divided into 4
300ml/¹/₂pt soured cream
2tsp chilli powder
1tbls paprika
oil, for greasing

- *Serves 4*   ①£

- *440cals/1850kjs per serving*

1 Using a small, sharp knife, make several deep slits in the flesh of each piece of chicken. Put in a shallow dish.

2 Mix together the soured cream with the chilli powder and paprika and pour over the chicken pieces. Turn the pieces to coat them with the mixture and marinate overnight in the refrigerator.

3 Remove the chicken from the refrigerator at least 1 hour before cooking to allow it to come to room temperature. Prepare the barbecue.

4 Remove the chicken pieces from the marinade and scrape off any excess. Reserve the marinade. Put the pieces on the oiled grill rack and put the rack about 7.5cm/3in above the hot coals. Cook for about 40 minutes, turning often, until the juices run clear when the flesh is pierced.

5 Pour the reserved marinade into a small saucepan, bring to the boil and simmer gently for 5 minutes, then serve with the chicken. (Or heat the sauce on the kitchen stove.)

Chilli chicken

Stew-pendous Casseroles

Meaty casseroles cannot be hurried – but they offer infinite creative opportunities and often taste even better when reheated

*C*ASSEROLE COOKERY IS a wonderfully easy way to make even the most economical cuts of meat taste delicious. Casseroles are time-consuming to cook, but after the initial preparations, there is no need to watch the clock too closely. A few minutes more or less in the cooking time will make little difference to the finished result – it will be just as delicious.

The secret of a good meat casserole is long, slow cooking. This is needed to tenderize the meat and to give the flavours time to blend and develop – which, in turn,

accounts for the charm of the dish. To tenderize the meat before it is cooked, just marinate it in wine, olive oil and herbs for a few hours.

Casserole cuts

Use a casserole to cook any cuts that you wouldn't risk roasting. The long, slow cooking will tenderize the toughest of meats. Most roasting and grilling cuts will make superb casseroles but, paradoxically, some prime cuts – such as fillet of beef or veal – are not well suited to the long, slow cooking.

Beef: the best cuts to casserole

are chuck and blade. The top part of the shin and flank are also very tasty but need much longer cooking. Chuck and blade are generally sold as 'braising steak'.

Veal: shoulder, breast, knuckle and shin all make wonderful casseroles as they take kindly to the long, gentle cooking in a well-flavoured sauce. Veal chops and cutlets are also excellent cooked this way.

Lamb: many classic lamb or mutton casseroles, such as Lancashire hot pot and Irish stew, are usually

Breton lamb fricassee (page 154)

151

made with really bony cuts such as middle neck, scrag and breast of lamb. But, if entertaining, go for cuts with less bone in them, such as shoulder meat or neck cutlets.

Pork: shoulder is usually a good, lean cut suitable for casseroles, and loin chops are excellent.

Preparing the meat

Cut the boneless meat into 2.5cm-4cm/1in-1½in cubes, making the cubes all the same size so that they will cook evenly. Cut away any gristle and fat as you go along.

Have the meat at room temperature and dry it on absorbent paper – wet meat will steam in the pan and not brown properly when fried. If the recipe tells you to dust the meat with flour, do so only at the last moment. If left too long, the flour draws out the moisture and makes the meat damp and tacky.

Cooking a casserole

After browning the meat and vegetables, remove them from the pan and stir the liquid into the remaining fat and sediment in the pan, scraping the bottom and sides clean with a wooden spoon. Bring to the boil and let it reduce a little before returning the meat and vegetables to the pan.

More casseroles are ruined by excessive heat than by anything else. Keep the casserole – throughout its cooking time – at a faint, barely perceptible simmer. If using the oven, a setting of 150C/300F/gas 2 or 170C/325F/gas 3 is usually about right.

The finishing touch

When the casserole is cooked, the sauce may need thickening. The simplest method of thickening is by reduction. Lift the meat and vegetables out with a slotted spoon and skim the sauce of any fat. Boil the sauce briskly, stirring, until reduced to the desired consistency.

Another simple method of thickening is a starch liaison. Blend some arrowroot or cornflour with a little cold water in a small bowl to a smooth paste. Spoon some of the casserole sauce into the liaison, blend well, then pour it into the casserole, stirring. Bring to the boil, then simmer for 2-3 minutes.

Beef stew with dumplings

● *Preparation: 45 minutes*

● *Cooking: 2¾ hours*

1.4kg/3lb chuck or blade
3tbls seasoned flour
25g/1oz butter
2tbls oil
700ml/1¼pt beef stock
150ml/¼pt red wine
salt and pepper
12 button onions
18 small carrots
beurre manié made with 25g/1oz
    butter and 2tbls flour (see
    opposite)
For the dumplings:
100g/4oz flour, sifted
2tsp baking powder
25g/1oz butter
2tbls chopped parsley
1 small egg, beaten
25ml/1fl oz milk

● *Serves 6-8*   🍴 ££ 🕐 ❄

● *710cals/2980kjs per serving*

1 Cut the meat into 5cm/2in pieces, discarding the fat and gristle. Toss in seasoned flour and shake off the excess.

2 In a large, flameproof casserole, heat the butter and oil. Sauté the meat on all sides until lightly browned. Pour in the stock and wine and bring to the boil. Season, cover and simmer for 1¼ hours.

3 Add the button onions and carrots to the casserole, cover and simmer for a further 30 minutes. 🕐

4 Meanwhile, prepare the dumplings. In a bowl sift together the flour, baking powder and ½tsp salt. Cut in the butter and rub in until the mixture resembles breadcrumbs, and stir in the parsley. In another bowl, combine the beaten egg and milk. Add enough of this mixture to the flour mixture to make a soft dough. Form into 12 dumplings the size of a walnut.

5 Drop the dumplings into the stock round the meat and vegetables, leaving a little space at the sides of the pan for the steam to circulate. Cover and steam gently for 15-20 minutes or until the dumplings are cooked.

6 To serve, spoon the meat and vegetables into a heated serving dish, using a slotted spoon, and arrange the dumplings around. Bring the cooking liquid to a boil and whisk in the beurre manié. Cook, stirring, until the sauce has thickened. Pour over the beef and serve.

Cook's tips

Note that although the dumplings are the size of a walnut before cooking, they swell to about twice their original size.

How to ··· *thicken a sauce with beurre manié*

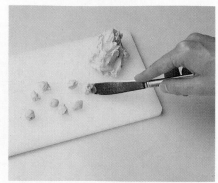

Lift the meat and vegetables out of the casserole and skim the sauce of fat by wiping the surface gently with sheets of absorbent paper.

In a small bowl, combine equal amounts of softened butter and flour and mash them to a smooth paste. Cut the mixture into pea-sized pieces.

Stir them gradually into the simmering sauce. Bring the sauce to the boil and simmer for 3-4 minutes to ensure the flour is cooked.

Apple and pork casserole

- ● *Preparation: 30 minutes*
- ● *Cooking: 2¾ hours*

25g/1oz butter, plus extra for greasing
2 onions, chopped
½tsp dried sage
salt and pepper
900g/2lb pork fillet, trimmed and cubed
2 cooking apples, peeled, cored and thinly sliced
700g/1½lb potatoes, chopped
2tbls hot milk
sage leaves, to garnish

- ● *Serves 4-6*   ① ££ ◷ ❄
- ● *390cals/1640kjs per serving*

1 Heat the oven to 170C/325F/gas 3. Grease a large ovenproof casserole with a little butter.

2 Mix the onions, sage and salt and pepper to taste in a small bowl. Layer the pork, onion mixture and apples in the casserole, finishing with a layer of pork. Add 3tbls water.

3 Cover the casserole and cook in the oven for 2-2½ hours or until the pork is tender. ◷

4 Meanwhile, cook the potatoes in boiling salted water until tender. Drain and mash with half the butter and the milk.

5 When the pork is cooked, spread the potatoes around the edges of the

casserole and mark a pattern with a fork. Dot with the remaining butter and cook for a further 15 minutes to brown the potatoes. Garnish with sage leaves and serve immediately.

Variations

Instead of topping this casserole with mashed potatoes, serve it on a bed of rice or noodles, if preferred.

Breton lamb fricassee

A fricassee consists of meat or poultry casseroled in a white sauce

- **Preparation: 20 minutes**

- **Cooking: 1 hour 45 minutes**

40g/1½oz butter
1tbls oil
700g/1½lb lean lamb, trimmed of
*   excess fat, cut into 4cm/1½in*
*   cubes*
350g/12oz button onions or
*   shallots*
2 garlic cloves, crushed
1 lemon
1tbls flour
300ml/½pt chicken stock
1 bay leaf
salt and pepper
2 egg yolks
100g/4oz small button
*   mushrooms, trimmed*
2tbls chopped parsley

- **Serves 4**

- **445cals/1870kjs per serving**

1 Heat 25g/1oz butter and the oil in a large casserole and fry the meat over moderate heat, stirring often, until it is sealed on all sides. Remove with a slotted spoon. Do this in batches, if necessary. Fry the onions or shallots and garlic, stirring, for 3-4 minutes.

2 Meanwhile, grate the zest from the lemon in long slivers, reserving some for the garnish. Squeeze the lemon juice and reserve.

3 Stir the flour and lemon zest into the onions and cook for 1 minute, stirring constantly. Pour in the stock, stirring. Add the lamb and bay leaf, bring to the boil and season to taste with salt and pepper. Cover the pan and simmer for 1½ hours or until the lamb is tender. Remove the bay leaf from the casserole.

4 Beat together the egg yolks and lemon juice. Pour in about 3tbls of the hot stock, mix well and return to the pan, stirring constantly. Simmer very gently for 5 minutes or until the sauce thickens.

5 Meanwhile, melt the remaining butter in a small pan and fry the mushrooms over moderate heat for 3 minutes, shaking them occasionally.

6 Stir the mushrooms and parsley into the lamb and adjust the seasoning. Turn into a heated serving dish and sprinkle with lemon zest. Serve hot.

Pork goulash with sauerkraut

- **Preparation: 35 minutes**

- **Cooking: 2½ hours**

900g/2lb boneless lean pork
*   shoulder*
salt and pepper
paprika
50g/2oz butter
1tbls oil
2 large onions, thinly sliced
1 garlic clove, finely chopped
400g/14oz canned tomatoes
2tbls tomato purée
pinch of cayenne pepper
450g/1lb canned or bottled
*   sauerkraut, drained*
150ml/¼pt soured cream

- **Serves 4-6**

- **555cals/2330kjs per serving**

1 Cut the pork into neat 2.5cm/1in pieces, discarding any fat and gristle. Season generously with salt and pepper and toss in 1tbls paprika.

2 In a large, flameproof casserole, heat the butter and oil. When the foaming subsides, sauté half the pork until brown all over. Remove the pork cubes with a slotted spoon and keep warm. Repeat with the remaining pork.

UNEASY LIAISON

An egg yolk and cream liaison is used to give a smooth, rich finish to a sauce. This type of thickening is tricky to add, as it can curdle.

First remove the cooked casserole from the heat and skim off excess fat. Next blend the egg yolk(s) and cream together in a small bowl, stirring them with a fork until thoroughly mixed. Spoon 2-3tbls of the hot sauce from the casserole into the egg yolk mixture to warm it slightly, then stir the whole lot into the casserole. Return the casserole to very low heat and cook carefully, stirring all the time, until the sauce thickens. Do not let the sauce boil or the yolk will curdle.

3 Add the onions and garlic to the fats remaining in the pan. Sauté for 7-10 minutes or until soft, stirring occasionally. Return the pork to the casserole. Stir in the tomatoes and their juice and the tomato purée. Season with salt, pepper and a pinch of cayenne. Cover and simmer for 1½-2 hours, or until the pork is tender, stirring occasionally.

4 Stir the drained sauerkraut into the goulash and simmer for a further 10 minutes. Stir in the soured cream, reserving a little, and heat through gently; do not boil. Correct the seasoning. Spoon the remaining cream over the top. Sprinkle with a little extra paprika, if wished, and serve immediately.

Veal chops with herbs

- **Preparation: 20 minutes**
- **Cooking: 50 minutes**

50g/2oz butter
2tbls olive oil
4 veal chops, each weighing
   350g/12oz
salt and pepper
150ml/¼pt chicken stock
6tbls dry white wine
2 shallots, finely chopped
1tbls finely chopped parsley
1tbls finely chopped chervil
1tbls finely chopped tarragon

- **Serves 4**
- **520cals/2185kjs per serving**

1 In a large frying pan, heat 25g/1oz butter and 1tbls olive oil. Season the chops with salt and pepper. When the foaming subsides, brown two of the chops on both sides. Transfer to a flameproof casserole. Add the remaining butter and oil to the pan and brown the other chops. Transfer to the casserole.

2 Add the chicken stock and white wine to the frying pan, stir to remove the sediment from the base of the pan, bring to the boil and pour over the chops. Sprinkle with the shallots, cover the casserole and cook over a low heat for 20-30 minutes or until the meat is tender.

3 With a slotted spoon, transfer the chops to a heated serving dish and keep warm. Boil the juices left in the casserole to half their original quantity. Stir in the chopped parsley, chervil and tarragon. Correct the seasoning and pour the sauce over the chops. Serve hot.

Cook's tips

The best result will be obtained if you use fresh herbs for this casserole. If you are unable to get them, use dried herbs and halve the quantities.

RING THE CHANGES

If you are getting bored with your standard casseroles as they all seem to taste similar, try one or a combination of the following additions:
 – a bit of crumbled stock cube
 – 4tbls wine, boiled to reduce it by half, or dry white vermouth
 – 1tsp wine vinegar
 – a few drops of Tabasco, Worcestershire sauce, mushroom ketchup or some Dijon mustard
 – 1tbls redcurrant jelly
 – grated zest and juice of an orange
 – 2tbls tomato purée.

Beef Burgundy

- **Preparation: 45 minutes, plus overnight marinating**
- **Cooking: 2¼ hours**

1.1kg/2½lb topside of beef
225g/8oz unsmoked bacon, diced
12 button onions
12 baby carrots
1tbls flour
4 garlic cloves, crushed
1 bouquet garni
salt and pepper
25g/1oz butter
12 button mushrooms
finely chopped parsley, to garnish
For the marinade:
600ml/1pt red wine
225g/8oz carrots, sliced
25g/1oz shallot, finely chopped
50g/2oz onion, finely chopped
2 sprigs of thyme
1 bay leaf

- **Serves 4-6**
- **885cals/3715kjs per serving**

1 Cut the beef into bite-sized pieces, discarding any fat and gristle. Put the beef pieces in a large bowl, add the marinade ingredients, then toss to mix. Cover and chill overnight.

2 Reserving the marinade, remove the meat from the bowl and drain well on absorbent paper.

3 In a flameproof casserole, gently heat the diced bacon until the fat starts to run. Add the button onions and baby carrots and sauté for 6 minutes or until lightly coloured, stirring occasionally. Transfer to a plate with a slotted spoon.

4 Add the beef to the casserole in several batches, if necessary. Sauté for 8-10 minutes or until evenly browned, turning occasionally. Sprinkle over the flour. Stir to blend, then strain in the liquid from the marinade. Add 65ml/2½fl oz water. Bring to the boil, stir and scrape well to remove the sediment from the base ▶

BEST OF BOTH WORLDS

For browning meat and vegetables, fresh beef and pork dripping are suitable. Butter on its own may burn, while oil gives an even browning. A mixture of butter and oil gives the best of both worlds – a butter flavour with little danger of burning.

of the pan. Return the sautéed bacon mixture to the pan, add the crushed garlic and bouquet garni and season to taste with salt and pepper. Lower the heat. Cover and simmer gently for 1½ hours or until the meat is tender and the sauce has reduced by half.

5 Towards the end of cooking, melt the butter in a small frying pan. Add the button mushrooms and toss until browned. Add to the meat and cook for a further 10 minutes. 🕐 Serve very hot from the casserole, garnished with the parsley.

Mediterranean veal stew

● *Preparation: 40 minutes*

● *Cooking: 2¼ hours*

75g/3oz butter
3tbls olive oil
*900g/2lb boned shoulder of veal,
    cut into 2.5cm/1in cubes*
salt and pepper
1 large onion, thinly sliced
2 garlic cloves, thinly sliced
1 green pepper, seeded and sliced
100g/4oz mushrooms, sliced
400g/14oz canned tomatoes
225ml/8fl oz dry white wine
2tsp dried oregano
1tsp dried rosemary
grated zest of 1 lemon
*450g/1lb courgettes, cut into
    5mm/¼in slices*

● *Serves 4-6* ⑪ ££ 🕐 ❄

● *540cals/2270kjs per serving*

1 In a flameproof casserole, heat 25g/1oz butter and 2tbls olive oil. Season the veal cubes with salt and pepper. When the foaming subsides, put in enough meat to cover the base of the pan and sauté until lightly browned on all sides. Remove the veal with a slotted spoon and set aside on a plate; repeat with the rest of the meat.

2 To the fat remaining in the casserole add 15g/½oz butter and 1tbls oil. Add the onion, garlic and green pepper and sauté for 7-10 minutes or until the onion is soft and translucent but not browned. Stir in the mushrooms and the canned tomatoes with their juice and cook for a further 3 minutes.

3 Add the wine, oregano, rosemary, and lemon zest and season to taste with salt and pepper. Bring to the boil and stir to remove any sediment from the sides of the casserole, then add the meat. Bring the mixture back to the boil, reduce the heat to very low, cover the casserole and simmer gently for 1½ hours or until the veal is tender. 🕐

4 Meanwhile, melt the remaining butter in a frying pan and sauté the courgette slices until slightly coloured and just tender. Remove with a slotted spoon and drain them well on absorbent paper.

Beef Burgundy (page 155)

5 Remove any grease from the casserole, add the courgettes, correct the seasoning and cook for a further 2-3 minutes. Serve hot.

THE BEST STOCK

For casseroles, use a good-quality stock – home-made is best, but one made from cubes will do. If using wine, choose an inexpensive one that is smooth and matured.

Fair Game

A simple roast of game, with traditional accompaniments,

is a delightful way to revive the cooking of bygone days and

to enjoy the meat's rich and subtle flavours

A GOOD RULE to remember when deciding how to cook game is that only the finest, most tender young game should be roasted. Unlike other methods, roasting does not provide a built-in safeguard against drying out the precious juices.

Choosing game for roasting
A good retailer, on whose advice you can rely, is worth his weight in gold. However, with experience, you can tell from its appearance whether the game is young and tender. A young bird has smooth legs, moist, supple feet and tender wing tip feathers.

You can buy quail, guinea fowl and pigeon (which are all farmed) all year round, together with hare and venison. Grouse, partridge, pheasant and wild duck are in stock only in season, although you may be able to buy frozen birds out of season. Snipe and woodcock will always need to be ordered specially.

Preparing game
If you buy game it will already be hung and dressed ready for cooking. If you are given it, you should hang it in a dry, airy place until you can get a poulterer or butcher to prepare it for you.

The length of time for hanging depends on the weather and your taste. Most birds are ready for eating when the tail feathers pull out easily. Rabbits are usually hung for only one day and hares for up to a week. Venison can hang for at least a week. Before cooking, wipe game birds inside and out with absorbent paper.

Roast mallard with port sauce (page 159)

Keeping game moist

Game meat is by nature dry, even in young birds, and it grows drier with age. However, there are various methods of counteracting this.

Barding keeps the flesh moist during cooking and is advisable for all game. Use thin sheets of fat salt pork, pork fat or fat, unsmoked bacon, and wrap them round the bird or joint, tying them in position with string. When the fat melts, it runs down the meat, providing constant basting.

Larding is a type of internal barding in which strips of fat are pushed through the length of the joint.

Marinating moisturizes, tenderizes and improves the flavour of the game.

Roasting game

Most game birds should be trussed (see All trussed up, opposite) before roasting to keep the body compact for cooking and carving.

Roast game birds as quickly as possible at a high temperature, so they do not have time to dry out. Larger game should be cooked more slowly otherwise the joint will be dry and fibrous on the outside by the time it is cooked all the way through. Use a small roasting tin for small birds so the juices do not spread out too much. Take care not to overcook as game will quickly become tough and it will be impossible to save the dish.

Serving game

Game is usually served with certain traditional garnishes and accompaniments such as game chips, bread sauce and sharp fruit relishes such as redcurrant jelly or cranberry sauce. Seasonal fresh vegetables, such as broccoli, carrots, swede and potatoes, are always good with game and a full-bodied red wine will round off the meal.

SPLENDID SALMIS

A salmis is one of the classic gourmet dishes in which a game bird is first part-roasted, then cut up. Cooking is completed in a rich sauce. This is traditionally done at table in a chafing dish.

BUYING AND ROASTING GAME BIRDS

Bird	Best time to eat	Hanging time	Temperature and roasting time
Grouse	August-October	2-4 days	190C/375F/gas 5 35 minutes
Partridge	October-November	3-5 days young birds 10 days older birds	220C/425F/gas 7 30 minutes
Pheasant	November-December	3 days young birds 10 days older birds	220C/425F/gas 7 50-60 minutes
Pigeon	August-October	Not hung (empty crop quickly)	220C/425F/gas 7 20 minutes
Snipe	November	3-4 days	220C/425F/gas 7 6-15 minutes undrawn
Mallard	November-December	2-3 days	220C/425F/gas 7 50-60 minutes
Teal	December	2-3 days	220C/425F/gas 7 10-15 minutes
Widgeon	December	2-3 days	220C/425F/gas 7 15-25 minutes
Woodcock	November-December	3 days	220C/425F/gas 7 15-20 minutes undrawn

How to ... *lard game*

Cut fat salt pork into 5cm/2in long strips, or lardons. Insert a strip in a larding needle. Thread the lardon through 1cm/½in of the meat, across the grain. Insert another strip of fat into the needle and continue with strips.

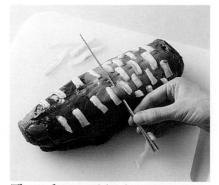

Thread several lardons across the meat to make a row. Add new rows behind the first, but not in line with it, so that the meat is covered with a chequer-board effect. The fat will keep the meat moist during roasting.

Roast mallard with port sauce

There are three kinds of wild duck: mallard, teal and widgeon

- **Preparation: 30 minutes**

- **Cooking: 1 hour 15 minutes**

2 mallard, dressed
salt and pepper
2tsp dried thyme
1 orange, unpeeled, coarsely
　chopped
1 tart apple, unpeeled, coarsely
　chopped
1 large onion, coarsely chopped
8 thin rashers of unsmoked streaky
　bacon
300ml/¹/₂pt port
orange slices, to garnish
watercress, to garnish
For the sauce:
2tbls flour
juice of 2 oranges
juice of 2 lemons
6-8tbls port
salt and pepper

ALL TRUSSED UP

To truss game birds, lay the bird on its breast with the neck end facing you. Bring round the wings and lay them flat across the back. Draw the neck skin over the body. Pass a skewer through one wing, through the neck skin and through the other wing. Turn the bird on its back. Tie the legs together with string, draw the string under the 'parson's nose' and tie it tightly. Place the ends of the legs into the vent.

- **Serves 4**

- **830cals/3485kjs per serving**

1 Heat the oven to 220C/425F/gas 7. Rub the cavities of the ducks with salt, pepper and thyme.

2 Mix together the chopped orange, apple and onion and use to stuff the ducks, keeping the remainder for the roasting tin. Sew up the cavities and truss the birds.

3 Place the ducks, breast sides up, on a rack in a roasting tin. Cover the breasts with bacon and pour the port into the tin. Add the remaining stuffing mixture. Roast the duck for 20 minutes, basting several times with the port.

4 Remove the bacon slices. Baste the duck well with the pan juices and continue roasting for 40 minutes or until the ducks are cooked: the juices should run clear when the inside of a leg is pierced with a skewer. Remove the trussing strings and skewers. Transfer the ducks to a heated serving dish.

5 To make the sauce, skim most of the fat from the pan juices and discard. In a small bowl, blend the flour to a smooth paste with the orange and lemon juices. Stir the mixture into the roasting juices and place over a high heat, stirring until all the crusty bits from the pan are incorporated into the sauce and the sauce thickens. Add the port and salt and pepper to taste. Heat through and strain into a heated sauceboat. Garnish with orange.

Partridge salad

- **Preparation: 25 minutes,
　plus marinating**

- **Cooking: 30 minutes**

2 partridges, dressed
salt and pepper
15g/¹/₂oz butter
2 rashers unsmoked streaky
　bacon
125ml/4fl oz olive oil
4tbls finely chopped shallots
1¹/₂tbls wine vinegar
¹/₂tsp dry mustard
4tbls finely chopped chervil or
　parsley
2 apples, peeled and diced
2 celery stalks, chopped, leaves
　reserved for garnish
watercress sprigs, to garnish

- **Serves 4**

- **710cals/2980kjs per serving**

1 Heat the oven to 220C/425F/gas 7. Season the partridges' cavities with salt and pepper. Put 7.5g/¹/₄oz butter inside each bird. Place bacon rasher over each partridge and put in a pan.

2 Roast for 30 minutes, basting frequently. Remove the bacon for the last 10 minutes of cooking time, to allow breasts to brown.

3 Cut each partridge into four pieces, then remove the skin. Combine the oil and shallots in a bowl. Place the partridge joints in this mixture and marinate in the fridge for at least 12 hours, or overnight.

4 Remove the partridge joints with a slotted spoon, reserving the marinade. Combine the vinegar and mustard with the marinade to make a vinaigrette. Add the herb, apples and celery and season with salt and pepper to taste. To serve, toss the partridge joints in the vinaigrette and place in a serving dish. garnish with celery leaves and watercress sprigs.

Pheasant en papillote

- *Preparation: 20 minutes*
- *Cooking: 55 minutes*

1tbls olive oil, plus extra for
*   greasing*
15g/¹/₂oz butter
1 young pheasant, halved
salt and pepper
pinch of dried thyme
1 thin slice of Spanish onion
1 ring of cooking apple, cored
sprig of thyme, to garnish

- *Serves 2* (❦) (££)

- *560cals/2350kjs per serving*

1 Heat the oven to 220C/425F/gas 7. Grease your hand with oil and run it inside and out a strong white or glazed brown paper bag large enough to hold the pheasant halves comfortably.

2 Heat the butter and 1tbls oil in a frying pan large enough to take the two pheasant halves side by side. When the foaming subsides, sauté the pheasant halves until well browned on both sides. Remove to a plate with a slotted spoon. Sprinkle with salt and pepper and a generous pinch of thyme, and reserve.

3 Separate the onion slice into rings. Using the fat remaining in the pan, sauté the onion and the apple for 1-2 minutes each side or until golden. Remove from the pan with a slotted spoon and arrange on top of the pheasant.

4 Carefully slide the pheasant halves into the oiled paper bag, taking care not to tear or pierce it in any way. Seal the bag tightly with string or a wire tag and place on a wire rack in a roasting tin. Roast for 30 minutes, then remove from the oven.

5 Crumple some foil and use it to line the tin so it fits tightly round the bag. Slit the bag open and fold the paper back.

6 Return to the oven for a further 15 minutes or until the top is browned and the bird is cooked through but still juicy. The juices should run clear when you pierce the thickest part of the leg with a skewer. Place the pheasant in its bag on a heated serving dish and serve immediately, garnished with a sprig of thyme.

Roast pheasant (see right)

BREAD SAUCE

Pour 300ml/¹/₂pt of milk into a saucepan. Add a bay leaf and an onion stuck with two cloves. Bring to the boil. Stir in 100g/4oz fresh white breadcrumbs and simmer for 20 minutes, stirring occasionally. Remove the onion and bay leaf and whisk in 1tbls double cream. Season to taste with salt, pepper and cayenne. Remove from the heat and stir in 15g/¹/₂oz butter.

Cook's tips

To make beurre manié, mash together 15g/¹/₂oz butter with 1tbls flour. Break off tiny pieces and use to enrich and thicken the stock.

Roast pheasant

● **Preparation: 45 minutes**

● **Cooking: 1 hour 10 minutes**

1 plump young cock pheasant,
   dressed
salt and pepper
thin strips of pounded salt pork fat
   or unsmoked fat bacon
15g/¹/₂oz butter, softened
175ml/6fl oz red wine
175ml/6fl oz chicken stock
1tbls redcurrant jelly
2tbls fresh white breadcrumbs
1 dessert apple, to garnish
For the stuffing:
1tbls olive oil
2tbls finely chopped onion
1 cooking apple
1tsp lemon juice
50g/2oz butter, softened
salt and pepper

● **Serves 4**

● **635cals/2665kjs per serving**

1 Heat the oven to 220C/425F/gas 7. To
make the stuffing, heat the oil in
small pan and add the onion. Sauté until
soft and lightly coloured. Remove the
onion with a slotted spoon and transfer to
a bowl. Peel and core the apple and grate
it coarsely into the bowl with the onion.
Quickly add the lemon juice and toss with
the apple and onion. Add the softened
butter. Blend the stuffing ingredients
together and season to taste.

2 Pack the stuffing into the pheasant's
body cavity, pushing it right in – the
handle of a wooden spoon makes a good
utensil. Sew up the stuffed cavity with a
trussing needle and fine string.

3 Sprinkle the bird lightly with pepper.
Cover the breast completely with
strips of fat, then truss the bird. Spread
the bird with softened butter and place it
in a small roasting tin. Meanwhile, mix
together 6tbls red wine and 6tbls chicken
stock in a small jug.

4 Roast the bird for 50-60 minutes,
basting every 10 minutes, the first
time with some of the wine and stock
mixture, then alternately with pan juices
and more wine and stock. Do not overcook
the pheasant – it is ready when the juices
run clear from the thickest part of the leg
when pierced with a skewer.

5 Lift the pheasant out of the roasting
tin, letting the juices from the body
cavity run back into the tin. Place it on a
heated serving dish. Remove the trussing

strings, skewer and the remains of the
barding fat. Keep warm.

6 Skim the roasting juices of all fat.
Place the tin over moderate heat. Add
the remaining stock and wine and bring to
simmering point, stirring and scraping the
tin with a wooden spoon. Stir in jelly and
breadcrumbs and continue to simmer,
stirring constantly, until thickened. Season
to taste and pour into a heated sauceboat.

7 To make the apple garnish, cut a slice
off the side of the apple so it will
stand firmly. On the side directly opposite
that slice, using a very sharp knife, cut a
small V into the apple without going right
down to the core. Leave the cut piece in
place. Now cut two more larger Vs outside
the first, making the third cut right to the
core. Stand the apple on the serving dish
alongside the pheasant and push the cut
pieces forward to make a 'beak'. Serve at
once, with the gravy.

Saddle of hare with grapes

● **Preparation: 50 minutes, plus
48 hours marinating**

● **Cooking: 1³/₄ hours**

100g/4oz piece of pork fat
2 large saddles of hare
225g/8oz white grapes, peeled and
   seeded
4tbls brandy
4tbls double cream
25g/1oz butter
1 large onion, very finely chopped
20g/³/₄oz flour
300ml/¹/₂pt Macon or other red
   wine
1tbls wine vinegar

1tbls Dijon mustard
1 clove
large pinch of grated nutmeg
salt and pepper
bunches of grapes, to garnish
For the marinade:
2 garlic cloves, crushed
2 small shallots, chopped
1 bay leaf
150ml/¹/₄pt Macon or other red
   wine
1tbls brandy

● **Serves 4**

● **715cals/3005kjs per serving**

1 Cut the pork fat into thin pieces and
thread half of these through the flesh
of the saddles with a larding needle (see
page 170). Reserve the remaining pork fat.

2 Combine the ingredients for the marinade in a dish large enough to hold
the saddles. Place them in the marinade,
turn until coated, then cover and leave in
the refrigerator for 48 hours, turning
occasionally.

3 Finely chop the reserved pork fat,
place in a roasting tin in the oven and
heat to 180C/350F/gas 4. Remove the
saddles from the marinade, reserving the
marinade. Lay the saddles on the fat in the
tin and surround the meat with the grapes.
Roast for 1½ hours or until tender.

4 Meanwhile, make the sauce. Melt the
butter in a small pan and fry the onion
gently until pale golden, stirring occasionally. Stir in the flour and cook for 1
minute. Whisk in the wine, vinegar, mustard and strained marinade.

5 Bring the mixture to the boil, whisking
all the time, add the clove and
nutmeg and season with salt and pepper
to taste. Boil until reduced by half.

6 Warm the brandy, pour it over the saddles in the tin and ignite. When the flames die down, transfer the joints and grapes to a warm serving dish and keep hot.

7 Press the sauce through a sieve into the ingredients remaining in the tin and stir well. Place over moderate heat, add the cream, stir well again and bring almost to boiling point. Pour a little of the sauce over the saddles and serve the rest in a sauceboat. Garnish with grapes.

Serving ideas

Braised red cabbage would be an ideal accompaniment to this dish as it cuts the richness of the hare.

Roast venison with cream sauce

- **Preparation: 35 minutes, plus marinating**

- **Cooking: 1¼ hours**

½ saddle well-hung venison, 1.6-1.8kg/3½-4lb dressed weight
100g/4oz piece of fat salt pork
150ml/¼pt olive oil
juice of 1 lemon
1tsp juniper berries
salt and pepper
1 onion, sliced
7.5cm/3in strip of pared lemon zest
2tbls wine vinegar
4tbls melted butter
350ml/12fl oz whipping cream
1tbls cornflour
flat-leaved parsley sprigs, to garnish

- **Serves 4-6**

- **900cals/3780kjs per serving**

1 Ask your butcher to remove the tough outer membrane and to cut away the sinews from the saddle of venison. Lard the venison with the salt pork, allowing two rows on each side.

2 In a large bowl, beat together the oil and lemon juice with a fork. Add the venison and turn it until thoroughly coated. Cover and leave in the refrigerator to marinate overnight, then remove from the fridge 2 hours before cooking to allow to come to room temperature.

3 Heat the oven to 180C/350F/gas 4. Drain the venison and pat dry with absorbent paper. In a mortar, crush the juniper berries and 1tsp salt with a pestle. Rub the mixture into the venison.

4 Place the saddle, meaty side up, in a roasting tin. Scatter the sliced onion around it and add the lemon zest. Pour the vinegar and the hot melted butter over the venison and put it in the oven.

5 Meanwhile, put 300ml/½pt of the cream in a small saucepan and warm it gently, stirring. After 15 minutes, baste the venison with half of the warmed cream. Return it to the oven for a further 20-30 minutes, basting once or twice with the pan juices.

6 Turn the saddle over, pour over the rest of the warmed cream and roast for a further 15 minutes. Increase the oven temperature to 220C/425F/gas 7 and turn the saddle meaty side up again. Roast for 10 minutes longer (see Cook's tips).

7 Transfer the venison to a heated serving dish and keep warm while making the sauce.

8 Strain the sauce from the roasting tin into a saucepan, reserving the onions.

In a small bowl, blend the cornflour with 2tbls cold water, stir in 2tbls sauce and return it to the saucepan. Bring to the boil and simmer for 1-2 minutes. Add the remaining cream, season to taste with salt and pepper and simmer gently.

9 Discard the lemon zest, spread the onion on top of the saddle and garnish with parsley. Hand the sauce round separately in a warmed sauceboat.

Cook's tips

If the venison is too rare for your taste, add no more than 3tbls of water to the pan and continue roasting until the venison is cooked to your liking.

Serving ideas

The venison would be good served with plainly boiled new potatoes to mop up the delicious sauce.

Out of the Frying Pan

Pan frying is one of the simplest ways of preparing a meal, and one of the most delicious. It is ideal for tender cuts of beef and veal

*A*LTHOUGH PAN FRYING is a simple technique it needs to be done with care, using the right materials and ingredients. Four things are essential: a good frying pan, the right cut of meat, the right fat and perfect timing.

The frying pan

Pan frying is carried out rapidly, so you need a good heavy-based pan to make sure that the meat cooks evenly and does not burn. Iron is the professionals' choice, and inexpensive, but it needs to be wiped over with oil after each use to prevent rust.

For domestic cooks who do not fry every day a modern pan with a non-stick coating is a better choice — but it must be a top-quality, heavy-gauge one. And again you must look after it — once the coating is damaged the pan is no longer non-stick. A non-stick pan has another advantage: less fat is needed to cook the food. The size depends on the numbers being fed — 25cm/10in diameter is the largest commonly available. So to serve four with large steaks or escalopes you will need to use two pans or fry two batches.

If you have weak wrists don't buy a large cast-iron pan — you won't be able to lift it easily. A lid can be useful; some frying pans have their own — otherwise use a large saucepan lid.

If the pan is for steaks and chops only you might choose a non-stick dry frying pan. These have ridges on the bottom which enable very little fat to be used, and hold the meat clear of any fat produced during cooking. They also give it a professional looking pattern of brown stripes if used very hot.

Choosing the meat

Beef for frying should be top-quality steak: sirloin (entrecôte), rump or fillet, cut to an even thickness. Fillet steaks should be about 3cm/1¼in thick, rump and sirloin steaks at least 2cm/¾in thick.

Veal cuts suitable for frying are loin, rib or shoulder chops; fillet for

Veal medallions (page 165)

cutting into medallions; or escalope, a thin slice off the fillet end of the leg.

Most cuts should be well trimmed to remove surplus fat, but veal chops need a thin layer around them to moisturize the meat. Slash this in three or four places with a sharp knife to stop it curling up during cooking. Allow at least 200g/7oz trimmed weight per serving, except for escalopes where 100g/4oz is sufficient.

Pan frying pointers

The pieces of meat must be of even thickness or they will not all be ready at the same time. Do not overcrowd the pan or the temperature of the fat will drop and the meat will simmer in its own juices instead of frying. If necessary use two pans, or fry two batches.

Heat the butter and oil until the butter sizzles and the foaming subsides. Put in the meat and fry over high heat for 2 minutes; turn and cook for 2 minutes on the other side. This initial cooking gives the appetizing brown colour. Lower the heat to medium and continue cooking to taste, turning the meat once or twice. Use tongs or a fish slice; do not spear the meat or the juices will escape.

Rare beef, still red in the centre, is perfectly safe, wholesome and tender, but you may prefer it medium or well done. Ensure you get just the right degree of cooking by meticulous timing – see the chart on page 166. Never overcook or the meat will be dry and tough.

Veal is started off at high heat in the same way as beef, but very thick chops may need longer – say 3-4 minutes each side. Then it is best to cover the pan and cook slowly for 6-8 minutes, or until the juices run clear. Veal should be reasonably well cooked, with just a hint of pink. But again, never overcook, or it will be extremely dry instead of juicy.

Medallions of veal need only about 2 minutes' cooking because they are cut from the fillet, which is extremely tender.

Economical escalopes

Veal escalopes are an excellent way of serving this expensive meat

as it is batted out thin, then coated with egg and breadcrumbs, which makes a satisfying portion with a small amount of meat. Prepare escalopes by putting the meat between two sheets of stretch wrap and beating with a meat hammer or the end of a rolling pin until about 5mm/¼in thick all over.

Pat dry, season and coat lightly with flour. Then dip in beaten egg, drain off excess and coat with day-old breadcrumbs. If possible chill for 30-60 minutes to set the coating before frying.

Pan-fried sirloin steaks

- **Preparation: bringing to room temperature, then 5 minutes**

- **Cooking: 10-15 minutes**

4 sirloin steaks, 150-175g/5-6oz each
salt and pepper
25g/1oz butter
2tbls olive oil
4tbls hot beef stock
juice of ½ lemon
1tbls finely chopped parsley
1tbls finely chopped chervil
chervil sprigs, to garnish

- **Serves 4**   (¶) (£££)

- **515cals/2165kjs per serving**

1 Wipe the steaks dry with absorbent paper and season with pepper. Leave to come to room temperature. Just before cooking season again by shaking salt and pepper over the steaks.

2 Heat the butter and oil in a heavy frying pan. When the butter is sizzling put in the steaks and fry over high heat for 2½ minutes on each side if you like rare steak. If not, lower the heat to medium and cook for a further ½-1 minute each side for medium-done; 2½-3 minutes for well-done. Transfer to a heated serving dish.

3 Add the hot beef stock and lemon juice to the pan, stir to incorporate the pan juices and heat through. Pour over the steaks. Sprinkle on a line of chopped parsley and chervil, garnish with chervil sprigs and serve at once.

Serving ideas

Accompany the steaks with straw potatoes and tomatoes grilled with thin slices of cheese inserted in them.

FATS FOR FRYING

Butter gives the best flavour but burns at low temperature, so use a little oil as well – about 2tbls to every 25g/1oz butter – as it has a higher burning point.

Do not use fat skimmed from stock or from a roasting tin for frying as it is full of moisture and will spit once heated up. Keep such fat for slow browning.

Use just enough fat to coat the bottom of the pan, except with escalopes which need more as the coating absorbs it.

Veal medallions

- **Preparation: bringing veal to room temperature, then 20 minutes**

- **Cooking: 15 minutes**

8 2.5cm/1in thick medallions of
   veal (see below)
salt and pepper
25g/1oz seasoned flour
50g/2oz butter
4tbls olive oil
¼ Spanish onion, finely chopped
100g/4oz frozen leaf spinach,
   defrosted and strained
1-2tbls double cream
2 tomatoes, skinned, seeded and
   diced

- **Serves 8**

- **465cals/1955kjs per serving**

1 Wipe the veal dry, tie a piece of string around the middle of each. Just before cooking season and coat in seasoned flour.

TEMPERATURE AND TASTE

Take the meat out of the refrigerator at least 2 hours before cooking to allow it to come to room temperature, otherwise it will lack flavour. Wipe dry with absorbent paper and season with pepper only (salt would draw moisture out again). Season again with salt and pepper before cooking.

2 Heat 25g/1oz butter and 2tbls oil in a small frying pan. Add the onion and fry over low heat until transparent, stirring occasionally. Add the spinach and cream, cook for 1-2 minutes longer and set aside.

3 Heat 25g/1oz butter and 2tbls oil in another heavy frying pan. When the foaming subsides put in the veal medallions and fry for 1-2 minutes, turning once.

4 Meanwhile add the tomato to the spinach mixture, season with salt and pepper to taste and heat through gently.

5 To serve spread a portion of the spinach mixture on each of four heated serving plates. Remove the strings from the veal medallions and put them on top of the spinach. Serve at once.

Hamburgers

- **Preparation: making the sauce, then 15 minutes**

- **Cooking: 5 minutes or longer**

1kg/2lb rump steak, minced
4tbls beef marrow (optional)
4tbls double cream
1 small onion, very finely chopped
salt and pepper
40g/1½oz butter
3tbls olive oil
300ml/½pt tomato or barbecue
   sauce
parsley sprigs, to garnish

- **Serves 4-6**

- **715cals/3005kjs per serving of meat**

1 Put the minced steak in a bowl and combine with the very finely chopped beef marrow (if using), cream and onion. Season with salt and pepper to taste. Form the mixture into eight hamburgers about 5cm/2in across.

2 Heat the butter and oil in a heavy frying pan. When the foaming subsides fry the hamburgers for 1½ minutes on each side over high heat. This gives them a crisp outside and rare centre. If you want them cooked through, reduce the heat to medium and continue frying.

3 Transfer the hamburgers to a heated serving platter. Pour the hot sauce (if using) over them and garnish with parsley sprigs and chopped parsley. Serve hot with a green side salad. ▶

How to ... cut veal medallions

Cut the fillet of veal into 2.5cm/1in slices and trim the medallions into neat rounds.

Encircle each round with string and knot it firmly to keep it in shape while cooking.

Rare-cooked hamburgers must be made from very fresh minced beef, or there is a health risk. So buy the steak in a piece and either mince it yourself or get the butcher to do it on the spot – do not buy ready-minced steak.

The beef marrow adds a fine flavour, but can be omitted if your butcher cannot supply a piece of marrow bone.

Serving ideas

Serve the hamburgers with a green salad made with chicory, endive and spring onions; and French fries or mini chips.

Veal chops with mushrooms

- **Preparation: bringing chops to room temperature, then 30 minutes**

- **Cooking: 30 minutes**

4 × 225g/8oz veal chops
salt and pepper
16 button onions
100g/4oz bacon, diced
100g/4oz button mushrooms, quartered
50g/2oz butter
2tbls olive oil
4tbls beef stock
2tbls finely chopped parsley

- **Serves 4**

- **555cals/2330kjs per serving**

1 Trim the chops, leaving only a narrow border of fat. Slash this in three or four places so that the chop does not curl up during cooking. Wipe the meat dry with absorbent paper, season with pepper and leave to come to room temperature.

2 Put the onions and bacon in a saucepan of cold water, bring to the boil, then drain immediately.

3 Heat 25g/1oz butter with the oil in a heavy frying pan over high heat. Season the chops with salt and pepper. When the butter stops foaming put the chops in the pan and brown for 2 minutes on each side. Then reduce the heat to medium, cover the pan and cook the chops gently for 6-8 minutes.

4 Meanwhile melt 25g/1oz butter in another heavy frying pan and sauté the onion and bacon mixture for 5 minutes, shaking the pan frequently. Add the

mushrooms and cook turning twice for a further 2-3 minutes.

5 Transfer the veal chops to a heated serving dish and keep hot. Stir the beef stock into the pan juices. Add the onion, bacon and mushroom mixture; season with salt and pepper to taste. Pour the mixture over the veal chops, sprinkle with parsley and serve at once.

Cook's tips

Peeling the button onions will be easier if plunged briefly in boiling water.

TIMINGS FOR PERFECT STEAKS

Cut	Weight	Thickness	Frying time each side*	Result
Fillet	100-175g/4-6oz	3cm/1¼in	4 minutes	rare
			7-8 minutes	medium
			9½-10 minutes	well-done
Tournedos	100-175g/4-6oz	5cm/2in	5½-6 minutes	rare
			7 minutes	medium
			8½ minutes	well-done
Châteaubriand (serves 2)	450g/1lb	4.5cm/1¾in	3½ minutes	rare
			4-4½ minutes	medium
			5-5½ minutes	well-done
Sirloin	150-175g/5-6oz	2cm/¾in	2½ minutes	rare
			3-3½ minutes	medium
			5-5½ minutes	well-done
Thick sirloin (serves 2)	325-350g/11-12oz	4cm/1½in	3½ minutes	rare
			4-4½ minutes	medium
			6-6½ minutes	well-done
Rump	200-225g/7-8oz	2cm/¾in	2½ minutes	rare
			3½-4 minutes	medium
			4½-5 minutes	well-done
Thick rump (serves 2)	450g/1lb	3-4cm/1¼in-1½in	4 minutes	rare
			7-8 minutes	medium
			9½-10 minutes	well-done
T-Bone	450g/1lb (weight including bone)	3cm/1¼in	3½-4 minutes	rare
			7-8 minutes	medium
			9½-10 minutes	well-done

*Including initial 2 minutes at high heat on each side

Variety Meats

The American name for offal is very apt: take your pick from quickly cooked liver and kidney; slowly-braised heart or tripe; or gourmet dishes based on sweetbreads and brains

*M*EAT WHICH COMES from the inside of an animal has everything to recommend it: tender, tasty, nutritious, low-fat, and generally inexpensive. But people are put off by its origin, and the British name offal (meaning 'off fall' – the parts that are cut away from the carcase). Think of it by the American name variety meat, and learn to appreciate the versatility of liver, kidney and heart, which can provide anything from hearty breakfast to gourmet supper. You may end up esteeming sweetbreads as highly as the French; or loving tripe as much as they do in the North of England and Normandy.

Liver and kidney

The big plus point for liver is that it is rich in iron, vitamin A and several important B group vitamins. Dieticians recommend eating it every week. It is also very quick to prepare and cook.

Lamb's and pig's liver are very similar, though pig's is slightly darker and stronger-tasting; also cheaper. Calf's liver is the finest and most expensive, but hard to get. To cook any of these, slice thinly, coat in seasoned flour and fry for not more than 2-3 minutes on each side. Any longer and the meat becomes tough, dry and grey. Liver and bacon and liver and onions are classic combinations. Add some wine to the pan juices and you have a gourmet sauce. Ox liver is coarser and too strong for some tastes; but very cheap. Try soaking it in milk before casseroling or braising.

To prepare liver simply remove any outer skin and cut out any large veins before slicing.

Kidney: lambs' kidneys are tiny – allow at least two per serving – with a very delicate flavour. Pigs' kidneys are about twice as big and stronger tasting. To prepare, remove any outer skin and cut out

Kidneys Dijonnaise (page 170)

the white central core. (The outer covering of suet is rarely seen nowadays.) Lambs' kidneys are usually halved lengthways, then fried or used for dishes such as Kidneys Dijonnaise (see recipe). Pigs' kidneys can be halved or cut in thick slices; use in the same way as lambs'.

Veal and ox kidneys are differently shaped, consisting of numerous segments. Veal kidney is very choice, but hard to get. It can be sliced, fried and served in a sauce, or baked whole in its suet covering. Ox kidney has a very strong flavour and is mainly chopped up and used as partner to beef in steak pies and puddings, in a ratio of 1:4.

Sweetbreads, brains and tripe

Sweetbreads come from the thymus gland and pancreas of the animal. The pale, soft meat is considered a great delicacy, especially in France – *ris de veau* is a classic dish. They are usually braised in stock before being used as required – for example in Sweetbread vol-au-vents (see right).

Brains too are pale and soft, with a delicate flavour. They are most commonly sliced and shallow fried, either plain, floured or coated in egg and breadcrumbs.

Tripe comes from the stomach lining of a steer or cow. It is white, and rubbery when raw; there are different types, but all taste similar. It tastes good, but the slithery texture puts many people off. Most tripe has already been prepared and precooked, so does not need very long cooking – in Savoury tripe with mushrooms (page 170) it is marinated for 1 hour, then cooked for 30 minutes.

Buying and storing

Liver, kidney and heart from pigs, lambs and oxen are widely available at butchers and supermarkets. For those from calves, you may have to find a butcher specializing in veal. Brains and sweetbreads usually need ordering in advance, though you may find them frozen in a large supermarket. Those from calves are not currently on sale in Britain. Tripe is quite common in the North, but hard to find in many

parts of the South unless frozen.

All offal must be very fresh: avoid anything that looks dull or dry, has a bluish tinge or smells unpleasant. Fresh brains and sweetbreads should be plump and moist, greyish-pink in colour. Tripe should be pure white, never slimy or grey-looking.

Don't delay getting offal into the refrigerator. As with all meat, remove it from the plastic wrappings and store on a plate with a piece of stretch wrap or foil laid on top to stop it drying out. Eat all fresh offal on the same day, or at least within 24 hours.

Brain fritters with sauce Robert

- **Preparation: 35 minutes**

- **Cooking: 20 minutes**

*450g/1lb lamb's brains, soaked and
   blanched*
1tbls lemon juice
salt and pepper
oil, for deep-frying
8 parsley sprigs
4 lemon wedges
For the batter:
150g/2oz flour
1 large egg
150ml/¼pt milk
2tsp oil
For the sauce:
25g/1oz butter
1 small onion, finely chopped
150ml/¼pt wine vinegar
150ml/¼pt beef stock
3 gherkins, chopped
1tsp French mustard
1tsp chopped parsley or tarragon

- **Serves 4**   (¶¶) (££)

- **600cals/2520kjs per serving**

1 Make the batter by sieving the flour and salt together into a bowl. Make a well in the centre, drop in one egg yolk, then add the milk, Whisk well until thick and creamy. Stir in the oil and allow to stand for 30 minutes.

2 Meanwhile prepare the sauce: melt the butter in a saucepan and add the onion. Stir for a few seconds, add the vinegar and reduce by half over high heat.

Add the stock, simmer for 15 minutes and keep hot.

3 Drain the brains and dry on absorbent paper, then divide into eight pieces. Sprinkle with the lemon juice, salt and pepper. Set aside.

4 Heat the oil in a large saucepan or deep-fat fryer to 180C/350F, when a cube of bread browns in 60 seconds.

5 When the batter has rested whisk the egg white until light and fluffy and fold it in with a large metal spoon.

6 Drop the brains into the batter, lift out each piece with a fork and deep-fry, a few pieces at a time, until golden brown. Remove and drain on absorbent paper.

7 Dry the parsley sprigs thoroughly, drop into the hot fat for a few seconds and drain well on absorbent paper. Arrange on a heated serving dish with the brains and lemon wedges.

8 Stir the gherkins, mustard and parsley or tarragon into the sauce. Pour into a heated sauceboat and serve at once to accompany the brain fritters.

Sweetbread vol-au-vents

- **Preparation: 25 minutes, plus chilling pastry**
- **Cooking: 40 minutes**

225g/8oz puff pastry, defrosted
1 egg, beaten
450g/1lb lamb's sweetbreads, soaked and blanched
300ml/½pt chicken stock
2tbls sherry
50g/2oz butter
100g/4oz mushrooms, sliced
1tsp lemon juice
25g/1oz flour
4tbls double cream
1 slice cooked ham, diced
salt and pepper

- **Makes 4 medium or 24 small vol-au-vents**
- **595cals/2500kjs per serving**

1 Roll out the pastry 1-2cm/½-¾in thick. Use a 10cm/4in round cutter if the vol-au-vents are for a main course, or a 5cm/2in one for small ones. Cut out twice the appropriate number of rounds, then use a smaller cutter to make a hole 3cm/1¾in across in half the smaller rounds or 8cm/3¼in across in half the larger rounds. You now have bases, borders and lids. Brush each base with beaten egg, put a border on top and press lightly. Brush the lids with egg. Put them on dampened baking trays and chill.

2 Heat the oven to 180C/350F/gas 4. Cut the sweetbreads into small pieces and put in an ovenproof dish. Add the stock and sherry.

3 Melt 25g/1oz butter in a small saucepan and sauté the mushrooms for 1-2 minutes. Add to the sweetbreads and cook in the oven for 15 minutes. Remove the dish from the oven but don't turn it off.

4 Drain the sweetbreads and reserve the liquid. Sprinkle the sweetbreads with the lemon juice. Melt the remaining 25g/1oz butter in a saucepan over low heat. Add the flour and cook for about 2 minutes, stirring, until it froths. Add the reserved liquid and whisk until smooth. Boil for 1 minute, remove from the heat and stir in the cream, ham, sweetbreads and mushrooms. Taste and adjust the seasoning and keep warm. Turn the oven up to 220C/450F/gas 8.

5 Remove the vol-au-vent cases from the refrigerator and bake in the centre of the oven for about 20 minutes (or 10 minutes if making small cases). When the pastry has risen and is golden brown remove from the oven and scrape out any soft pastry from the centre. Fill with the braised sweetbreads, top with the lids.

Cook's tips

Always fill vol-au-vents just before serving, otherwise the pastry will become soggy and the taste spoiled.

Plan ahead

The vol-au-vents can be prepared several days in advance, cooled on a wire rack and kept in an airtight tin. Reheat in an oven before serving.

SOAK AND BLANCH

Sweetbreads and brains need preparing before cooking.
Sweetbreads: soak in cold water for 1 hour, changing it several times, to remove all blood. Drain and rinse under cold water. Then blanch: put in a saucepan, cover with cold water and add 1tbls lemon juice and 1tsp salt. Bring slowly to the boil, simmer for 15 minutes, then drain and plunge into cold water to firm. Remove the tubes and outer membrane.
Brains: soak in cold water for 1-2 hours, then gently pull away the covering membrane, removing any white matter. Soak in fresh water until ready to use. Unless braising, blanch as for sweetbreads, adding a small onion and a bay leaf. Simmer for 15-30 minutes depending on size. Cool in the cooking liquid, or drain and put in cold water to firm up.

How to… *skin and core kidneys*

Pull the protective fat away from the kidney with both hands. Try not to break the skin at this stage. The butcher may do this for you.

With a sharp knife cut the skin at the core of the kidney. Carefully peel the thin skin away either with your fingers or a knife.

Cut the kidneys in half lengthwise. Remove the central core with sharp scissors or a knife, use halved or sliced.

Kidneys Dijonnaise

- *Preparation: 15 minutes*
- *Cooking: 20 minutes*

550g/1¼lb lambs' kidneys
2tsp flour
50g/2oz butter
50g/2oz flour
50g/2oz shallot or onion, finely chopped
150ml/¼pt dry white wine
1tbls lemon juice
150ml/¼pt double cream
1½tbls Dijon mustard
salt and pepper
chopped parsley, to garnish
350g/12oz rice, boiled, to serve

- *Serves 4*   🍴 ££
- *755cals/3170kjs per serving*

1 Remove any skin or core from the kidneys. Cut each one in half lengthways. Dust lightly with the flour.

2 Melt the butter in a large shallow frying pan. When it sizzles, put in the kidneys and fry fairly briskly for 2-3 minutes, turning so that they seal and change colour on each side. Remove with a slotted spoon and reserve.

3 Add the shallots or onion and fry very gently for 2-5 minutes until golden.

4 Add the wine and lemon juice and boil rapidly until they are reduced to one quarter of their original quantity.

5 Off the heat, stir in the cream and mustard. Return the kidneys and their juices to the pan and season lightly with salt and pepper. Reheat gently, without boiling, for 5 minutes, stirring frequently. Serve at once, sprinkled with parsley, on a bed of plain boiled rice.

HEART TO HEART

Hearts need long slow cooking but emerge deliciously tender, and produce wonderful rich, fat-free gravy. Lambs', pigs' and calves' hearts are small, and are stuffed, sewn up and braised. Ox hearts, being much bigger and tougher, are usually sliced, then casseroled.

To prepare hearts, wash inside and out under cold running water, cut out any tubes or gristle and pat dry on absorbent paper.

Savoury tripe with mushrooms

- *Preparation: 30 minutes, plus 1 hour marinading*
- *Cooking: 45 minutes*

700g/1½lb partly cooked tripe
3tbls vinegar
3tbls oil
50g/1oz butter
100g/4oz mushrooms, sliced
1 large onion, cut into thin rings
1tbls flour
400g/14oz canned tomatoes
½tsp oregano
salt and pepper
50g/2oz fresh breadcrumbs
1tbls chopped parsley

● *255cals/1070kjs per serving*

1 Cut the tripe into strips about 5cm/2in long and soak in a mixture of the vinegar and oil for about 1 hour to tenderize, turning from time to time. Drain and dry on absorbent paper.

2 Heat the oven to 180C/350F/gas 4. Melt 50g/1oz butter in a frying pan and cook the sliced mushrooms and onion over low heat for about 4 minutes, then remove with a slotted spoon to a plate.

3 Add the flour to the pan and brown slightly, scraping the bottom of the pan with a wooden spoon. Purée the tomatoes in a blender, food processor or vegetable mill. Add to the pan with the oregano and stir well. Season with salt and pepper to taste and turn off the heat.

4 Grease a casserole with 15g/½oz butter and cover the bottom with half the tripe. Lay the mushrooms and onion on top and cover with about one-third of the breadcrumbs. Top the casserole with the marinated tripe.

5 Pour the tomato sauce over the tripe, sprinkle with the remaining bread-crumbs and dot with the remaining butter. Cook in the oven for about 30 minutes, then put the mushroom caps on top, upside down, and cook for a further 5 minutes. Sprinkle with chopped parsley.

Stir-fried liver

● *Preparation: 20 minutes, plus 15 minutes standing*

● *Cooking: 10 minutes*

450g/1lb pig's liver, in one piece
1tbls cornflour
1tsp salt
1tsp ground ginger
1tbls medium-dry sherry
5tbls oil
1 large garlic clove, crushed
1½tbls coarsely chopped spring onion tops
For the sauce:
1½tbls soy sauce
1tbls medium-dry sherry
1tbls tomato purée
1½tbls chicken stock
1tsp sugar

● *325cals/1365kjs per serving*

1 Trim away all traces of thin outer skin or veins from the liver. Using a sharp knife, cut down into 3mm/⅛in thick slices, then into 2.5cm/1in strips.

2 Put the cornflour in a bowl and mix with the salt and ginger. Stir in 2tbls water, the sherry and 1tbls oil; mix until smooth.

3 Add the liver slices and gently turn to coat with the cornflour mixture. Leave to stand for 15 minutes.

4 Put all the sauce ingredients into a mixing bowl and stir until well blended.

5 Heat the oil in a frying pan over medium heat. When it sizzles, add the liver, spreading the pieces evenly over the pan. Increase the heat and cook briskly, stirring, for 30 seconds.

6 Sprinkle in the garlic and spring onion and continue stir-frying for another 30 seconds. Pour the sauce mixture into the pan, bring to the boil and cook, stirring constantly, for a further 30 seconds. Serve hot with boiled rice.

Steak and kidney pudding

- **Preparation: 30 minutes**

- **Cooking: 4 hours**

For the suet crust pastry:
butter, for greasing
225g/8oz self-raising flour
100g/4oz shredded suet
¼tsp salt
For the filling:
450g/1lb stewing beef
175g/6oz ox kidney
1½tbls flour
salt and pepper
1 onion, finely chopped
150ml/¼pt beef stock

- **Serves 4**

- **660cals/2770kjs per serving**

1 Thoroughly butter the inside of an 850ml/1½pt pudding bowl and a piece of double thickness greaseproof paper large enough to cover the top

How to ... cover a pudding

Fold a pleat in a square of greaseproof paper which is larger than the top of the basin. Tie over the basin.

Fold a pleat in a similar sized piece of foil. Fold over the first layer of paper and twist the edges tightly.

generously. (see the pictures above).

2 Make the suet crust: mix the flour, suet and salt together in a mixing bowl, then add just enough cold water to make a soft, elastic but dry dough.

3 Turn the dough onto a lightly floured surface, knead briefly, then roll into a circle about 5cm/2in larger all round than the bowl top. Cut out one quarter and reserve for the lid. Line the bowl with the rest, damping the joining edges. The pastry should extend to just above the rim of the bowl.

4 Cut the beef into 2.5cm/1in cubes, removing any fat and gristle. Remove the core from the kidney and cut the kidney into small pieces.

5 Season the flour and toss the steak and kidney pieces in it. Pack the meat tightly into the pastry-lined bowl, adding a layer of onion at intervals. Add enough stock to come halfway up the bowl.

6 Turn the pastry edges down over the meat and brush with water. Roll the remaining pastry into a circle to fit exactly inside the top of the basin. Dampen the edges and press together to seal.

7 Pleat the greaseproof paper down the centre to allow the pudding to expand while cooking and cover the bowl with it. Then cover the paper with the foil. Twist the edges to form a tight cap, or tie with string. Lower the bowl into a large saucepan containing fast boiling water to reach halfway up the bowl. Cover tightly with the lid.

8 Boil steadily for 3½-4 hours (the longer the better), topping up the pan with boiling water as necessary.

9 To serve remove the bowl from the pan and stand it on a plate. Uncover, make a hole in the crust and pour in any remaining stock. Knot a clean tea-towel or table napkin round the bowl and serve at once with cooked vegetables.

Roast Birds of a Feather

Roast chicken and turkey make relatively inexpensive festive fare, but can be dry and lacking in flavour. A little know-how can easily overcome these problems

OLDER COOKS WILL remember the times when chicken and turkey were rare and expensive. Now nearly everyone can afford chicken any weekend, and turkey is the most popular Christmas roast. But the mass production methods which have led to poultry for all, have also led to a loss of flavour. A plain roasted bird is not the delicacy it used to be, especially if frozen. Unless you are lucky enough to be able to get fresh free-range birds, you need to add other ingredients and roast with care to give them an exciting flavour and keep the flesh moist and tasty.

The first step is to ensure that the bird is not only completely thawed if it was frozen, but has come to room temperature: cooking while still chilled reduces flavour. Take a thawed chicken out of the refrigerator at least 1 hour before cooking; allow at least 2 hours for a big turkey. For health reasons both chicken and turkey must be well done. Continue cooking until a skewer inserted into the thickest part of the leg produces clear juices. Another test is to gently pull on a leg; it should move freely. Also remember that stuffings should be cold or at least cool,

and be put in the bird only at the last minute, not too tightly packed. This is to prevent any bacteria from multiplying before the bird is cooked through.

It is now considered safer to cook stuffing separately.

Choicer chicken

Essentially simple techniques will ensure a succulent tasty roast every time. The easiest is to blend butter with lemon juice, herbs and spices and spread the mixture over the outside, as well as putting a

Turkey with pomegranates (page 174)

little inside, before roasting. To enhance the flavour always add a stuffing, either in the neck cavity, or more unusually, in between the breast skin and flesh.

Always start roasting a chicken breast side down, or on its side, so that the breast does not dry out. A French anti-dryness technique is to lay the bird on a wire rack and pour 300ml/½pt of water into the tin. Add the giblets, some onion slices, parsley stalks and a bay leaf and roast as usual, basting with the liquid, which makes good gravy.

As a general rule roast a chicken in a moderate oven – 180C/350F/gas 4. An average-sized chicken to serve four will need about 1¼ hours if stuffed. Baste frequently to get a crisp golden skin and turn the bird over from time to time.

Tastier turkey

When the turkey has been stuffed and trussed rub the skin with lemon and cover the breast with streaky bacon. Alternatively spread it all over with a paste of softened butter and salt and cover with a dome of aluminium foil. Remove this 20 minutes before the end of the cooking time to brown the skin. Unless you bought a self-basting turkey (these are injected with butter) baste every 15 minutes.

Traditionally two stuffings are used for turkeys, one in the body cavity and one at the neck end. Never fill the body cavity more than half full, to ensure that the bird cooks fully. If using only one stuffing, put it in the neck. Popular stuffings are sausage meat, with or without chestnuts; veal forcemeat or herb and celery. Allow 60-100g stuffing per kg turkey, or 1-1½oz per lb. If preferred small turkeys can be plain roasted as they are often cheaper than joints for family meals. Place an onion cut in half in the cavity with a knob of butter mixed with fresh or dried herbs.

Roast turkeys for 15 minutes at 220C/425F/gas 7 to brown, then turn down to 170C/325F/gas 3 to complete cooking. Calculate the time required after stuffing the bird. Allow 43 minutes per kg/20 minutes per lb. Cover the breast with foil to avoid overcooking.

How to ··· truss a turkey

Lay the bird breast up; pass a needle and string through the left thigh, just above the joint of drumstick and thigh. Push the needle through the bird and out the other leg.

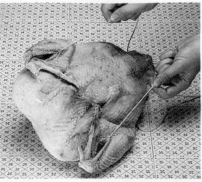

Push the legs close to the body and pull the string out with a length on each side. Turn the bird over. Carry each string down to a wing and loop it completely round the elbow joint.

Pull the turkey's neck skin carefully over the back, then tuck the wing tips over to hold them. Holding the strings taut, pull them round and cross in the middle of the back.

Take the strings down to the tip of the drumsticks. Wind the string twice around the parson's nose and the leg tips, pulling it tightly. Tie securely and cut the ends from the strings.

Roast turkey with pomegranates

● **Preparation: 20 minutes**

● **Cooking: 2 hours 15 minutes**

2.4-2.7kg/5-6lb turkey, with giblets reserved for preparing the sauce
75g/3oz butter
½ lemon
salt and freshly ground black pepper
100g/4oz unsmoked streaky bacon, thinly sliced
4tbls vegetable oil
3 pomegranates
2tbls brandy

● **Serves 6-8**

● **520cals/2185kjs per serving**

1 Heat the oven to 190C/375F/gas 5. Wash the turkey under cold running water, if necessary, and dry it thoroughly with absorbent paper. Put the butter, lemon, salt and pepper into the cavity of the bird. Cover the breast with the bacon and truss the bird with thin string.

2 Put half the oil, then the turkey in a roasting tin, place it in the centre of the oven for two hours. Turn the bird and baste it with the pan juices every 20 minutes so that the meat cooks evenly.

3 Squeeze 1½ pomegranates on a citrus press to remove the pips. Halfway through cooking pour the juice over the turkey and continue basting.

4 Meanwhile, remove any fat or green portions from the reserved liver, wash it under cold water, pat dry and cut the liver into small pieces. Wash the heart, dry it and cut it into four pieces.

5 Put the heart and liver in a small saucepan with the remaining oil and sauté for two minutes over low heat. Pour over the brandy, raise the heat and cook until the brandy has just evaporated, then remove from the heat.

6 Squeeze the remaining half pomegranate and add the juice to the liver. Scoop out the seeds from the third pomegranate with a metal spoon. Add to the liver and heart. Place the pan over low heat, bring back to a simmer, cook for 10 minutes, then remove from the heat.

7 Fifteen minutes before the turkey is done, remove the bacon to brown the breast. Serve with the turkey, rather like crackling, or reserve for another recipe.

8 When the turkey is cooked, transfer it to a warm dish, place it in the oven and turn off the oven, leave the door slightly ajar.

9 Skim most of the fat from the tin juices and add the rest to the liver and pomegranate sauce. Check the seasoning, reduce the sauce by a third by boiling it uncovered, over medium heat, then pour it into a warmed sauceboat. Serve the turkey and sauce separately with buttered French beans or sautéed sliced courgettes.

Cook's tips

There are a wide variety of turkeys to choose from around Christmas. The fresh birds in the supermarkets are ready-prepared but look for one with a plump breast. If you prefer to buy your turkey from the butcher it is advisable to order in advance to make sure you have the size you want. Ask for a hen turkey as they have more breast meat and are generally more tender.

Roast poussins with dill stuffing

● **Preparation: 20 minutes**

● **Cooking: 45-50 minutes**

2 x 450g/1lb oven-ready poussins with giblets
50g/2oz butter
dill sprigs, to garnish
For the dill stuffing:
25g/1oz butter, softened

2 eggs, separated
50g/2oz dry white breadcrumbs
3-4tsp finely chopped fresh dill
salt and pepper

● *Serves 4* (♦♦) (££)

● *410cals/1720kjs per serving*

1 Heat the oven to 180C/350F/gas 4. Wipe the poussins inside and out with absorbent paper. Clean the livers, chop finely and reserve them for the stuffing. (Use the remaining giblets for stock or soup.)

2 Make the stuffing: put the butter in a bowl with the egg yolks and beat with a wooden spoon to blend. Stir in the breadcrumbs, chopped livers and dill; season with salt and pepper to taste. Whisk the egg whites until stiff but not dry and fold gently into the breadcrumb mixture.

3 Loosen the skin all over the breast of each poussin by easing your fingers between skin and flesh, being careful not to tear the skin. If necessary use a sharp knife to cut it free.

4 Push enough of the stuffing between the skin and breast of each poussin to cover the entire breast with a thin even layer. Divide the remaining stuffing between the poussin cavities. Skewer or sew up the cavities, making sure that the stuffing cannot slip out from under the breast skin. Truss as shown on page 226.

BREAD SAUCE

This is the traditional accompaniment to both roast chicken and roast turkey, and very easy to make. Quarter a small onion and put in a saucepan with 425ml/¾pt milk, 4 peppercorns, 2 cloves and a bay leaf. Bring to the boil, then remove from the heat, cover and leave to infuse for 20 minutes. Strain and return to the pan with 100g/4oz fresh breadcrumbs, 25g/1oz butter and a pinch of salt. Simmer gently to reheat, stirring occasionally. Serve hot.

5 Put a large roasting tin over medium heat, add the 50g/2oz butter and heat until foaming. Turn the poussins in the butter until evenly coated. Lay them in the tin on their backs and roast for 45 minutes or until done, basting frequently with the cooking juices.

6 Remove the poussins from the tin and, using a large sharp knife, cut each one in half right down the middle. Put the two halves back together again and arrange the poussins on a heated serving dish. Garnish with dill sprigs. Strain the pan juices into a heated sauceboat and serve at once with the roast poussins and new potatoes.

Cook's tips

If you cannot get any fresh dill use dried dill to make the stuffing and garnish the poussins with flat-leaved parsley.

Roast chicken with saffron and lemon

- **Preparation: 15 minutes**

- **Cooking: 1 hour 10 minutes**

1.6kg/3½lb oven-ready chicken
salt and pepper
75g/3oz butter, softened
good pinch powdered saffron or
    crushed saffron strands
1 garlic clove, finely chopped
juice of ½ lemon
flour, for dusting
watercress sprigs, to garnish
For the sauce:
50g/2oz butter
100g/4oz button mushrooms,
    sliced
rind and juice of ½ lemon
2 egg yolks
150ml/¼pt double cream
4tsp sugar
6tbls dry white wine

- **Serves 4**

- **770cals/3235kjs per serving**

1 Heat the oven to 220C/425F/gas 7. Wipe the chicken clean inside and out with absorbent paper. Season the cavity with salt and pepper.

2 Put the butter in a small bowl and, using a wooden spoon, work in the saffron, garlic and lemon juice. Season generously with salt and pepper. Put half of this seasoned butter inside the chicken.

3 Truss the chicken as shown on page 226. Spread the remaining butter over the breast and thigh; sprinkle with salt and pepper.

4 Lay the chicken on its side in the roasting tin and put in the oven for about 20 minutes, until slightly browned. Turn onto the other side and roast for another 20 minutes. Remove it from the

THAW POINTS

Complete defrosting is essential for all poultry to avoid any risk of salmonella. In the refrigerator is safest, but allow plenty of time, especially for turkey.

Turkey weighing	Time
2.3-3.6kg/5-8lb	20-36 hours
3.6-5kg/8-11lb	36-42 hours
5-5.9kg/11-13lb	42-48 hours
9-11.3kg/20-25lb	60-72 hours
Chicken weighing	**Time**
1.5-2.5kg/3-5lb	24 hours

oven and reduce the temperature to 180C/350F/gas 4.

5 Turn the chicken onto its back and sift a dusting of flour over the breast. Spoon over 3-4tbls boiling water and roast for a further 30-35 minutes, or longer if necessary, basting frequently until done.

6 Meanwhile prepare the sauce. Melt the butter in a saucepan and fry the mushrooms lightly. Remove with a slotted spoon and reserve. Blanch the lemon rind by putting it in boiling water for 2 minutes; drain.

7 Put the egg yolks in a bowl with the cream, reserved mushrooms, lemon juice and blanched rind. Mix the ingredients together lightly.

8 Put the sugar in a small heavy pan and melt over low heat, then bring to the boil and boil to make a rich brown caramel. Holding the pan at arm's length, add 2tbls water. Then stir over low heat until the caramel has dissolved and continue cooking until the mixture is syrupy. Stir the caramel into the egg yolk mixture.

9 Remove skewer and string from the chicken and drain the juices into the roasting tin. Transfer the chicken to a heated serving dish.

10 Pour off most of the fat from the roasting tin. Add the wine, put the tin over high heat and bring to the boil, stirring and scraping the tin to dislodge the sediment. Boil for 3-5 minutes, until the liquid is reduced by half.

11 To finish the sauce put the cream in the top of a double boiler or in a bowl set over boiling water. Strain the contents of the roasting tin into the cream and whisk for about 5 minutes, until it has thickened slightly. Do not allow to boil or it will curdle. Season with salt and pepper to taste, pour into a heated sauce boat and serve with the roast chicken, garnished with watercress sprigs.

CONVENIENCE TURKEY

Whole birds are too large to buy for everyday meals, but nowadays you can enjoy turkey at any time by buying a rolled turkey breast from the supermarket. These usually weigh about 1kg/2¼lb and serve 4-6. They benefit from being marinaded in a little oil, wine and herbs before roasting at 180C/350F/gas 4. Alternatively they can be pot-roasted on a bed of onions with oil and wine.

Fast Fish

Grilling is the ideal way to cook fresh fish: it's fast and seals in all the oils and juices. Almost any fish can be grilled, from expensive salmon or halibut to everyday cod or herring

Grilled halibut with anchovies (page 179)

GOOD-QUALITY FRESH fish needs the minimum of cooking — overcooking ruins it — and fast grilling is the preferred method. Grilled fish can be served with very simple accompaniments, such as boiled new potatoes and a salad, or dressed up with a rich sauce, like Grilled halibut with anchovies (page 179). Such a dish, or a large handsome fish cooked whole, like the Grilled sea bass with almonds, makes an excellent,

easy-to-cook centrepiece for a dinner party or Sunday lunch. For everyday occasions, fish such as herring or mackerel, whole or filleted, make quick, inexpensive and nutritious family meals.

Grilled fish is ideal barbecue food and cooking outdoors over charcoal makes it even more delicious. Extra flavour can also be introduced by marinating the fish before cooking or by serving a flavoured butter.

Preparing to grill

Have the fish cleaned, with heads left on or taken off as you prefer. Red mullet should be cleaned with the liver left in to flavour the fish. Remove any scales by scraping the skin with a sharp knife, working towards the head. Small fish may be grilled whole; larger ones are more commonly cooked as steaks or fillets. A meaty fish can be cut into cubes and skewered with other ingredients; shellfish such as scallops are especially good cooked this way.

When cooking small fish such as mackerel whole, slash them diagonally with a sharp knife in two-three places on both sides to allow the heat to reach the centre. Season the fish with salt and pepper or coat it with seasoned flour. The latter is good for white fish, which develops very little colour during cooking, giving it an appetizing crispy golden brown exterior. Brush with oil to prevent the fish from drying out while cooking. Large flat fish such as Dover sole are first dipped in milk, then in seasoned flour.

Grilling the fish

Preheat the grill thoroughly and grease the grid before putting the fish on it. Keep the fish close to the heat (7.5-12.5cm/3-5in away) so that it cooks fast, otherwise it will become flabby; turn. (Delicate fillets can be cooked without turning, at a higher temperature.)

Pieces, steaks or fillets should be basted frequently with butter, oil or any marinade to keep them moist. Whole fish, being protected by their skin, need be basted only at the beginning and after turning.

To test when the fish is cooked, stick a fork into it and press gently. When cooked the flesh will flake slightly, and the juices will look milky. With thick whole fish or steaks; cooked to the bone.

Serve the fish piping hot, garnished with parsley to give colour. A slice or wedge of lemon is essential with fish such as herring to act as a counterpoint to the taste of the rich oily flesh.

Grilled herrings with mustard

- **Preparation: 20 minutes**

- **Cooking: 15 minutes**

4 herrings, cleaned with heads removed
1kg/2lb new potatoes, scraped
2tbls flour
salt and pepper
1tbls oil
2tbls French mustard
4tbls fresh breadcrumbs
4tbls melted butter
dill or parsley sprigs, to garnish

- **Serves 4**

- **650cals/2730kjs per serving**

1 Heat the oven to 240C/475F/gas 9. Also heat the grill to high.

2 If scales remain on the herrings, scrape them off with a sharp knife, working towards the head. Wash the fish and dry carefully on absorbent paper.

3 Cook the potatoes in boiling salted water for 15-20 minutes or until tender when tested.

4 Season the flour with salt and pepper, then dip the herrings in it, and put on a well-oiled baking tray. Grill for 3-4 minutes on each side, or until cooked.

5 Arrange the herrings in a shallow heatproof dish. Spread them liberally with mustard, then sprinkle with the breadcrumbs and melted butter. Bake for 5 minutes. Serve in the dish accompanied with the drained potatoes.

Cook's tips

Fresh new potatoes can simply be scrubbed clean, cooked and eaten skins and all. This not only gives extra flavour, but added fibre and vitamins.

Variations

Coat the herrings with seasoned medium oatmeal instead of flour for a crunchier coating for grilling or frying.

Grilled halibut with anchovies

- **Preparation: 30 minutes**
- **Cooking: 30 minutes**

2 garlic cloves, finely chopped
2tbls finely chopped parsley
12 anchovy fillets
6 × 150g/5oz slices halibut
1tbls olive oil
For the sauce:
2tbls olive oil
1 onion, finely chopped
400g/14oz canned tomatoes
50g/2oz black olives, stoned and halved
2 garlic cloves, crushed
1 bouquet garni
grated zest and juice of 1 lemon
1½tsp sugar
¼tsp dried oregano
4 drops hot pepper sauce
4 anchovy fillets
2tbls grated Parmesan cheese
2tbls single cream
black pepper
For the garnish:
12 anchovy fillets
25g/1oz anchovy butter
(see Buttering up, page 180)
finely chopped parsley
6 cocktail gherkins, cut into fans

- **Serves 6**
- **295cals/1240kjs per serving**

1 Mix the garlic and parsley on a plate and roll the 12 anchovy fillets in the mixture. Cut the fillets into lengths to match the thickness of the halibut slices.

2 Make incisions in the fish slices and insert the anchovy strips right through the fish. Brush the slices with oil.

3 Make the sauce: heat the oil in a heavy saucepan and fry the onion for about 5 minutes until golden but not brown. Add the tomatoes, olives, garlic, bouquet garni, lemon zest and juice, sugar, oregano and hot pepper sauce. Bring to the boil, stirring occasionally, then simmer gently, uncovered, for 10-15 minutes until the sauce is reduced by about one-third.

4 Crush the four anchovy fillets to a paste with a fork. Stir the Parmesan cheese into the sauce together with the cream and crushed anchovy. Season with pepper to taste. Heat the grill to high.

5 When ready to grill the fish, brush the grill grid with a little oil. Put the fish slices on the grid and grill 12.5cm/5in away from the heat for 5 minutes on each side or until the fish flakes easily with a fork. Baste from time to time with the cooking juices.

6 Arrange the fish slices on a heated serving platter. Garnish each slice with two anchovy fillets and a round of anchovy butter. Pour the sauce around the fish and garnish with chopped parsley and gherkin fans.

Grilled mackerel with fennel (page 180)

Cook's tips

Halibut is an expensive fish and deserves this special treatment for a dinner party. You will need three tins of anchovies all together.

How to... fillet a fish

To make two fillets, cut along the backbone from head end to tail through the flesh; split the fish and remove the bone.

To split open a gutted, headless fish, cut the fish through the belly cavity through to the tail. Turn over and press down to open.

Lift up the backbone from the head end. Cut it free just above the tail, keeping the tail on if the recipe requires. The fish can then be layered flat or rolled.

Grilled mackerel with fennel

- **Preparation: 30 minutes, plus marinating**
- **Cooking: 15 minutes**

4 × 275g/10oz mackerel, cleaned
salt and pepper
225g/8oz dried fennel stalks
6tbls olive oil
6 lemon slices, halved
2 lemons, cut into quarters

- **Serves 4**
- **515cals/2165kjs per serving**

1 Cut off the fins and season the fish generously with salt and pepper.

2 Arrange a bed of half the fennel stalks in a dish large enough to hold the fish in a single layer. Sprinkle over 3tbls oil, lay the fish on top and cover with the remaining fennel stalks. Sprinkle with another 3tbls oil and marinate the fish for at least 1 hour.

3 Heat the grill to high. When ready to grill, brush the grill grid with a little oil. Transfer the fennel stalks on the top of the fish to the grill grid.

4 Cut three diagonal slits in the flesh of each mackerel on each side. Put the fish on the fennel stalks; brush over with oil from the marinade. Reserve the remaining fennel for topping.

5 Grill the mackerel 12.5cm/5in from the heat for 8 minutes on each side or until the fish flakes easily with a fork. Baste with the pan juices after turning the fish to cook the second side.

6 Arrange the reserved fennel stalks on a warmed serving dish. Lay the mackerel on top, put half a lemon slice in each slit and garnish with the lemon wedges. Set the fennels stalks alight – this gives the fish a unique barbecued flavour – and serve.

Cod steaks with cheese topping

- **Preparation: 15 minutes, plus standing**
- **Cooking: 15 minutes**

4 × 175g/6oz cod steaks
salt and pepper
3tbls melted butter
50g/2oz Gruyère cheese, grated
50g/2oz Cheddar cheese, grated
1tbls Dijon mustard

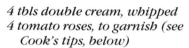

4 tbls double cream, whipped
4 tomato roses, to garnish (see Cook's tips, below)

- **Serves 4**
- **390cals/1640kjs per serving**

1 Heat the grill to high. Using a sharp knife, remove the skin and small centre bone from each cod steak. Season each one generously with salt and pepper. Leave the cod steaks to stand at room temperature for 15 minutes.

2 Use some of the butter to grease a shallow heatproof dish large enough to take the steaks comfortably in one layer. Lay them in side by side and pour the remaining melted butter over them. Put under the grill and grill 7.5cm/3in from the heat for 5 minutes. Turn over and grill for a further 3 minutes.

3 Meanwhile put the grated cheeses in a bowl, beat in the mustard and season to taste with pepper. Fold in the whipped cream.

CLARIFIED BUTTER

Place the butter in a small heavy-based saucepan and melt it very slowly. The butter will foam and the foam will fall gently to the bottom of the pan, leaving the clarified butter as clear as oil. Pour into a bowl carefully, without disturbing the sediment. Keep the clarified butter in the refrigerator and use as needed.

BUTTERING UP

Make flavoured butters to serve with grilled fish well in advance and chill ready for use. Or make a double quantity, cut into portions, wrap individually and freeze until required.

To make, cream the softened butter with the flavouring and season with salt and pepper to taste if needed. Roll into a sausage shape and wrap in foil. Chill and cut into thick slices before serving.

Anchovy butter Use 25g/1oz butter and 1tsp anchovy essence or 2tsp mashed anchovy fillets.

Parsley butter Use 50g/2oz butter, 1tbls chopped parsley, 1tbls lemon juice and ¼tsp paprika. Parsley may be replaced by tarragon, fennel and dill.

Watercress butter Use 25g/1oz butter, 1tbls chopped watercress and ½tsp onion juice creamed together.

4 Spread the cheese topping over the cod steaks and grill for a further 3 minutes or until golden brown. Garnish with a tomato rose and serve at once.

Cook's tips

To make a tomato 'rose', thinly peel the skin from a firm tomato. Roll it up and ease out into a rose shape. Alternatively garnish the fish with wedges of tomato; or two small tomatoes, halved and grilled.

All Wrapped Up

A golden pastry crust wrapped round meat or fish turns a plain dish into something spectacular. It also makes expensive cuts go further

*B*AKING *EN CROUTE* was invented in the days of cooking over open fires to protect meat from the fierce heat and keep it moist and succulent. The crust was just flour and water paste, discarded before the meat was eaten. Once cooking became more sophisticated and took place in an oven, this was replaced by an edible puff or flaky pastry crust.

Because the glossy, golden brown, elaborately decorated crust makes a dish look very imposing and is best suited to large pieces of meat or fish, baking *en croûte* is mainly used for party dishes to serve at least six people. On the other hand, the humble Cornish pasty is a form of baking en croûte. This is designed to make a little meat go a long way; and the same holds true for the expensive items such as fillet of beef or fresh salmon used for the party dishes. As well as adding a portion of pastry, the case allows other ingredients to be included along with the meat. The Russian dish Coulibiac (page 183) is a fine example as it includes vegetables, rice and hard-boiled eggs to stretch a relatively small amount of salmon.

A pastry crust has still more advantages: again like the Cornish pasty, originally consumed at the bottom of a tin mine, it makes the food easily portable and convenient to eat in the fingers. So *en croûte* dishes are ideal for grand picnics or for buffet parties.

Flavoursome fillings
Many foods lend themselves to being cooked *en croûte*: meat, poultry, game and fish, combined

Boeuf en croûte (page 183)

with vegetables, a coating sauce or spicy stuffing. If shortcrust pastry is used, the filling can be wrapped up raw and cooked inside it. With some foods this may mean that the pastry starts to brown too much before the filling is cooked, but it can easily be protected with crumpled foil. If flaky or puff pastry is used the cooking time for the pastry is too short for any raw filling except fish, so it must be precooked, as in Boeuf en croûte (see right). Make absolutely sure that cooked fillings and any sauce or stuffing are completely cold before being wrapped up; warmth would spoil the pastry.

All wrapped up

It's important to use just the right amount of pastry so that it rolls out thick enough to encase the filling safely without being unpleasantly thick. Pastry quantities are usually expressed by the amount of flour used to make them: 225g/8oz shortcrust or flaky pastry means pastry made with that amount of flour. But with puff pastry, which is usually bought or made in bulk at home, a made weight is given.

Puff and flaky pastry really should be rolled out until almost too thin to handle, otherwise the underneath will not cook. These are the best ones to use for party dishes; but for a more ordinary dish like the Meat loaf en chemise (see right) you could substitute shortcrust pastry, especially if you feel nervous about the technique. This can be a little thicker – up to 5mm/¼in is usual.

Roll the pastry out to roughly the shape required and put the cold filling on top. Trim the pastry and reserve the trimmings. Brush the edges with egg glaze and fold the pastry up neatly, just like a paper parcel, sealing the edges with egg or water and tucking in ends.

Use the trimmings to decorate the crust with leaves, flowers, tassels and other shapes (see page 72). These are functional as well – use them to disguise joints and any holes you cut for steam to escape. Stick them in place with egg glaze, then glaze the whole crust so that it looks rich and glossy when borne to the table.

Meat loaf en chemise

- **Preparation: 30 minutes, plus cooling**

- **Cooking: 1¼ hours**

15g/½oz butter, plus extra for greasing
1 large onion, very finely chopped
3 slices stale white bread
about 150ml/¼pt beef stock
225g/8oz lean minced beef
225g/8oz lean minced pork
2tbls finely chopped parsley
1tsp Worcestershire sauce
hot pepper sauce or cayenne pepper
salt and pepper
225g/8oz puff pastry, defrosted
4tbls.French mustard
beaten egg, to glaze
tomato sauce (see Linguini steps 1, 2 and 3, page 33)
parsley sprigs, to garnish

- **Serves 4-6**

- **615cals/2585kjs per serving**

1 Heat the oven to 220C/425F/gas 7. Melt the butter in a heavy frying pan and fry the onion over low heat until soft, stirring occasionally.

2 Trim the crusts off the bread. Soak the slices in a little beef stock or water, then squeeze out as much moisture as possible.

3 Put the onion and bread in a large bowl along with the beef, pork,

chopped parsley, Worcestershire sauce and a little hot pepper sauce or cayenne pepper to taste. Mix thoroughly until smoothly blended, adding generous amounts of salt and pepper.

4 Generously butter an 850ml/1½pt loaf tin. Pack the meat mixture into it and level off the top with spatula. Cover with foil and bake for 45 minutes. Remove from the oven and leave to cool completely before turning out.

5 When ready to proceed heat the oven to 200C/400F/gas 6. Roll out the pastry into a 30cm/12in square. Turn the meat loaf out of the tin, scrape off any excess fat and spread it liberally with the French mustard.

6 Set the meat loaf in the centre of the pastry and wrap it up like a parcel. Brush the seams lightly with water; seal them tightly and trim away the excess pastry. Use the scraps to make a decorative lattice of strips over the top. Brush all over with beaten egg and cut small vents on top to allow steam to escape.

7 Transfer the parcel to an ungreased baking tray and bake for 30 minutes or until the pastry is puffed, crisp and golden. Meanwhile make the tomato sauce to accompany the meat.

8 Serve the meat loaf hot, cut in thick slices, garnished with parsley sprigs and accompanied with the sauce.

Plan ahead

Make the meat loaf first thing in the morning, or even the day before, so that it is quite cold before you wrap it in pastry.

How to … make a pastry parcel

On a lightly floured surface, roll out the pastry very thinly to the required size and trim the edges to form a rectangle.

Brush the edges with beaten egg and wrap around the filling. Cut a piece of pastry from each end and fold in the corners to seal.

Use any remaining pieces of pastry to make decorate leaves, tassels and berries. Brush with egg and press lightly into place.

Boeuf en croûte

- **Preparation: 45 minutes, plus cooling and chilling**

- **Cooking: 55 minutes**

1kg/2¼lb fillet of beef
black pepper
225g/8oz puff pastry
25g/1oz butter
100g/4oz mushrooms, thinly sliced
1tsp mixed herbs
1tsp finely chopped parsley
beaten egg, to glaze
watercress sprigs, to garnish

- **Serves 6**

- **405cals/1700kjs per serving**

1 Trim any excess fat from the fillet and tie the meat into a neat shape with string. Sprinkle generously with pepper. If using frozen pastry begin to defrost it.

2 Fry the meat quickly in the butter to brown it on all sides, then reduce the heat to medium and fry for 15 minutes longer, turning occasionally. Remove from the pan and leave until completely cold.

3 Fry the mushrooms in the butter left in the pan for 2 minutes. Season with the mixed herbs and parsley and continue frying until the liquid from the mushrooms is completely reduced. Remove from the heat and leave until cold.

4 Roll out the pastry into a rectangle about 10cm/4in larger all round than the beef. Spread half the mushroom mixture over the centre of the pastry.

5 Remove the string from the beef and put the meat on the centre of the pastry. Brush the pastry edges with beaten egg. Wrap over the long sides and press the seam to seal. Then lift up the short sides to encase the meat completely and pinch the seams together. Put on baking tray with the seams underneath.

6 Roll out any trimmings and cut them into decorative shapes such as leaves and tassels. Stick them onto pastry with beaten egg. Chill the parcel for 2 hours to relax the pastry.

7 Heat the oven to 200C/400F/gas 6. Brush the pastry with beaten egg and bake in the centre of the oven for 25-30 minutes until the pastry is well risen and golden brown. Transfer to a heated serving platter, garnish with watercress sprigs and serve at once.

Coulibiac

- **Preparation: making pastry, then 30 minutes plus cooling and chilling**

- **Cooking: 15 minutes, then 30 minutes**

25g/1oz butter
½ Spanish onion, finely chopped
salt and pepper
flour, for rolling
225/8oz flour-quantity Puff or Rough puff pastry (page 50)
225g/8oz cooked rice, cooled
3 hard-boiled eggs, sliced
2tbls finely chopped fennel, dill or parsley
450g/1lb fresh salmon fillet, skinned
1 egg yolk, beaten with 1tbls water
300ml/½ pt mousseline (page 77) or Béchamel sauce (page 16)
flat-leaved parsley, to garnish

- **Serves 6**

- **450cals/1890kjs per serving**

1 Melt the butter in a small frying pan and fry the onion over low heat for 2-3 minutes until transparent, stirring now and then. Add the mushrooms and fry for 10 minutes or until their moisture has evaporated. Season with salt and pepper to taste. Spread on a plate and cool.

2 Put the pastry on a lightly floured work surface and roll out as thinly as possible. Put it upside down on a baking tray and brush off any excess flour.

3 To assemble, put half the cold rice in the centre of the pastry, cover with a layer of sliced egg and season with salt and pepper. Sprinkle with 1tbls finely chopped fennel, dill or parsley and lay the salmon on top. Sprinkle with the remaining fennel, dill or parsley, season and cover with the remaining egg slices.

4 Trim the pastry to an even rectangle and brush the edge with some of the egg mixture. Fold the edges of the pastry over the filling to make a neat parcel. Press the edges together to seal in the filling. Decorate with pastry trimmings, covering the seam. Chill for 30 minutes.
🕐 Heat the oven to 220C/425F/gas 7.

5 Brush the pastry with egg glaze. Bake for 30 minutes or until the pastry is puffed and golden. Meanwhile make the tomato sauce.

6 Serve on a warmed serving plate, garnished with flat-leaved parsley and accompanied by the sauce.

Chicken pillows

- **Preparation: defrosting pastry, then 40 minutes**

- **Cooking: 1 hour**

6 chicken thighs
3 boned chicken breasts
about 8tbls flour
4tbls olive oil
100g/4oz butter
salt and pepper
300ml/½pt chicken stock
350g/12oz button mushrooms
9tbls Madeira
4-6tbls double cream
350g/12oz puff pastry, defrosted
1 egg yolk

- **Serves 6**　　　　🍴 💷 🕐

- **790cals/3320kjs per serving**

1 Prepare the chicken and sauce well in advance to allow cooling time. Bone the thighs and cut the breasts in half to make two large, flat, thin rounds. Roll the 12 pieces up tightly into sausage shapes.

2 Dust the chicken with flour. Heat 2tbls oil and 50g/2oz butter in a heavy flameproof casserole and fry the pieces until golden brown all over; season with salt and pepper.

3 Skim off the excess fat from the pan, then pour the stock over the chicken.

Cover and simmer for 20 minutes; leave until completely cold.

4 Slice the mushrooms thinly and fry in 2tbls oil and 25g/1oz butter until golden. Season with salt and pepper, moisten with 6tbls Madeira and leave to cool on a dish.

5 Make the sauce: melt 25g/1oz butter in a heavy saucepan. Add 3tbls flour and stir over medium heat to make a deep golden roux. Remove from the heat; beat in 3tbls Madeira and the juices from the cooked chicken. Return to the heat and stir in the cream. Bring to the boil, stirring constantly. Fold in half the mushrooms and simmer for 10 minutes, adding a little more stock if the sauce becomes too thick.
🕐 Allow to cool.

6 Heat the oven to 220C/425F/gas 7. Divide the pastry into six pieces. Roll each piece out and cut into an 18cm/7in square. Cut decorative leaves and tassels from the trimmings.

7 Lay one piece of breast and one piece of thigh diagonally on each pastry square. Cover with one-sixth of the remaining mushrooms. Moisten the filling with a little mushroom juice. Then fold the other corners over so that they meet in the middle, overlapping slightly, like an envelope. Brush the seams with beaten egg yolk and seal tightly.

8 Put the pastry pillows on a baking tray with the seams underneath. Glaze with beaten egg yolk. Decorate with pastry leaves and tassels; glaze these as well.

9 Bake for 20-25 minutes or until the pillows are well risen and golden. Reheat the Madeira sauce and serve it separately in a jug.

Pot Luck

Use pot roasting and braising to make joints of meat which could be tough if roasted meltingly tender and to raise prime cuts to new heights of excellence

POT ROASTING AND braising are almost identical ways of cooking meat. But there should be very little liquid in a pot roast, whereas a braise has quite a bit. Both are slow, gentle methods, used to tenderize less fine cuts of meat or to make a change from roasting. Cooking can be done on top of the stove or in the oven, but the latter is more common as it provides all round heat and cuts out any risk of burning.

Choosing the meat

Pot roasting is used for whole joints of meat, as in the recipes given here. For braising, the meat can be cut into chunks or slices – see page 188. For economy, choose any of the less fine joints which will benefit from moist slow cooking. But make sure they are reasonably lean or trim before cooking, as too much fat will make the sauce or gravy unpleasantly greasy to eat.

Beef: look for well-trimmed topside, top rump or silverside, boned and rolled. Finer cuts such as sirloin or fillet are not improved by pot roasting; keep these for traditional roasting in the oven.

Pork: hand and spring are good economical joints; or use leg or loin. Leg and foreleg should be boned and rolled as they are very large; loin can be left on the bone if preferred. But remember that a joint on the bone will cook more quickly than one that is solid meat. Spare rib is also good, although rather more fatty (strip off the rind), but belly pork has too much fat – dry roasting ensures that this drains away. Braising pork tenderloin, a prime cut, makes it sheer magic as the result is so succulent.

Swiss veal (page 186)

Lamb: joints of lamb are always tender, but a pot roasted or braised leg or shoulder makes a change from the usual roast.

Veal: pot roasting is an ideal way to cook veal, which can be dry and bland, ensuring that it remains moist and succulent. Stuff with raw ham and Gruyère cheese (see Swiss veal, below) for extra flavour.

Choosing the pot

The best pot to use is a flameproof casserole with a tight-fitting lid so that no steam can escape. A heavy base is desirable, and is in fact essential if the cooking is carried out on the top of the stove since it will prevent the contents from burning on the bottom. It should be just large enough to take the meat and accompaniments, otherwise the liquid will be dissipated over the pan surface and boil away.

If the lid does not fit tightly, insert a layer of foil or buttered greaseproof paper underneath it. If the casserole is not flameproof, brown the meat in a frying pan and transfer it to the casserole afterwards. Make sure to boil the cooking liquid in the frying pan to collect the tasty sediment.

Cooking technique

For both pot roasting and braising, start by braising the joint all over in olive oil or butter. Or use fat trimmed from the joint – heat it in a frying pan to release the liquid fat, then discard the bits.

Remove the meat and brown the diced vegetables; these then form a bed on which the meat rests while cooking. Add other flavourings such as bacon and herbs.

Return the meat to the pan and add the liquid – usually stock, with a little wine added for flavour if available. Beer or cider can be used instead; a spoonful or two of flamed brandy works wonders. Always bring the liquid to the boil before adding it to the meat. If cold it will extract flavour and moisture from the meat while heating up.

Whether cooking in the oven or on the stove top, regulate the heat so that the liquid is just at a gentle simmer. If it boils the meat will harden and the liquid is likely to boil away before cooking is complete.

How to ··· bone and stuff lamb

With a sharp boning knife, release the blade bone gradually from the meat working towards the socket.

When the bone is free as far down as the socket, hold it firmly with a cloth and twist until it comes out.

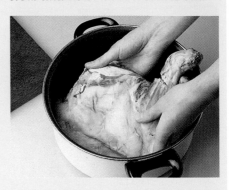

The pocket in the shoulder is now free from bone and can be stuffed with various flavoured stuffings.

Sew the end with fine string to secure and place in the pan on a bed of vegetables ready for braising.

Swiss veal

- **Preparation: 1 hour, plus chilling and bringing to room temperature**

- **Cooking: 1 hour 40 minutes**

1.4kg/3lb boned and rolled veal leg or loin
salt and pepper
grated nutmeg
12 thin slices (50g/2oz) raw ham
12 thin slices (175g/6oz) Gruyère cheese
150g/5oz streaky bacon rashers
100g/4oz butter
2 carrots, finely chopped
2 onions, finely chopped
300ml/½pt dry white wine
1 garlic clove, finely chopped
3tbls brandy
30 baby onions, peeled
1tbls caster sugar

24 small button mushrooms, thickly sliced
150ml/¼pt double cream
flat-leaved parsley, to garnish

- **Serves 8**

- **595cals/2500kjs per serving**

1 Lay the veal on a work surface and cut it into 12 even slices without separating them completely. Open the slices out carefully and season generously with salt, pepper and a pinch of nutmeg. Lay a slice of raw ham and Gruyère cheese in each cut slice.

2 Pull the joint together again. Cover it with bacon rashers and tie up securely with string, first lengthways and then horizontally in several places.

3 Melt half the butter in a flameproof casserole large enough to hold the joint comfortably and fry it until browned all over. Remove and keep warm.

4 Fry the carrots and onions in the same fat until golden brown. Meanwhile ▶

186

◀ combine the wine and garlic in a small pan and bring to the boil.

5 Lay the veal on top of the vegetables. Warm the brandy, then pour it over the veal and set alight. When the flames die down moisten the veal with the wine and garlic. Cover the casserole and simmer over the lowest possible heat for 1-1¼ hours or until the veal is tender.

6 Meanwhile fit the baby onions in the bottom of a heavy pan that will take them in one layer. Add the sugar, 15g/½oz butter and season with salt and pepper. Cook for 12-15 minutes over medium heat, shaking the pan frequently, until evenly golden brown.

7 In another pan, melt 25g/1oz butter and fry the mushrooms for 4-5 minutes until tender. Season and set aside.

8 Remove the veal from the casserole, discard strings and bacon and keep the meat hot on a heated serving dish.

9 Strain the sauce through a fine sieve, pressing some of the flavouring vegetables through as well. Return the sauce to the casserole, stir in the cream and reheat gently. Taste and adjust the seasoning.

10 Heat the remaining 15g/½oz butter in a large frying pan and toss the onions and mushrooms to heat them through.

11 To serve garnish the veal with the parsley, onions and mushrooms. Spoon some of the cream sauce over the veal and serve the remainder in a heated sauceboat.

Cook's tips

Choose a long thin-shaped joint. Chill well before slicing and filling, then bring to room temperature before cooking.

Lamb provençale

- **Preparation: 30 minutes**

- **Cooking: 1¼ hours**

2 garlic cloves
1.4kg/3lb shoulder of lamb
salt and pepper
4tbls olive oil
2 large onions, finely chopped
1 carrot, finely chopped
300ml/½pt boiling hot beef stock
3 large ripe tomatoes, skinned,
   seeded and finely chopped

2tbls tomato purée
½tsp dried thyme
100g/4oz black olives, stoned
flat-leaved parsley, to garnish

- **Serves 6**

- **850cals/3570kjs per serving**

1 Cut the garlic cloves into thin slivers. Make slits all over the lamb with a sharp-pointed knife and push in the garlic slivers. Season well with salt and pepper.

2 Heat the oil in a large flameproof casserole and brown the lamb all over. Remove the meat and add the onions and carrot; fry until golden.

3 Add the stock, tomatoes and tomato purée, season with salt and pepper to taste and bring to the boil. Return the lamb to the casserole and sprinkle with thyme.

4 Cover the casserole and simmer over low heat until the lamb is tender; about 1 hour for medium rare. Add the olives about 10 minutes before the end of the cooking time.

5 Transfer the lamb to a heated serving dish. Skim the fat from the sauce and spoon vegetables and sauce around the lamb. Garnish with parsley and serve.

Portuguese beef

- **Preparation: marinating, then 15 minutes**

- **Cooking: 3¼ hours**

425ml/¾pt red wine
juice of ½ lemon
4tbls olive oil
2 garlic cloves, finely chopped
1tsp paprika
2 bay leaves
2 cloves
12 black peppercorns
1.6kg/3½lb silverside of beef, rolled
salt and pepper
1 beef stock cube, crumbled
2tbls tomato purée
beurre manié *made from 15g/½oz butter and 1tbls flour*
For the garnish:
900g/2lb boiled new potatoes
350g/12oz cooked peas
12 cooked asparagus tips

- **Serves 6**

- **835cals/3505kjs per serving**

1 Put the wine in a large bowl with the lemon juice and 2tbls oil. Flavour with the garlic, paprika, bay leaves, cloves and peppercorns. Add the beef and turn to coat. Cover and marinate in the refrigerator overnight.

2 Remove the joint from the refrigerator and bring to room temperature, then drain and pat dry with absorbent paper, reserving the marinade. Heat the oven to 150C/300F/gas 2.

3 Season the meat with salt and pepper. Heat the remaining 2tbls oil in a large flameproof casserole and brown the meat on all sides.

4 Remove the meat and add the reserved marinade, stock cube and tomato purée. Bring to the boil, add the

meat, cover and cook in the oven for 2½-3 hours or until the meat is tender but pink in the centre.

5 Transfer the meat to a heated dish, remove the string and keep hot. Bring the sauce to the boil and boil for 5 minutes to reduce by about one-third.

6 Pass the sauce through a sieve into a saucepan, bring to the boil and gradually whisk in the *beurre manié*. Continue to boil for another 3-4 minutes, stirring, until thick. Check the seasoning by tasting, add more salt and pepper if necessary.

7 To serve, slice half the beef thinly and lay the slices on a heated serving dish with the remaining piece of meat at one end. Spoon a little sauce over the slices and pour the remainder into a sauceboat. Garnish the dish with separate piles of potatoes, peas and asparagus tips.

MINI-BRAISES

Braising can also be used to cook good-quality stewing steak, large thick (pork or lamb) chops and slices of liver or heart (lamb's or pig's). Follow the basic cooking method, using enough liquid to just cover the meat. Cover tightly and cook over low heat or in a 180C/350F/gas 4 oven.

FLAVOUR ENHANCER

To ensure that a pot roast or braise emerges deliciously moist, marinate the meat first. Combine olive oil, wine, herbs and spices in a dish just large enough to hold the joint. Put in the joint, spoon over the marinade and leave to marinate overnight in the refrigerator. Remove 1-2 hours before cooking to allow the meat to come to room temperature. Remove from the marinade and pat dry with absorbent paper before browning. Reserve the marinade and use it as the cooking liquid.

English pork loin

- **Preparation: 30 minutes**
- **Cooking: 2 hours**

2.2kg/4½lb loin of pork, chined
5tbls olive oil
75g/3oz butter
2 onions, finely chopped
450g/1lb white breadcrumbs
25g/1oz suet
1-2tbls chopped thyme
6tbls chopped parsley
450g/1lb cooking apples, finely chopped
salt and pepper
1 large egg
1-2tbls lemon juice
1-2tbls milk, if needed

150ml/¼pt dry cider
425ml/¾pt chicken stock
3 red dessert apples
6-8 parsley sprigs

- **Serves 6**
- **980cals/4115kjs per serving**

1 Heat the oven to 190C/375F/gas 5. Trim the joint of fat, leaving a 2cm/¾in thickness. Heat 4tbls oil in a frying pan and brown the joint on all sides, then remove from the pan.

2 To make the stuffing, melt 50g/2oz butter in the pan and fry the onions gently until soft. Remove the onion and put into a large bowl along with the breadcrumbs, suet, thyme, 4tbls parsley and the cooking apples. Season with salt and pepper to taste. Add the egg and lemon juice and mix to a paste. If the mixture is dry and crumbly, add a little milk.

3 To stuff the joint separate the loin into chops by cutting down almost to the bone. Fill the space between each chop generously with stuffing – the stuffing band should be as wide as the chop. Use long skewers horizontally to keep the chops together. Season the top of the joint with salt and pepper and sprinkle the stuffing bands with the remaining chopped parsley.

FINISHING TOUCH

Pot roasting and braising produces delicious juices which make wonderful gravy or sauce. The simplest type is made just by skimming off the fat from the juices left in the pan and straining the gravy into a sauceboat. If there is too much liquid, reduce and thicken it by boiling rapidly. Flavouring vegetables can be partly or wholly incorporated into a sauce by pressing them through a sieve along with the liquid, then reheating it carefully, perhaps with a small amount of added cream for extra flavour.

To thicken a large amount of sauce use *beurre manié*, as in Portuguese beef (see left) or a paste of cornflour and water.

4 Pour the cider and stock into a roasting tin and bring to the boil on the stove top. Put the joint in the tin, cover with foil and cook in the oven for 45 minutes. Remove the foil and cook for a further ¾-1 hour. ▶

5 When the pork is almost done, core but do not peel the dessert apples and cut them into rings. Fry in the remaining butter and oil until golden.

6 To serve, transfer the pork to a heated serving dish and remove the skewers. Garnish with the fried apples and parsley sprigs. Skim the fat from the pan juices and serve in a heated sauceboat.

Belgian pork tenderloin

- **Preparation: marinating, then 20 minutes**

- **Cooking: 40 minutes**

2 pork tenderloins (1.1kg/2½lb together)
1 thyme sprig, plus extra to garnish
1 parsley sprig
2 bay leaves
salt and pepper
grated nutmeg
1 garlic clove, sliced
200 ml/7fl oz red wine
1 tbls olive oil
25g/1oz butter
1 tbls French mustard
1 tbls redcurrant jelly
tarragon vinegar
1 tsp cornflour

- **Serves 6**

- **355cals/1490kjs per serving**

1 Put the tenderloins into a deep dish. Add the thyme, parsley and bay leaves; sprinkle with pepper and nutmeg. Add the garlic and pour over the wine and oil. Cover and leave in a cool place for 2 days, turning the meat from time to time.

2 Remove the meat from the marinade and dry with absorbent paper; reserve the marinade. Heat the oven to 190C/375F/gas 5.

3 Melt 20g/¾oz of the butter in a deep baking tin large enough to hold the meat. Add the tenderloins and fry over medium heat for about 4 minutes, turning to seal them on all sides.

4 Cover the dish with foil and cook in the oven until the pork is tender – about 20-25 minutes, depending on the thickness of the tenderloins. Check at regular intervals after the first 15 minutes; do not cover. ⏱ Transfer the meat to a heated serving dish and keep warm.

5 Strain the marinade into the baking tin. Put over low heat and simmer gently, stirring to incorporate the sediment, until reduced by a quarter.

6 Stir in the mustard, redcurrant jelly and vinegar. Add 2tbls water to the cornflour, stir until smooth, then stir into the marinade.

7 Bring the sauce back to the boil over a low heat to thicken it. Stir in the remaining butter and season with salt. Strain the sauce, if necessary, then pour some over the meat and the rest into a heated sauceboat. Garnish the pork with thyme sprigs and serve hot with the sauce.

Golden Wonders

Chicken and turkey are ideal meats for deep-frying. Given a protective coating and plunged briefly into boiling hot oil they emerge crisp and crunchy outside, tender and juicy within

Whether left as whole portions or cut into small pieces the fine-textured flesh of chicken and turkey cooks through to perfection when deep-fried. This is achieved by coating it, usually with egg and breadcrumbs, to protect the meat from the fierce heat of the oil and stop it drying out and hardening.

Deep-frying lends itself to a wide range of dishes, suitable for every occasion from a family meal to an elegant dinner party. The joints can be coated and deep-fried in a matter of minutes; or elaborately boned out and rolled round a savoury stuffing. Left-over roast poultry can be deep-fried in the form of croquettes.

Use ready-prepared chicken joints for deep-frying or buy a chicken of up to about 1.6kg/3½lb in weight and quarter it. Turkey joints are too large to cook through and are best cooked as escalopes or boned out first.

Preparing

Take the meat out of the refrigerator about 2 hours before cooking to allow it to come to room temperature. Dry thoroughly with absorbent paper. Remove all skin and any bones that stick out awkwardly. For special occasions, and with turkey, remove all the bone.

To make escalopes put the boned-out portions between two sheets of stretch wrap and beat to an even thickness with a meat hammer or rolling pin. Different types of stuffings or cheese slices can be layed on to the flattened meat. Roll up tightly and then secure with a cocktail stick.

Chicken Kiev (page 192)

Protective coatings

The simplest coating, frequently used when the meat is deep-fried in small pieces, is a light dusting of flour or cornflour. This is enough to protect during the cooking time.

Larger portions need a stronger coating, usually a mixture of egg and breadcrumbs (see page 136). This will stop the surface from burning for as much as 15 minutes if necessary. Use seasoned flour to dry the surface and give it immediate protection. Then dip the portion in lightly beaten egg and roll in fresh white breadcrumbs. Do not use dry or browned breadcrumbs – fresh ones will fry to a crisp golden crunch. Pat them on firmly so that they adhere well to the sticky egg. For extra protection, usually when the food inside is rolled and might unfurl during cooking, the entire coating process can be repeated to give a thicker, firmer coating.

A short chilling time – 15 minutes – helps to set the coating and prevent any tendency for it to shed when put into the hot oil. Do not leave in the refrigerator longer, or the cooking time will be affected.

Batter is not generally used for coating poultry as it is too thick and stops it from cooking through. Only use on poached poultry.

Frying

Observe the same basic rules for deep-frying poultry as for fish and seafood (see pages 136-8). Use enough oil just to half-fill the pan, and make sure it reaches the specified temperature by testing with bread cubes or a thermometer if you do not have a thermostatically controlled deep-fat fryer. The temperature must not rise too high or the poultry will burn before being cooked through. Most dishes are cooked at 160-180C/ 320-350F.

As with other foods avoid overcrowding the pan, which would lower the temparature too much. Use the basket for chicken portions and large quantities of cubed meat. For small pieces or quantities use a slotted spoon – the open-meshed wire sort sold in Chinese supermarkets drains better than the common ones. Heat the basket or spoon in the oil before adding food. Always check the oil temperature before cooking a second batch.

Drain poultry well on absorbent paper before frying. Keep hot in a low oven, uncovered.

Chicken Kiev

- *Preparation: making and chilling butter, then 1 hour*

- *Cooking: 20 minutes*

100g/4oz butter
2tbls lemon juice
1-2 garlic cloves, crushed
1tbls finely chopped parsley
salt and pepper
4 chicken breasts, with the wing bone
25g/1oz flour
2 large eggs, beaten
fresh white breadcrumbs, for coating
oil, for deep-frying
lemon twists and parsley sprigs, to garnish

- *Serves 4*

- *685cals/2875kjs per serving*

1 Several hours in advance cream the butter with half the lemon juice, garlic and parsley. Season with salt and pepper to taste. Form into a rectangular block abvout 6.5cm/2½in long, enclose in stretch wrap and chill until very firm.

2 Prepare the chicken breasts: cut off the wings below the first joint. Remove the rib bones and breast cartilage but leave the wing bone. Remove and discard the skin.

3 Lay the chicken breasts out flat, cut side up. Remove the loose fillet from each one. Cut the sinew at the wing end and flatten the breasts with a meat hammer until about 15cm/6in across. Flatten the fillets as well. Season with salt and pepper and rub with the remaining lemon juice.

4 Cut the chilled butter into four fingers and put one on each breast. Put the flattened fillets on the butter, then wrap the breast meat around them.

5 Spread the flour on a large plate and season generously with salt and pepper. Coat the breasts all over; shake off any excess flour. Dip the breasts in beaten egg, drain, then coat with breadcrumbs, patting them on firmly.

6 Repeat the egg and breadcrumbing process, then chill the breasts for 15 minutes to set the coating.

7 Heat the oil to 160C/320F. Lower the joints carefully into the hot oil two at a time and fry for 10 minutes or until golden brown. Drain on absorbent paper and keep hot while frying the remaining two chicken portions.

8 Slip a cutlet frill on each wing tip and serve piping hot, garnished with lemon twists and parsley sprigs.

Cook's tips

To save time you can buy breasts ready prepared for making Chicken Kiev.

How to ··· *prepare chicken Kiev*

Beat out the breast and fillet thinly using a meat hammer or rolling pin. Put a finger of chilled butter in the centre.

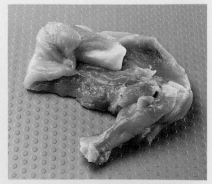

Lay the fillet over the finger of butter, then fold in the end and the two sides so as to form a neat parcel.

Deep-fried turkey packets

- **Preparation: 30 minutes**

- **Cooking: 30 minutes**

50g/2oz no-soak dried apricots
50g/2oz walnuts, chopped
1 garlic clove, finely chopped
2 large egg yolks
salt and pepper
4 turkey escalopes
25g/1oz flour
1-2 large eggs, lightly beaten
fresh white breadcrumbs
oil, for deep-frying
lemon wedges and parsley, to
  garnish
tossed green salad, to serve

- **Serves 4**

- **540cals/2270kjs per serving**

1 Put the apricots in a pan and add just enough water to cover. Bring to the boil, then simmer gently for 20 minutes or until tender.

2 Strain the apricots and chop them up. Put them in a bowl and combine with the walnuts, garlic and egg yolks. Season with salt and pepper to taste.

3 Put each turkey escalope between two pieces of stretch wrap and beat with a meat hammer until 3mm/⅛ in thick.

4 Cut each escalope in two and fill with 1tbls of the apricot stuffing. Fold the edges over to cover the filling and make a square packet; or shape into a roll, depending on the shape of the escalope.

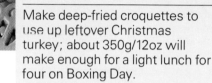

5 Put the flour, egg and breadcrumbs in separate shallow dishes; season the flour liberally with salt and pepper. Coat the turkey packets with flour, shaking off the excess. Dip them in egg, drain well, then coat with breadcrumbs; make sure the ends are well coated. Repeat with egg and breadcrumbs, then chill for 15 minutes to set.

6 Heat the oil to 170C/325F. Using a wire spoon, deep-fry two turkey packets for 4 minutes. Remove from the oil, drain on absorbent paper and keep hot. Fry the remaining packets in the same way and drain them well on absorbent paper.

7 Arrange the turkey packets on a heated serving platter and garnish.

CRACKING CROQUETTES

Make deep-fried croquettes to use up leftover Christmas turkey; about 350g/12oz will make enough for a light lunch for four on Boxing Day.

Finely chop the meat and mix with 100g/4oz finely chopped mushrooms, 150ml/¼pt white sauce, 1tbls chopped parsley, a good pinch of cayenne pepper plus salt and pepper to taste. Shape into balls or cakes with floured hands and coat with flour, egg and breadcrumbs. Chill for at least 1 hour before deep-frying.

Twice-fried chicken

- **Preparation: 35 minutes**

- **Cooking: 5-10 minutes**

1.6kg/3½lb chicken
4tbls soy sauce
8tbls dry sherry
1tsp sugar
1tsp finely chopped fresh ginger
  root
oil, for deep frying
2-3tbls cornflour
To serve:
225g/8oz long-grain rice, boiled
100g/4oz coarsely grated carrot
1tsp finely grated orange zest
50g/2oz butter
salt and pepper
4 spring onion tops

- **Serves 4**

- **840cals/3530kjs per serving**

1 Bone and skin the chicken completely and cut the meat into even-sized 2.5cm/1in cubes.

2 Put the soy sauce into a large bowl and combined with the sherry diluted with 1tbls water, the sugar and ginger root. Put in the chicken cubes, turn to coat and marinate for at least 2 hours.

3 Heat the oil to 160C/320F. Drain the chicken cubes well, put half of them in the wire basket and deep-fry for 1 minute. remove from the oil and drain on absorbent paper. Repeat with the remaining chicken cubes.

4 Return all the fried chicken cubes to the marinade and allow to stand for at least 15 minutes.

5 Reheat the oil to 180C/350F. Make the orange rice: fold the grated carrot and orange zest into the hot rice. Add the butter and season with salt and pepper. Keep hot while refrying the chicken cubes.

6 Drain the chicken pieces. Dust them lightly with cornflour and refry in two batches for 30 seconds or until crisp and golden brown. Drain on absorbent paper and serve at once, garnished with a spring onion top and accompanied by the rice.

Deep-fried chicken with tarragon mayonnaise

- *Preparation: 30 minutes, plus marinating and chilling*

- *Cooking: 25 minutes*

1.6kg/3½lb chicken
salt and pepper
cayenne pepper
juice of 1 lemon
2tbls olive oil
25g/1oz flour
1-2 large eggs, lightly beaten
fresh white breadcrumbs
oil, for deep-frying
watercress sprigs, to garnish
For the tarragon mayonnaise:
½ × Basic mayonnaise
(page 21)
1½tbls Dijon mustard
1tbls capers
1tbls finely chopped fresh tarragon
2 gherkins, finely chopped

- *Serves 4*

- *900cals/3780kjs per serving*

1 Joint the chicken into four portions, removing the protruding bones from the breast pieces. Cut away all the skin.

2 Put the chicken pieces in a shallow bowl and season generously with salt and pepper, plus a pinch of cayenne. Add the lemon juice and olive oil, stir to coat the joints in the marinade, cover and leave for at least 2 hours.

3 Meanwhile make the mayonnaise and mix in the mustard, capers, tarragon and gherkins. Season with salt and pepper to taste, stir well and chill.

4 Put the flour, beaten egg and breadcrumbs into separate shallow dishes. Season the flour well with salt and freshly-ground pepper.

5 Remove the chicken pieces from the marinade, drain on absorbent paper and dip each one in the flour. Shake off the excess and dip in the beaten egg; drain well and coat with breadcrumbs. Pat the breadcrumbs on firmly and chill for 15 minutes or until needed.

6 Heat the oil to 160C/320F. Lower the chicken legs into the hot oil and fry for 15 minutes or until the coating is golden. Remove, drain well and keep hot.

WEIGHT WATCHING?

Deep-fried food is definitely not slimming. However, chicken cooked this way is always skinned first, which reduces the damage considerably. A 175g/6oz chicken breast yields 215 calories if fried with skin on; only 150 if skinned first. But of course the delicious crispy coating accounts for still more calories . . . better keep deep-fried chicken as an occasional treat!

7 Check the temperature of the oil, then add the chicken breasts. Fry these for 10 minutes or until the coating is golden, then remove and drain.

8 Arrange the chicken portions on a heated serving platter and serve hot, garnished with watercress sprigs. Serve the tarragon mayonnaise separately.

Simply Delicious

If you want to entertain without spending hours in the kitchen away from your guests, pan frying tender cuts of lamb and pork is the answer

Pork chops with apple (page 197)

P*AN FRYING IS* both quick and easy and the perfect answer to what to give dinner guests if you want something that's guaranteed fail-safe and delicious. If you have an open-plan dining room with adjoining kitchen you can cook the main course while still chatting to your guests and serve it fresh from the pan at the peak of perfection.

Choosing the meat

For pan frying the meat must be young and tender: pork and lamb chops and fillet, pork escalopes and best end of neck of lamb are all suitable. (For Steak, see page 164).

Lamb: Buy small cutlets from the best end of neck, slightly larger ones from the loin, or chump chops from the top of the leg, which are the meatiest. Lamb chops should be fairly thickly cut, otherwise they are inclined to shrivel in the high heat of the frying pan.

Pork: Buy tender chops, fillet or escalopes. Tenderloin chops are the smallest and usually the most tender. Loin chops are slightly larger; middle loin chops often include a piece of kidney which many people consider a bonus. Chump chops, taken from between the loin and the leg, are large and meaty, but still very tender. Pork fillet or tenderloin is an extremely delicate, tender cut with no fat at all. A whole fillet weighs about 350g/12oz and can be cut into medallions in the same way as lamb. Pork escalopes are much cheaper than veal, which some of your guests may not wish to eat anyway, and virtually indistinguishable from it once egg-and-breadcrumbed.

Although not cheap, these cuts are nowhere near as expensive as their equivalents in beef or veal – and are very tasty – all the accompaniment they need is a sauce quickly made from the pan juices and a colourful garnish. The frying time can be as short as 8 minutes; 20 minutes is the longest.

Preparing and cooking

If the meat has been frozen, make sure it is completely thawed before cooking. When you take it out of the refrigerator, wipe it dry with absorbent paper, and season with pepper only; salt would draw more moisture out. Leave for 2 hours to come to room temperature and season with salt just before cooking: add more pepper if liked.

Ask the butcher to trim off any sharp corners of bone from chops, so that they will lie really flat in the pan and brown evenly. Trim chops well, but leave a thin layer of fat to keep them moist. For medallions or noisettes ask the butcher to bone the meat but not roll it. Prepare medallions as shown opposite; for noisettes, remove the skin but leave the fat on.

Use a heavy pan and a mixture of butter and olive oil for pan frying pork and lamb, exactly as for pan frying beef and veal (see page 163). Pork is also good fried in lard, which is rendered pork fat and intensifies the 'porky' flavour. If you have a non-stick frying pan and like to use a minimum of fat, just

heat it and wipe round with a piece of the fat trimmed off the meat.

Fry fairly fast and briefly, using the charts as a guide, so that the meat has a crisp brown outside and a tender juicy centre. Keep the meat hot while making the sauce. This can be something as simple as the pan juices, deglazed with a little water, stock or wine. Adding a small knob of butter will give it a professional-looking gloss.

COOKING PERFECT PORK CHOPS
*Marinated chops will take about 1 minute longer on each side

Cut	Weight	Thickness	Cooking time each side*	Result
Chump chop	350-400g/12-14oz	3-4cm/1¼-1½in	6 minutes	well-done but juicy
Tenderloin chop	175g/6oz 300g/10oz	1cm/½in 2.5cm/1in	7-8 minutes 10 minutes	well-done but juicy well-done but juicy
Loin chop	275-300g/9-10oz 350g/12oz	2cm/¾in 2.5cm/1in	7 minutes 8 minutes	well-done but juicy well-done but juicy

* Including initial 2 minutes at high heat on each side

COOKING PERFECT LAMB CHOPS
*Marinated chops will take about 1 minute longer on each side

Cut	Weight	Thickness	Cooking time each side*	Result
Chump chop	about 175g/6oz	2.5cm/1in	3-3½ minutes 4 minutes	slightly pink well-done
Loin chop	about 150g/5oz	2.5cm/1in	3 minutes 4 minutes	slightly pink well-done
Best end of neck cutlet	about 75g/3oz	2.5cm/1in	3 minutes 4 minutes	slightly pink well-done

*Including initial 2 minutes at high heat on each side

How to ··· cut lamb medallions

Bone a best end of neck and strip off all the skin. Roll the meat up tightly with the thick side or eye of meat inside.

Tie securely with fine string in several places. Sear in butter and olive oil, then cut between the strings into 2.5cm/1in slices.

Pork chops with apple rings

- *Preparation: bringing chops to room temperature, then 10 minutes*

- *Cooking: 25 minutes*

4 pork chops, 2.5cm/1in thick
salt and pepper
2 large crisp tart dessert apples
2tbls Demerara sugar
25g/1oz butter
4tbls apple juice
flat-leaved parsley, to garnish

- *Serves 4* (♍) (££)

- *315 cals/1325 kjs per serving*

1 Trim the fat off the chops, leaving a thin layer to protect the meat. Reserve the fat. Wipe the chops with absorbent paper and season with pepper. Leave to come to room temperature. Season with salt just before cooking.

2 Chop the reserved pork fat and put it in a large frying pan over medium heat until the fat has melted and the pieces are shrivelled and crisp.

3 Remove the fat pieces with a slotted spoon and discard. Add the chops and fry over medium-high heat for 5 minutes on each side.

4 Meanwhile core the unpeeled apples and slice them thickly into rings. Toss in a bowl with the sugar.

5 When the chops are well browned on both sides and almost cooked through, remove them from the pan and keep warm.

6 Melt the butter in the pan and fry the apple rings for 2-3 minutes until coloured on both sides and softening.

7 Return the chops to the pan, burying them in the apple rings, and continue

to fry for a further 2-3 minutes or until the chops are cooked through, turning once. Some of the apple rings will start off under the chops; see that you exchange them with those on top when turning the chops.

8 Transfer the chops to a heated serving dish and garnish with the apple rings. Keep warm.

9 Add the apple juice to the juices in the pan. Bring to the boil over medium heat, scraping the pan clean with a wooden spatula or spoon. Pour the sauce over the chops and serve at once.

NOISETTE OR MEDALLION?

Best end of neck of lamb is delicious cut into little round steaks similar to tournedos of beef. These can be noisettes or medallions. In both cases the meat is boned and rolled up with the eye or thick side inside, tied at intervals with string and sliced into rounds. The noisette is left with a thin covering of fat, which protects it during cooking, and cut about 4cm/1½in thick. The medallion is completely fatless, and cut only 2.5cm/1in thick, so that it cooks very quickly.

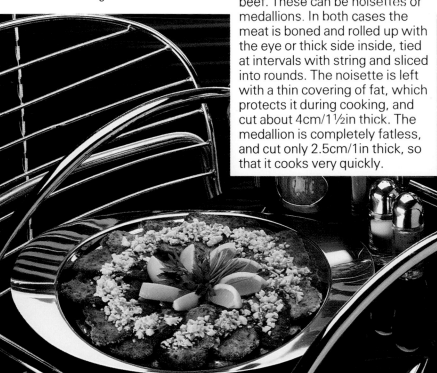

Pork escalopes mimosa

- *Preparation: 15 minutes*

- *Cooking: 8 minutes*

500g/18oz pork tenderloin, trimmed
well-seasoned flour, for dusting
1 large egg
75g/3oz dry white breadcrumbs
1tbls oil
25g/1oz butter
1 large lemon, cut into 8 wedges
chives
flat-leaved parsley
For the mimosa garnish:
1 large egg, hard-boiled, yolk sieved and white finely chopped
1tsp finely grated lemon zest
1tbls snipped chives or spring onion tops

- *Serves 4* (♍) (££)

- *380 cals/1595 kjs per serving*

1 Cut the pork across into 8mm/⅓in slices. Lay each slice flat between two pieces of dampened greaseproof paper and beat gently with a meat hammer or wooden rolling pin.

2 Dust each escalope lightly on both sides with seasoned flour. Beat the egg with 2tsp water, dip each escalope in the egg and then toss in the breadcrumbs until well coated. Lay flat on greaseproof paper and press on the coating with a palette knife. If possible, chill the meat for 30 minutes to allow the coating to firm.

3 When ready to cook heat the oil and butter in a large frying pan. When sizzling fry as many of the escalopes as the pan will hold for 3-4 minutes on each side, until golden and cooked through. Drain on crumpled absorbent paper and keep warm while cooking the rest.

4 Meanwhile make the mimosa garnish. Combine the hard-boiled egg, lemon zest and chives or spring onion tops. When all the escalopes are cooked pile them on a heated serving platter and sprinkle with the garnish. Arrange the lemon wedges in the centre with the chives and parsley.

GLAMOROUS GARNISHES

Especially with dinner-party food, never omit the finishing touch: a garnish to add colour or texture contrast to the meat.

Choose fresh green herbs like parsley or watercress; or small crisp vegetables. Button mushrooms, cut into pretty shapes and quickly fried, are ideal. Or use raw or fried tomatoes for their vivid colour. For texture contrast use tiny fried bread croûtons: fry in advance and keep hot.

Lamb chops with wine

- ● *Preparation: bring chops to room temperature, then 15 minutes*
- ● *Cooking: 35 minutes*

8 x 150g/5oz loin lamb chops, each 2.5cm/1in thick
salt and pepper
75g/3oz butter
2tbls olive oil
3tbls finely chopped onion
150ml/¼pt dry white wine
1tbls finely chopped fresh tarragon or chives, or a combination
2tbls finely chopped parsley
4tbls chicken stock
For the garnish:
1tbls finely chopped onion
1tsp finely chopped parsley
1 parsley sprig

- ● *Serves 4*
- ● *535 cals/2245 kjs per serving*

1 Heat the oven to 170C/325F/gas 3. Trim the chops, leaving a small border of fat around the meat. Wipe dry with absorbent paper, then season generously with pepper. Leave to come to room temperature and season with salt just before cooking in the pan.

2 Heat 25g/1oz butter and the oil in a frying pan large enough to take the chops in one layer. When the foaming subsides, lay the chops in the pan and brown them over medium heat for 3 minutes on each side. Transfer to a large flameproof casserole.

3 To make the sauce pour off and discard the fat from the frying pan and melt the remaining 50g/2oz butter. When it starts sizzling add 3tbls onion and cook for 2 minutes, stirring occasionally. Pour in the wine and chopped herbs and simmer for 2-3 minutes, scraping the brown crusty bits from the pan surface into the sauce.

4 Season and pour the sauce over the chops, bring back to a simmer. Cover and put in the oven for 15 minutes, turning the chops and basting them with the sauce from time to time.

5 Transfer the chops to a heated serving dish and keep warm. Add the chicken stock to the casserole and boil rapidly for 5 minutes or until the sauce has thickened slightly. Strain the sauce and pour it around the chops. Sprinkle the remaining very finely chopped onion and remaining chopped parsley over the chops, garnish with the parsley sprig and serve at once.

Rich Roasts

Whether you roast pork English style, with crisp crackling, or in the more subtle French style, either way you'll create a meal to remember

French-style loin of pork (page 201)

PORK IS SO rich and succulent that nearly all cuts can be roasted, even the less expensive ones, and it lends itself to being cooked in many different ways. It can be roasted on the bone, for maximum flavour; or boned and rolled with a tasty stuffing inside, for easy carving. It can be roasted English style, with the rind left on and finely scored to make crackling; or French style, with the rind removed and the fat flavoured in various ways. It can be left plain, or cooked and served with delicious accompaniments. And if there's any left over it will if anything be even more delicious cold.

Buy top-quality pork for roasting, whatever the cut. It should be sweet-smelling with a pale pink colour, smooth fine-grained texture and a fair proportion of very white fat. The skin should not be too thick. Allow 100-175g/4-6oz of boned meat per person; or one chop if serving a loin. For meat with bone, allow 175 - 275g / 6 - 10oz bought weight per person.

Pork is never served rare. This

199

can be dangerous to health, but nowadays the main reason is that it tastes best when well cooked. Pork attains maximum flavour when cooked slowly and thoroughly in an uncovered roasting tin.

Suitable cuts

Leg is the prime cut, very lean and with little waste. A whole leg is a very large joint; it is usually divided into four or more smaller pieces. Fillet end is the most expensive; knuckle end slightly less so.

Loin is a popular cut, easier to carve than leg if properly prepared. Ask the butcher to chine the joint: cut through the bone at the base which holds the chops together. He should also score the skin finely to produce thin strips of crackling. A boned and rolled loin makes a more elegant joint which only needs slicing into rounds. If you buy it ready-boned ask the butcher for the bones and add them to the roasting tin to give extra flavour.

Fillet, often called tenderloin, is the tenderest and most expensive cut of pork, the equivalent of fillet steak, and completely fat free.

Spare rib and shoulder joints are fairly lean and moderately priced. They make good small roasting joints. Shoulder can be bought on the bone or boned and rolled.

Blade is cut from behind the head, on top of the foreleg. Although

inexpensive it makes a delicious roast, boned and stuffed.

Hand and spring is a large, inexpensive roasting joint, cut from the foreleg; ideal for big families. Or it can be bought divided into two smaller cuts, hand and shank.

Belly is the cheapest cut, rather fatty for today's tastes, but full of flavour.

Preparation and cooking

Allow 2-3 hours at room temperature for a refrigerated joint to lose its chill and develop flavour. Wipe with a clean damp cloth and trim off any excess fat. Season the whole joint with pepper, but only the fat with salt. Do not add any extra fat, by barding or larding the joint, spreading it with fat or adding some to the roasting tin. Pork has sufficient natural fat for perfect roasting.

Use a rack if the joint is boned and rolled. Weigh the joint and calculate the cooking time – 30 minutes to every 450g/1lb and 30 minutes over. Make sure the meat is cooked through at the end by inserting a skewer into the centre: if the juices do not run clear give it a few more minutes. If using a meat thermometer, this should register 85C/190F for well done.

After cooking, allow the joint to settle for 5-10 minutes in a warm place; this makes it easier to carve.

Tenderloin stuffed with gooseberries

- **Preparation: 30 minutes**
- **Cooking: 45 minutes**

2 × 450g/1lb pork tenderloins
175g/6oz green gooseberries
25g/1oz butter
1 onion, finely chopped
75g/3oz fresh wholemeal
   breadcrumbs
1tbls chopped parsley
1tbls chopped marjoram
pinch ground cloves
2tbls dry white wine
2tbls clear honey
For the gravy:
150ml/¼pt dry white wine
150ml/¼pt ham stock

- **Serves 4**
- **325cals/1365kjs per serving**

1 Heat the oven to 200C/400F/gas 6. Slit through each tenderloin lengthways, leaving it uncut down one side. Open each one out flat, like a book, and beat with a meat hammer or rolling pin.

2 Top and tail the gooseberries and finely chop 100g/4oz of them. Cut the remainder in half lengthways; reserve.

3 Melt the butter in a frying pan over low heat and cook the onion until just transparent. Stir in the gooseberries and cook until the onion is soft.

4 Remove the pan from the heat and stir the breadcrumbs, herbs, cloves and 2tbls wine into the onion mixture. Spread the mixture on the pork tenderloins, then reshape each piece and tie up like a parcel with fine string.

5 Cook the tenderloins side by side on a rack in a roasting tin for 30 minutes.

6 Take the tin out of the oven and remove the rack. Carefully remove the string from the pork and put the pork in the bottom of the tin. Spoon the honey over each piece and arrange the reserved halved gooseberries on top. Mix together the wine and stock and pour round the meat. Return to the oven for 15 minutes.

7 Place the tenderloins on a heated serving platter and carve at the table.

Serving ideas

Tenderloin with gooseberries is expensive but good for dinner parties.

French-style loin of pork

- **Preparation: 45 minutes, plus soaking and standing times**
- **Cooking: 1¼ hours**

6 dried mushrooms
2 large garlic cloves
1.4kg/3lb loin of pork (6 large chops), skinned and chined
salt and pepper
For the stuffed vegetables:
15g/½oz butter
3tbls finely chopped onion
225g/8oz pork sausagemeat
6tbls grated Parmesan cheese
1tbls finely chopped parsley
½tsp each finely chopped fresh tarragon and chives
6 large ripe tomatoes
175g/6oz large button mushrooms

- **Serves 6**
- **480cals/2015kjs per serving**

1 Soak the dried mushrooms in warm water for 30 minutes. Pour mushrooms and liquid into a small pan and simmer gently until the mushrooms are soft and swollen and the water has almost evaporated. Reserve three mushrooms and cut the rest into four strips. Cut one garlic clove into 12 slivers.

2 Weigh the joint and calculate the cooking time. Allow 35-40 minutes per kg/18 minutes per lb. Make 12 deep slits in the fat and push in a strip of mushroom and a sliver of garlic. Season the joint all over with pepper; sprinkle only the fat with salt. Leave to stand at room temperature for 2 hours to absorb flavours. Towards the end heat the oven to 230C/ 450F/gas 8.

3 Transfer the joint to a roasting tin and roast for 20 minutes, then reduce the temperature to 150C/300F/gas 2 and roast for the calculated cooking time, basting occasionally with the juices in the tin. Add a little water if the juices start to dry up.

4 Meanwhile prepare the stuffed vegetables. Finely chop the remaining garlic clove. Melt the butter in a small pan and fry the onion and garlic for 3-4 minutes until soft but not coloured; cool.

5 Finely chop the reserved dried mushrooms and put them in a bowl with the onion mixture, sausagemeat, Parmesan cheese, parsley, tarragon and chives. Mix well and season to taste.

6 Slice the tops off the tomatoes and scoop out the seeds. Lightly sprinkle inside with salt and leave upside down on a rack for a few minutes to drain. Wipe the mushrooms and remove the stalks. Stuff the tomatoes and mushroom caps with the sausagemeat mixture.

SUPER STUFFING

Home-made sage and onion stuffing is easy to make and streets ahead of the packet variety. Just boil two large onions for 5 minutes, then chop finely and mix with 1tsp dried sage, 1tbls olive oil, 50g/2oz fresh breadcrumbs plus salt and pepper to taste.

7 About 25 minutes before the end of the cooking time put the stuffed tomatoes in the tin around the joint. Add the mushrooms 15 minutes later.

8 Transfer the roast pork to a hot serving dish and surround it with the stuffed vegetables. Pour off excess fat from the tin and moisten the pork and vegetables with the juices. Serve at once.

Loin of pork with orange

- **Preparation: 20 minutes**
- **Cooking: 2 hours 5 minutes**

1.4kg/3lb loin of pork, weighed after skinning and boning (keep skin and bones if possible)
salt and pepper
1-2 garlic cloves, finely chopped ▶

How to ... make crackling

To make successful crackling it is necessary to make deep scores in the pork fat.

Paint over the pork fat with a light coat of oil. Some people consider this unnecessary and use only salt.

Press cooking salt all over the pork fat. Only sprinkle pepper on the meat surfaces.

2tbls finely chopped parsley
1tsp chopped fresh marjoram or
  ½tsp dried
2tbls oil
200ml/7fl oz chicken stock
juice of 1 large orange
3-4tbls orange liqueur
1tbls French mustard
3tbls dry white breadcrumbs
1tbls soft light brown sugar
For the garnish:
2-3 seedless oranges, segmented
watercress sprigs

• **Serves 8**

• **300 cals/1260 kjs per serving**

1 Heat the oven to 170C/325F/gas 3. Sprinkle the inside of the pork with salt, pepper, garlic, parsley and marjoram. Form it into a neat roll, fat side out, and tie at intervals with string.

2 Heat the oil in a flameproof casserole into which the meat fits closely. When it sizzles, brown the meat lightly.

3 Gently heat the chicken stock, add to the casserole with the bones and pieces of skin, if available. Cover and cook in the oven for 1¾ hours.

4 Discard the bones and skin. Pour the orange juice and liqueur over the meat, spread thinly with mustard and sprinkle with breadcrumbs and sugar. Return to the oven and cook, uncovered, for 15 minutes or until the juices run clear and the topping is crisp and golden.

5 Lift the meat out, remove the string and allow to settle in a warm place for 10 minutes before carving into thick slices. Pour excess fat off the pan juices, add the orange segments and heat for 2 minutes, turning once.

6 Arrange the meat slices on a heated serving platter. Using a slotted spoon, arrange the orange sections in groups around the meat. Tuck watercress sprigs in between the groups. Check the gravy for seasoning and pour into a heated sauceboat. Serve at once.

Aromatic roast pork

• **Preparation: 30 minutes, plus marinating**

• **Cooking: 1½ hours**

SIMPLE SAUCES

The rich succulence of pork calls for a sharp, slightly acidic sauce. Apple is the traditional one. To make enough for four cook 450g/1lb of cooking apples in just enough water to stop them burning, until soft and pulpy. Rub through a sieve and add a very little sugar – no more than 25g/1oz – reheat and serve hot.

Or try Cranberry sauce: boil 225g/8oz cranberries with 150ml/¼pt water, crushing with a spoon, until tender. Rub through a sieve, sweeten to taste and pour into a small mould. Leave for 12 hours before using, when the mixture will have jellied.

1.4kg/3lb boned loin of pork
  with all but a thin sheet of
  surface fat removed
4tbls olive oil
150ml/¼pt dry white wine
1-2tbls Pernod
salt and pepper
25g/1oz butter
fennel leaves, to garnish
**For the aromatic herb
  flavouring:**
20 sprigs fresh fennel, chopped
2tbls finely snipped fresh chives
4 garlic cloves, finely chopped

• **Serves 6**

• **435cals/1825kjs per serving**

1 First make the aromatic herb flavouring: put all the ingredients in a small bowl and mix well.

2 Wipe the untied meat and pierce it deeply on the inside in 12 places. Force generous amounts of the flavouring into the holes; there must be enough to marble the roast with colour when carved.

3 Rub the joint outside with oil and sprinkle with the remaining herb flavouring. Put in a bowl and add the wine and Pernod. Cover loosely with foil and leave in a cool place for 3-4 hours to marinate, turning the meat several times.

4 When ready to roast remove the pork from the marinade and drain thoroughly in a colander placed over the bowl. Reserve the marinade and pat the meat dry. Weigh it and calculate the cooking time, allowing 35-40 minutes per kg/16-18 minutes per lb. Heat the oven to 190C/375F/gas 5.

5 Season the meat generously with salt and pepper, roll up and tie in 4-6 places. Heat the butter in a small flameproof roasting tin and sear the meat all over by turning in the butter until golden brown.

6 Put the meat on a rack in the roasting tin and roast for 20 minutes less than the calculated cooking time. Then remove the meat from the oven and raise the temperature to 220C/425F/gas 7. Drain off excess fat from the pan and add the reserved marinade. Return to the oven and cook for the remaining 20 minutes.

7 Transfer the joint to a warmed serving platter and remove the string. Leave it in the turned-off oven while making the gravy. Add 150ml/¼pt water to the pan and bring to a gentle boil. Taste and adjust the seasoning and strain into a warm jug. Skim off all excess fat and serve with the pork. Garnish the pork with fennel leaves.

Poultry in the Pot

Casseroled, pot-roasted or braised poultry dishes are easy to cook and ideal for trouble-free entertaining as they need little or no last minute attention

GENTLE, MOIST COOKING methods – casseroling, pot-roasting and braising – are ideal for modern mass-produced chickens, ducks and turkeys. Not so much to tenderize them, as being killed young they are rarely tough, but to add flavour and succulence to meat which can be tasteless and dry.

Pot-roasting and braising are ancient cooking methods, dating from the days when few people had ovens – meat was either spit-roasted, or put in a covered pot on the fire. They are used for whole young birds; only a small amount of liquid is added, and the bird cooks in its own juices for a comparatively short time.

For casseroling or stewing, the bird is cut into portions and well covered with liquid. A tough old boiling fowl would be cooked for several hours to tenderize it; the birds usually available today cook much more quickly.

Poultry and pots

A factory-farmed frozen chicken will benefit most from this type of cooking, but if you use a free-range or maize-fed bird the result will be even more delicious. Ducks are also suitable, but as they are so much fattier it is essential to prick the skin and drain off excess fat when browning them. Turkey joints are so large that the meat is usually removed from the bone and cubed.

Originally pot-roasting and braising was carried out on top of the stove, in a special pot with a concave lid. This was heaped with

Chicken with mange-tout (p.204)

embers to provide all-round heat — today we simply put the dish in the oven. Casseroles and stews are also best done in the oven. (Both *can* be done over very low heat on top of the stove, but the risk of burning, even with a heavy-based pan, is much greater.) Any kind of casserole dish can be used; a flameproof one is convenient, as the preliminary browning can be done in it, but lacking this do the browning in a frying pan and transfer the ingredients to the casserole. For pot roasts and braises the casserole should be of a size to fit snugly round the bird, otherwise precious juices will evaporate away. For all methods, a tight-fitting lid is essential — if it's loose, put a layer of foil underneath.

Pot roasts and braises

However varied with different vegetables, spices and cooking liquids, the basic method is simple. Wipe the bird dry with absorbent paper and season inside and out with salt and pepper. Stuff it if wished, and truss to keep it in a neat shape while cooking (see page 174).

Brown the bird in oil and butter for about 10 minutes, turning it carefully with two spoons. Never use a fork, which would pierce the skin and allow juices to escape. Remove it and fry any flavouring

vegetables, then pour off excess fat — with duck there will be a lot. Return the bird to the casserole and pour on *hot* stock — cold liquid draws flavour out of the bird. Add any wine, herbs and spices, cover tightly and simmer very gently until the juices run clear when the inside of a thigh is pierced with a skewer or sharp knife. Reduce and/or thicken the sauce.

Casseroles

Prepare a chicken by cutting it into four or eight portions, depending on size (see below). Chicken portions are convenient, but if you buy a whole one, with giblets, you get the basis for chicken stock at no extra cost.

There is very little meat on the legs of a duck, so divide this by halving it first, then dividing each half in two. Leave a portion of the breast with each leg. Take turkey meat off the bone and cut evenly.

Proceed as for pot-roasting and braising and cook very gently in a tightly covered casserole.

Chicken with mange-tout

- **Preparation: 15 minutes**

- **Cooking: 45 minutes**

1.6kg/3½lb chicken, cut into 4 portions
25g/1oz butter
2tbls olive oil
1 large onion, chopped
425ml/¾pt chicken stock (page 36)
salt and pepper
2 celery stalks, chopped
2 leeks, sliced
100g/4oz mange-tout

- **Serves 4**

- **475cals/1195kjs per serving**

1 Heat the oven to 190C/375F/gas 5. Put the butter and oil in a large flameproof casserole over medium heat. When the foaming subsides, add the chicken por-

How to ... portion a chicken

Cut through the meat on the breast along one side of the breastbone; ease the flesh away and remove breast and wing as one portion; or if the bird is large divide into two.

Repeat on the other side to obtain two or four more joints, leaving the carcass bare. Cook this with the giblets to make a tasty stock (see page 36).

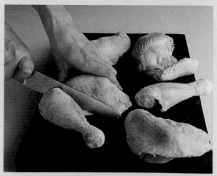

Cut the legs from the body, severing the hip joint with the knife point. Separate drumstick from thigh if the bird is large and cut off the end joint if still in place.

tions and fry until golden brown all over.

2 Remove the chicken and add the onion. Cook for 2-3 minutes until transparent, stirring occasionally.

3 Pour off the fat in the casserole and add the stock. Bring it to the boil and season with salt and pepper. Add the chicken portions, cover and put in the oven for 25 minutes.

4 Add the celery and leeks to the casserole, making sure they are covered in stock, and scatter the mange-tout over the chicken. Cover and return to the oven for a further 15 minutes or until the chicken is tender and the mange-tout tender but still crisp. Check the seasoning.

Cook's tips

When mange-tout are out of season, use fresh green beans instead.

Duck curry

- **Preparation: 20 minutes**

- **Cooking: 1 hour 40 minutes**

2tbls olive oil
1.8kg/4lb duck, cut into 4 serving
*   pieces*
1 tsp mustard seeds
1 large onion, finely chopped
2 garlic cloves, finely chopped
4cm/1½in piece fresh ginger root,
*   peeled and finely chopped*
1 green chilli, seeded and finely
*   chopped*
1 tsp each ground cumin, chilli
*   powder and turmeric*
1tbls ground coriander
salt and pepper
3tbls vinegar
50g/2oz desiccated coconut
boiled rice, to serve

- **Serves 4**

- **635cals/2665kjs per serving**

1 Heat the oil in a flameproof casserole. Prick the duck skin all over with a fork and fry the pieces in the oil for 4-5 minutes on each side or until they are golden brown. Remove from the casserole and pour off the excess fat, leaving about 3 tablespoons behind.

2 Add the mustard seeds to the casserole, cover the pan and fry over low heat for 2 minutes. Add the onion and fry for 20 minutes until golden brown, stirring occasionally. Add the garlic, ginger and green chilli and fry for 2-3 minutes stirring constantly on a low heat.

3 Put all four spices in a small bowl and add ½tsp salt. Add the vinegar and mix to a paste; put this in the casserole. Fry over a medium heat for 4 minutes, stirring constantly.

4 Add the duck pieces and turn them over several times so they are coated with spices. Continue frying for 2-3 minutes.

5 Meanwhile bring 300ml/½pt water to the boil and stir in the desiccated coconut. Pour the coconut milk over the duck pieces and stir to mix into the spices.

6 Cover and simmer for 40-50 minutes or until the duck is tender and the sauce has thickened.

7 Skim off excess fat, taste and adjust the seasoning and serve hot with rice.

FLAVOUR-SEALED

FLAVOUR-SEALED

An old-fashioned but very effective way of ensuring a casserole turns out perfectly is to seal the lid on with luting paste, made with 50g/2oz flour and enough cold water to make a stiff mixture. Put on the lid, then spread the paste thickly over the join between lid and side. This ensures that every bit of aromatic moisture is trapped inside and penetrates the poultry. You cannot look at the dish during cooking, but there's no need – it's foolproof. Break the seal at the table to get the full impact of the heady aroma.

Duck with figs

- *Preparation: 20 minutes*
- *Cooking: 2¾ hours*

1.8kg/4lb duck, with giblets
salt and pepper
1 garlic clove, sliced
2 bay leaves
1 orange, quartered
1 tbls olive oil
425ml/¾pt dry white wine
225g/8oz fresh figs, quartered
thyme sprigs, to garnish
For the stock:
duck giblets
1 onion, sliced
2 carrots, thickly sliced
2 garlic cloves, crushed
½tsp each dried marjoram and
   thyme
½tsp salt
4 black peppercorns

- *Serves 4*
- *405cals/1700kjs per serving*

1 Put the duck stock ingredients in a saucepan, cover with 425ml/¾pt water and bring to the boil. Lower the heat, cover and simmer for 45 minutes, skimming regularly, until the liquid is reduced to half its original quantity. Strain.

2 Heat the oven to 170C/325F/gas 3. Rub the cavity of the duck with salt and pepper. Put the garlic, bay leaves and orange quarters inside, then truss the duck (see Masterclass page 226) and prick the skin all over.

3 Heat the oil in a flameproof casserole and lightly brown the duck all over. Pour off the excess fat.

4 Pour the wine and duck stock into a saucepan. Bring to the boil, then pour into the casserole. Cover and cook in the oven for 1½-2 hours or until the juices run clear when the inside of the leg is pierced.

5 Transfer the duck to a heated serving plate; remove the strings. Keep warm.

6 Skim as much fat as possible from the sauce. Add the figs and bring the sauce back to the boil. Taste and adjust the seasoning. As soon as the figs are heated, pour the sauce over the duck. Garnish and serve.

Plan ahead

Cook the casserole to the end of step 4 the previous day. Cool and skim the fat carefully from the top.

Catalan chicken

- *Preparation: 30 minutes*
- *Cooking: 1½ hours*

1.4kg/3lb chicken
75g/3oz butter
3tbls olive oil
1 onion, chopped
3 red peppers, seeded and diced
150g/5oz Spanish chorizo or other
   mild Italian spicy sausage, diced
225g/8oz long-grain rice
1 bouquet garni
salt and pepper
100g/4oz frozen peas
75ml/3fl oz dry white wine
200ml/7fl oz chicken stock
   (page 36)

- *Serves 4-6*
- *960cals/4030kjs per serving*

1 Wipe the chicken inside and out with absorbent paper. Heat the oven to 180C/350F/gas 4.

2 Melt 25g/1oz butter and 1tbls oil in a large frying pan. Add the onion and peppers and fry over low heat for 2 minutes or until the onions are transparent, stirring constantly. Add the chorizo or other sausage and cook for 1 minute.

3 Stir in the rice and add 850ml/1½pt water and the bouquet garni. Bring to the boil, season with salt and pepper, then cover and simmer gently for 18 minutes, until the rice is tender and the liquid has been absorbed. Meanwhile cook the peas.

4 When the rice is done add 15g/½oz butter and stir it in with a fork, then stir in the peas. Taste and season.

5 Take out a quarter of the rice mixture and spread it on a large plate to cool. Keep the remainder warm, covered. Stuff the chicken cavity with the cooled rice and truss (see page 174).

6 Heat the remaining 40g/1½oz butter and 2tbls oil in a flameproof casserole. Season the chicken with salt and pepper and brown it evenly all over.

7 Put the wine and stock in a saucepan, bring to the boil and pour over the chicken. Cover and put in the oven for 45-50 minutes or until tender.

8 Transfer the chicken to a heated serving dish, remove the trussing strings and keep it warm. Skim the fat off the sauce, check the seasoning and pour it into a heated sauceboat. Arrange the reserved rice mixture around the chicken and brush the bird with a little of the sauce just before serving.

Chicken with black cherries

- *Preparation: 30 minutes*

- *Cooking: 1¾ hours*

1.4kg/3lb chicken
salt and pepper
2tsp dried rosemary
2tbls olive oil
25g/1oz butter
300ml/½pt chicken stock
  (page 36)
400g/14oz canned black cherries
2tsp cornflour
2tsp lemon juice

- *Serves 4*

- *470cals/1975kjs per serving*

1 Heat the oven to 170C/325F/gas 3. Wipe the chicken inside and out with absorbent paper. Rub the cavity with salt, pepper and the dried rosemary. Truss the chicken (see page 174). If already trussed, season outside.

2 Heat the oil and butter in a flameproof casserole and fry the chicken over medium heat for 10 minutes or until golden brown all over.

3 Bring the chicken stock to the boil and pour it into the casserole. Cover and cook the chicken for 1¼ hours in the oven, or until the juices run clear when the inside of the leg is pierced with a skewer or sharp knife.

4 Transfer the chicken to a heated serving plate, remove the trussing strings and keep warm.

5 Skim off excess fat from the sauce and strain in the cherry juice. Bring the sauce to the boil. Put the cornflour in a small bowl and mix with 1tbls cold water. Add a little of the hot sauce to the cornflour mixture, then stir it into the casserole. Simmer until the sauce has thickened, stirring constantly.

6 Add the cherries and cook for a further 2 minutes until they are heated through. Add the lemon juice a little at a time, stirring while it is being added then correct the seasoning.

7 Pour a little of the sauce over the chicken and serve at once with the rest of the sauce in a heated sauce boat.

Plan ahead

Cook the chicken the previous day to the end of step 3. Cool, carve and reheat carefully. Pour the juice into a jug, cool and refrigerate, then skim off the fat.

Hungarian chicken

- *Preparation: 20 minutes*
- *Cooking: 50 minutes*

4 chicken portions
salt and pepper
100g/4oz butter
1 large onion, finely chopped
1tbls paprika
1tbls flour
300ml/½pt chicken stock
*   (page 36)*

1tbls tomato purée
150ml/¼pt double cream
juice of ½ lemon
watercress sprigs, to garnish

- *Serves 4*

- *595cals/2500kjs per serving*

1 Season the chicken portions with salt and pepper. Melt the butter in a flameproof casserole, add the onion and fry over medium heat for 2-3 minutes until soft and transparent.

2 Stir in the paprika and flour. Add the chicken portions and cook over low heat until golden all over. Then cover and continue cooking for 10 minutes.

3 Bring the stock to the boil and pour it over the chicken. Add the tomato purée and season with salt and pepper. Return to the boil, then cover and simmer very gently for 30 minutes.

4 Remove the chicken pieces to a warmed serving dish. Stir the cream and lemon juice into the casserole; stir well and simmer for 5 minutes. Taste and adjust the seasoning and pour the sauce over the chicken. Serve at once garnished with watercress sprigs.

Variations

For a more spicy version of this recipe, add finely chopped, deseeded chilli to the onion and ¼tsp cayenne pepper to the paprika and flour. Soured cream can be used instead of double cream.

Poached to Perfection

Poaching is the ideal method of cooking fish. It is quick and simple and captures the delicate flavour and texture which is so often lost

Trout in red wine (page 210)

FISH IS EASILY ruined by poor cooking, whether it has been boiled in water until tough and tasteless, or coated in breadcrumbs and fried until hard and dry. Poaching is a method which avoids all these problems; it is not at all difficult, but only requires careful attention, particularly to timing.

Choosing and storing
Almost any kind of fish can be poached, either whole or in steaks or fillets. But, as with poached eggs, it must be super-fresh. Look for whole fish with rounded, bright eyes, red gills and stiff firm bodies.

Fillets or steaks should be moist, with a fresh colour; both should have a mild pleasant smell.

Storing is best avoided – buy the fish on the day you plan to eat it. Or at least eat it next day. To store, wash and pat dry, then wrap loosely in greaseproof paper and put in the refrigerator until ready to cook. If there are delicately flavoured foods such as cream and desserts in the refrigerator put the fish in a polythene bag or plastic container to avoid any transfer of smells.

Poaching techniques

The golden rule for poaching is to keep the heat really low, so that the poaching liquid is just below simmering and barely moves. With very delicate fish like sole fillets, a buttered paper laid over the top, slit to allow steam to escape, helps to keep it moist and full of flavour.

When the fish is to be served cold, the heat can be turned off once the liquid comes to the boil. Tightly covered, the fish will be cooked by the time it begins to cool down – see Italian poached cod, page 211. This method is also used for large fish like salmon when served cold. The larger the fish the larger the quantity of water needed, and so the longer the time it takes to cool, during which it is still cooking. Do not remove the fish until it is quite cold, to ensure that it is done, and also to reduce the risk of breakage, as it will have had a chance to set.

A flavourful liquid will add to the character of the final dish. This need not be complicated, but something better than milk or plain salted water is called for. For smaller pieces of fish, the simplest method is to use water with added salt, peppercorns and lemon juice. Then add flavourings – a dissolved fish, chicken or vegetable stock cube, bay leaf, a couple of tablespoons of sliced onion and some crushed peppercorns. Bring to the boil, then simmer very gently until the fish is opaque and flakes easily with a fork: then remove it to prevent any further cooking.

For a special occasion, use wine instead of water, or a mixture of both. Chopped shallots are an ideal flavouring for poaching liquids, being small and less harsh than ordinary onions – Spanish onions are also good. A wine-based poaching liquid is not wasted, but makes the perfect base for a rich sauce to finish the dish.

Alternatively, poach the fish in a court bouillon, the classic French method. The name means 'quick stock', which it is (see opposite). Use fish stock from the freezer, if you have any, or fish trimmings (page 37).

Oven-poaching: this is a different method of poaching, suitable for fish fillets and small fish steaks or cutlets. Butter an ovenproof dish and sprinkle with chopped mushroom stalks and shallot. Season, sprinkle with lemon juice and lay in the dish. Sprinkle with more mushroom and shallot and 2–4tbls wine or fish stock. Cover with buttered foil and cook in an oven preheated to 230C/450F/gas 8 for 8–12 minutes. Remove the fish and thicken the liquid.

Trout in red wine

- **Preparation: 30 minutes**
- **Cooking: 30 minutes**

4 × 275g/10oz trout, cleaned, and
  with heads cut off
salt and pepper
butter, for greasing
4 shallots, finely chopped
600ml/1pt red wine
150ml/¹/₄pt Hollandaise sauce
  (page 76)
4tbls double cream
watercress sprigs, to garnish

- **Serves 4**
- **665cals/2795kjs per serving**

1 Heat the oven to 150C/300F/gas 2. Season inside the trout with salt and pepper, then lay them in a buttered flameproof dish. Sprinkle with the shallots and pour over enough red wine to cover – add a little water if necessary.

2 Put the dish over medium heat and bring the wine to a gentle simmer. Cover the fish with buttered foil, transfer the dish to the oven and poach for about 20 minutes or until the flesh flakes easily with a fork.

3 Meanwhile make the Hollandaise sauce and keep it warm over warm (not hot) water.

4 Lift the fish carefully out of the wine onto a board. Remove the skin with a sharp knife and dab the fish dry with absorbent paper. Arrange on a heated serving dish and keep warm.

5 Pour 300ml/1¹/₂pt of the hot wine into a large saucepan and boil rapidly until reduced to 4tbls (this will take about 10 minutes). Strain and leave to cool slightly.

6 Fold the reduced wine and cream into the Hollandaise sauce and season with salt and pepper to taste. Stand over warm water but do not allow the bowl to touch the water.

7 To serve, coat the head ends of the trout with a quarter of the sauce and garnish with watercress.

How to ··· poach fish

There are several methods and liquids suitable for poaching fish as described above. Here a court bouillon (see opposite) is made ready to poach a salmon trout.

A fish kettle is ideal for poaching large fish or several medium ones. Arrange the fish on the grid and lower into the court bouillon. To serve cold, cool in the liquid.

Poached sole with grapes

- **Preparation: making stock and sauce, then 35 minutes**
- **Cooking: 25 minutes**

4 sole fillets
softened butter
3 shallots or 1 small onion, finely chopped
salt and pepper
150ml/¼pt dry white wine
150ml/¼pt fish stock (page 37)
175g/6oz seedless white grapes

For the cream sauce:
150ml/¼pt Béchamel sauce (page 76)
4tbls double cream
1 large egg yolk, beaten
few drops lemon juice

- **Serves 4**
- **405cals/1700kjs per serving**

1 Make the stock and Béchamel sauce. Butter a shallow flameproof casserole generously and sprinkle with the shallots or onion. Season the sole, roll up, fasten with cocktail sticks and put in the pan. Pour over the wine and stock.

2 Cut a piece of foil the same size as the pan and cut a small whole in the centre. Butter the foil and lay it buttered side down over the fish.

3 Put the pan over medium heat and bring to the boil, then reduce the heat, cover the pan and poach the fish very gently for 10–12 minutes, until it flakes easily with a fork.

4 Remove the fish rolls from the pan, discard the cocktail sticks and arrange the rolls on a heated flameproof serving dish. Keep warm.

5 Return the pan of poaching liquid to a high heat and boil rapidly until reduced to about one-quarter of its original quantity. Meanwhile mix 2tbls of the cream with the egg yolk and stir into the Béchamel sauce. Heat through gently. Add the sauce to the reduced poaching liquid with a few drops of lemon juice and heat through without boiling, stirring constantly. Heat the grill to high.

6 If seedless grapes are unobtainable, use ordinary ones, peeling them and removing the pips. Melt 15g/½oz butter in a small saucepan. Reserve two small clusters of grapes for the garnish and cook the remainder in the butter for a few minutes to heat them through. Pour the grapes and butter round the fish rolls.

7 Whip the remaining cream until just thick and fold it into the sauce. Pour the sauce over the fish and grapes and brown under the grill. Serve hot, garnished with the reserved grapes.

COURT BOUILLON

Although this must be made in advance, it can be completed within 30 minutes. Make just enough to cover the fish in a pan or dish in which it fits snugly. For about 1L/1¾pt water, add a sliced carrot, small onion stuck with 2 cloves, parsley sprig or crushed stalk, bay leaf and 2 crushed peppercorns. To sharpen the taste, add a slice of lemon and 75ml/3fl oz wine. Replace the water with wine or dry cider.

Bring the court bouillon to the boil and simmer very gently, covered, for 15 minutes. Strain and it is ready to use.

Italian poached cod

- **Preparation: 25 minutes, plus chilling**
- **Cooking: 15 minutes**

4 × 175g/6oz cod steaks
salt and pepper
juice of 1 lemon
4 tomatoes, thinly sliced, to serve
chives and flat-leaved parsley, to garnish

For the sauce:
4tbls finely chopped Spanish onion
4tbls finely chopped parsley
2 garlic cloves, crushed
8tbls olive oil
juice of ½ large lemon

- *Serves 4*
- *390cals/1640kjs per serving*

1 Put the cod steaks in a large frying pan with enough salted water to cover. Add the lemon juice and pepper to taste. Bring to the boil, then turn off the heat, cover the pan with a lid or foil and leave to stand for 10–12 minutes, until the fish flakes easily with a fork.

2 Carefully remove each cod steak from the pan with a fish slice and, holding it on the fish slice, dab with absorbent paper. Arrange the cod steaks on a serving dish, cool and then chill for about 2 hours. Mix together the sauce ingredients; cover and chill until ready to serve the dish.

3 To serve, pour a portion of sauce over each cod steak and accompany with slices of tomato garnished with coarsely-snipped chives and a sprig of parsley.

Cook's tips

This refreshing dish should be prepared at least 2½ hours in advance. Serve it with a variety of salads.

Poached hake with lemon garlic butter

- **Preparation: 30 minutes, plus chilling**

- **Cooking: 30 minutes**

4 × 200g/7oz thick slices of hake
1 chicken stock cube
1 onion, very thinly sliced
1 bay leaf
1 bouquet garni
For the lemon garlic butter:
50g/2oz unsalted butter
1–2 garlic cloves, crushed
salt and pepper
1 tbls finely chopped parsley
1 tbls lemon juice
For the garnish:
8 small new potatoes
4 tbls finely chopped parsley
1 lemon, thinly sliced
watercress sprigs

- *Serves 4*
- *285cals/1195kjs per serving*

1 First make the lemon garlic butter. Cream the butter until smooth, add the garlic and parsley and mix well. Season with the lemon juice and pepper. Roll into a sausage shape, wrap and chill.

SALMON IN SPLENDOUR

Cold poached salmon is the perfect buffet party dish as it looks magnificent and tastes superb. Cook the salmon in a court bouillon as shown on page 210. Lift out very carefully with 2 fish slices and transfer the whole fish to a large long serving dish. Gently strip off the upper skin. Garnish as elaborately as you like, using thinly sliced cucumber and/or radish and slices of lemon to eat with the fish, plus parsley sprigs and lettuce for colour contrast. Serve with mayonnaise and salad.

When the exposed side of the fish has been eaten, remove the whole back bone carefully and serve the remaining fish.

2 Steam the new potatoes for the garnish in their skins for 30 minutes or until done.

3 Remove any thin black membrane from inside the fish slices, but leave the skin on to hold them together. Put the fish in a wide flameproof casserole or baking dish with a lid. Season with pepper.

4 Dissolve the chicken stock cube in 600ml/1pt boiling water and pour over the fish. Add the onion, bay leaf, bouquet garni and bring to the boil. Lower the heat, cover and poach or 10 minutes until the fish flakes easily with a fork.

5 Remove the fish to a work surface with a fish slice and remove the centre bones. Transfer to a heated serving dish and keep warm.

6 Turn the heat up to high and boil the pan juices to reduce to half their original quantity. Strain over the fish.

7 Garnish the dish with the steamed new potatoes sprinkled with parsley, lemon slices and watercress sprigs. Top each slice of fish with two thin rounds of garlic butter.

Cook's tips

This way of serving hake is equally good with other firm white fish steaks or fillets such as cod, conger or whiting.

FREEZER

If you only have frozen fish available to you, defrost it in the refrigerator and cook as soon as possible after it has thawed. Small pieces such as fingers or fillets can be cooked from frozen. Never refreeze fish once thawed without cooking it first to avoid food poisoning.

Looking at Lamb

Lamb makes a wonderful roast for beginners: easy to cook, always tender, cheaper than beef and infinitely versatile, blending well with other flavours

LAMB CAN BE plainly roasted English or French style; turned into dinner-party specials; or boned and stuffed with exotic mixtures of fruit, herbs and spices. As well as being much cheaper than beef, lamb is easier to roast, as the timing is less critical, and a successful result is virtually guaranteed. It is also a very succulent, juicy meat, so there is often no need to make gravy, especially if the joint is stuffed; just spoon over some of the cooking juices.

Cuts to choose

Almost all lamb cuts can be roasted. Check when buying that there is a high proportion of meat to bone and fat — always inspect both sides of the joint. Allow 225-375g/8-12oz uncooked weight of meat and bone per person.

Leg is the most expensive, but economical as it is the leanest cut. It can be either partially or completely boned to take a stuffing. As the year advances and the lambs get larger buy half legs — fillet or knuckle end — to serve a small number of people.

Loin produces one of the finest and most delicately flavoured roasts. It divides into two parts, middle loin and chump end. A saddle or double loin — both sides attached by the backbone — makes a spectacular dinner party roast. Ask the butcher to chine a loin to avoid carving problems. This entails sawing through the bone running the length of the joint so that when it is cooked the bone can be removed, leaving nothing more to do than run a knife between the chops to separate them.

Best end of neck, also known as rack, is cheaper than loin and provides small, delicately flavoured cutlets — allow two per person. A pair of best ends can be presented

Crown roast of lamb (page 215)

in two attractive ways: shaped into a ring and stuffed to make a crown roast, or interlocked and stuffed to make a guard of honour (see Rack of lamb Italian style, below).

This joint should be chined like loin for easy carving. The tips of the bones should be trimmed clean of meat, which would char during roasting, and shortened. For a crown roast they are decorated with cutlet frills. Alternatively a best end can easily be boned. Run a sharp knife down the cutlet bones and across the bottom to lift out the meat. Can be stuffed and rolled.

Shoulder is many people's favourite, with excellent flavour. It can be plainly roasted, or boned and stuffed. Larger shoulders can be divided into two – blade and knuckle end joints – ideal for two. Knuckle is easiest to carve.

Breast is the cheapest cut, tender and flavoursome, but very fatty. It is usually boned, stuffed and rolled; some butchers sell ready-prepared joints. Buy more of this cut per person to allow for the extra fat.

Preparing and roasting

Cover the joint loosely with foil and store it in the coldest part of the refrigerator. It will keep for up to six days, and if it has not been hung by the butcher two days' storage will even improve the flavour.

Always remember to take the joint out of the refrigerator about 2 hours before roasting, so that it is at room temperature. Otherwise it will spend some of the cooking time losing its chill rather than roasting. Wipe it clean with absorbent paper and cut away lumps of excess fat, but leave the covering layer of fat in place to protect it during roasting. Leave the papery outer skin (the fell) to help keep the joint in shape, unless it is to be coated in breadcrumbs.

Season the meat with salt and pepper, confining the salt to the fat sides – if put on the meat it will draw out the juices. Rub with a cut clove of garlic if liked and spread with a little butter. To roast stand the joint on a rack set over a roasting tin so that it stands clear of the pan juices (except for best end, where the bones will keep it clear of the bottom).

How to ... prepare a shank end

Hold the shank end of the leg of lamb, where the meat tapers away to the bone. Pare the meat away from the tip of the bone with a sharp knife carefully.

Saw off 15cm/6in of the bare protruding bone with a clean hacksaw. Tuck in the ends of the meat and secure with skewers or stitch with string.

Rack of lamb Italian style

- ● *Preparation: 15 minutes*
- ● *Cooking: 55-65 minutes*

2 best ends of neck of lamb (about 450g/1lb each), chined and trimmed
salt and pepper
65g/2½oz butter, softened
75g/3oz fresh white breadcrumbs
3tbls grated Parmesan cheese
½tsp each dried marjoram and thyme
¼tsp dried oregano
finely grated zest of ½ lemon
1 small egg, beaten
watercress sprigs and whole grilled tomatoes, to garnish

- ● *Serves 4*
- ● *720cals/3025kjs per serving*

1 When removing the best ends from the refrigerator strip off the skin covering the fat. Season the fat and allow the meat to stand, lightly covered, to come to room temperature.

2 Heat the oven to 200C/400F/gas 6. Put a frying pan over high heat and lay the best ends in it, fat side down. Sear until the fat takes on a little colour.

3 Spread 25g/1oz of the butter over the best ends. Stand them up in a roasting tin with the rib bones interlaced and roast for 20 minutes. Remove the tin from the oven and set the meat aside while preparing the topping. At this stage do not switch off the oven.

4 Make a paste with the breadcrumbs, Parmesan cheese, herbs, lemon zest,

beaten egg and the rest of the softened butter. Use half the mixture to coat the fatty side of each best end. Return to the oven for a further 30 minutes for pink meat, 40 minutes for well done. Baste occasionally towards the end of the cooking time.

5 Transfer the lamb to a well-heated serving platter, carve and serve each portion well garnished with grilled tomatoes and watercress sprigs.

Variation

For an alternative topping omit the oregano and replace the Parmesan cheese with finely chopped parsley.

Cook's tips

For a guard of honour roast two best ends in the same position, omitting the coating and filling the centre with a stuffing of your choice.

Shoulder of lamb Moroccan style

● **Preparation: 1 hour**

● **Cooking: 40-65 minutes**

1.4kg/3lb shoulder of young lamb, boned
75g/3oz sugar
salt and pepper
For the stuffing:
225g/8oz no-soak prunes
225g/8oz no-soak dried apricots
75g/3oz fresh white breadcrumbs
25g/1oz butter, softened
2 egg yolks
1 large onion, finely chopped
4tbls finely chopped parsley
1/4tsp dried chopped rosemary
1/4tsp dried thyme
grated zest of 1 lemon
good pinch cayenne pepper

● **Serves 6**

● **525cals/2205kjs per serving**

1 When taking the lamb out of the refrigerator to come to room temperature cut it so that it can be opened out flat in one piece and any large pieces of fat can be easily removed.

2 Meanwhile make the stuffing. Stone the prunes and chop 75g/3oz of them coarsely. Also chop 150g/5oz of the apricots. Put the chopped fruit in a large

bowl with the remaining stuffing ingredients. Season generously.

3 Heat the oven to 190C/375F/gas 5. Lay the lamb out flat on a work surface, skin side down. Spread with the stuffing, fold in any scrappy ends of meat and roll the shoulder neatly from the long edge. Tie the roll with string in about five places. Stitch along the join with a large needle.

4 Put the sugar in a saucepan with 150ml/1/4pt water and stir over low heat until the sugar has dissolved. Heat to simmering point, then add prunes and apricots, simmer for 5 minutes.

5 Line a roasting tin with foil. Season the roll all over with salt and pepper and lay it in the tin. Put the apricots and prunes round the joint and spoon the poaching syrup over them.

6 Roast the lamb for 30 minutes, then increase the temperature to 200C/400F/gas 6. Continue to roast for about 30 minutes for pink meat or 45 minutes for well done, basting occasionally. If the meat starts to brown too quickly draw the foil up to cover it loosely.

Crown roast of lamb

● **Preparation: 45 minutes**

● **Cooking: 1 hour 20 minutes**

2 best end joints, each with 6-8 cutlets
salt and pepper
2tbls fresh rosemary, crushed, or 1tbls dried
25g/1oz butter
watercress sprigs and orange segments, to garnish
For the stuffing:
425g/15oz canned apricot halves, drained
grated zest and juice of 1 orange
2 orange, peeled and segmented
grated zest and juice of 1 lemon
225g/8oz cooked rice
100g/4oz white breadcrumbs
1 onion, finely chopped
1/2tsp ground cinnamon

● **Serves 6** ▶

1 When taking the best ends out of the refrigerator to come to room temperature cut off the skin and trim the meat from the tops of the bones. Weigh the joints and calculate the cooking time at 44 minutes per kg/20 minutes per lb.

2 Sew one end of each joint together with fine string, around the last bone of each one. Stand the tied joints upright and bend them round until the other ends meet. Stitch these together to form a crown. Tie around the base to hold the crown in shape. Season inside and out with salt and pepper and sprinkle a little of the rosemary inside.

3 Heat the oven to 190C/375F/gas 5. Reserve 12 apricot halves. Chop the rest and mix with the stuffing ingredients; season with salt and pepper.

4 Melt the butter with the remaining rosemary in a roasting tin, then put in the lamb. Spoon the stuffing loosely into the centre of the crown. Cover the bone ends with foil and roast for the calculated time, basting occasionally. Cover the stuffing with foil if it becomes too brown.

5 Put the lamb on a warmed serving dish. Remove string and foil and put cutlet frills on the bone ends. Garnish with reserved apricot halves, watercress sprigs and orange segments.

Leg of lamb in pastry

● **Preparation: 40 minutes, plus cooling**

● **Cooking: 70-85 minutes**

1.4kg/3lb leg of young lamb, boned
225g/8oz made-weight puff pastry
4 lamb's kidneys
50g/2oz butter
100g/4oz button mushrooms, thinly sliced
50g/2oz fresh white breadcrumbs
good pinch each dried thyme and rosemary
salt and pepper
2tbls brandy
50g/2oz pâté de foie gras
1 egg, lightly beaten

● **Serves 4-6**

● **915cals/3990kjs per serving**

1 When removing the lamb from the refrigerator to come to room temperature remove most of the fat, leaving just a thin layer. Defrost the pastry.

2 Prepare and dice the kidneys. Melt half the butter in a frying pan and fry the kidneys for 1 minute, stirring to brown all over. Drain off most of the fat, then add the mushrooms, breadcrumbs, herbs and salt and pepper to taste. Fry for a further 3-4 minutes, until the breadcrumbs are a pale golden colour.

3 Remove the pan from the heat. Pour the brandy over the kidney mixture, stand back and set it alight with a match. Let the flames die down, then leave the mixture until lukewarm. Blend the pâté into the kidney mixture and leave the mixture until cold.

4 Heat the oven to 190C/375F/gas 5. Stuff the lamb with the kidney mixture, pressing it firmly into the space left by the bone. Ease back into shape and tie up securely, or sew along the seams with a large needle and fine string.

5 Put the lamb on a rack in a roasting tin and roast for 45-60 minutes depending on how well cooked you want it to end up. Remove from the oven, place on a plate, and leave until cold.

6 Heat the oven to 230C/450F/gas 8. Remove the string and spread the lamb with the remaining butter. Roll the pastry to a rectangle about 35 × 40cm/14 × 16in. Lay the lamb on top and fold the pastry up to enclose it, sealing the edges with beaten egg. Reserve any trimmings.

7 Transfer the pastry parcel to lightly dampened baking tray, joins downward. Make two or three holes in the top to allow steam to escape and decorate round them with pastry leaves, securing

HIGH OR LOW?

Large joints of lamb can be roasted at high temperature, which seals in flavour and gives a rich brown crust. But as this also causes shrinkage, a small joint is best roasted more gently, giving a juicy, tender joint with minimum loss of weight. Alternatively the joint can be started at one temperature and finished at another – see different recipes.

For a plain roast heat the oven to 170C/325F/gas 3. Allow 45-50 minutes per kg/20-23 minutes per lb for pink lamb, or up to 66 minutes per kg/30 minutes per lb for well done. Transfer the lamb to a hot serving platter and let stand in a warm place for 10-15 minutes before carving – use the front of the turned-off oven with the door ajar, warming compartment or stove top. This allows the meat to settle and makes it easy to carve. Meanwhile make gravy if required.

with beaten egg. Brush the pastry all over with cold water.

8 Cover the pastry leaves with small pieces of foil so they do not get too brown and bake for 10 minutes. Then remove the foil, brush the pastry all over with beaten egg and bake for a further 10 minutes until the pastry is puffed and golden. Serve hot.

Desserts and cakes

*I*n these days of healthier life-styles, puddings and cakes are more of a treat than a necessity; however, on special occasions and for people with hearty appetites, they are the perfect ending for a meal.

Desserts are not necessarily unhealthy – or fattening. The first chapter includes lots of ideas for fresh fruit salads, the lightest of desserts (if served without cream!). There are tips on how to plan ahead for the best results, how to keep the salads light and healthy, and how to prepare the fruit. There are serving suggestions too – you will discover how to make fruit salads look especially magnificent and tempting, piled into pineapple or melon shells.

Frozen desserts are also light, though not always in calories. There are two separate chapters: one on ice cream and the other on water ices, sorbets and granita – an Italian variation that is served still slushy. Discover all these different types and how to freeze them, before serving them imaginatively with a wonderful variety of sauces, both hot and cold.

Working with gelatine is not difficult, but to ensure its successful use, there is a step-by-step guide in the cheesecake chapter. Not all cheesecakes or mousses are set with gelatine; most European recipes call for baking, so there is information on oven temperatures and tin types.

Meringues are delicious to eat and fabulous to look at. Best of all, they can be made well in advance, so they are ready for both impromptu meals or planned dinner parties. Cooking with Confidence provides a step-by-step guide on how to whisk the egg whites, and how to pipe the meringue to create a really professional masterpiece. Recipes include such classics as Tropical Pavlova (see page 249) and Baked Alaska (see page 248).

The chapter on baking contains recipes for both simple and elaborate cakes. Some can be served with tea, others make a perfect dessert at the end of a meal. There are recipes for both creamed and fat-free sponges as well as all-in-one cakes. Information on baking tins and how to prepare them is included, along with facts about oven temperature and determining when the cake is properly cooked, and tips on turning out, cooling and storing.

Fresh and Fruity

Use the exciting colours and textures of fresh fruit to make beautiful desserts that are mouthwateringly light and low in calories — the perfect finish to a rich meal

WHETHER YOUR DESSERT is plain or fancy the fruit must be in prime condition, fresh and perfectly ripe. A few blemishes don't matter if the fruit is to be cut up for a fruit salad, but for a fruit bowl it must be unmarked and perfect in shape as well. Presentation is everything: the shapes, colours and textures of the fruit should contrast and complement one another.

Fruit salads

These are most spectacular served in pineapple or melon shells, but they also look good in glass dishes, which allow the colours of the fruit to be seen. Here you can ring the changes between a large serving dish and individual bowls, goblets or glasses. Small dishes are particularly good for decoratively arranged fruit salads.

Although the bulk of the fruit should be fresh, one or two canned fruits, such as lychees or figs, will add variety. Raisins or sultanas are useful for adding extra sweetness and colour contrast; soak them in boiling water first to plump them up. Use a mixture of four or five different fruits to give a pleasant contrast of texture and colour, allowing a total of 450g/1lb to serve four.

Before starting to prepare the fruit, squeeze the juice of a lemon into the bowl or bowls. This serves three purposes: it helps to stop fruit such as bananas and apples from turning brown; it draws out the juices; and gives the salad a pleasant sharp tang to contrast with the sweetness of the fruit and sugar.

Use a very sharp knife to prepare the fruit, so you can cut neat pieces, and make sure it has a stainless steel blade, as carbon steel reacts with the acid in fruit to produce off flavours. Prepare citrus fruit first, so that its acid juice works with the lemon juice.

Prepare the salad up to 6 hours ahead, to give the flavours time to blend and develop. But do not add bananas or soft berry fruits until

Celebration salad (page 222)

just before serving as they will soften too much. As you put the fruit into the bowl, sprinkle each layer with a little icing or caster sugar and fresh orange juice. (For special occasions use sweet or medium dry wine or a fruit-based liqueur instead.) Be sparing with the sugar — more can always be added at the table. Cover with foil, put in the bottom of the fridge and leave until about 30 minutes before eating.

Serve fruit salads with a topping of chopped or flaked nuts for crunch, or accompany with crisp biscuits.

MAKING SUGAR SYRUP

Traditionally fruit salads were dressed with syrup. This has fallen out of favour into today's health-conscious age, but you might like to try it for a party.

To make syrup for a good-sized fruit salad, put 300ml/½pt water into a saucepan with 100g/4oz sugar. Stir over a low heat until the sugar dissolves. Then bring to the boil and allow to boil for 2-3 minutes without stirring. Remove from the heat and leave to cool. Flavour the syrup with fruit juice, and liqueur or wine if liked.

When cold pour the syrup over the prepared fruit and turn the pieces gently until coated all over. Cover the bowl and put on the bottom shelf of the fridge for 2-3 hours or longer if possible.

Melon flower salad

- **Preparation: 45 minutes, plus chilling**
- **Cooking: 5 minutes**

1 Galia melon or cantaloupe
juice of 1 lemon
1 red-skinned apple
1 pear
1 orange
1 peach
50g/2oz cherries, stoned
50g/2oz strawberries
1 mint sprig, to decorate
For the paprika dressing:
6tbls unsweetened pineapple juice
4tbls lemon juice
1 large egg, beaten until pale
75g/3oz sugar
¾tsp paprika

- **Serves 6-8**
- **120cals/505kjs per serving**

1 Prepare a melon flower (see below). Brush the melon flesh with some of the lemon juice. Wrap the melon flower in stretch wrap or foil and chill until required.

2 Make the paprika dressing: combine the pineapple and lemon juices with the beaten egg, sugar and paprika in the top pan of a double boiler. Set over boiling water and cook, whisking constantly with a wire whisk, for about 5 minutes or until thick. Pour the dressing into a serving jug, leave to cool, then chill.

3 Quarter, core and dice the apple and pear, leaving the skins on. Put in a large bowl with some of the remaining lemon juice; mix well. Cover; chill briefly.

4 Peel and slice the orange and cut each slice in half. Put in a separate bowl. Peel and stone the peach, slice and add to the bowl along with any juice from the orange. Cover and chill briefly. Chill the cherries and strawberries separately.

5 Just before serving, put the melon flower on a large plate. Drain the diced apple and pear and combine with the other chilled fruit. Pile the mixture into the melon; any left over can be arranged round the base. Decorate with a mint sprig.

6 To serve, cut wedges of melon to accompany each portion of fruit salad. Hand the dressing separately.

How to ··· *make a melon flower*

Cut a very thin slice from the base of the melon to make it stand up firmly.

Cut lengthways into six or eight sections. Do not cut more than two-thirds of the way down.

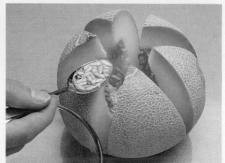

Carefully scrape out the seeds and membrane. Wrap the melon flower tightly and chill until required.

Pineapple boats

- **Preparation: 50 minutes, plus chilling**

2 small pineapples
1 small melon
2 apricots
1 nectarine
1 banana
2tsp lemon juice
For the sauce:
225g/8oz full-fat soft cheese,
  at room temperature
100ml/3¹/₂fl oz milk
1tbls caster sugar
¹/₂tsp ground cardamom

- **Serves 4** ①

- **280cals/1175kjs per serving**

1 Prepare four pineapple boats (see below), reserving half the pineapple flesh for another dish. Cut the melon into balls. Peel, slice and stone the apricots; stone and slice the nectarine. Peel and slice the banana; toss it in the lemon juice.

2 Mix the fruit gently in a large bowl. Divide between the pineapple boats, cover and chill for about 30 minutes.

3 To make the sauce, put all the ingredients in a small bowl and beat until smooth. Transfer to a serving jug and hand separately.

Cook's tips

Use left-over pineapple, alternating with chunks of Cheddar on cocktail sticks, as an appetizer to go with drinks.

Preparing a pineapple boat

Using a large, sharp knife, cut the pineapple in half vertically through its spiky top. With a smaller knife, cut round each half between the shell and the flesh, then cut out and dice the flesh, removing the woody 'eyes' and the hard central core.

MELON SENSE

Always wrap melon in stretch wrap or foil before chilling. This will stop the smell from permeating everything else in the fridge.

Red fruit bowl

● **Preparation: 20 minutes,
  plus chilling**

225g/8oz strawberries
100g/4oz raspberries
225g/8oz redcurrants
100g/4oz mulberries or
  blackberries
450g/1lb red cherries
For the syrup:
100g/4oz sugar
1tbls lemon juice
2tbls brandy

● **Serves 6**

● **140cals/590kjs per serving**

1 First prepare the sugar syrup: put the sugar in a small saucepan with 300ml/½pt water. Bring to the boil, then boil for 2-3 minutes, without stirring, until the mixture has a syrupy consistency. Stir in the lemon juice and brandy and leave until cold.

2 Prepare the fruit. In a glass bowl, combine the fruit and syrup and toss very gently to coat. Chill for at least 30 minutes before serving.

Cook's tips

To prepare berry fruit: place in a colander, run cold water gently over, then leave to drain. Spread between sheets of absorbent paper to dry. Gently hull strawberries.

HEALTH HINTS

Fresh fruit is a much healthier dessert than puddings or pastries, lacking their refined carbohydrates and fats, and containing plenty of vitamins and dietary fibre. Most fruits, except bananas, are very low in calories. But watch out for dried fruits of all kinds; these are high in calories because their sugar content is so concentrated.

Avoid adding a lot of extra calories by using just enough sugar to make the fruit palatable. If you have a sweet tooth use an artificial sweetener, or try a little concentrated apple juice (from health food shops). Serve the fruit with yoghurt or *fromage frais* rather than cream or ice cream.

Celebration salad

● **Preparation: 50 minutes,
  plus soaking and chilling**

2 ripe pears
2 peaches
juice of 2 oranges
½ small pineapple
75g/3oz grapes or 3 kiwi fruit
175g/6oz red plums or red cherries
225g/8oz raspberries or
  strawberries
100g/4oz vanilla sugar
250ml/9fl oz sweet sparkling wine
1 kiwi fruit, sliced, to decorate

● **Serves 8**

● **145cals/610kjs per serving**

1 Peel and core the pears and cut into chunks. Skin and stone the peaches and chop the flesh into chunks. Put the fruit in a large shallow dish, pour over the orange juice and toss.

2 Peel the pineapple and cut into chunks. Seed the grapes, or peel the kiwi fruit and cut into chunks. Halve and stone the plums or cherries.

3 Add half the raspberries or strawberries, and the remaining fruit, including their juices, to the dish. Spoon the orange juice over the fruit and sprinkle with the

FRUIT BOWLS

The best fruit bowls consist of top-quality ripe fruits of the season, arranged with just a few unusual varieties to add interest. Strawberries, however, look stunning served in a bowl on their own. Whichever fruits you choose, arrange them attractively in a fruit bowl or on a fruit stand, with a few strawberry or blackcurrant leaves to add a decorative flourish.

sugar. Cover and leave to soak for 1-2 hours.

4 Purée the reserved raspberries or strawberries through a sieve. Divide the purée between eight large, tall glasses, then fill them up with the fruit and juice.

5 Not more than 1 hour before serving, top up each glass with sparkling wine. Chill, then decorate with kiwi fruit slices just before serving.

Cook's tips

Vanilla sugar is made by storing a vanilla pod in a jar of caster sugar. It can be used in baking or whenever a hint of vanilla is required. Sachets of vanilla sugar can be bought in Italian delicatessens; alternatively add a few drops of vanilla essence to the orange juice.

The Big Chill

Home-made ice cream, rich and lusciously flavoured, is a luxury dessert, surpassing anything you can buy and amazingly easy to make

MANY PEOPLE THINK you need special equipment to make ice cream, but this is not the case. The real thing, made with cream and often eggs, requires nothing more specialized than a freezing compartment and a wire whisk.

Making ice cream

There are many different ways of making ice cream but almost all depend mainly on cream. This can be mixed with milk or other ingredients, but the more cream the smoother the result.

Whipped cream ices: the simplest ice creams are made by whipping double cream, folding in a flavouring and freezing. Another simple version can be made by incorporating whisked egg white with the whipped cream. This makes a slightly less rich mixture, and is cheaper as it goes further.

Dissolved sugar ices: To make a completely smooth ice cream the sugar is dissolved by heating it in some of the cream before adding the rest of the cream and freezing. If the sugar is just stirred in, it gives an unpleasant granular texture to the ice cream when frozen.

Syrup-based ices: alternatively, the sugar may be incorporated as a syrup made with water. This must be a heavy syrup, otherwise it will separate out from the cream while freezing, so it's important to boil the syrup to the stated temperature.

Custard-based ices: many ice creams have a base of custard made with egg yolks. This can be made from double cream only or with milk or single cream, and may be mixed with fruit purée for flavour and colour.

Freezing ice cream

Unless you make ice cream often and in large quantities, an electric ice cream maker or hand churn are

Ice cream stripe (page 228)

not necessary. But it does help if you have a freezer. Although ice cream can be made perfectly well in the freezing compartment of the refrigerator, there may not be much space in it. Also you must turn the refrigerator to its coldest setting about an hour before starting, and remove anything that you do not want to get too cold (eggs and cheese, for example). Unless you want a moulded ice cream, use a shallow container, preferably metal, for freezing it, as this speeds up the process; the faster the freezing, the smaller the ice crystals will be, and the smoother the ice cream. If using a mould, chill it beforehand for the same reason.

Pour the prepared mixture into the container, cover with foil and – for most ice creams – freeze until hardened to a depth of about 2.5cm/1in around the edges. This will take about 1 hour for 1L/1¾pt ice cream. Then, working quickly, beat the mixture vigorously with a fork or wire whisk to break down the ice crystals and freeze again until solid. This takes anything from 2-5 hours, depending on the temperature of the freezing compartment. A big freezer will do the job more quickly than the small freezing compartment of a refrigerator. Some ice creams (usually whipped cream ices) do not need beating.

Serving ice cream

Most ice creams should be transferred from the freezer to the refrigerator about 30 minutes before serving to let them soften slightly. This lets through the flavour and true texture.

Turning out: if the ice cream is in a mould, invert it onto the serving plate and put a cloth wrung out in hot water over the mould for a few seconds. This should loosen the ice cream without spoiling it.

Slices: if the ice cream has been made in a square or oblong container or small charlotte mould, turn it out as above and slice to serve.

Scoops: ice cream always looks attractive served in balls, which are easily produced if you have an ice cream or potato scoop. Dip the scoop in warm water before each use so that the ice cream comes away cleanly.

Butterscotch ice cream

- ● *Preparation: 15 minutes, plus cooling and freezing*

- ● *Cooking: 10 minutes*

75g/3oz soft light brown sugar
50g/2oz golden syrup
50g/2oz butter
300ml/½pt double cream
25g/1oz butterscotch pieces, crushed, for the ice cream (optional)
25g/1oz butterscotch pieces, crushed, to decorate

- ● *Serves 4*

- ● *530cals/2225kjs per serving*

1 Place the sugar, golden syrup and butter in a small saucepan. Heat gently until the butter has melted and the sugar has dissolved. Raise the heat, bring to the boil and boil for 2 minutes.

2 Remove the pan from the heat and stir in 2tbls hot water. Take care, as the mixture will splutter at first. Set aside until cool, about 1 hour.

3 Whip the cream lightly, then fold in the cooled butterscotch sauce. Stir in the crushed butterscotch pieces, if using. Pour into a shallow freezerproof container, cover with foil and freeze for 4-5 hours or until solid.

4 Serve straight from the freezer, spooned into individual glasses. Decorate each serving with a little crushed butterscotch.

TWO DIMENSIONAL

Colourful sauces add a whole new dimension to an ice cream dessert. Chocolate and butterscotch are very popular, and the classic Melba sauce made with crushed raspberries is hard to beat. A hot sauce on cold ice cream makes a wonderful contrast. Finally, add a texture contrast to your ice cream with chopped nuts or praline scattered over the top, and a crisp wafer or biscuit.

How to...
line a bombe mould

Spoon about 3tbls ice cream into the chilled mould. Smooth it evenly across the base using the back of the spoon.

Add more ice cream and work up the sides of the mould. The layer should be an even thickness of about 2.5cm/1in all the way up.

ICE CREAM BOMBES

These dome-shaped frozen desserts consist of an outer layer of ice cream with a contrasting centre. This can be a different-coloured ice cream, a sorbet, or a mousselike mixture as used in the Strawberry-pistachio bombe (right). They make ideal dinner-party desserts as they look so impressive, both whole and sliced, and because they can be made well ahead.

The authentic shape requires a proper bombe mould, but any similar-shaped china or plastic basin can be used. Make sure to get these well chilled before lining with the ice cream.

Strawberry-pistachio bombe

- **Preparation: 1 hour plus freezing**
- **Cooking: 15 minutes**

For the strawberry ice cream:
700g/1½lb ripe strawberries
100g/4oz icing sugar
juice of ½ lemon
600ml/1pt double cream, lightly whipped

For the bombe mixture:
4 egg yolks
50g/2oz caster sugar
150ml/¼pt double cream
green food colouring (optional)
almond essence (optional)
25g/1oz pistachio nuts, skinned and chopped
50g/2oz glacé cherries, chopped

- **Serves 10-12**
- **405cals/1700kjs per serving**

1 Purée the strawberries with the sugar and lemon juice until smooth. Push through a nylon sieve to remove pips. Fold the purée into the whipped cream until evenly combined.

2 Pour into a shallow freezerproof container and freeze for 1 hour or until frozen to a depth of 2.5cm/1in around the edges. Remove from the freezer and place in a chilled bowl. Beat vigorously then return to the container and freeze for a further 2-3 hours or until solid.

3 About 30 minutes before assembling the bombe, chill a 1.1L/2pt bombe mould and put the ice cream in the refrigerator to soften.

4 Line the mould evenly with a 2.5cm/1in layer of ice cream, smoothing it with the back of the spoon. (Return the remaining ice cream to the freezer.) Cover with foil and freeze for 1 hour or until firm.

5 Meanwhile, prepare the bombe mixture. Whisk the egg yolks until pale and very thick. Put the sugar in a small saucepan with 2tbls water and heat gently until the sugar dissolves. Boil, without stirring, for 1 minute or until the syrup reaches 110C/230F on a sugar thermometer. Allow to cool slightly, then slowly pour onto the egg yolks, whisking constantly until the mixture becomes cold.

6 Whip the cream until soft peaks form, then fold into the egg mixture. If liked, tint pale green with food colouring and flavour with a few drops of almond essence. Fold in the nuts and cherries.

7 Spoon the bombe mixture into the cavity in the ice cream. Smooth the surface, cover and freeze for 3-5 hours or until firm. Put a serving plate in the refrigerator to chill.

4 Tip the mixture into a chilled bowl and beat vigorously, then cover and freeze again until firm, about 2-3 hours.

5 About 30 minutes before serving, transfer the ice cream to the main part of the refrigerator to allow it to soften.

Cook's tips

A vanilla pod gives a finer flavour than vanilla essence, and can be used many times over, as long as you wash and dry it well after use. But if you prefer, add 2-3 drops of vanilla essence to the cooked custard instead.

Variations

Chocolate ice cream: *break into pieces 225g/8oz plain chocolate and melt it in a bowl set over simmering water. Stir into the custard while it is still warm. Cool, then fold in the whipped cream.*

Coffee ice cream: *dissolve 4tbls instant coffee and 2tbls sugar in 2tbls hot water. Cool, then stir into the cold custard. Fold in the whipped cream.*

 8 Unmould the bombe about an hour before serving. Invert the plate over the mould. Soak a cloth in hot water, wring it out and wrap round the mould. Sharply reverse mould and plate and slide off the mould. Put the bombe into the refrigerator to soften.

9 Cut the bombe into neat slices to serve it.

Cook's tips

The strawberry ice cream will serve 8-10 people on its own.

Vanilla ice cream

- **Preparation: 20 minutes, plus cooling and freezing**
- **Cooking: 20 minutes**

400ml/14fl oz milk
1 vanilla pod, broken up
8 egg yolks
100g/4oz caster sugar
400ml/14fl oz double cream

- **Serves 6-8**
- **440cals/1850kjs per serving**

HEALTH HINT

Once you have taken ice cream out of the refrigerator, serve it quickly and put any left over straight back into the freezer. This both preserves the texture of the ice cream and prevents any harmful bacteria from developing. Never refreeze ice cream which has melted or even become very soft. Home-made ice cream can be kept in the freezer for up to two months.

1 Put the milk and the vanilla pod in a saucepan and bring to the boil. Turn off the heat and reserve.

2 Whisk the yolks and sugar in a bowl or the top pan of a double boiler until pale and very thick. Pour the hot milk and vanilla pod onto the yolks and cook over very gently simmering water, stirring constantly with a wooden spoon, until the mixture thickens and coats the back of the spoon – 5-10 minutes. Leave to cool, then remove the vanilla pod.

3 Whip the cream until slightly thickened and fold it into the cold custard. Spoon the mixture into a shallow freezer-proof container, cover with foil and freeze. Leave for 1 hour or until the mixture has frozen to a depth of 2.5cm/1in around the edges.

Peppermint and chocolate ice cream

- **Preparation: 20 minutes, plus freezing**

- **Cooking: 15 minutes**

75g/3oz sugar
3 large egg yolks
600ml/1pt double cream
5-6tbls crème de menthe
75g/3oz plain chocolate, chopped

- **Serves 6**

- **835cals/3505kjs per serving**

1 About an hour before starting, chill an 850ml/1½pt jelly mould (preferably plastic).

2 Put the sugar in a small saucepan with 50ml/2fl oz water and stir over low heat until dissolved. Then boil until the syrup reaches 101C/215F on a sugar thermometer, or forms a thread when pulled between two spoons. Allow to cool slightly.

3 Whisk the egg yolks lightly in a bowl. Pour in the syrup in a thin stream, whisking constantly, until the yolks become pale yellow.

4 In another bowl, whip the cream until soft peaks form. Fold in the yolks, crème de menthe and chocolate. Pour the mixture into a shallow freezerproof container, cover with foil and freeze for about an hour, or until the mixture has frozen to a depth of 2.5cm/1in around the sides of the container.

5 Remove from the freezer and beat vigorously with a fork to break down the ice crystals. Spoon into the chilled mould, press it in firmly, then cover and freeze again until firm, about 3-5 hours.

OVER THE TOP

As an alternative to a sauce, top the ice cream with a suitably flavoured liqueur. Use Curaçao or another orange-flavoured one for orange or tangerine ice cream; kirsch goes with almost any fruit flavour; try crème de menthe with vanilla, or apricot brandy with an apricot-flavoured ice cream. One tablespoon per serving is ample.

6 About 30 minutes before serving, unmould the ice cream. Invert over a flat serving plate and cover with a cloth wrung out in hot water. Leave for a second or two, then carefully remove the mould. Place the ice cream in the main part of the fridge to soften slightly.

Tangerine ice cream

- **Preparation: 30 minutes, plus cooling and freezing**

- **Cooking: 10 minutes**

12 tangerines
100g/4oz caster sugar
600ml/1pt double cream
small shiny leaves, to decorate (optional)

- **Serves 6-8**

- **480cals/2015kjs per serving**

1 Grate the zest from six of the tangerines very finely and stir into the sugar.

2 Put the flavoured sugar into a small saucepan along with half the cream. Heat the mixture to to just below boiling point, stirring until the sugar has dissolved. Remove from the heat and leave to cool.

3 Meanwhile, squeeze the juice from all the tangerines. When the cream is cold strain the tangerine juice into it and stir well. Whip the remaining cream until soft peaks form and fold into the flavoured cream. Pour into a shallow freezerproof container, cover with foil and freeze for 1 hour or until the mixture is firm to a depth of 2.5cm/1in around the sides of the container.

4 Beat the ice cream vigorously to break down the ice crystals, re-cover and freeze again until completely firm; about 2-3 hours.

5 Transfer to the refrigerator for 30 minutes before serving to soften. Serve in scoops in glass dishes, decorated with shiny leaves, if wished.

Cook's tips

Close relatives of the tangerine, such as clementines and satsumas, can be used to make this ice cream. Sometimes these come with leaves, which are ideal for the decoration. Otherwise use any small shiny leaves you can get. Wash and dry before use, and make sure they are not eaten – ivy leaves in particular are quite poisonous.

Ice cream stripe

- **Preparation: making ice creams, then 20 minutes plus freezing**
- **Cooking: 10 minutes**

$1/2 \times$ *Chocolate ice cream (page 226)*
$1/2 \times$ *Vanilla ice cream (page 226)*
$1/2 \times$ *Coffee ice cream (page 226)*
150ml/¼pt double cream, whipped, to serve (optional)
For the praline:
50g/2oz almonds, in their skins
100g/4oz caster sugar
oil, for greasing

- **Makes 10-12 slices**
- **480cals/2015kjs per serving**

1 Make up the three batches of ice cream and freeze. Put them in the main part of the refrigerator to soften about 30 minutes before assembling the dessert, and chill a 900g/2lb loaf tin.

2 Meanwhile, make the praline: put the almonds and sugar in a small pan over low heat and cook without stirring until the sugar caramelizes. Brush a sheet of foil with oil, turn the mixture onto it and leave to set. Then either crush it with a rolling pin between sheets of greaseproof paper or put it through an electric grinder.

3 Working quickly, spoon the chocolate ice cream into the base of the loaf tin and level the top. Sprinkle with half the praline. Continue with a layer of vanilla ice cream and the remaining praline. Finish with the coffee ice cream.

4 Return to the freezer for 3-4 hours or until firm. Invert the tin over a flat serving plate and cover with a cloth wrung out in hot water. Leave for a few seconds and unmould. Serve sliced, decorated with whipped cream, if wished.

Variations

For a simpler dessert, use bought ice creams: you will need 425ml/15fl oz of each flavour.

WHAT WENT WRONG?

Lumpy texture: it is essential to beat the ice cream vigorously when semi-frozen to make sure the texture will be smooth.
Curdled custard: when making custard-based ice cream, don't overcook the custard or the eggs will curdle.

Banana ice cream

- **Preparation: 40 minutes, plus cooling and freezing**
- **Cooking: 20 minutes**

5 very ripe bananas, peeled and sliced
grated zest and juice of 1 lemon
150ml/¼pt double cream, lightly whipped
75g/3oz crystallized ginger, finely chopped
For the custard:
100g/4oz caster sugar
300ml/½pt milk
150ml/¼pt double cream
4 large egg yolks

- **Serves 6**
- **425cals/1785kjs per serving**

1 First make the custard. Put the sugar, milk and cream into the top pan of a double boiler and bring slowly to the boil over direct heat, stirring constantly to dissolve the sugar. Remove from the heat.

2 Put the yolks in a bowl and beat lightly with a wire whisk. Gradually pour in the hot cream mixture, whisking all the time, until well combined.

3 Return the custard to the pan and cook over simmering water, stirring, for 5-10 minutes or until the custard thickens and coats the back of a wooden spoon. Pour into a bowl, cover and chill.

4 Purée the bananas in a blender or food processor, adding a little custard if necessary, or press them through a nylon sieve. Stir the lemon zest into the chilled custard with the banana purée and the strained lemon juice. Then fold in the lightly whipped cream.

5 Pour the mixture into a shallow freezerproof container, cover with foil and freeze for 1 hour or until frozen to a depth of 2.5cm/1in around the sides of the container. Beat the ice cream vigorously with a fork or wire whisk to break down the ice crystals, cover and freeze until firm, about 3-5 hours.

6 Transfer the ice cream to the main part of the refrigerator about 30 minutes before serving to allow it to soften slightly.

7 To serve, scoop the ice cream into individual serving dishes or sundae glasses and sprinkle with finely chopped crystallized ginger.

Scrumptious Sponges

Ritual baking days may have gone out of fashion, but everyone still loves a sponge. At tea or as an any-time treat, try one of these classic cakes and revive an old tradition

YOU DON'T HAVE to be a master baker to make perfect sponge cakes. With a little care and patience, you will achieve excellent results every time.

Baking a sponge
First set the oven to the required temperature.

Prepare the tins before you start mixing (see Preparing the tin, page 230). A cake mixture that is kept waiting will not rise properly.

Fill the tins with the cake mixture and place the tins in the centre of the oven (unless the recipe states otherwise). If you have to use two shelves you may need to switch the tins over halfway through, or once the cakes have set.

Don't open the oven door unless it's absolutely necessary; if you must, close it carefully.

Is it cooked?
A sponge is ready when it is well risen, and shrinks away slightly from the sides of the tin. It should also spring back into shape when you press lightly with your finger.

Turning out
Sponge cakes should be left for 3 minutes to settle before being turned out of their tins. Then turn out, peel off the lining paper and invert onto a wire rack so that the cake cools resting right side up, otherwise you will have the marks of the rack on top of your sponge.

Storing sponges
Butter-rich sponges can be stored for two to three days in an airtight tin. Whisked sponges, which contain no fat, tend to dry out very quickly, so they should be eaten on the day of baking.

Sponges, without fillings or decorations, freeze well: whisked sponges and Swiss rolls for up to 3 months; creamed sponges for up to 6 months. Defrost in their wrappings for 2-2½ hours at room temperature, then fill or decorate and eat the same day. It hastens staling to refrigerate a sponge, so add cream fillings and decorations as close to serving time as possible.

All-in-one lemon cake (page 230)

All-in-one lemon cake

● *Preparation: 30 minutes*

● *Cooking: 1 hour, plus cooling*

melted butter and flour, for the tin
175g/6oz self-raising flour
½tsp baking powder
175g/6oz butter, softened, or
*   soft margarine*
175g/6oz caster sugar
3 eggs, lightly beaten
finely grated zest of 1 lemon
1-2tbls lemon juice
crystallized lemon slices and
*   angelica, to decorate (optional)*
For the glacé icing:
200g/7oz icing sugar
2tbls lemon juice
few drops of yellow food colouring
*   (optional)*

● *Serves 6-8*   ⑪ ££ 🕐 ❀

● *605cals/2540kjs per serving*

1 Heat the oven to 170C/325F/gas 3. Prepare a deep 18cm/7in round cake tin (see Preparing the tin, right).

2 Sift the flour with the baking powder into a large bowl. Add the butter or margarine, caster sugar, eggs, lemon zest and lemon juice. Beat with an electric mixer for 1 minute or with a wooden spoon for 2 minutes, just until blended.

3 Turn the mixture into the prepared tin. Level the surface, then make a shallow hollow in the centre. Bake the cake in the oven for 50-60 minutes or until done, covering with greaseproof paper towards the end of baking to prevent overbrowning.

4 Leave to settle, then turn the cake out of the tin and peel off the lining paper. Turn the cake, the right way up, on a wire rack and leave until cold. 🕐

5 For the glacé icing, sift the icing sugar into a bowl, then slowly stir in the lemon juice, and a few drops of colouring if you are using it, and blend until smooth. Place a tray underneath the rack. Pour the icing over the top of the cake and allow it to trickle down the sides. If using decorations, add these in a pattern when the icing is beginning to set; then leave to set completely.

Cook's tips

This cake can also be baked in a 15cm/6in square tin. The cooking time remains the same.

PREPARING THE TIN

Brush the base and sides with melted butter. Line the base with a circle or rectangle of greaseproof paper and brush that with melted butter. Dust the sides and base lightly with flour, knocking the tin against the table to shake off the surplus.

Chocolate Victoria sandwich

● *Preparation: 40 minutes*

● *Cooking: 30 minutes*

melted butter and flour, for the tins
225g/8oz butter or block
*   margarine, softened*
225g/8oz caster sugar
½tsp vanilla essence
4 large eggs
200g/7oz flour
25g/1oz cocoa
2tsp baking powder
For the filling and topping:
150g/5oz plain chocolate
150ml/¼pt soured cream
roasted hazelnuts, to decorate

● *Serves 6*   ⑪ ££ 🕐 ❀

● *800cals/3360kjs per serving*

1 Heat the oven to 180C/350F/gas 4. Prepare two 21.5cm/8½in sand-

wich tins (see Preparing the tin, left).

2 In a large bowl, cream the butter, caster sugar and vanilla essence until light and fluffy.

3 In another bowl, whisk the eggs until light and frothy, then whisk, a few spoonfuls at a time, into the butter mixture. Do not add the eggs too quickly as this would make the mixture curdle.

4 Sift the flour, cocoa and baking powder into a bowl and sprinkle over the creamed mixture a little at a time, folding it in lightly but thoroughly with a large metal spoon. Divide the mixture evenly between the prepared tins and level the tops lightly with a spatula. Bake for 25 minutes or until cooked.

5 Remove the cakes from the oven and leave to settle, then turn them out. Peel off the greaseproof paper and invert the cakes onto a wire rack to cool, right sides up. 🕐

6 To make the filling and topping, break the chocolate into a bowl and place over a pan of just-simmering water. Add the soured cream and stir until the chocolate has melted. Remove from the heat and leave to cool. Use half to sandwich the cakes together, and spread the rest over the top of the cake. Decorate with roasted hazelnuts.

How to ··· *make a whisked sponge*

Put the egg yolks, caster sugar, lemon juice and salt in a bowl and whisk for about 5 minutes, until it is light and fluffy and leaves a trail when the whisk is lifted.

Sift the flour and cornflour mixture, a little at a time, over the surface of the egg yolk mixture, folding it in with a cutting motion to disperse the flour evenly.

Whisk the egg whites until soft peaks form, tip them onto the sponge mixture and fold in gently but thoroughly, cutting with the side of a large metal spoon.

Jam and cream sandwich

- ● *Preparation: 40 minutes*

- ● *Cooking: 25 minutes, plus cooling*

6tbls jam
150ml/¼pt double cream, whipped
icing sugar, for dusting
For the whisked sponge:
melted butter and flour, for the tins
50g/2oz flour
25g/1oz cornflour
4 large eggs, separated
175g/6oz caster sugar
1½tbls lemon juice or water
large pinch of salt

- ● *Serves 6* ⑪ ££ ❄

- ● *360cals/1510kjs per serving*

1 Heat the oven to 180C/350F/gas 4. Prepare two 20cm/8in deep sandwich tins (see Preparing the tin, opposite).

2 Sift the flour and cornflour together three times onto greaseproof paper. Put the egg yolks, sugar, lemon juice or water and salt in a bowl. Whisk with an electric whisk at high speed for 5 minutes. If whisking by hand, whisk steadily until the mixture is light and fluffy.

3 Resift the flour and cornflour a little at a time over the surface of the egg yolk mixture, at the same time folding it in lightly but thoroughly with a large metal spoon.

4 Put the egg whites in another bowl, which must be spotlessly clean and dry. Wash and dry the whisk carefully and then whisk the egg whites until soft peaks are formed. Fold into the sponge mixture. Divide the mixture evenly between the prepared sandwich tins. If necessary, level the tops lightly with a spatula. Bake for 20-25 minutes or until done.

5 Remove the cakes from the oven and leave to settle. Then turn out. Peel off the greaseproof paper and invert the cakes onto a wire rack to cool.

6 Just before serving, sandwich with jam and cream and dust the top of the cake with icing sugar.

Making a Swiss roll

Turn the cake out quickly onto sugared greaseproof paper, peel off the lining paper and trim the crusty edges with a sharp knife.

Lay a sheet of greaseproof on top and, while the cake is still warm, roll it up carefully from a short end with the paper inside.

HINTS AND TIPS

Eggs: take eggs out of the fridge well before you intend to use them as they should be at room temperature.

Fats: some people prefer butter for making sponges for its flavour. Soft margarine is excellent in all-in-ones — though you must take care not to over-cream it — while block margarine is best for creamed mixtures. Allow one hour at room temperature to soften butter or block margarine; soft margarine can be used straight from the fridge.

Mandarin Swiss roll

- *Preparation: 40 minutes*

- *Cooking: 10 minutes, plus cooling*

melted butter and flour, for the tin
75g/3oz caster sugar, plus extra for dredging
3 large eggs
65g/2¹/₂oz flour
1tsp ground mixed spice
pinch of salt
15g/¹/₂oz ground almonds
150ml/¹/₄pt whipping cream
100g/4oz canned mandarin segments, well drained and chopped
icing sugar and orange segments, to decorate

- *Serves 8*

- *175cals/735kjs per serving*

1 Heat the oven to 200C/400F/gas 6. Prepare a 33cm × 23cm/13in × 9in Swiss roll tin (see Preparing the tin, page 22). Dredge a large sheet of greaseproof paper with caster sugar.

2 In a large bowl, whisk together the eggs and sugar until the mixture is pale and the whisk leaves a trail on the surface.

3 Sift together the flour, spice and salt and stir in the ground almonds. Gradually and lightly fold this into the egg mixture. When evenly combined, pour into

WHAT WENT WRONG?

Air bubbles under the top crust and crumbly edges: the mixture was over-creamed.
Cake rises in a cone in the centre, the top is badly cracked and a hard crust forms over the top: the oven was too hot.
Cake sinks in the middle and is either coarse and close-textured or dry and crumbly: the oven was too cool.
Cake is cracked and overbrown on the top but still level: the oven is much hotter at the top than the bottom.
Cake rises lopsidedly: the oven is hotter on the side that has risen the highest.

the prepared tin, level the surface and bake for 8-10 minutes, until it is just firm to the touch and there is no bubbling sound.

4 Invert the cake onto the sugared greaseproof, peel away the lining paper and trim the edges. Place another sheet of greaseproof on top, roll up firmly and leave to cool.

5 Just before serving, lightly whip the cream. Carefully unroll the cake and remove the top sheet of the paper. Spread the cream evenly over the surface, leaving a border of 5mm/¹/₄in around the edge

6 Scatter the mandarins over the cream. With the aid of the base paper, reroll the cake. Sift icing sugar over the cake and serve as soon as possible, decorated with orange segments.

Dreamy Cheesecakes

The delectable contrast between soft creamy filling and crunchy crust makes cheesecakes irresistible – and the most delicious can be made at home

CHEESECAKES OF ONE kind or another have a long history. Ancient Greeks and Romans loved them, and they are still tremendously popular today. Variations on the basic theme are legion, and in America they have hundreds of different recipes, many handed down by Italian and German immigrants. The cheesecakes eaten in Britain today are mostly American-inspired, but in the 16th century 'maids of honour', small curd cheese tartlets, were popular.

Although there are so many variations, there are just two basic kinds, with either a cooked or an uncooked filling. The European cheesecake is baked, usually in a shortcrust pastry case, and the cheese filling is set with flour and/or eggs. Sometimes a biscuit crust or sponge cake mixture is used instead of shortcrust. In the American-style cheesecake, the filling is set with gelatine, and the base usually consists of crushed biscuits bound with butter.

The traditional technique for making a cheesecake consists of beating all the filling ingredients together. Using an electric mixer, blender or food processor will speed up the process and make a smoother, lighter cake.

The filling
Different cheeses can be used for making cheesecakes, which results in a variety of tastes and textures, which are further varied according to whether the cheese is cooked or not.

Marbled coffee cheesecake (page 234)

233

Curd cheese: this gives a good flavour, but may need whisking before use to make it smooth. It may also need squeezing in muslin to remove excess water.

Full-fat soft cheese: this contains 45% fat and produces a rich cake with superb texture. Medium or low-fat soft cheese can also be used to make a less rich cake.

Cottage cheese: being a low-fat cheese (only around 4% fat), this makes a low-calorie filling. The lumps must be removed by first sieving or beating. Some recipes add cottage cheese to full-fat soft cheese to lighten and also sharpen the filling.

Marbled coffee cheesecake

- **Preparation: 45 minutes, plus chilling**

- **Cooking: 5 minutes**

175g/6oz digestive biscuits, crushed
50g/2oz walnuts, finely chopped
75g/3oz melted butter
butter for greasing
whipped cream, to decorate
  (optional)
plain chocolate beans,
  to decorate (optional)
For the filling:
450g/1lb full-fat soft cheese
100g/4oz caster sugar
2 egg yolks
¹/₂tsp vanilla essence
150ml/¹/₄pt single cream
15g/¹/₂oz powdered gelatine
  (1 sachet)
2tbls instant coffee granules
1tbls sugar

- **Serves 6-8**   ⚙ ££ 🕐 ❄

- **630cals/2645kjs per serving**

1 Stir together the biscuits, nuts and melted butter. Butter an 18cm/7in square loose-bottomed cake tin. Press the mixture into the base. Chill until firm.

2 Beat the cheese and caster sugar in a large bowl until smooth. Beat in the egg yolks, vanilla essence and cream.

3 Place 2tbls cold water in a small bowl and sprinkle over the gelatine. Leave to soften for 5 minutes, then place the bowl in a pan of hot water and heat gently

until dissolved. Leave to cool slightly.

4 Pour the gelatine into the cheese mixture, stirring until blended.

5 Mix the coffee and sugar with 1tbls hot water and stir until dissolved.

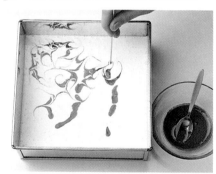

6 Pour the cheese filling into the tin. Trickle over the coffee, then use a skewer to marble it into the filling. Chill for 2 hours or until set. 🕐

7 To serve, remove the cake from the tin and decorate with piped whipped cream and chocolate beans, if wished.

Orange-almond cheesecake

- **Preparation: 35 minutes, plus chilling**

butter, for greasing
75g/3oz melted butter
225g/8oz almond macaroons,
  crushed
For the filling:
225g/8oz curd cheese

Orange-almond cheesecake

150ml/¹/₄pt yoghurt
2 eggs, lightly beaten
2tbls clear honey
juice and grated zest of 1 orange
15g/¹/₂oz powdered gelatine
  (1 sachet)
50g/2oz almond macaroons,
  crushed
25g/1oz flaked almonds, toasted

- **Serves 6**   ⚙ ££ 🕐 ❄

- **475cals/1995kjs per serving**

1 Butter a 20cm/8in fluted flan ring and stand it on a flat serving plate.

2 Combine the melted butter and crushed macaroons and mix well. Tip the mixture into the flan ring and press it down smoothly to cover the base and sides. Chill while you make the filling.

3 Beat together the cheese and yoghurt until they are completely smooth. Then beat in the eggs and honey.

4 Put the orange juice into a cup and sprinkle on the gelatine. Leave to soften for 5 minutes, then put in a pan of hot water and heat until the gelatine has dissolved and the liquid is quite clear. Remove from the heat and allow to cool slightly.

5 Pour the gelatine mixture steadily into the cheese mixture, stirring well. Stir in the orange zest and crushed macaroons.

6 Pour the mixture into the prepared case and chill for about 2 hours or until the filling has set. 🕐 Remove the flan ring and decorate with toasted almonds.

How to ··· dissolve gelatine

Pour a little cold water or fruit juice into a small heatproof bowl. Sprinkle on the gelatine and leave to soften for 5 minutes without stirring or until it has absorbed all the liquid – it may end up quite solid in consistency.

Put the bowl in a pan of hot water and heat gently until the gelatine has dissolved and the liquid is clear. Swirl this around occasionally but do not stir, or the undissolved gelatine will stick to the spoon.

FREEZING CHEESECAKES

Both cooked and uncooked cheesecakes freeze well, though any fruit toppings or decorations should be put on after defrosting. Remove from the tin, wrap well, then freeze for up to 1 month. Defrost at room temperature for 4-6 hours.

Strawberry cheesecake

This cheesecake has an unusual soft, mousse-like consistency.

- **Preparation: 1 hour, plus chilling**
- **Cooking: 15 minutes**

butter, for greasing
175g/6oz shortbread biscuits, finely crushed
50g/2oz melted butter
225g/8oz strawberries
grated zest of ¹/₂ orange
2tbls orange juice
15g/¹/₂oz powdered gelatine (1 sachet)
350g/12oz curd cheese
100g/4oz caster sugar
2-3 drops of vanilla essence
4tbls yoghurt
150ml/¹/₄pt double cream, lightly whipped
1 egg white
halved strawberries, to decorate

- **Serves 8**

- **515cals/2165kjs per serving**

1 Heat the oven to 180C/350F/gas 4. Lightly butter an 18cm/7in spring-release or loose-bottomed cake tin.

2 Add the crushed biscuits to the melted butter and stir until evenly coated. Spoon the mixture into the tin and press firmly and evenly over the base. Bake for 8-10 minutes or until lightly browned, then leave to cool.

3 Meanwhile, put the strawberries in a bowl, sprinkle with the orange zest and juice and crush to a pulp with a fork. Sprinkle the gelatine over 3tbls cold water in a small bowl and leave to soften for 5 minutes.

4 Beat the cheese with the sugar, vanilla essence, yoghurt and cream until smooth and then stir in the crushed strawberries.

5 Place the bowl of gelatine in a pan of hot water and heat gently until completely dissolved, then leave to cool. Pour the gelatine into the cheese mixture, stirring constantly until the gelatine is thoroughly incorporated.

6 Softly whisk the egg white. Gently fold into the cheese mixture, then turn into the prepared tin and smooth the surface. Cover loosely and chill for 3-4 hours or until set. Just before serving, remove the sides of the tin and decorate.

How to ··· *make a crumb crust*

Crush the biscuits thoroughly with a rolling pin until they are reduced in texture to fine, even crumbs.

Mix the crumbs with melted butter and any other ingredients. Tip into a buttered spring-release tin or flan ring.

Press the mixture down smoothly to cover the base or base and sides of the tin evenly. Chill or bake before filling.

Black Forest cheesecake

● *Preparation: 45 minutes, plus chilling*

● *Cooking: 10 minutes*

350g/12oz full-fat soft cheese
75g/3oz caster sugar
2 eggs, separated
1tbls kirsch
15g/¹/₂oz powdered gelatine (1 sachet)
300ml/¹/₂pt whipping cream
425g/15oz canned stoned black cherries in syrup
1tbls arrowroot or cornflour
kirsch or lemon juice
chocolate curls, to decorate
For the base:
75g/3oz plain chocolate, broken up
65g/2¹/₂oz butter, plus extra for greasing
250g/9oz plain chocolate digestive biscuits, crumbled

● *Serves 8-10*   ❚❚ ££ 🕐 ❋

● *875cals/3675kjs per serving*

1 Line and grease the base of a 23cm/ 9in spring-release or loose-bottomed cake tin. In a small saucepan, melt the chocolate and butter over low heat; mix them with the biscuit crumbs. Spread evenly over the base of the tin and chill.

2 In a large bowl, cream the cheese and sugar. Beat in the yolks and kirsch.

3 Pour 2tbls cold water into a small bowl and sprinkle on the gelatine. Leave for 5 minutes to soften, then stand the bowl in a pan of hot water and heat

until dissolved. Leave to cool slightly.

4 Whip the cream until it just holds soft peaks. Whisk the egg whites until stiff. Beat the gelatine mixture slowly into the cheese, taking care not to let lumps form. Using a large metal spoon, gently fold in the cream, then the egg whites.

5 Drain the cherries, reserving the syrup. Cut them in half and spread a third over the chilled crumb base. Turn the cheese mixture gently on top and spread evenly. Chill for 3-4 hours or until set.

6 Make a cherry sauce: blend the arrowroot or cornflour with a little of the reserved syrup. Pour the remaining syrup into a pan, adding kirsch or lemon

juice to taste. Bring slowly to the boil, then stir in the arrowroot mixture. Stir until it thickens and clears. Cool under a piece of dampened greaseproof paper. 🕐

7 Remove the cheesecake from the tin. Decorate with a ring of the remaining halved cherries and spoon a little sauce over them. Arrange chocolate curls round the edge and serve with the remaining sauce handed separately in a sauceboat.

Cook's tips

To make chocolate curls, shave long, thin strips off a block of plain chocolate with a potato peeler or sharp knife.

Cherry cheesecake

- ● *Preparation: 1 bour, plus chilling*

- ● *Cooking: 1½ bours*

150g/5oz flour
4tbls icing sugar
1tsp grated lemon zest
75g/3oz softened butter
2 egg yolks
For the filling:
600g/1¼lb full-fat soft cheese
150g/5oz sugar
2tbls cornflour
1½tsp grated lemon zest
½tsp vanilla essence
3 eggs
2tbls double cream
For the topping:
400g/14oz canned stoned red cherries
2tsp arrowroot or cornflour

- ● *Serves 8-10*

- ● *540cals/2270kjs per serving*

1 First make the pastry: sift the flour and sugar into a large bowl and stir in the lemon zest. Make a well in the centre and add the softened butter and egg yolks. Rub the mixture with your fingertips to form a mixture resembling breadcrumbs, then bring it all together to make a soft dough.

2 Form the pastry into a ball, wrap in stretch wrap and chill for 15 minutes. Then use to line a 24cm/9½in spring-release tin so that the pastry comes halfway up the sides. Chill again for 30 minutes.

3 Heat the oven to 200C/400F/gas 6. Prick the pastry with a fork, then bake blind for 15-20 minutes or until golden, removing the beans for the last 5 minutes. Leave to cool. Reduce the oven temperature to 140C/275F/gas 1.

4 Make the filling: beat the cheese until soft. Add the sugar, cornflour, lemon zest and vanilla essence and beat until blended. Beat in the eggs one at a time, beating lightly after each addition. Gently beat in the cream.

5 Pour the filling into the pastry case and bake for 1 hour. Turn off the heat, let the cheesecake cool in the oven for another hour, then chill overnight in the refrigerator.

6 Drain the cherries, reserving the syrup. Remove the cake from the tin and arrange the cherries in neat circles on top.

TIN TYPES

Cheesecakes are fragile and so are best made in a spring-release cake tin to make quite sure that they are not broken when removed from the tin. A loose-bottomed cake tin can also be used, but is less easy to manage.

If the cheesecake is a no-cook variety and the case is made of biscuit crumbs, you can line an ordinary cake tin with stretch wrap, leaving some extending at the top. This can be used to lift out the cheesecake after chilling.

For a cooked cheesecake, line an ordinary cake tin with foil and use this to lift it out. Make sure the foil is smooth.

7 To make the topping: measure 300ml/½pt of the reserved syrup, making up with water if necessary. Blend the arrowroot with a little of this syrup, then pour into the remaining syrup. Pour into a saucepan and bring to the boil, stirring constantly, then boil until the glaze becomes transparent. Cool until tepid, ▶

◀ then spoon the glaze over the cherries. Chill the cake for at least 3 hours before serving as a dessert or at teatime.

Viennese cheesecake

- **Preparation: 1 hour, plus chilling**

- **Cooking: 1½ hours**

350g/12oz shortcrust pastry, defrosted if frozen
100g/4oz softened butter
4 large eggs, separated
150g/5oz icing sugar, sifted, plus extra to decorate
450g/1lb curd cheese
juice and grated zest of 1 large lemon
about ½tsp vanilla essence
2tbls flour
25g/1oz raisins or sultanas
25g/1oz chopped candied peel

- **Serves 8**

- **550cals/2310kjs per serving**

1 Roll out the pastry 3mm/⅛in thick. Line the base and the sides of a 23cm/9in loose-bottomed flan tin with a fluted edge. Prick the base all over with a fork. Chill for 30 minutes.

2 Heat the oven to 200C/400F/gas 6. Line the pastry case with greaseproof paper and fill with baking beans.

3 Bake the flan case blind for 15 minutes, then remove the beans and paper and bake for another 10-20 minutes or until the pastry is cooked through and lightly coloured. Leave to cool. Reduce the oven temperature to 190C/375F/gas 5.

4 Beat together the softened butter, the egg yolks, icing sugar and curd cheese until thoroughly blended.

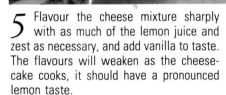

5 Flavour the cheese mixture sharply with as much of the lemon juice and zest as necessary, and add vanilla to taste. The flavours will weaken as the cheesecake cooks, it should have a pronounced lemon taste.

6 Sift the flour over the raisins or sultanas and the chopped candied peel. Toss to coat them well, then fold into the cheese mixture.

7 Whisk the egg whites until stiff but not dry. Using a large metal spoon, fold gently, but thoroughly, into the cheese mixture. Fill the baked pastry case with the mixture and smooth the surface.

8 Bake for 30-35 minutes or until the cheesecake is firm in the centre and well risen. Cool in the tin before lifting out carefully onto a serving dish. Dust the top with icing sugar. Serve either warm or chilled.

CHEESECAKE CHOICE

Crushed biscuits make the easiest base for a cheesecake. Digestive biscuits, plain or chocolate coated, are very popular, but you can also use shortbread, muesli biscuits or gingernuts. Or try cornflakes, puffed rice or muesli (as long as it doesn't contain whole nuts or lumps of dried fruit).

For variety, add some chopped nuts, desiccated coconut or a little ground cinnamon, ginger or mixed spice to the base.

WHAT WENT WRONG?

Cracked or sunken top: oven temperature too high.
Filling soft and sunken: the cheese was not drained well enough.
Filling rubbery: too much gelatine used, or beaten egg white not folded in gently.

Frozen Assets

Cooling and good to look at, inexpensive and simple to make, water ices and sorbets are both excellent refreshers and elegant desserts

A WATER ICE is usually a simple sugar syrup flavoured with fruit juice or purée, or with an essence such as strong coffee. The absence of any fat in the syrup results in large ice crystals forming; the ice therefore has to be beaten vigorously during freezing to break down the crystals as they form and keep the ice smooth.

Granita, an Italian speciality, is a variation on a simple water ice. For a granita the crystals are allowed to form more roughly and the ice separates slightly so that the top is rough-textured, icy crystals, while the bottom is slushy almost to the point of being liquid.

A sorbet is another variation, smoother than the basic water ice.

To achieve the smoothness, whisked egg whites are beaten into the mixture when it is partially frozen.

Making the sugar syrup

Always use the amount of sugar recommended in the recipe for making the sugar syrup. If you use less, the ice will freeze too hard and will lack flavour; if you use too much, the sugar will stop it firming up at all. Any type of white sugar can be used, though granulated is the cheapest. Avoid brown sugars as they give the ice a poor colour.

To keep the water ice smooth, always dissolve the sugar in the water before adding the flavourings. Put the sugar and the water in

a heavy-based saucepan and place the pan over low heat to begin with. Stir gently with a wooden spoon until all the sugar crystals are dissolved, then raise the heat and boil for the specified time without stirring again. This will give you a really smooth syrup with no grains in it. If you use a flavouring such as lemon juice or zest, strain the syrup through a muslin-lined sieve.

The proportion of sugar to water varies both with the type of ice you are making – for example a slushy granita or a firmer water ice – and with the amount of liquid in the flavouring. Some fruits contain

Melon and ginger sorbet (page 241)

more water than others and this will affect the amount of water needed in the syrup.

Flavourings

Most water ices are flavoured with the puréed flesh of a fruit or vegetable. Sometimes the fruit has to be cooked first to soften it, others will purée easily in a blender. For citrus fruit ices, use the juice only, but flavour the sugar syrup with a little pared zest. Sieve fruit purées and juices to ensure that they are completely smooth. Other flavourings such as coffee, tea or wine can also be used.

There is one important rule to remember when making water ices – prior to freezing the mixture should, if anything, taste over-flavoured and over-sweet. You will be surprised how much flavour is lost with freezing. Keep subtle flavours for rich ice creams.

Water ices are best made with the stronger flavoured fruits such as citrus and currants. Raspberries and strawberries are good, too, and the autumn fruits such as apples and pears. Some vegetables make good ices too, for serving as a first course. Tomato and carrot are particularly good as the flavours are strong.

If you are using alcohol to flavour a water ice, choose one that complements the flavour of the main ingredient.

Freezing the ice

If you are using the frozen food compartment of your refrigerator, start by turning it to its coldest setting at least 1 hour before you start. Any food in the refrigerator that you do not want to freeze by accident should be moved to the bottom of the refrigerator.

Most freezers need no special adjustment. The temperature of −18C/0F, which is the standard storage temperature in a domestic freezer, is low enough for freezing water ices without setting the fast freeze switch.

Serving a water ice

Fifteen minutes to 1 hour before serving, transfer the ice to the ordinary chilling compartment of the refrigerator to soften it slightly

(reset the controls back to normal if you have been freezing in the frozen food compartment).

A water ice or sorbet should be just one stage harder than slushy when served, just firm enough to hold a shape in the scoop. A granita should still be positively slushy.

Red berry sorbet

- *Preparation: 30 minutes, plus cooling and freezing*

- *Cooking: 15 minutes*

900g/2lb strawberries
225g/8oz sugar
juice of 1 lemon
*¹/₂tsp red food colouring
  (optional)*
4 large egg whites
900g/2lb raspberries
6tbls kirsch

- *Serves 8-12*

- *200cals/840kjs per serving*

1 Rub the strawberries through a fine nylon sieve into a bowl and discard the pips.

2 In a heavy-based saucepan, combine the sugar with 600ml/1pt water. Stir over low heat until the sugar dissolves, then bring to the boil. Boil for 10 minutes. Remove from the heat and stir in the lemon juice. Strain the syrup through a muslin-lined sieve and leave to cool.

3 Combine the strawberry purée and the syrup and add enough red food colouring to make a pink ice, if wished. Pour into a shallow, freezerproof container, cover and freeze for 1 hour, or until firm to a depth of about 2.5cm/1in all round the edges of the container.

4 Remove the ice from the freezer and whisk vigorously to break up the ice particles. Cover and freeze for 30 minutes.

5 Whisk the egg whites until stiff. Remove the ice from the freezer, whisk again until smooth then whisk in the stiffly beaten egg whites. Return to the container; freeze for 2 hours until firm.

6 About 1 hour before serving, transfer the sorbet to the refrigerator to soften.

7 To serve, scoop into 12 balls and arrange in a single layer in a large, flat, chilled serving dish. Cover the sorbet with a thick layer of raspberries, sprinkle with the kirsch and serve.

Freezer

Both water ices and sorbets can be stored in the freezer in a rigid container for up to two months, though they are at their best eaten within a week of making.

WHAT WENT WRONG?

The ice won't freeze: too much sugar or alcohol was used in the mixture.
The ice sets like concrete: too little sugar was used in the mixture.
The ice isn't smooth: it wasn't whisked often enough during freezing.

Claret granita

- **Preparation: 15 minutes, plus cooling and freezing**
- **Cooking: 5 minutes**

200g/7oz sugar
75cl bottle of claret
juice of 1 orange
juice of 1 lemon
mint leaves, to decorate

- **Serves 6**　　　　🍴 ££

- **225cals/945kjs per serving**

1 Put the sugar and 200ml/7fl oz water in a heavy-based saucepan and stir over gentle heat until the sugar is dissolved. Boil for 1 minute, then cool.

2 When the syrup is cold, add the wine, the orange and lemon juices, and mix together with a small whisk. Strain the mixture through a muslin-lined sieve into a shallow, freezerproof container and freeze

for 1-1½ hours or until it is frozen to a depth of 2.5cm/1in all round the sides.

3 Turn the claret ice into a large bowl and whisk until smooth with an electric mixer. Pour back into the freezer

LUSCIOUS LIQUEURS

Liqueurs are added to ices either at the final beating or poured over just before serving. Choose a liqueur that goes well with the fruit used in the recipe. Kirsch teams happily with all fruits, crème de cassis goes with blackcurrants, Drambuie and peach brandy with peaches, Cointreau with oranges and apricot brandy with apricots.

container and freeze again until lightly set and a mass of small, light crystals.

4 Stir the granita and spoon it into six claret glasses, shaping it into domes with a spoon. Garnish and serve.

Cook's tips

A granita should be served immediately it is frozen to the right consistency, but for convenience you can make it in advance: leave to soften in the fridge for 1 hour, whisk thoroughly with a fork and serve immediately.

How to ... *make a water ice*

Prepare the fruit, then purée it through a fine nylon sieve. Discard any pips and fibres left over from the fruit.

Dissolve the sugar in the water over low heat, then boil. Add lemon juice, if necessary, and strain through a muslin-lined sieve.

Add the cold syrup to the purée. Pour into a shallow freezerproof container, cover and freeze until slushy.

Stir the mixture vigorously with a fork, then freeze again. Repeat every 30 minutes until half frozen, then freeze hard.

Melon and ginger sorbet

- **Preparation: 25 minutes, plus cooling and freezing**
- **Cooking: 10 minutes**

100g/4oz sugar
½tsp powdered gelatine dissolved in 1tbls water
1 ripe honeydew melon, about 900g/2lb
¼tsp ground ginger
2 egg whites
stem ginger strips, to decorate

▶

● *Serves 4*

● *135cals/565kjs per serving*

1 Put the sugar and 300ml/½pt water in a pan and heat gently until the sugar has dissolved. Boil for 5 minutes, then remove from the heat and leave to cool for about 10 minutes. Stir in the dissolved gelatine and leave until completely cold.

2 Meanwhile, cut the melon in half and remove the seeds. Scoop out the melon flesh, put it in a blender or food processor with the ginger and blend to a smooth purée.

3 Whisk the cold sugar syrup and 300ml/½pt melon purée together, then pour into a shallow, freezerproof container and freeze until slushy – about 30 minutes. Remove from the freezer and whisk vigorously.

4 Whisk the egg whites until stiff, then whisk into the half-frozen mixture until evenly blended. Return to the freezer and freeze for several hours until solid.

5 Transfer the sorbet to the refrigerator 15 minutes before serving.

6 To serve, scoop the slightly softened sorbet into coupe glasses and decorate with strips of stem ginger.

Blackcurrant water ice

● *Preparation: 20 minutes, plus cooling and freezing*

● *Cooking: 40 minutes*

450g/1lb blackcurrants
175g/6oz sugar
2tsp lemon juice
6tbls crème de cassis, to serve (optional)

● *Serves 6*

● *175cals/735kjs per serving*

1 Put the blackcurrants in the top pan of a double boiler with 6tbls water. Cook slowly over simmering water for about 30 minutes or until the blackcurrants have released their juice. Strain through a nylon sieve, pressing out as much juice as possible with the back of a spoon.

2 Put the sugar and 300ml/½pt water in a heavy-based saucepan and heat gently, stirring, until the sugar is dissolved, then boil for 10 minutes. Add the lemon juice and strain the syrup through a muslin-lined sieve into a bowl; cool.

3 Combine the sugar syrup with the blackcurrant juice in a measuring jug. Make up to 700ml/1¼pt with water. Pour it into a shallow, freezerproof container, cover and freeze for 1 hour or until it is frozen to a depth of about 2.5cm/1in all round the sides.

4 Whisk the mixture vigorously, then freeze again. Repeat every 30 minutes until half frozen. Cover and leave for a further 2–3 hours until frozen hard.

5 Transfer the water ice to the refrigerator about 1 hour before serving.

6 Arrange scoops of water ice in each of six individual glass dishes. Spoon 1tbls crème de cassis over each helping, if liked, and serve immediately.

Peach water ice

● *Preparation: 30 minutes, plus cooling and freezing*

● *Cooking: 15 minutes*

225g/8oz sugar
juice of ½ lemon
4 peaches, weighing about 450g/ 1lb
sliced black grapes and mint sprigs, to decorate

● *Serves 6*

● *190cals/800kjs per serving*

1 Put the sugar and 600ml/1pt water in a heavy-based saucepan and heat gently, stirring, until the sugar is dissolved. Boil for 10 minutes, then add the lemon juice and strain the syrup through a muslin-lined sieve into a bowl; cool.

2 Skin, stone and quarter the peaches. Purée the peach flesh in a blender and rub it through a fine nylon sieve until you obtain 300ml/½pt purée (work quickly or the peaches will turn brown). Add the cold syrup to the peach purée. Pour it into a shallow, freezerproof container, cover and freeze for 1 hour or until it is frozen to a depth of 2.5cm/1in all round the sides.

3 Whisk the mixture vigorously, then freeze again. Repeat every 30 minutes until the ice is half frozen. Cover the ice and leave for a further 2–3 hours until frozen hard.

4 Transfer the water ice to the refrigerator about 1 hour before serving to soften slightly.

5 Arrange scoops of water ice in six individual glass dishes. Garnish with sliced black grapes and mint sprigs. Serve immediately.

PREPARING PEACHES

To skin peaches, immerse in a bowl of boiling water and leave briefly. Drain and plunge into cold water, nick the skin near the stalk and peel away in downward strips. To stone peaches, cut round the fruit with a small sharp knife through to the stone, then twist apart.

Set Fair

Moulded mousses, cold soufflés and sparkling jellies all make ideal dinner party desserts, prepared well in advance and needing little or no cooking

Cold lemon soufflé (page 245)

M OUSSES, COLD SOUFFLÉS and jellies rely almost entirely on gelatine to hold their shape. Modern powdered gelatine is easy to use and very reliable, but it is important to use it exactly as directed, so that the mixture sets just firmly enough to hold its shape, without being rubbery.

Using gelatine

In Britain, gelatine is almost always the powdered variety, in 50g/2oz packets containing five sachets, or in 225g/8oz packs of loose powder. Normally 15g/½oz gelatine will set 600ml/1pt of liquid, but in warm weather a little extra may be advisable. The sachets weigh fractionally less then 15g/½oz, but are still designed to set 600ml/1pt. If using loose powder, use 3 level imperial teaspoons or 4 level 5ml spoons.

Leaf gelatine is rarely seen, though common in France; it is also used in the same way.

For successful results, gelatine *must* be used in the prescribed two-stage manner, first being soaked, then heated gently until dissolved. First, put 3-5tbls cold water into a small bowl, sprinkle the gelatine over it and leave for 5 minutes to soften. If the recipe contains fruit juice, you can use that, but not milk, as it will curdle. The gelatine will absorb the liquid and probably become quite solid again. Second, stand the bowl in hot water until the gelatine has dissolved; swirl it around from time to time but do not stir as the undissolved gelatine will stick to the spoon.

In recipes where the gelatine is combined with a hot mixture, the second stage can be omitted. It must never be boiled, as this makes it taste unpleasant. All cooking must be finished and the pan removed from the heat before the gelatine is added.

For best results, the gelatine liquid and base mixture should both be lukewarm when combined. If the mixture is too cold, the gelatine may set into lumps before being blended in.

Soufflés and mousses

A cold soufflé is not really a soufflé at all, but a mousse of eggs, sugar and cream. It just looks like one, being set in a soufflé dish and moulded to stand above its rim. A mousse is set in a mould and turned out like a jelly.

Mousse mixtures are made with whole eggs or egg yolks, whisked together until thick and fluffy. Preparing this over a pan of simmering water helps achieve maximum volume and a good thick texture. This base is then stiffened with gelatine, flavoured as required, and enriched with whipped cream. To lighten it still further, whisked egg white may be folded in.

For best results, whip cream softly so that it is about the same consistency as the base mixture and will fold in smoothly. Similarly egg whites should be whisked to the soft peak stage; do not let them become stiff or dry.

Moulded jellies

The plainer the mould, the easier it is to turn out. Metal ones are the most common as they enable the jelly to set quickly and be turned out easily. Thick earthen-ware or glass moulds are a bit more difficult to turn out as the warmth of the water used to loosen the jelly does not spread so evenly or quickly. But they are good for jellies made with acid fruit such as blackcurrants which can react with metal to give an unpleasant taste; alternatively use a plastic mould. Wetting a mould before pouring the syrupy jelly in helps to make sure it unmoulds cleanly.

Gelatine reaches its optimum setting power after about 12 hours. A jelly that is to be unmoulded and turned out needs the full 12 hours, so it is best to make it the day before it is needed. But do not make jellies too far in advance; after about 24 hours, the texture begins to deteriorate, becoming tough and rubbery. Also do not freeze.

For unmoulding see page 116. Turn the jelly out onto a flat lightly wetted plate so that if it isn't prefectly centred it can be slid into place. Allow jellies to stand at room temperature for ½-1 hour before serving to take off the chill.

SOUFFLE SECRETS

To enable the soufflé to stand above the rim of the dish, cut a band of double thickness grease-proof paper long enough to fit round the dish and wide enough to stand 7.5cm/3in above it. Secure it with string, tape or pins.

Spoon the mixture in carefully to avoid crumpling the paper collar. When it is set, remove the collar very carefully so as not to pull off chunks of soufflé. Undo the fastenings and hold a long-bladed knife against the side of the dish and close to the join. Carefully peel away the paper against the back of the knife.

The exposed rim of the soufflé can be left bare to show off the airy texture, or decorated by pressing on chopped nuts or grated chocolate. Remove the soufflé from the refrigerator 30 minutes before serving. Decorate before serving.

How to ...finish a cold soufflé

When the soufflé is set, unwrap the greaseproof collar. Use a warmed palette knife to prevent sticking.

Even the edge carefully with the palette knife, then arrange toasted chopped nuts around the soufflé edge.

Pipe whipped cream around the edges. On a lemon soufflé, decorate with strips of peel and slices of lemon.

Cold lemon soufflé

- **Preparation: 40 minutes, plus cooling and setting**

- **Cooking: 20 minutes (eggs)**

1 sachet powdered gelatine
3 large eggs, separated
200g/7oz caster sugar
finely grated zest and juice of 3
    lemons
300ml/½pt double cream
For the decoration:
150ml/¼pt double cream, whipped
chopped toasted nuts
julienne strips of blanched orange
    rind

- **Serves 4-5**

- **685cals/2875kjs per serving**

1 Fit a collar of greaseproof paper around a 1.5L/2½pt soufflé dish to come at least 7.5cm/3in above the rim. Put 3tbls cold water into a small bowl, sprinkle the gelatine over it and leave for 5 minutes to soften.

2 Put the egg yolks in a large bowl and add the sugar, lemon zest and juice. Put the bowl over a saucepan of barely simmering water and whisk vigorously until the mixture is thick, light and fluffy and the beaters leave a trail when lifted.

3 Remove the egg yolk mixture and the pan of water from the heat. Stand the bowl of softened gelatine in the hot water to soften it. Meanwhile continue whisking the egg yolk mixture until lukewarm.

4 Remove the gelatine from the hot water when dissolved and allow to cool slightly, then stir it gently into the egg yolk mixture.

5 Stir the mousse mixture until it begins to set (put it over ice if possible).

6 Whip the cream until it just holds a trail and has about the same texture as the yolk mixture. Whisk the egg whites in a clean dry bowl until soft peaks.

7 Using a large metal spoon fold the cream into the egg yolk mixture, followed by the egg whites, working as quickly and lightly as possible.

8 Stand the prepared dish on a plate and carefully pour in the soufflé mixture. Chill until set; allow 3-4 hours.

9 Just before serving peel off the paper collar. Decorate with swirls of piped whipped cream and press chopped toasted nuts around the sides. Finish with the orange julienne strips.

Cold chocolate soufflé

- **Preparation: 40 minutes plus cooling and setting**

- **Cooking: 5 minutes**

1 sachet powdered gelatine
150g/5oz plain chocolate, broken
    up
finely grated zest and juice of 1
    orange
1tbls instant coffee, dissolved in
    3tbls boiling water
6 large eggs, separated
100g/4oz caster sugar
300ml/½pt double cream
1-2tbls brandy, rum or liqueur
    (optional)
chopped and halved walnuts, to
    decorate

- **Serves 6**

- **510cals/2140kjs per serving**

1 Fit a collar of greaseproof paper round a 1L/2pt soufflé dish to come 7.5cm/3in above the rim. Put 3tbls cold water into a small bowl, sprinkle the gelatine over it and leave for 5 minutes to soften.

2 Put the chocolate in a bowl and combine with orange zest, juice and coffee over a pan of hot water until melted and blended.

3 Meanwhile put the egg yolks in another bowl with the sugar. Put over a saucepan of simmering water without allowing the bottom to touch the water. Whisk until the mixture is light and bulky and leaves a trail when the beaters are lifted. Remove and continue whisking.

4 Take the saucepan under the chocolate and stand the bowl of gelatine in the hot water until it dissolves, remove.

5 Whisk the chocolate mixture lightly to ensure it is lump free. When both are just warm, mix together

6 Whip the cream until it just barely holds a trail on the surface. Using a large metal spoon quickly and lightly fold the chocolate-gelatine mixture into the egg yolk mixture. Then fold in the cream, together with the alcohol, if using. Stop folding as soon as no streaks appear.

7 If possible, stand the bowl over another bowl filled with ice. Stir until it is on the point of setting. Then whisk the egg whites in a clean dry bowl to soft peaks. Fold into the chocolate mixture.

8 Stand the soufflé dish on a plate. Carefully pour in the soufflé mixture and chill for 3-4 hours until set.

9 Just before serving peel off the paper collar. Gently press the chopped walnuts round the sides of the soufflé with a palette knife; put walnuts in the centre.

White lady jellies

- **Preparation: 20 minutes, plus cooling, setting and coming to room temperature**

1 sachet powdered gelatine
125ml/4fl oz lemon juice
125ml/4fl oz gin
175ml/6fl oz Cointreau
1-2tbls sugar
350g/12oz black grapes, halved
    and seeded
4 unpeeled orange slices, quartered

- **Serves 8**

- **145cals/610kjs per serving**

1 Put 3tbls cold water into a bowl, sprinkle the gelatine over it and leave for 5 minutes to soften. Stand the bowl in hot water until the gelatine has dissolved. ▶

2 Combine the lemon juice, gin, Cointreau and 175ml/6fl oz water. Add 1-2tbls sugar to taste – the jelly should be quite tart. Add cooled gelatine and mix.

3 Divide the mixture between eight wetted 60ml/2½fl oz ring moulds and chill until set; allow at least 12 hours.

4 To unmould the jellies turn each mould upside down on an individual plate and wipe with a cloth wrung out in hot water. Shake plate and mould to release the jelly and remove the mould. Leave for 30 minutes at room temperature.

5 Fill the centres of the jellies with grapes and orange quarters.

Cook's tips

If you don't have any small ring moulds, use plastic cups or mousse containers. Arrange the grapes around the jellies.

Oriental mousse

- **Preparation: 30 minutes, plus cooling and setting**

100g/4oz preserved stem ginger in syrup
1 sachet powdered gelatine
600ml/1pt whipping cream, or half single and half double cream
3tbls lemon juice
4 kiwi fruit, thinly sliced
2 large egg whites

- **Serves 6**

- **435cals/1825kjs per serving**

1 Drain the ginger, reserving 150ml/¼pt of the syrup. Chop the ginger.

2 Put 3tbls cold water into a small bowl, sprinkle the gelatine over it and leave for 5 minutes to soften. Stand the bowl in hot water until the gelatine has dissolved, then allow it to cool slightly.

3 Whip the cream until just stiff enough to hold a trail. Fold in the ginger, dissolved gelatine, reserved syrup and the lemon juice. Put over a bowl of ice, if possible, and stir until the mixture is on the point of setting.

4 Meanwhile line six 300ml/½pt stemmed glasses with slices of kiwi fruit.

5 Whisk the egg whites in a clean dry bowl until soft peaks form. Fold into the ginger mixture with a large metal spoon. Spoon the mousse into the glasses and chill until set; allow 3-4 hours.

Apple apricot mousse

- **Preparation: overnight soaking, then 15 minutes plus cooling and setting times**

VEGETARIAN VERSION

Gelatine is out for vegetarians as it is made from animal hides and bones. Fortunately there is a substitute – agar-agar – which is obtained from red seaweed. It can be bought as powder flakes or in long strands and dissolves only in boiling water. Use 5ml/ 1tsp per 600ml/1pt of liquid. Buy the substitute from health food or whole food shops.

- **Cooking: 20 minutes**

225g/8oz apricots, soaked overnight
450g/1lb cooking apples
finely grated zest and juice of ½ lemon
1 sachet powdered gelatine
2 large eggs, separated
75g/3oz sugar, or to taste
150ml/¼pt double cream
1-2 drops almond essence
whipped cream and toasted almond slivers, to decorate

- **Serves 6**

- **305cals/1280kjs per serving**

1 Drain the soaked apricots and measure off 300ml/½pt of the liquid into a saucepan. Add the apricots. Peel and core the apples, chop coarsely and put in the pan with the apricots, together with the lemon zest and juice. Bring to the boil over medium heat, cover and simmer gently for 20 minutes or until the apricots are very soft and the apples disintegrating.

2 Meanwhile put 3tbls cold water into a small bowl, sprinkle the gelatine over it and leave for 5 minutes to soften. Stand the bowl in hot water until the gelatine has dissolved, then leave to cool slightly. Also beat the egg yolks lightly.

3 When the fruits are cooked, purée them in a blender or food processor with all their juices. Mix the egg yolks into the hot fruit purée and sweeten to taste.

4 Pour the fruit purée into a 1L/1¾pt measuring jug. Leave until lukewarm, then beat in the dissolved gelatine. If necessary, stir in a little cold water to make the mixture up to 850ml/1½pt. Pour into a large bowl and stir until just on the point of setting.

5 Whip the cream lightly, until the same consistency as the fruit purée. Whisk the egg whites in a clean dry bowl until standing in soft peaks. Using a large metal spoon, fold the cream into the fruit purée, followed by the egg whites. Flavour to taste with almond essence.

6 Pour the mousse into a wetted 1.5L/ 2½pt mould and chill ⏰ for 12-24 hours until perfectly firm.

7 Thirty minutes before serving dip the mould briefly into hot water and turn the mousse out onto a flat plate. Leave at room termperature. Decorate just before serving with rosettes of whipped cream and toasted almond slivers. Fresh apricots also make an ideal topping with the whipped cream

Magical Meringues

Light as air, crisp and crunchy, meringues make the perfect dessert. Everyone loves them — but not everyone knows how easy they are to make

SERVED ON THEIR own with just a little whipped cream or as part of all sorts of hot and cold desserts, meringues are always clear winners. And they are simple to make, as long as you observe a few precautions and master the technique of whisking egg whites.

Ingredients
No meringue can be made without eggs. Always use medium-sized eggs, EEC size 4 or 5. Very fresh eggs are best as the white is very thick and whisks up easily. Whisk whites at room temperature as you get a greater volume.

The other essential ingredient for a meringue is sugar. Caster sugar is the type most commonly used, though for some types of meringue, icing, granulated or brown sugar is preferred.

Salt and cream of tartar are sometimes added to a meringue mixture to stabilize it. Either of these ingredients, added in very small quantities just before you start to whisk, helps to achieve a good volume of whisked mixture and prevents it from collapsing too quickly once you have stopped whisking.

Types of meringue
The simplest meringue is known as *meringue suisse*. For this the egg whites are whisked and then caster sugar is whisked in. Variations containing chopped or ground nuts are popular.

American meringue, for example Pavlova, includes cornflour and lemon juice or vinegar. This makes a crisp meringue with a soft, marshmallowy inside.

Meringue cuite, used by professional bakers, involves whisking icing sugar into the egg whites over a low heat, whereas *meringue italienne* is made by whisking hot sugar syrup into beaten whites.

Making meringues
First set the oven to the required temperature, then butter and line your baking sheet. Separate the eggs carefully, putting the whites into a large bowl. Some chefs use a copper bowl because a chemical reaction between copper and egg whites leads to greater volume, but this isn't necessary. Do make sure, though, that the bowl you use is scrupulously clean and large enough to take the volume of whites after whisking. It is also important that the bowl and whisk are dry, as water is a great enemy of whisked whites.

Raspberry nut meringue (page 252)

247

When selecting a whisk you can choose between a balloon whisk, a rotary or an electric whisk. There is no question that a balloon whisk gives the greatest volume of whisked egg white — but only after a long and tiring session. A little volume is lost using an electric whisk, but the result will still be perfectly acceptable.

If you are using a hand whisk it helps to tip the bowl to one side; this gives you maximum room to move the whisk and makes it easier to get a good volume. Take care not to overbeat — the egg whites should still look rather moist on the surface. This is usually described as 'stiff but not dry'.

Add the sugar, 1tbls at a time, or according to the recipe, whisking well after each addition. The meringue should look smooth and glossy. Sometimes only a certain amount of the sugar is actually whisked in, with the remainder being folded in at the end to give a slightly more chewy texture. But don't handle the mixture more than is necessary or you will beat out some of the air you have so carefully beaten in.

Shaping meringues

Spoon or pipe the mixture onto the prepared baking sheet. If piping, a plain 1cm/½in nozzle is the most usual choice, fitted into a large piping bag. Hold the bag at a right angle to the baking sheet and, as you pipe, take care not to flatten the meringue by pressing down with the nozzle. Finish piping by releasing the pressure, giving a sharp upward pull.

If shaping by hand, either spread the meringue into a flat disc with a palette knife or, for shell shapes, use two spoons. Scoop up a portion of the mixture with one spoon and, with the second, ease it off onto the baking sheet so it makes a neat oval with a ridge on top.

Cooking meringues

For crisp white meringues with a slightly soft centre, dry them out in a very low oven for several hours or as directed in the recipe. For slightly drier meringues with a pale caramel colour, cook at 150C/300F/gas 2 for 1 hour then turn the oven off and leave them for 10–15 minutes to finish drying out.

Meringues containing nuts should be cooked at a higher temperature, as the oil in the nuts might make the mixture spread if it is cooked slowly.

If you are using a meringue mixture as a topping for a hot dessert, the meringue is cooked very quickly, and at a high temperature. This colours the surface but leaves the underlying layer still soft.

Baked alaska

- **Preparation: 45 minutes,
  plus 30 minutes soaking**

- **Cooking: 45 minutes,
  plus cooling and freezing**

225g/8oz strawberries, quartered
4–5tbls brandy
700ml/1¼pt vanilla ice cream
4 egg whites
75g/3oz caster sugar
sifted icing sugar, for dusting
For the cake:
melted butter, for greasing
50g/2oz flour
3 eggs, separated
100g/4oz caster sugar
½tsp lemon juice
salt

- **Serves 6–8**

- **360cals/1520kjs per serving**

1 To make the cake, heat the oven to 180C/350F/gas 4. Brush a 23cm/9in sandwich tin with melted butter and line the base with a circle of non-stick baking paper. Sift the flour three times. Put the egg yolks, sugar, lemon juice and a pinch of salt in a large bowl and whisk until light and fluffy. In another bowl, whisk the egg whites until soft peaks form. Sift the flour over the egg yolk mixture and fold in with a large metal spoon. Fold in the egg whites. Turn into the prepared tin and bake for 30–40 minutes, or until a skewer inserted in the centre comes out clean. Turn onto a wire rack, remove the lining paper and leave to cool.

2 Place the berries in a bowl with the brandy and soak for 30 minutes.

3 Place the sponge on an ovenproof serving dish and prick with a fork.

4 Heat the oven to 220C/425F/gas 7. Cover the centre of the cake with the strawberries and their juices, leaving a 1cm/½in rim around the edge. Slice the ice cream and cover the fruit with it. Place in the freezer for 5–10 minutes while you make the meringue.

5 In a large bowl, combine the egg whites with a pinch of salt and whisk until stiff but not dry. Add the caster sugar, 1tbls at a time, and continue whisking to a smooth, glossy meringue. Spread over the ice cream and sides of the cake, covering the cake completely, and form peaks all over with the flat side of a knife. Dust generously with sifted icing sugar.

6 Bake at once for 3–6 minutes, or until the tips of the peaks are slightly browned. Serve immediately.

How to ··· *whisk egg whites*

Separate the eggs, making sure no trace of egg yolk gets into the whites or they will not whisk up stiffly. Using a scrupulously clean whisk, whisk the whites until soft peaks form.

Gradually add the caster sugar, 1tbls at a time, beating well after each addition. If using an electric whisk, start off at slow speed. As the whites begin to foam, increase the speed slightly.

Continue whisking the mixture until the meringue is stiff in texture – it will hold its shape on the whisk – and glossy in appearance. Don't overwhisk. The meringue is now ready to be used; shape at once.

Tropical pavlova

● **Preparation: 30 minutes**

● **Cooking: 2½ hours, plus cooling**

melted butter, for greasing
4 egg whites
225g/8oz caster sugar
2tsp cornflour
1tsp lemon juice
For the filling:
300ml/½pt double cream
1tbls icing sugar
1tbls kirsch
½ mango, sliced
½ small pineapple, chopped
1 kiwi fruit, sliced and halved

● **Serves 6**

● **300cals/1260kjs per serving**

1 Heat the oven to 100C/200F/gas low. Grease a large baking sheet. Using a 23cm/9in plate as a template, draw a circle on a piece of non-stick baking paper. Place, pencilled side down, on the greased baking sheet.

2 In a large bowl, whisk the egg whites until stiff but not dry. Sift together the caster sugar and the cornflour. Sift half this mixture over the egg whites, a spoonful at a time, whisking in each addition. When the mixture is smooth and glossy fold in the remaining sugar and cornflour with a large metal spoon. Fold in the lemon juice.

3 Spoon the meringue mixture into the centre of the circle and use the spoon to push and mould the mixture into a round with a slightly hollowed centre.

4 Bake for 2–2½ hours or until the meringue is firm on the outside and dry underneath. Turn off the oven and leave the meringue until cold. Remove the meringue from the oven and carefully peel off the paper.

5 To assemble, whip the cream to soft peaks, then fold in the sugar and kirsch. Put the meringue on a serving dish and spoon the cream into the centre of it; put the prepared fruit on top and serve within 30 minutes.

WHAT WENT WRONG?

'Plaster of Paris' meringues: this is caused by too dry a mixture, either from too much sugar or from overbeating. About 50g/2oz sugar per medium egg white is the norm.
Rubber meringues: this is the result of undercooking. Allow plenty of time to dry out even if you think they look done.
Weepy mixture: liquid will collect at the bottom of the bowl if the meringue mixture is allowed to stand after whisking, so cook it immediately.

Chocolate meringue gateau

- *Preparation: 1 hour 10 minutes*

- *Cooking: 2½ hours, plus cooling*

melted butter, for greasing
4 egg whites
pinch of salt
225g/8oz caster sugar
600ml/1pt double cream
175g/6oz plain chocolate
chopped toasted almonds,
   to decorate

- *Serves 6–8*   (Ⅲ) (££) (🕒)

- *810cals/3405kjs per serving*

1 Heat the oven to 130C/250F/gas ½. Grease three baking sheets with melted butter. Mark two 20cm/8in circles on two pieces of non-stick baking paper and place, pencilled sides down, on two of the greased baking sheets. Place a third piece of paper on the remaining sheet.

2 Whisk the egg whites and salt in a clean, dry bowl until stiff but not dry. Add half the sugar, 1tbls at a time, whisking well after each addition, then fold in the remaining sugar. Fit a piping bag with a 2cm/¾in plain nozzle and spoon a third of the mixture into the bag.

3 Pipe a spiral of meringue from the inside to the outer edge of the pencilled circle. Repeat this procedure with the other circle, refilling the bag. With the remaining mixture, pipe 18 even-sized drops onto the third baking sheet.

4 Place all three sheets in the oven and bake until crisp and dry. The drops will take about 1-1½ hours, and the circles 2–2½ hours. Leave to cool on a wire rack,

Filling a piping bag

Insert a nozzle into the piping bag. Fold the top third of the bag over and spoon in the mixture. Alternatively rest the bag over a tall jug so that both hands are free to spoon in the meringue.

then remove the paper. (🕒)

5 Whip the cream until thick enough to hold its shape. Break up the chocolate and melt in a bowl over hot water.

6 When the small meringue drops are cool, dip the base of each one in the chocolate, then set aside to allow the chocolate to harden.

7 Fit a piping bag with a star nozzle. Pipe a third of the cream over one of the meringue circles, and then place the other circle on the top. Spread half the remaining cream over the top of the gateau and trickle the remaining chocolate over the top. Swirl it into the cream using a skewer, making circular movements for an attractive design.

8 Using some of the remaining cream, sandwich pairs of the meringue drops together with piped rosettes. Sprinkle the chopped nuts over the centre of the gateau. Pipe the rest of the cream in rosettes around the gateau and arrange the meringue drops on the serving dish. Serve as soon as possible.

Plan ahead

Meringues can be made up to a month in advance. Store them in an airtight container, then assemble and decorate them just before serving, or as directed in the recipe.

Piping a meringue circle

Draw a circle with a pencil on a piece of non-stick baking paper and place, pencilled side down, on a greased baking sheet. Pipe a spiral of meringue from the inside of the circle to the outer edge.

EGG SENSE

Never throw egg yolks away — they can always be used for sauces, custards, ice cream, mayonnaise, for glazing pastry or enriching scrambled eggs. Put them into a bowl and cover with a little cold water; they will keep in the refrigerator for 3–4 days. Alternatively, beat them lightly with a pinch of salt or sugar and freeze for up to three months.

Ice cream hearts

- ● *Preparation: 50 minutes*

- ● *Cooking: 4¼ hours,*
  plus cooling and chilling

375ml/13fl oz hazelnut ice cream
crystallized violets, to decorate
For the meringues:
melted butter, for greasing
1 egg white
small pinch of salt
40g/1½oz soft light brown sugar
For the mocha sauce:
75ml/3fl oz sweetened condensed
milk
½tsp instant coffee granules
1tbls hot water
1tsp drinking chocolate powder
3tbls double cream

- ● *Serves 4*

- ● *370cals/1550kjs per serving*

1 Grease a baking sheet. Cut a heart-shaped template measuring about 7.5cm x 10cm/3in x 4in from a piece of thin card. Use this template to outline four heart shapes with a pencil on a piece of non-stick baking paper, then place the paper, pencilled side down, on the baking sheet.

2 Heat the oven to 100C/200F/gas low. In a large bowl, whisk the egg white with the salt until stiff but not dry. Add 1tbls of the sugar, 1tsp at a time, whisking well after each addition.

3 Fold in the remaining sugar with a large metal spoon. Fit a piping bag with a 5mm/¼in plain nozzle and fill with the meringue mixure.

4 Pipe heart shapes onto the prepared paper and bake for 3–4 hours to dry the meringues out completely. Transfer them carefully to a wire rack and allow them to cool, then peel off the lining paper and reserve the meringues.

5 Make the mocha sauce: place the milk in a small saucepan. Dissolve the coffee in the hot water, then add to the milk. Mix together the chocolate powder and cream and stir this into the milk. Heat gently, stirring, just to warm the ingredients. Do not boil. Allow the sauce to cool, then chill it.

6 To serve, arrange the meringue hearts on individual serving plates. Scoop out 12–16 balls of ice cream using a melon baller, then top each heart with three or four balls. Pour the sauce over the top, decorate with crystallized violet petals and serve at once.

Freezer

Small meringues will freeze for up to six months. Pack them in a rigid container to prevent breakage. Defrost for 15 minutes at room temperature.

Larger meringues can pick up moisture and lose crispness, and are more likely to break, so freezing isn't recommended.

Almond-topped meringue cake

- **Preparation: 40 minutes**
- **Cooking: 2¼ hours, plus cooling**

melted butter, for greasing
50g/2oz butter
100g/4oz caster sugar
4 egg yolks
100g/4oz flour
1tsp baking powder
5tbls milk
few drops of vanilla essence
300ml/½pt double cream,
    whipped
225g/8oz strawberries, sliced
icing sugar, for dusting
For the meringue:
4 egg whites
pinch of salt
225g/8oz caster sugar
2tbls flaked almonds

- **Serves 8** ⓧ £££ 🕐
- **400cals/1680kjs per serving**

1 Heat the oven to 150C/300F/gas 2. Brush two baking sheets with melted butter. Mark two 23cm/9in circles on two sheets of non-stick baking paper and place, pencilled sides down, on the sheets.

2 Make the meringue: in a large bowl, whisk the egg whites and salt until stiff but not dry. Whisk in the sugar, 1tbls at a time, until smooth and glossy. Divide between the circles, spreading to cover them evenly. Sprinkle one with the almonds. Bake for 1–1½ hours or until crisp but still slightly soft inside, reversing the sheets halfway through. Turn out onto a wire rack, cool, then remove the paper.

3 Increase the oven temperature to 190C/375F/gas 5. Grease and base-line two 23cm/9in round sandwich tins and make the sponges: cream the butter and sugar until light and fluffy. Beat in the egg yolks, one at a time. Sift together the flour and baking powder and add to the butter mixture alternately with the milk and vanilla essence. Mix until smooth. Divide between the tins. Bake for 35–40 minutes or until a skewer inserted in the centre comes out clean, changing the positions of the tins halfway through. Carefully remove from the tins, remove the paper and cool on a wire rack. 🕐

4 Place the plain meringue upside down on a serving plate. Top with a sponge layer, then the cream and strawberries, then the second sponge layer. Finish with the almond-topped meringue and dust with icing sugar. Keep cool.

Raspberry nut meringue

- **Preparation: 35 minutes**
- **Cooking: 1 hour 20 minutes, plus cooling**

melted butter, for greasing
5 egg whites
pinch of salt
275g/10oz caster sugar
1tsp white wine vinegar
100g/4oz ground walnuts

For the filling and decoration:
350g/12oz raspberries
2tbls icing sugar
2tsp kirsch
600ml/1pt double cream
10 walnut halves
mint or raspberry leaves,
    to decorate

- **Serves 8–10** ⓧ £££ 🕐
- **535cals/2245kjs per serving**

1 Heat the oven to 170C/325F/gas 3. Grease two 20cm/8in sandwich tins and base-line with non-stick baking paper.

2 Whisk the egg whites with the salt until stiff but not dry, then whisk in 1tbls sugar. Gradually fold in the remaining sugar, then the vinegar and walnuts. Spoon the mixture into the tins, smoothing it with a spatula. Bake for 1–1¼ hours or until crisp but still slightly soft inside.

3 Loosen carefully with a knife and remove from the tins. Cool on a wire rack; then remove the paper.

4 Reserve about 25 raspberries. Gently cook the remainder with the icing sugar and kirsch for 5–7 minutes or until soft. Purée in a blender, sieve and cool. 🕐

5 To assemble, whip the cream until soft peaks form. Reserve a third and fold the rest into the purée. Spread over one meringue, then cover with the second.

6 Fit a piping bag with a large star nozzle and pipe the plain cream around the edge of the top meringue, then arrange some of the raspberries on top. Fill the centre with walnut halves. Decorate the base with the remaining berries and the leaves. Serve as soon as possible.

INDEX

ACKNOWLEDGEMENTS

The publishers extend their thanks to the following agencies, companies and individuals who have kindly provided illustrative material for this book. The alphabetical name of the supplier is followed by the page and position of the picture/s.

Abbreviations: b = bottom;
c = centre; l = left; r = right; t = top.

All pictures from Marshall Cavendish Picture Library: Bryce Attwell 28tr, 98br, 111tr; Jan Baldwin 15cc; Tom Belshaw 48br, 160tr, 208bl; Martin Brigdale 138tl; Paul Bussell 13br, 25b, 30tl, 30/31bc, 54t, 62br, 66/67cc, 101tl, 102/103bc, 117tr, 119c & 188/189bc, 129br, 150tr, 152tr, 154tr, 159tl, 167b, 170br, 173b, 175tr, 183br, 193tr, 199cc, 206/207bc; Chris Crofton 9b, 26/27bc, 32bl, 47tr, 232tr, 249br; Ray Davies 89bl; Alan Duns 121b; Ray Duns 22tl, 45b, 95b, 145cr, 223b; Laurie Evans 40/41bc, 49cc, 96tr, 99b, 139b, 140tr, 148tr, 156tr, br, 185b, 191b, 201tr, 205br, 217c & 236br, 229b, 246bl; Melvin Grey 24tr; Jon Hall 141b, 176bl; Christine Hanscombe 34tl; John Hollingshead 94bl, 135b, 239b; James Jackson 35b, 42/43tc, 91b, 92br, 100br, 106tr, 124tr, 131b, 153br, 168/169bc, 182tr, 193bl, 194br, 203b, 207tr, 237t, 247b, 252t; John Kevern 189tr; Chris Knaggs 7c & 44tr, 39b, 63b, 77b, 112/113bc, 127tl, 155bl, 165tr, 178br, 179bl, 197tr, bl, 202bl, 211tr, 213b, 224br, 241tr; Jess Koppel 86tr; Don Last 233b, 238br, 243cc; David Levin 144b, 146tl; Michael Michaels 16br, 18br, 21tr, 29b, 38tl, 133bl, 134tr; Peter Myers 12t, 19b, 20tr, 51tr, 52/53bc, 58br, 62tc, 78/79tc, 84/85tc, 85bc, 93br, 107br, 109b, 125cc, 128tr, 136/137tc, 142br, 157b, 160b, 162br, 164br, 187b, 198b, 200bl, 209cc, 219b, 221bl, 226/227bc, 231cr, 234br, 240br; Alan Newnham 81c & 90tr; Roger Phillips 149tr, 235bl; Grant Symon 10/11tr, 17cr, 72br, 151b; Paul Webster 143b, 163b, 166tr, 172bl, 195cc, 211br, 226tl; Andrew Whittuck 69b 71t, 73t, 122/123tc, 230tr, 251tr; Paul Williams 26tr, 36/37bc, 57tl, 59cc, 68cc, 70br, 75b, 80cc, 83bc, 86br, 97br, 104br, 115b, 117bl, 118tl, br, 137bl, 208tr,214br, 215br, 225tr, 245tr, 248cr; Peter Williams 161br.

Index compiled by INDEXING SPECIALISTS, Hove.